D1551896

Oracle Database 11g Release 2 High Availability

About the Authors

Scott Jesse (Colorado Springs, Colorado) has worked for Oracle since 1996 and is currently Customer Support Senior Manager for the Oracle RAC Assurance Team. He has worked with the Oracle RAC Assurance Team since 2007. Prior to this assignment, Scott's primary focus was on clustering technologies. He has served as a Global Team Lead and as a member of the Advanced Resolution and Escalations Team within Oracle Support, providing him with a unique insight into the needs of Oracle technology customers. Scott is the coauthor of *Oracle Database 10g High Availability with RAC, Flashback, and Data Guard* and *Oracle9i for Windows 2000 Tips & Techniques*, both by McGraw-Hill/Oracle Press.

Bill Burton (United Kingdom) joined Oracle from Computer Associates in 1998, spending two years with the Oracle UK product support group for Database before transferring to the U.S. Gold Support Team in October 2000. He spent time in the Oracle HA Support group, dealing with Oracle RAC and Oracle Data Guard, before joining the Bug Determination and Escalation group (BDE) for those products. He has been a member of the Oracle RAC Assurance Development Team since 2007. Together with Josh Ort, he wrote and presented the Upgrading to 11gR2 Session at Oracle OpenWorld 2010.

Bryan Vongray (Beaver, Pennsylvania) has more than nine years of experience implementing and supporting all aspects of the Oracle Database. He specialized in Oracle High Availability with specific focus in Oracle Real Application Clusters (Oracle RAC), Oracle Data Guard, Streams, backup and recovery, as well as Grid Control. As a Senior Consultant for Oracle Consulting Services, Bryan had planned and implemented Oracle Maximum Availability Architecture (MAA) Solutions for numerous Oracle customers. Bryan is now putting his Oracle MAA expertise to use as a member of the Oracle RAC Assurance Team within Oracle Global Customer Support.

About the Contributor

Hagen Herbst (Germany) is an OCP-certified DBA with more than a decade of experience in Oracle products. Prior to joining the Oracle RAC Assurance Team within Oracle Global Customer Support, he spent years installing and upgrading countless databases, mainly Oracle RAC and Failsafe Systems in Europe, the Middle East, and Africa. Hagen has also served as the senior Oracle DBA in a data center, utilizing all aspects of Oracle's Maximum Available Architecture.

About the Technical Editors

Farouk Abushaban is a Senior Principal Engineer at Oracle. He is a founding member of the Center of Excellence Team and is the Global Technical Lead for Enterprise Manager High Availability implementations. He spent 22 years in customer support and information systems. Farouk works directly with strategic

Oracle customers and partners to improve product utilization and performance in large deployments. He has a bachelor's degree in Electrical Engineering from the University of Colorado in Colorado Springs and completed his master's degree in Management of Information Technologies with emphasis on Project Management and Security from Colorado Technical University. Farouk has been with Oracle since 1997.

Jiong Dai (Daedal) has worked with Oracle for more than ten years. He started in Advanced Product Support, where he supported Oracle RDBMS, Oracle Developer, Oracle Designer, and Oracle Application Server, delivering onsite OPS design, Oracle backup/recovery strategy review, and database performance review. He became an Oracle Certified Professional in 2000. In 2004, he worked with Intel Server Performance Scalability Lab, publishing the world's leading TPC-H results and world leading MAPI Messaging Benchmark 3 (MMB3) results, and working for the enterprise workload character analysis on TPC-C, SPECjAppServer (Java Application Server), SJBB, and so on. In 2006, he moved to the Oracle HA Product Support Team and eventually moved on to the Oracle RAC Assurance Team in 2009. Currently, he provides support to critical Oracle RAC customers to assure their successful implementation on Oracle RAC. He is the author of *RAC Assurance Support Team: RAC Starter Kit and Best Practices (AIX) (Linux)*.

Michael Smith is a principal member of the technical staff in Oracle's Maximum Availability Architecture (MAA) Team in Server Technologies. Mike has been with Oracle for 12 years, previously serving as the Oracle Data Guard Global Technical Lead within Oracle Global Support. Mike's current focus is developing, validating, and publishing HA best practices using Oracle Data Guard in an integrated fashion across all Oracle Database HA features. His Oracle Data Guard technical specialties focus on network transport, recovery, role transitions, Oracle Active Data Guard, and client failover. He has published a dozen MAA Best Practice Papers for Oracle 9*i*, 10*g*, and 11*g*. He has been a contributing author to previous Oracle Press publications. Mike has also been speaker at three Oracle OpenWorld events held in San Francisco. His "What They Didn't Print in the DOC" Best Practice Presentations covering Oracle Data Guard and MAA are a favorite among Oracle users, with attendance at the top of all Oracle Database technology presentations.

Paul Tjhang, Principal Technical Support Engineer, Oracle Corporation, worked as a system administrator and support engineer before becoming an Oracle DBA. He is responsible for maintaining the Oracle RAC Assurance Support Team's Starter Kit and Best Practices documentation. He has reviewed many Oracle RAC configurations and provided feedback for best practices configuration. He is also actively supporting Oracle customers with Oracle RAC-related issues.

Oracle Press™

Oracle Database 11g Release 2 High Availability

Maximize Your Availability with Grid Infrastructure, Oracle Real Application Clusters, and Oracle Data Guard, Second Edition

Scott Jesse
Bill Burton
Bryan Vongray

New York   Chicago   San Francisco
Lisbon   London   Madrid   Mexico City   Milan
New Delhi   San Juan   Seoul   Singapore   Sydney   Toronto

The McGraw·Hill Companies

Cataloging-in-Publication Data is on file with the Library of Congress

McGraw-Hill books are available at special quantity discounts to use as premiums and sales promotions, or for use in corporate training programs. To contact a representative, please e-mail us at bulksales@mcgraw-hill.com.

Oracle Database 11g Release 2 High Availability: Maximize Your Availability with Grid Infrastructure, Oracle Real Application Clusters, and Oracle Data Guard, Second Edition

1 2 3 4 5 6 7 8 9 0   QFR QFR   1 0 9 8 7 6 5 4 3 2 1

ISBN   978-0-07-175208-4
MHID   0-07-175208-0

Sponsoring Editor
Wendy Rinaldi

Editorial Supervisor
Janet Walden

Project Manager
Vastavikta Sharma,
Glyph International

Acquisitions Coordinator
Stephanie Evans

Technical Editors
Farouk Abushaban, Jiong
Dai (Daedal), Michael Smith,
Paul Tjhang

Copy Editor
Lisa Theobald

Proofreader
Susie Elkind

Indexer
Karin Arrigoni

Production Supervisor
George Anderson

Composition
Glyph International

Illustration
Glyph International

Art Director, Cover
Jeff Weeks

Cover Designer
Pattie Lee

I would like to dedicate this to my father, Larry Jesse, who has fought for his entire adult life for what he has believed to be right and true. I will never fully understand the struggles he has faced, but I have learned to appreciate them more as I have grown older.
–Scott

For Mum and Dad, though sorely missed you remain an inspiration; also for Molly (6) and Izzy (4), whose ability to adapt to change and boundless imagination never cease to amaze me.
–Bill

This book is dedicated to my wife, Joleen, and my two children, Hayden (8) and Delaney (1).
–Bryan

Contents at a Glance

PART II
Oracle Real Application Clusters (Oracle RAC)

PART III
Disaster Planning

PART IV
Enhancing Availability with Additional Features

Contents

PART I
Oracle's Grid Infrastructure

PART II

Oracle Real Application Clusters (Oracle RAC)

PART III
Disaster Planning

PART IV
Enhancing Availability with Additional Features

Acknowledgments

All of the thanks for this project go to Bill Burton, Bryan Vongray, and Hagen Herbst. They have shown tremendous tenacity in seeing this project through, and I am grateful to them for their hard work. In particular, Bill was truly the driving force behind making this whole thing happen, in spite of the hectic and crazy pace of the last several months, and then Bryan really stepped in and solidified the team, followed by Hagen. I have an enormous amount of respect for their knowledge and work ethic, as well as for the entire team, including Jiong Dai, Paul Tjhang, Mike Smith, and Farouk Abushaban, who provided invaluable inputs in the technical review of the book. I am very honored to be able to be a member of the Oracle RAC Assurance and Oracle RAC Support teams and a part of the Oracle RAC Community as a whole, as there are many tremendous talents within the Oracle RAC Community. In my opinion, the Oracle RAC Community is the strongest and most vibrant community of technologists within Oracle, thanks to the great minds who strive to work with and know and understand Oracle's RAC and Clusterware technology. There are so many good people in that list that it is impossible to name them all, but anyone who has ever ventured onto Helprac knows who the go-to people are, and I am grateful to all of the input they have provided over the years.

Also, although this is the third book I have participated in, it has also been the most difficult project for various reasons. Having said that, I could not have made it through without the careful prodding and cajoling of the McGraw-Hill team. They have almost infinite patience, for which I am grateful, and without which this project may never have been completed. Although no longer with McGraw-Hill, Lisa McClain was an invaluable asset for getting this off the ground, and I wish her all the best in her future endeavors. Huge thank yous to the entire McGraw-Hill team!

Finally, what are we without family? I am extremely blessed with the family that I have, both immediate and extended, and I owe everything to them, My wife, Tricia, is an incredible person whom I adore and without whom none of this would be possible. I am stunned that my three children (Erica, 16; Amanda, 14; and Mitchell, 12) have grown so quickly. It seems like yesterday that I was writing about them in acknowledgments as just wee tots—to me, they always will be, even though Erica is now driving. Along with Tricia they are the lights of my life. Thank you to my entire family, my parents, and my wife's parents for all of the tremendous support they have given us and me through the years. That support is what keeps us going through tough times, but so often, we forget to stop and say thank you, so please know that you are loved and remembered daily.

—Scott Jesse

During a hectic three-month period last year (2010), I had a major move at home; the Colorado Springs Grizzlies rugby team, for which I was president, coach, and player, made the National Championships; and I lost my mother, who lived 5,000 miles away. So, coauthoring a book at the time seemed not to be the greatest idea I had ever had. Of course, most of these things you cannot predict, so you just have to deal with it. And the only way you can do that is with a lot of help, support, and considerable understanding from your family, friends, and all those involved on the project.

I simply could not have done this without the support of my wife, Mandy, who kept things together while I was stuck in the office tapping away on my keyboard, and my children, Molly and Izzy, for understanding that "in a minute" did not always really mean that. You will always be an inspiration to me and I will always love you. Thanks to my sisters, Jenny and Sue, brothers-in-law, Jeff and Richard, as well as Auntie Lynne, for nagging me when we were in Italy to stop lazing around and get working. Finally, I have to thank my brother, Peter, for being himself, which is a good thing.

Outside of the family I have to thank the McGraw-Hill team, and especially Stephanie Evans whose understanding and patience were wonderful during that three-month period. I would like to thank our copy editor, Lisa (Red Ink) Theobald, for making me realize how poor my English really is. I will try harder next time!

I thank Scott Jesse for suggesting that we could do this, and for then organizing and coordinating the authors' efforts, as well as for being a thoroughly nice bloke. Scott also brought Bryan Vongray on board, which was an inspired decision, and Hagen Herbst, which meant we had some excellent eyes on the work before it even got to our tech editors. The tech editors—Farouk, Jiong, Mike, and Paul—did a great job and pointed me back in the right direction a number of times. I also have to thank Anil Nair for checking my work and suggesting some very useful additions. There are too many people to mention here that have helped me within Oracle, but a few from my years in Support include Mike Ross, John Cahill, Walt Williams, Mike Smith, Mike Polaski, Cathy Scully, Bennett Leve, and Balaji Bashyam. I am privileged to work with brilliant people every day within the Oracle development organization, but I must mention my immediate team members—Bob Caldwell, Josh Ort, Mark Brewer-Tillotson, and Girdhari Ghantiyala (Giri)—who work constantly to make Oracle RAC and CRS adoption as easy as possible for new Oracle RAC customers, as well as helping existing customers stay on or get back on track. I would like to thank my Director, Sandesh Rao, for his continued support and for continuing to employ me and letting me write this book. Finally, of course, thanks to Angelo Pruscino for agreeing to let us write this book and for being the driving force behind Oracle RAC, ASM, and CRS.

—Bill Burton

Needless to say, having a 1-year-old in the house makes life move extremely fast. This, on top of keeping up with all the activities of an 8-year-old, while also trying to pass along, through coaching my son's ice hockey team, the ice hockey knowledge that my mentors and coaches passed on to me, doesn't leave much time for anything else let alone writing a book. That being said, I need to thank my wife, Joleen, for managing many of the family activities, which allowed me to put in the hours necessary to see this book through completion. I also need to thank my daughter, Delaney, and son, Hayden, for making me smile and taking my mind away from the writing of this book. The balance my family provided is what allowed me to overcome frustrating times that come with such a task. Keeping the focus on family, I would like to thank my mother, Cindy, and father, John, for supporting me throughout my life, even in the most difficult situations. Simply stated, this project would not have been completed without the support of my family.

Aside from my family, I would like to thank Scott Jesse and Bill Burton for giving me the opportunity to coauthor this book. Writing has always been a passion of mine, as is sharing my knowledge with others, so writing this book was essentially a dream come true. In addition, thanks to Hagen Herbst for his knowledgeable contributions to this book, as well as to Jiong Dai (Daedal), Farouk Abushaban, Michael Smith, and Paul Tjhang for catching my mistakes in the technical edit. You guys are all truly brilliant and it is a privilege to work with you on a day-to-data basis.

To close out, I would like to thank those at McGraw-Hill/Oracle Press for allowing this project to happen and for being so patient with us writers. A special thanks to Stephanie Evans for her assistance throughout this process, as well as to Wendy Rinaldi, Janet Walden, Vastavikta Sharma, and Lisa Theobald.

—Bryan Vongray

Introduction

n the first edition of this book, we focused on what we called the "High Availability Database Administrator." However, that term led to the question of just what is meant by *High Availability*? As a term bandied about among database administrators, this can have different meanings depending on who is interpreting it, who has to implement it, and who is requesting it. After all, how high is *high*? To many end users and management types, "High Availability" really means the same thing as "always available," period—no ifs, ands, or buts. But then reality hits, and we realize that there is a cost associated with "always available." Nothing comes for free. The more mission-critical your system, the more you are willing to invest in maintaining the uptime to achieve that goal of "always available." But even when budgets are tight (as all budgets are), you want to get the "Maximum" possible availability for your investment. So perhaps the best way to think of "High Availability" is that it is synonymous with Maximum Availability, where Maximum Availability means getting the "maximum possible" return on investment out of the resources at your disposal.

The parameters surrounding this principle are wide and complex, but the reality is simple: availability is defined, ultimately, by end users of your systems who have no notion of what HA requires, but simply expect the system to be up and available at all times. This goes well beyond the users who just want to buy books at midnight or check their 401(k) over the weekend, and it includes all manner of mission-critical systems that are needed to support an ever-shrinking world that never sleeps and requires 24/7/365 access. That means that any true availability solution must encompass the entire technology stack, from the database, to the application server, to the network. It goes without saying that this requires the cooperation of every aspect of a company's technology staff, working together in harmony.

Combine the need to "harmonize" all aspects of a corporate data center with the fact that oversized IT budgets are a thing of the past, and today's DBA or systems administrator is faced with the daunting challenge of keeping costs down while making systems available on an ever-increasing scale. In that respect, cost goes well beyond the simple cost of hardware or software, and must include the costs of implementation, maintenance, and integration necessary to achieve this harmony. The more disparate the different components of the corporate data center, the greater the costs will be in all three of these areas. While High Availability for the database remains a problem that rests primarily on the shoulders of the database administrator, maximizing availability for "the business" requires that every aspect of the data center and the entire IT infrastructure be synchronized to ensure the availability of the data that the business requires. Although this book is very much focused on database technologies for maintaining uptime, the goal of the book goes well beyond just the database.

What Is Maximum Availability?

Maximum Availability is the concept of getting the absolute most out of the resources available to you. As a database administrator or systems administrator, Oracle's *Maximum Availability Architecture (MAA)* refers to a set of best practices and blueprints, based on Oracle technologies, to achieve the optimum in availability for your environment. A DBA needs to plan and prepare for a number of interrelated issues:

- Hardware and software failures
- Human errors
- Natural and man-made disasters
- Database performance and manageability

Hardware and software failures, as well as the area of human errors, refers to the fact that the *DC* in *data centers* does not stand for divine creation. The reality is that hardware components and software are created by human beings. Human beings, by nature, are imperfect. As such, over time, we know that hardware components will fail—regardless of how much time and effort is put into the design, implementation, and testing of these components. By the same token, software is imperfect—the only software without bugs has either never been released (vaporware) or is obsolete (another word for useless). The business cycle cannot wait for perfect software—too much is to be gained from the timely release of the imperfect. You need to consider these imperfections when you're planning to maximize your availability.

IT systems are in fact managed and used by humans, and just as humans coding software can make mistakes, so can humans who are managing your environments. Perhaps a user inadvertently drops a table, deletes the wrong data, overwrites a critical file, or kills the wrong process. Regardless of where the fault lies, both the infrastructure and the processes must be developed to prepare for, mitigate, and overcome the consequences of these failures.

Clearly, these types of errors are preventable, and you can and should make every effort to prevent these failures from happening, along with using strategies that minimize their impact when they do occur. Unfortunately, in some cases, nothing can be done to prevent a disaster. Whether borne of earth, wind, fire, or flood, whether man-made or of the natural type, disasters happen and you need to have plans to mitigate and recover from disasters. Having a good disaster recovery plan if a disaster strikes means more than just mitigating the impact on your business or organization; it can often make the difference regarding the very survival of your business. This not only means having a failover system in case of complete system loss, but also having the technologies in place that can help recover from the more minor tragedies: user errors, bad memory, or database corruption.

In the performance area, it is not enough simply to ensure that the systems are up—it is crucial that you ensure that the information in those systems can be accessed in a timely fashion. A poorly performing system is often seen in the same light as a down system. In fact, a poorly performing system can impact your business just as much as a system that is completely down. So maintaining access to critical information in a timely fashion is key to maximizing your availability.

Finally, if an HA solution is overly complex, it can become too top-heavy and collapse in upon itself. If the management costs outweigh the benefits of availability, then what's the point? Manageability must therefore be considered a critical component of the overall MAA. Maximizing your availability *with the resources that you have available* means keeping control of costs of implementation, integration, and management of the environment, thereby allowing investments to be directed toward other areas as needed.

Oracle's Integrated Approach to Maximum Availability

Achieving harmony among all the components of your infrastructure is crucial. Proper integration leads to lower costs, easier implementation, and better manageability. To that end, Oracle Database 11*g* Release 2 and Oracle's grid infrastructure integrate many of the components necessary to achieve Maximum Availability under a single umbrella, simplifying the implementation, maintenance, and integration, and thereby simplifying the path to High Availability.

We have written this book to offer a foundation for Maximum Availability. Although not every aspect of Oracle's MAA technologies are covered in these pages, the technologies discussed here are the linchpins to success, from the underlying Grid Infrastructure stack, to the Grid Control tools used to monitor and manage your Maximally Available environment. Using the Oracle stack to its fullest potential involves many different aspects of an enterprise's IT infrastructure, but clearly the

DBA plays a central role in that. In fact, this book offers much helpful information pertinent to all members of the IT team.

Leverage What You Have

Oracle Database 11g provides a wide spectrum of HA technologies built into the core RDBMS that you already use. This book shows you how to leverage technologies that are integrated with the Oracle RDBMS, including technologies that you already have in your toolkit, but you may not be using yet. Although a multitude of HA options are available on the market, if you already paid for your Oracle license, you have a vested interest in exploring how much of the base functionality you can use before widening your scope of inquiry.

Granted, a "six of one or half a dozen of the other" argument can be made: Oracle-provided solutions can incur licensing fees, so money saved on hardware solutions might just be redirected. But we believe that leveraging the available database-centric HA technologies will give you the most cost-effective approach to HA, as well as making the tech stack manageable by the database administrators, which ends up saving your organization costs in the long run.

Integration Oriented

In addition to leveraging technologies already waiting at your fingertips, the MAA approach to HA also provides more opportunities to focus on the integration of multiple aspects of availability, instead of dealing with them in isolation. In keeping with the idea that Maximum Availability means maximizing the resources that you have at your disposal, this book focuses on explaining the individual HA technologies separately so that you can pick and choose all those that fit your needs.

We also emphasize the fully integrated package that can be provided by a database-centric HA strategy. We pair up Oracle Real Application Clusters (Oracle RAC) and Oracle Data Guard, and discuss the unique challenges that are overcome by this combined solution. We put a media backup strategy into the mix as well, showing how Recovery Manager (RMAN), Oracle RAC, and Oracle Data Guard work together to provide a full solution. We then incorporate Oracle Flashback technologies with Oracle Data Guard so that you can quickly leverage a database flashback to reinstate your original primary database after failover. The list goes on and on. When you focus on database availability tools, the challenges of integration quickly begin to disappear.

Welcome to "The Grid"

If you haven't been barraged by the publicity yet, you should probably know that the little "g" in 11g stands for "grid." Grid computing is a philosophy of computing that posits, simply, that computing needs should operate on the same principal as utility grids. You do not know where your electricity comes from, or how it is managed; all you know is that you can plug in your appliances—from a single lamp to an entire house of washers, dryers, and water heaters—and you get as much electricity as you need. Computing needs should be the same: you plug into the grid, and you get your computational needs, your information needs, and your application needs. You get as much as you need, and you do not worry where the computers are located or how they are managed.

Such a grid would be based, of course, on the kind of availability that we have come to expect from the utility grid. When the electricity grid goes down, even for a single day, it makes headlines all over the country *because it happens only every 30 years or so.* Thus, for grid computing, one of the foundational pillars must be Maximum Availability.

Cloud Computing

Cloud computing is another hot topic that has become a recent buzzword. According to Wikipedia, "Cloud computing is Internet-based computing, whereby shared resources, software and information are provided to computers and other devices on-demand, like the electricity grid." So, what is the difference between "cloud computing" and "the grid"? To our way of thinking, there is very little difference—the concept in both cases is the same: an "always-on" infrastructure that users can plug into to get the data (information) that they need to make the decisions to run businesses, households, and other organizations. Whether you call it "the grid" or "the cloud" makes little difference—either way, this shapeless "netherworld" of computing must be made up of actual hardware and software, backed by solid principles, and using the best technology to create a solid and manageable infrastructure. The grid guides us, but business dictates our actions.

And to that end, Oracle's grid infrastructure and Oracle Database 11*g* provide real solutions for current availability challenges. In all actuality, these solutions are a natural evolution of concepts and technologies that Oracle has been building toward since the days of Oracle Parallel Server (OPS), first released with Oracle 7. Oracle's grid infrastructure has evolved over several generations, from the early Oracle Cluster Manager releases for Linux and Windows in the Oracle 8*i* days, to Oracle Clusterware releases included with Oracle Database 10*g* and Oracle Database 11*g* Release 1. Oracle's grid infrastructure is the next generation in the evolution of this clustering software, combining the clustering aspects with the storage to provide that foundation for your grid computing needs.

What's Inside This Book

This book is about the Oracle technologies that are provided with Oracle Database 11*g* Release 2 and Oracle Clusterware to help achieve a highly available end-user experience. We have grouped these technologies into four parts:

- **Grid Infrastructure**   Laying the foundation for Maximum Availability

- **Oracle Real Application Clusters**   Building on this foundation at the database layer

- **Disaster Planning and Recovery**   Expanding availability beyond the data center

- **Enhancing Availability with Additional Features**

Grid Infrastructure

With Grid Infrastructure 11*g* Release 2, Oracle Automatic Storage Management (ASM) and Oracle Clusterware are installed into a single home directory, which is referred to as the *Grid Infrastructure home*. Part I, "Oracle's Grid Infrastructure," discusses the features that make up the underlying foundation of the Oracle grid—namely, the operating system, the Oracle Clusterware layer, and the storage grid. Our intent with this book is to provide a practical, no-nonsense approach to implementing Oracle solutions—but at the same time, we all like to have a little fun.

Chapter 1 begins with a series of hypothetical downtime situations that occur in a fictional startup company (LunarTrax) intending to provide space tourism services "to the Moon and beyond." With each downtime scenario, you are directed to the technology that would assist the sysadmin or DBA with that particular problem. This information shows you how the technologies discussed in the remaining chapters apply to real uptime challenges.

We embark on the journey into the world of Oracle VM in Chapter 2. We review the supported way of using OVM with Grid Infrastructure and offer DBAs a look at how they can cheaply set up a cluster using OVM for feature learning. We consider why and how to use Oracle VM for Oracle RAC installations and mention the difference between hardware virtualized and paravirtualized guests.

Chapter 3 provides an overview of Grid Infrastructure itself. We explain many of the new concepts introduced in 11*g* Release 2, such as Grid Plug and Play (GPnP) technology, the concepts of server pools, SCAN (Single Client Access Name) VIPs, and the like.

Chapter 4 details the actual installation and maintenance of a Grid Infrastructure environment, including best practices to set yourself up for success from the beginning. This chapter includes a look at OS prerequisites and preinstallation configuration, storage and networking considerations, and a patching discussion to prepare for ongoing maintenance. In addition, we discuss upgrading from earlier releases of Oracle Clusterware and ASM.

Chapter 5 discusses the storage grid in detail, with ASM, ADVM (ASM Dynamic Volume Manager), and ACFS (ASM Cluster File System) as the central focus of the storage grid. We introduce the concepts of ASM instances, ASM disks, and disk groups for those who are new to ASM and discuss new features such as ACFS and ADVM, as well as management tools such as ASMCMD (the command line interface for ASM Storage Administration) and AMSCA—the GUI ASM Configuration Assistant.

Oracle Real Application Clusters

Part II is dedicated in its entirety to the setup, configuration, and administration of Oracle RAC. The centerpiece of Oracle's database availability offerings, Oracle RAC provides a clustering solution that really took hold in Oracle9*i* and now has mushroomed into the de facto standard for enterprise database computing in Oracle Database 11*g*.

Chapter 6 is the definitive guide to Oracle RAC setup, starting with a beginner's guide to the basic architecture and moving through the Oracle RAC installation by building on the Grid Infrastructure configuration in Part I. The database configuration is illustrated step by step for quick Oracle RAC implementations, again including best practices for setting up the environment optimally from the outset.

Chapter 7 delves deeper into the Oracle RAC stack, discussing the finer points of administration and upkeep unique to clustered databases. For example, this chapter addresses points such as how redo and undo are handled in an Oracle RAC environment, how archiving is handled, and what are some of the additional utilities needed to monitor and maintain an Oracle RAC database. Availability requisites such as rolling patch upgrades, dropping nodes, and adding nodes, and policy-managed databases are discussed.

Chapter 8 takes more of an application viewpoint of the Oracle RAC database. Assuming that some aspect of your database is always up, how does your application best take advantage of things such as load balancing and transparently failing over if and when individual component failures occur in the grid on the back end? This chapter covers those questions and speaks to how both the database administrator and application developer can work together to ensure that the inevitable component failures will go unnoticed by the vast majority of "the business."

Disaster Planning and Recovery

Part III deals with those additional technologies provided with Oracle Database 11*g* Release 2, beyond just Oracle RAC, that are provided to minimize downtime from unforeseen problems. These problems can occur by way of a complete site loss due to man-made or natural disasters, or a smaller outage due to a faulty hardware component, leading to corrupt data on disk. Problems can also result from user errors: incorrect updates, logical application errors, or dropped tables. With these types of problems, the goal is to have prepared successfully, and then have all the pieces in place to deal appropriately with different types of disasters.

Chapter 9 takes an extensive look at the configuration and administration of Oracle's most frequently overlooked feature: Oracle Data Guard. A complete disaster recovery solution, Oracle Data Guard provides a rich toolkit for using a database's existing architecture to mirror a complete database to another site. Combined with Oracle RAC and Flashback Database, Oracle Data Guard is a superior business continuity tool to be used at times of total site loss or blackout.

Chapter 10 takes a look at Oracle's Oracle Recovery Manager (RMAN) utility and how you can use RMAN for media backups to provide a necessary partner to Oracle RAC and Oracle Data Guard in the fight against downtime. Topics include a primer on RMAN configuration and usage, taking advantage of features such as the Flash Recovery Area, and performing backups and recoveries when required. Advanced topics include the integration of RMAN into Oracle RAC clusters and using RMAN to offload backups in Oracle Data Guard environments.

Chapter 11 focuses on the suite of technologies that Oracle collectively refers to as "Flashback Recovery." This suite has been developed to provide minimal loss of time and data during those most dreaded of accidents: human error. Flashback Recovery comes in a few different flavors: Flashback Query, Flashback Versions Query, Flashback Transaction Query, Flashback Table, Flashback Drop (for undoing a dropped object), and Flashback Database.

Enhancing Availability with Additional Features

Part IV discusses the benefits of using the proper tools to manage and monitor the environment. The proper toolset greatly reduces the costs and complexity of managing the environment, while proper monitoring lets you rapidly identify and react to those "unforeseen" problems. To that end, Chapter 12 discusses the use of Oracle Data Guard Broker and Oracle Data Guard Manager (DGMGRL), which you can use to manage and automate Oracle Data Guard–related tasks. It also covers other tools, such as srvctl and crsctl, that you can use to manage and monitor your Oracle RAC and Oracle Data Guard environments.

Chapter 13 concludes with a discussion of using Oracle Grid Control to manage all aspects of the grid and using this information to maximize the availability of your systems. The chapter discusses the setup and configuration of Grid Control and offers hints and best practices for using it to monitor your systems. Some of the administration and monitoring tasks outlined in previous chapters, such as Oracle Data Guard role transitions, service creation, and other features, are demonstrated.

MAA Workshops

This book is organized to provide a conceptual understanding of how Oracle's Maximum Availability technologies work. We provides a fictitious, yet realistic, business scenario in which to demonstrate the functionality of these integrated offerings so that you can see them in action.

The MAA workshops offer step-by-step instructions that walk you through configuration and setup of different products. As readers of technical books ourselves, we know that these tried-and-tested recipes can be invaluable, because a configuration is not something you run through every day. Sometimes you just need the step-by-step instructions.

The workshops offer instructions for achieving a certain end, such as adding a new node to your existing cluster. The steps have been freed of any conceptual explanation and will just get you through the process.

So that you can access the MAA workshops quickly and easily, when you need them, every workshop in the book has been included in the book's table of contents. So after you read this book cover to cover and have found what you need, you can later return to the configuration steps for a quick guide to a setup, configuration, or administration technique.

Examples

When we began writing this book, we took a look at the breadth of topics involved and decided that, as with the previous edition, all examples would be appropriate for Linux systems. This decision was made easier by the fact that the Linux OS has become ubiquitous, particularly in the Oracle RAC arena, owing in large part to principles mentioned earlier in this introduction: ease of management, low overall cost, and the high level of integration with Oracle's products. Keep in mind, however, that in many cases, particularly with respect to the RDBMS, the information offered is generic in nature, so the platform is not important for many of the examples.

We also included OVM as part of our configuration, because of the flexibility it provides in creating a sandbox environment. We wanted to write a book that you can take into a simple test environment that has been configured on the cheap, so you can easily step through many of the examples here as a proof-of-concept on some of the availability techniques we discuss. For such environments, it only makes sense to use a cost-sensitive OS such as Linux, running on commodity-priced hardware. Adding OVM into the mix gives you even greater flexibility to create clusters and standby environments with multiple virtual nodes, while maintaining the low cost necessary for your sandbox environments. It also means that you can teach yourself how to use complex enterprise-computing concepts in the basement of your own home, since in many cases, there is just no substitute for the learning value of hands-on tinkering for comprehension.

It's time to discover how you can maximize your availability. The tech stack is often complex, and as with any endeavor worth doing, it is worth doing right. You will surely have a few setbacks, but the results will be impressive and worth all the effort. Happy tinkering!

PART
I

Oracle's Grid
Infrastructure

CHAPTER
1

Architecting the Oracle
Database Grid

s you have already discovered, or perhaps are about to discover, maintaining the Maximum Availability database is a tricky prospect. Hundreds of possible sources of downtime are hiding in the nooks and crannies of your enterprise. Outage situations cascade into catastrophes, as an attempt to resolve a problem creates another outage and quickly spirals out of control. But with careful planning or swift corrective action, almost all downtime scenarios can be prevented.

This book discusses numerous technologies that can prevent or drastically reduce a variety of database outages. What are these downtime scenarios? Which possible outages can you protect yourself against? The fact is that the Maximum Availability DBA lives by Murphy's Law: "Anything that can go wrong, will go wrong." Pure and simple. So to survive as a DBA, you must live by this maxim. Not only do you have to prepare for every eventuality—you have to expect it. Simply hoping that bad things or extreme scenarios will not happen is courting disaster. Putting things off with the mindset that things are working well so far is courting disaster. It is okay for you to hope for the best, but it is imperative that you plan for the worst, and this is never more true than in your role as a Maximum Availability DBA.

As discussed in the introduction to this tome, database availability is not defined by the database administrator; it is defined by the perception of the business—the users who expect the data they need to be accessible at the touch of a button. To illustrate the various types of situations that threaten the availability of your database, this chapter will walk through the planning stages of setting up a database grid meant to insulate the business and these end users from various types of problems that can ultimately cause data to be inaccessible, for whatever reasons. We will discuss different types of outages and the particular technologies you can use to protect against these problems, and we'll point you to the specific chapter in this book where the implementation of a particular technology is covered in detail.

LunarTrax: To the Moon and Beyond!

For the situations in this chapter, and for the workshops and examples throughout the book, we will use the database from the company LunarTrax, Inc., a fictitious startup company whose ambitious goal is to provide tourism to the moon. This company's primary databases hold several terabytes of data—everything from flight data, to solar flare forecast information, to marketing data for potential target customers, in addition to data used for internal accounting and human resources (HR).

The lead DBA and architect, Maximus Aurelias Anthony (known as Max to his friends), is a veteran of 1000 psychic wars and is taking no chances with the uptime and availability of his system. To ensure that the environment is as easily managed as possible, Max has implemented a consolidation strategy that reduces the original number of planned databases to a finite number. Once this strategy is implemented, the primary production databases will include one database for customer-facing data (external customers) and one for internal data/internal customers. This consolidation strategy greatly reduces costs, both from an initial investment standpoint and from a maintenance standpoint. However, from a database standpoint, it essentially puts all of the company's eggs into just two baskets. Therefore, along with this consolidation strategy, it is essential that Max put in place an infrastructure that will guard these "eggs" according to their true value.

As a veteran of many years in the DBA world, including some time spent in the technical support arena, Max is well aware of the potential for disaster from all corners. To combat this, he is determined to implement a database grid with complete redundancy and the ability either to avoid or quickly recover from any of the common (and less common) pitfalls that can afflict a database and ultimately impact the business.

Planning the Grid

In planning for his database grid, Max must account for several areas to ensure that the business continues to run smoothly and is not impacted by database operations or failures. Max believes it is imperative that the environment be set up so that planned maintenance activities occur on an ongoing basis, while minimizing the impact to the business. Planned maintenance is crucial, because technology never stands still. In particular, in this competitive industry, the ability to stay one step ahead of the competition often depends on the best use of the latest technology. Therefore, having the flexibility to upgrade systems, both from a hardware and software perspective, is a key component to Max's database grid.

Max is also keenly aware of the fact that component failures occur. This is just a fact of life. Hardware in particular has a finite lifespan—moving parts can continue moving for only so long before they give out. Whether a lower-cost commodity hardware solution or a so-called high-end hardware solution is used, the reality is that at some point, a component is going to fail.

In addition to hardware failures are the inevitable software failures that must be anticipated. Whether a software failure occurs because of a design limitation or some unintentional flaw (aka a software bug), the chances of encountering a software failure of some type are a practical guarantee. Failure to plan for this inevitability is nothing short of a plan to fail.

Perhaps more concerning to Max than the inevitable component or software failure is the unpredictability of his users. As any good DBA will attest, Max would feel most secure if no users were allowed into the database at all. Unfortunately, that would defeat its purpose. So, like a father turning over the car keys to his teenage daughter for the first time, Max has to accept the fact that at some point, he will need to turn over at least some of the keys to the database to his end user population. When that happens, any number of things could potentially go wrong. He knows that the database grid at LunarTrax must have resiliency to withstand and recover from user errors.

Another priority for Max is having the ability to expand in the future. As a startup in a new industry, LunarTrax has high hopes for a bright future, but a shoestring budget in the present. Therefore, Max must build in the ability to expand his database grid in the future to meet the anticipated increase in demand that will arrive with the success of this endeavor—but this future expansion cannot be allowed to impact the current systems.

Finally, Max realizes that his primary responsibility is to prepare for the worst-case scenario—total disaster. Whether something as simple as a cut utility line causing loss of power to the data center, or something as catastrophic as a flood that leaves your data center under three feet of water, disasters can break a business. Protecting against disasters of this type is vital, and Max knows that he must ensure that his database grid can withstand the extended loss of the primary data center. His plans must account for both failover and failback strategies in such a situation.

This chapter discusses various aspects of the grid from a theoretical perspective and lays the groundwork for the rest of the book, which delves into the specifics of Oracle technology and how it addresses many important concerns.

The Grid and Planned Maintenance

Max is keen on ensuring that his company, and specifically his corporate database infrastructure, can stay up-to-date with the latest hardware and software maintenance releases. From a database perspective, this means he must develop a strategy for maintaining the software.

His first step is regular, proactive application of patchsets and patchset updates (PSUs), but in the longer term, he must plan for database upgrades in a timely fashion. But he has other aspects to think about as well. Operating system maintenance must be considered—including both the patching and upgrading of the operating system, plus any third-party software and applications. Max knows from experience (particularly from his days in technical support), that these activities are too often avoided and postponed rather than embraced. In many IT departments, patching and other types of maintenance are not always viewed as part of the expected routine for a DBA, but something to be avoided at all costs until it is forced on the DBA by a crisis. In these situations, the lack of system upkeep is either the direct cause of the crisis or, at a minimum, it can become an insurmountable hurdle in diagnosing and resolving the issue. What subsequently occurs is a "fire drill," in which the DBA is forced to perform necessary maintenance in the middle of a crisis, without proper planning and preparation. This lack of planning and preparation can easily make things worse, even though the measures are required to resolve the primary issue. Avoiding these "fire drills" is a crucial component of Max's MAA strategy.

In addition to the software maintenance, the DBA must be able to update system hardware—whether that means adding components such as CPU or memory or implementing firmware or BIOS changes. In extreme cases, entire servers may need to be switched out, whether due to failure or simple obsolescence.

Based on past experience, Max is determined to embrace the maintenance of his environment aggressively. His plans are to incorporate the upkeep of all components of his database grid into the daily routine of his DBA staff. Even though many of these activities may not occur until well into the future, he knows that proper planning in the early stages can ensure that these future activities can be undertaken with minimal impact on the business, and the end result of this is an environment that can be sustained and healthy for the long term.

Oracle Technologies: Reducing the Impact of Maintenance

In terms of long-term planning, you have a few choices from an Oracle technology perspective that will help you keep up with the technology with minimal impact to your operations. This book focuses on two of the major technologies in this respect—Oracle Real Application Clusters (Oracle RAC) and Oracle Data Guard.

Oracle RAC and Planned Maintenance

We begin with a discussion of Oracle RAC. Oracle RAC is an Oracle feature based on clustering technology which provides simultaneous access to the database from every active node. This simultaneous access from live nodes is known as a "shared everything" architecture. Having "shared everything" access to your database from multiple nodes (servers), which is what Oracle RAC provides, is in many ways a boon to your database maintenance. You can apply many individual patches to the Oracle Database itself, including PSUs, in a rolling fashion by applying each patch to one node at a time. This lets you take advantage of the most critical short-term fixes without users losing access to the database.

In addition to database patches, Oracle RAC also lets you patch and even upgrade your operating system in a rolling fashion without incurring downtime. Whether you are applying a service pack (from RH4 U6 to RH4 U7, for example) or performing an actual operating system upgrade (such as an upgrade from Oracle Enterprise Linux, OEL 4 to OEL 5), it is possible to do this on a single node at a time in your Oracle RAC Cluster, without ever having to incur a full outage. Because of this (among other reasons), Max has chosen Oracle RAC to be a central component of the database grid at LunarTrax.

From a hardware perspective, implementing Oracle RAC also allows hardware maintenance to occur in a rolling fashion. Changes to BIOS or firmware can usually occur one node at a time, as well as replacement of individual components, either because of failure or due to an upgrade. Oracle RAC and patching specifics are covered in Chapters 6 and 7.

Oracle Data Guard and Planned Maintenance

Although Oracle RAC is clearly a central tenet of the database grid, it is not the be-all, end-all solution to every potential need. Applying patchsets to the Oracle Database or upgrading the database from one major release to another cannot be done in a rolling fashion with Oracle RAC alone. However, by combining Oracle RAC with Oracle Data Guard, you can achieve these upgrades in a rolling fashion with minimal downtime.

Converting a physical standby database to a logical standby allows you to perform the upgrade on the logical standby while logs are still being applied from the primary (where the business is still happily chugging away using the older release). After the upgrade of the logical standby, users can be migrated to the newly upgraded system with minimal impact, and the original primary can then be upgraded—again, while log files are moving between the two sites and everything is still synchronized. After users have migrated, the original primary system can be upgraded, and users (the business) can be switched back following the same process—all with minimal, if any, impact.

Therefore, Oracle Data Guard is another key component in Max's database grid strategy for LunarTrax. Oracle RAC and Oracle Data Guard combined allow Max the flexibility to perform ongoing maintenance of his environment, with minimal impact to the business. Specifics of implementing Oracle Data Guard are discussed in more detail in Chapters 9 and 12.

Additional Oracle Technologies

In addition to Oracle RAC and Oracle Data Guard, Max has evaluated technologies such as Oracle Streams and Oracle GoldenGate to solidify his database grid. Because Max has chosen to defer implementation of these technologies for later, we will not discuss them in this book but will include them in future editions as appropriate.

Recovering Quickly from Failures

Max's strategy of aggressively embracing and being proactive with maintenance will undoubtedly pay dividends by avoiding problems in the future. However, no one at LunarTrax is naive enough to assume that all problems will be avoided. No matter how diligent the LunarTrax DBA team is with patching, the possibility of encountering a bug in the software stack always exists, particularly because LunarTrax is intentionally pushing the boundaries of technology. And of course, as mentioned earlier, hardware component failures are a fact of life that cannot be avoided no matter how much you patch the software stack. Max hopes to eliminate downtime due to hardware component failures by ensuring redundancy throughout the system. This includes redundant network cards (network interface card [NIC] bonding), redundant disk access cards (multipathing), redundant storage (RAID), and even redundant servers (Oracle RAC).

In addition to this redundancy, a solid backup (and restore) strategy is imperative for any DBA. We'd like to say that this goes without saying, but Murphy's Law tells us to take nothing for granted. No matter how much redundancy exists in the system, data corruption or data loss can occur—so backups, as always, are a crucial component to any database grid.

Oracle Technologies at Play

To achieve the desired redundancy necessary to recover quickly from software failures or component failures, Max wants to ensure that he is using the best technology for his specific purposes. He is well aware that when it comes to backups, he has a plethora of options from which to choose. As an Oracle veteran, Max harkens back to the days of a database backup being as simple as an OS copy of a few gigabytes' worth of files while the database was shut down. But in the real world, with terabytes' worth of data, OS file copies no longer cut the mustard. Let's explore the Oracle technologies Max needs to achieve his goals.

Again with Oracle RAC

Clearly, Oracle RAC, with its shared everything architecture, is a key component to a redundant architecture. Any failure affecting an individual server's ability to function properly will not impact the entire database, because other nodes in the cluster will be able to continue the work seamlessly, even if an entire node is lost. Although other technologies such as Oracle Data Guard or Streams can achieve the same goal, they do so by keeping copies of the data in separate and distinct databases. This, however, implies a time delay in reacting to and recovering from relatively simple failures. Only Oracle RAC can provide this redundant access to the same database, so that even in an extreme case such as the complete failure of a node in your cluster, other nodes are up and running and actively accessing the same database even in the midst of the server failure. The remaining instances will automatically perform instance recovery for the instance that crashed, and any sessions that were connected to the downed server will be able to reconnect immediately to another instance that is already actively accessing the database.

Oracle Clusterware

The Oracle Clusterware component of Oracle's grid infrastructure is a necessary underpinning of an Oracle RAC Database. In addition to facilitating shared access to the actual database, Oracle Clusterware offers the benefit of monitoring for failures of critical processes such as instances, listeners, virtual IP addresses and the like, as well as monitoring node membership and responsiveness. When the Oracle Clusterware stack detects a failure of a critical component of the cluster, corrective action is taken automatically to restart the failed resource, up to and including the node itself. This architecture allows Max to meet his goal of recovering quickly from localized and relatively minor failures without impacting the business.

Oracle Recovery Manager (RMAN)

With respect to backups, too much is never enough. Max has determined that regular data pump exports will occur, but since a data pump export is only a point-in-time backup, his Oracle RMAN backup strategy is key to success. Because he will also be using Automatic Storage Management (ASM), the RMAN strategy is doubly important. RMAN allows you to take full or incremental backups, and lets you restore and recover as little as a single database block. Max knows that this type of flexibility in terms of backup and recovery is integral to maximizing the availability of the LunarTrax databases.

Flashback Database

Finally, Max decided early on to enable Flashback Database in all the environments. In days gone by, Max often found that he needed to perform an entire database restore to recover up to the time just prior to the occurrence of some critical error (such as an inadvertent deletion of data, some other logical corruption, or corruption of an online redo log). However, with the advent of Flashback Database, he knows now that he can alleviate the need to do this by essentially storing all of the blocks necessary both to redo and undo transactions for a specified period of time. This means that Max can do a "rewind" of the database without first doing a full restore, potentially saving immeasurable time in a crisis. Flashback Database and RMAN are discussed in more detail in Chapters 10 and 11.

Protecting Against and Recovering from User Errors

Speaking of inadvertently deleting data, the thing that most often keeps Max awake at night is the possibility of user errors causing data loss. Perhaps the most difficult outage situations are those tricky logical errors introduced by the users themselves—a user updates the wrong table or updates the wrong values, a developer thinks she is logged into the test system but is actually logged into the production system, or a user omits the where clause on a delete or update statement and 100,000 rows vanish or are logically corrupted. Max has been around long enough to see these problems happen over and over again—when months of work go down the drain.

This is a concern for Max particularly in the LunarTrax environment, where everyone works at a frenetic pace, and the company is not yet large enough to have clear lines of demarcation between production, development, and test environments. Max wants to be able to restrict access altogether to the production environments, but with the company's small development staff, and the rate at which changes are pushed through, this is just not practical.

Oracle Technology Checkpoint: Flashback Query and Flashback Table

Fortunately, the flashback features allowing recovery from serious errors are built into the database. The Flashback Query feature allows undo data stored in the Undo Tablespace to be read so that the DBA or anyone with appropriate access can "go back in time" and query the data as it existed before the incident. The Flashback Table feature also allows quick recovery if a table is inadvertently dropped, by maintaining a recycle bin, whereby dropped objects are essentially renamed and stored until space is needed. Max needs to ensure that enough storage exists to retain a sufficient amount of available undo, and a sufficient amount of free space must be available in user tablespaces to allow for upkeep of the recycle bin.

Beyond that, it is a matter of educating the developers and other users about the capabilities of Oracle Flashback technologies. The key is catching errors quickly—so full disclosure is important. Flashback technologies rely on data storage, and storage resources are not infinite. As long as errors are uncovered within a reasonable time period, Max and his DBA staff should be able to quickly recapture this type of data, and in some cases, the developers or users may be able to correct their own mistakes.

Again with the Flashback Database

Sometimes, however, serious database errors are tough to overcome. Typically, user errors do not occur in a vacuum, and an erroneous update can occur alongside hundreds of correct updates. Pretty soon, the bad data is buried by thousands of additional updates. How can you find just one of those transactions among thousands? Can you "rewind" the entire database back to a previous point in time? The answer is *yes*. Flashback Database is an important feature in Max's Maximum Availability Architecture (MAA) plans for the LunarTrax environment, and it can in fact "rewind" the database to allow for "do-overs." So in extreme cases, when Flashback Query is not enough, Flashback Database can help the MAA DBA retain his or her sanity in a world gone mad. Oracle Flashback features are covered in detail in Chapter 11.

Planning for Expansion and Future Growth

A key component in Max's Oracle database grid is the ability to grow the grid as LunarTrax grows. Max intends to budget as much as possible toward ensuring that a solid foundation is in place for development, testing, and quality assurance (QA) environments, as well as the production grid—but he knows his budget can't accommodate all of the planned capacity immediately. He hopes that, once the first launches get off the ground, more money will be available for hardware, just in time for the expansion that LunarTrax will need in its database grid. Max knows that he still needs to plan now, however, for that future growth. And as the requirements for the grid expand and the grid grows, that growth cannot be allowed to have a detrimental impact on the current operations—it must be as seamless and transparent as possible.

Oracle Technology: Automatic Storage Management

Technologies such as ASM and Oracle RAC play pivotal roles. By implementing ASM from the outset, Max will have the flexibility to grow his storage easily in the future, without the need to bring down operations. Because ASM allows both the addition and removal of disks as needed, Max can even remove/replace storage that becomes outdated in the future, again without impacting the day-to-day operations of the database, since this can all be accomplished online.

ASM also allows striping across all available disks; this means Max does not have to invest costly resources in determining manual file system layouts. In the past, Max had to spend time determining where the I/O hot spots were as part of his regular tuning; then he had to move files to different file systems on different disks to achieve the I/O performance necessary for his operations. With ASM, this is not necessary, because not only are all files automatically striped across all available disks, but "hot blocks" are also automatically moved to the "sweet spot" on the disk, to improve seek times. ASM is discussed in more detail in Chapter 5.

Again with the Oracle Clusterware

Beyond storage, capacity at LunarTrax may need to grow as well, with the addition of servers to provide more CPU, memory resources, or networking resources to the business. Business needs often cycle over time: users may find the database completely accessible, but when activity in some areas increases, resources may become restricted. Max anticipates that the database for internal customers will experience problems at the beginning of each month, when accounts receivable (AR) must close out the preceding month's accounts and run massive reports on the status of all opening and closing accounts. This month-end requirement sends the database processing needs of the AR department through the roof—but only for a week or so, and then it settles back into a more routine usage pattern. At the same time, HR typically finds its peaks near the middle and end of the month, as it processes employee hours, salaries, and payments.

By implementing Oracle Clusterware, which is part of Oracle's 11g Release 2 grid infrastructure stack, LunarTrax will be able to create *server pools*, which allow for the transition of servers between different grids depending on demand. In addition, instances from different databases can be allocated to run on more or fewer servers within the grid, as needed. In the future, if the total number of servers needs to be expanded due to an overall increase in demand, a new server can be added and the overall capacity of the grid can be expanded easily. By the same token, if older servers need to be retired or reallocated to new environments, this can be just as easily accomplished without impacting end users. This can all occur without taking the database offline, by adding nodes to or removing nodes from a cluster while the business continues to function as usual. Oracle's grid infrastructure and server pools are discussed in detail in Chapters 3 and 4.

Disaster Recovery

The next item on the agenda for Max and the LunarTrax staff is to plan for the ultimate: some type of disaster that renders the data center inoperable. During his time as a DBA and as a support tech, Max was exposed to all manners of issues that rendered an entire system (and in some cases, an entire data center) inoperable. These issues ranged from a simple power outage that extended beyond the capacity of the UPS, to full-blown flooding of the data center. Of course, hurricanes, earthquakes, and other natural disasters do occur, and the potential for terrorist attacks or sabotage is omnipresent. But a catastrophe in the data center itself is not always the cause of these disasters. Max recalls a scenario in which an inadvertent overwrite by the systems administrator of all the shared disks in a system rendered it completely useless. Although this did not impact the data center itself, the fact that Max's company had a disaster recovery site available for switchover, meant they were able to quickly recover from this type of error and keep the business going, saving several hours of downtime and countless thousands of dollars.

Oracle Technology: Oracle Data Guard

Based on their experience, Max and the LunarTrax crack staff have determined that an Oracle Data Guard environment should exist in two geographically separate locations. Given LunarTrax's plans to promote space tourism, Max intends to be the first person to implement a lunar Oracle Data Guard environment, but that is a long-term plan, dependent on some networking improvements. Near-term, the intent is to achieve geographic separation of at least 500 miles.

The LunarTrax DBA and networking teams have scouted appropriate terrestrial sites for a secondary data center to house their Oracle Data Guard environment. Given that their headquarters and primary data center are located in areas susceptible to hurricanes, they ultimately settled on the foothills of Colorado as an ideal secondary site, realizing that hurricanes, earthquakes, and other such natural phenomenon are relatively rare in Colorado. Nevertheless, the cautious nature of the DBA has induced the team to scout out tertiary sites as well, not necessarily to create cascaded standby sites, but to take advantage of the ability to sync up multiple standbys to a single primary. One site will have a delay implemented in the application of the logs to provide some lag time in synchronization. This will allow Max and the team time to intercept any unwanted changes in the redo stream before they are applied to the tertiary site, preventing the propagation of any logical corruptions to all sites, should it occur.

Not wanting to tie up all this hardware in waiting for the unlikely (but inevitable) need to use it, Max wants to maximize utility as well as availability. Therefore, the intent of the LunarTrax secondary and tertiary DR sites will be to run a combination of Oracle Active Data Guard and Logical Standby to allow access to these systems for reporting purposes. This additional capacity will allow Max to justify the expense of maintaining the disaster recovery systems beyond simple standby resources. Oracle Data Guard, Oracle Active Data Guard, and Oracle Logical Data Guard are discussed in more detail in Chapters 9 and 12.

What Next?

"What next?" is a question often asked by DBAs in the midst of a crisis. In this context, though, this is a good thing. Here it means: What's next in terms of the proactive work that must be undertaken to keep data available to the business? In this case, you are in control of the next step, rather than having events control you. After the architectural foundation is created for the database grid, testing and implementation can begin.

Test, Test, and Test Some More

Crucial to your success in planning for the worst is your ability to react quickly to different types of problems. In many cases, Oracle has automated the responses—but sometimes, even when automation is possible, the DBA prefers to leave those decisions in the hands of humans as opposed to machines.

Testing should not only encompass functional testing, but it should cover processes and procedures for reacting to certain situations. This ensures that you and your staff have the practice and expertise necessary not only to know what the correct decisions are, but also to be able to execute those decisions flawlessly and efficiently. In addition, it is crucial that test environments mimic production as closely as possible. A three-node Oracle RAC cluster in your production environment with a single-instance test environment is not going to allow you to test all aspects of the production environment. By the same token, having a production environment with Oracle Data Guard, and a testing or development environment without Oracle Data Guard, will also leave you wanting in terms of the ability to test real-life scenarios that could impact your production environment.

A DBA with the best of plans and a perfect understanding of the theory of a technology can still lack practical experience, that only testing and trial by fire can provide. Even if decisions are automated to a certain extent, testing is still crucial at all stages. Automation relies on software written by humans, and because humans have flaws, software has flaws. Couple this with a lack of practical experience and even the best theoretical systems can fail to live up to their expectations.

Test the Redundancy of Your Environment by Inducing Failures

As you know, when running Oracle's grid infrastructure and Oracle RAC, one of the primary goals is to achieve redundancy of various different hardware and software components. In many cases, recovery from certain failures is automated. But to be sure that redundancy works when needed and as expected, testing is a must. Testing uncovers configuration issues and defects that may cause the stack to fail to work as expected. If you have redundant network cards (aka bonding, or IP network multipathing [IPMP]), you can expect that if one card fails, the bonded pair will continue to act as one. By the same token, if you have enabled multipathing to your storage, how do you know that if one path fails, the other path will continue to provide unhindered access to your storage? You cannot just take this on faith. The answer is to test the environment. If you expect the system to recover from a failure automatically, testing by inducing failures prior to going into production will ensure that the system will perform as expected, or else allow you the opportunity to uncover configuration issues or software defects that prevent the stack from working as expected.

Test Your Backups by Restoring

In addition to testing the automated features of a clustered environment, you need to test the manual processes as well. In Max's time as a DBA and technical support specialist, he often encountered other DBAs who were adept at backing up their databases but had never practiced a restore or a recover operation. When something went wrong, and a restore was needed, they'd call Max. Even though he was happy to assist, the fact is that this cost time.

But what if this lack of experience costs you more than just time? If a restore and recovery have never been tested, how do you know it will work as expected? The middle of a crisis is not the time to find out that your backups were incorrectly configured, and now you need to do a full restore with only half of your files in the backup set. The middle of a crisis is not the time to learn that you don't have access to the tapes where your backups are stored. The middle of a crisis is not the time to find out that your database exports will actually take seven hours to import back in.

Max knows that the only way to ensure that a backup is successful is to restore that backup regularly to a test location. And the only way to know how long it will take to recover is to test it and measure it. It is not enough just to test prior to going into production, either. Things change in the production environment: the amount of data increases, the environment changes, and the situation changes. Even the people change. Regular testing not only validates the backup itself, but also the process.

Testing ensures that the DBAs on Max's team are skilled and practiced at restore and recovery operations, and when a crisis does occur, he can be confident that the necessary data will be available and the reaction to the crisis will be second nature. Furthermore, multiple solutions to a particular problem are often available. Some situations may call for using Flashback Database, while other situations call for a partial restore or perhaps a full restore. In other scenarios, Data Pump may be the most desirable solution. Knowing how long certain operations will take will allow you to make the correct decision as to which operation should be performed to keep the business up and running or to get it back online as quickly as possible.

Test Your Disaster Recovery by Switching to the DR Site

Beyond testing of backups, you need to test your disaster recovery scenario. The middle of a crisis is not the time to realize that you are unsure of the steps necessary to perform a switchover or failover. The middle of a crisis is not the time to find out that firewall issues exist between your application servers and the DR site on which the database is running. The middle of a crisis is not the time to realize that your network dropped a log file three weeks ago, and now your Oracle Data Guard environment is out of sync!

Max's database grid architecture is accompanied by test plans that include regular monitoring, regular testing of database backups by restoring to test systems from the production backup sets, and also regular switchovers of the production environment. Max intends to perform a planned switchover and switchback of the production environment between the primary site and the DR site at least twice per year, even after the production phase begins, to ensure that the necessary functionality is available when it is needed.

Sandbox Environments

So what exactly is meant by the "production system" anyway? "Production down" no longer means only the production system is affected. If a staff of testers or developers are idle while waiting on a "development" environment, then whenever that environment is down, it is costing the business money. Therefore, caution needs to be used even in these "lower environments" when introducing changes that might impact the productivity of any of your staff. A sandbox environment can be created to test basic patches and other scenarios that might impact any user base. A sandbox system does not necessarily need to be an identical copy of the production environment, but a system that can be used at will by the DBA staff is something that many businesses cannot afford to do without. It allows quick and immediate access to a production-like environment, where some basic sanity testing—such as checking for patch conflicts—can occur without impacting any users in the environment.

Go Forth and Conquer

The downtime scenarios illustrated in this chapter are the tip of the iceberg. You can see that many common, everyday situations can be fixed using the functionality provided by the full Oracle stack. In most cases, with Oracle Database 11g Release 2, this functionality is at your fingertips and you can leverage it immediately, with just a few steps outlined in the chapters that follow. Remember that planning, preparation, and testing are important to ensure that you are prepared to take advantage of the Oracle database grid to the full extent of its capabilities.

Now that we've explored a few of the situations that might cause angst for the MAA DBA, let's roll up our sleeves and dig into the technologies available to prevent (or significantly reduce) these disruptions. The ensuing chapters will provide the technical details you need to build your own database grid from the ground up. Go forth and conquer!

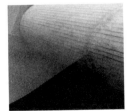

CHAPTER
2

Oracle VM

ou may wonder why this chapter is about a product that some consider a competitor to Oracle Clusterware and Oracle Real Application Clusters (Oracle RAC); however, Oracle VM has a role to play in maximum availability and is supported for some cluster configurations. When using single-instance databases, guest virtual machines (VMs) can be live-migrated (moved without shutdown) from one machine to another to allow for maintenance, and they can even be set up to relocate to another node when the current node fails. A failure scenario would of course result in a short outage, but imagine if VMs were actually running Oracle RAC databases—then the failure would simply mean one node down until it completes the move. You can even live-migrate a guest running an Oracle RAC instance in the latest versions, but even for older versions you can move a guest to new hardware when the current hardware fails.

This chapter covers how Oracle VM can be used to set up a low-cost test cluster for our DBA, Max, to hone his grid infrastructure and Oracle RAC skills well away from the production environment. Although the prior edition of this book focused on setting up a simple Oracle RAC cluster using firewire, we have found that for testing and demo purposes, Oracle VM and optionally iSCSI (using a server such as Openfiler) provide more flexibility and a superior sandbox environment.

Virtualization Basics

Virtualization allows multiple virtual machines to run on a single physical machine. Each virtual machine gets a share of the physical machine's resources, but it sees those shared resources as though they were its own memory, CPU, and storage.

Virtualization is used for many reasons. In a data center with many underutilized machines, it makes sense to reprovision some of the costly hardware and move applications to run as guests on a VM server. It is also possible to move guests to different physical VM servers, reducing application downtime when you're performing hardware maintenance. Max has, in fact, considered this for LunarTrax, but the company is currently growing rather than consolidating and is buying right-size machines as its user base increases. LunarTrax is also going to use Oracle Data Guard with Oracle RAC, and Max is particularly interested in virtualization, because it allows him to run multiple hosts on a single physical machine, thereby creating a cluster in a single reasonably priced box. This is a great environment in which to learn the new features in Oracle 11*g* Release 2 Clusterware and Oracle RAC.

Oracle VM

Oracle VM comes as two separate installable products, the manager and the server. The server can exist on its own without the manager and can be configured from the command line. The manager provides a browser-based GUI to manage Oracle VM.

Guest virtual machines that run on the server can be set up from scratch using the original installation media, or you can use preconfigured templates to set it up. Two types of guests can be configured for Oracle VM:

- **Hardware virtualized** With a hardware virtualized guest, you install and run an original copy of your operating system. The Hypervisor and the server hardware itself deal with making the guest work in a virtual environment. A **uname -a** on the guest O/S would look like any other Linux install.

- **Paravirtualized** With a paravirtualized guest, the operating system gets recompiled to incorporate the necessary paravirtualized drivers to work in a virtual environment. For Oracle VM, the running kernel name then becomes a Xen kernel.

```
[root]# uname -a
Linux host1 2.6.18-92.1.17.0.2.el5xen #1 SMP Tue Nov 18 04:11:19
EST 2008 i686 i686 i386 GNU/Linux
```

Oracle VM Server and Dom-0

Oracle VM Server is a complete Xen-based Linux kernel that provides the services to run your guest virtual machine. This Oracle VM Server machine is often referred to as the *hypervisor*, *Domain-0 (Dom-0)*, or the *management domain* and takes up a small amount of the physical machine resources. Dom-0 controls the creation and destruction of guest virtual machines and manages the presentation of physical resources to those guests. The installation is from a single disc and uses a standard configuration to make it simple and fast. The product is free to download from Oracle e-delivery at http://edelivery.oracle.com/oraclevm. For support patches and updates, you will need to license the Oracle Unbreakable Linux support service. This book is not intended to cover Oracle Virtualization in depth, so it sticks mostly to the simple default installation, but we'll look at some of the other options that apply.

Oracle VM Server Hardware Requirements

Not all servers are able to run virtual environments, although most modern machines are capable. The minimum requirements are shown in Table 2-1, but if you want to run multiple guests on the same server, you will need more memory at least.

NOTE
The information in Table 2-1 is from Oracle's published requirements; check the following site for any changes that may occur: www.oracle.com/technetwork/server-storage/vm/overview/index.html.

Supported Host Platforms	Systems with x86 or x86_64 processors that support PAE (Physical Address Extension)
Minimum Processor Class	I686 class
Minimum Memory	1GB
Recommended Memory	2GB
Number of Supported Guests	Based on the amount of physical memory in the server and the amount of memory allocated to each guest
CPUs Supporting Paravirtualized Guests	Intel Pentium-PRO or newer All AMD Athlon/Duron or newer
CPUs Supporting Hardware Virtualized Guests	Some Intel Pentium D, Core, Core2, and Xeon models (/proc/cpuinfo should include "vmx" among the flags)
	Some AMD Athlon and Opteron models (/proc/cpuinfo should include "svm" among the flags)
Maximum Number of CPUs	Oracle VM Server: 64 logical CPUs Guests: 32 logical CPUs
Maximum Memory	Oracle VM Server: 1TB Guests: x86 (32-bit): 63GB x86_64 (64-bit): 510GB
Supported Disks for VM files	SCSI, SAS, IDE/SATA, NAS, iSCSI, FC, FCoE
Supported Virtual Hardware	vDisk: 20 hda, 26 sda, 5 xvd (all tested for a single PV machine instance); maximum of 128 vDisk devices per VM pool
	vNICs: 31 for paravirtualized, 8 for hardware virtualized
Hypervisor Booting	From local drives, SAN, iSCSI, NFS, flash

TABLE 2-1. *Oracle VM Server Requirements*

Installing Oracle VM Server

The Standard Installation is similar to any other Linux install and should overwrite previous software from the system or partition. By default, the install will set up Dom-0 to take up 500MB of memory from the server machine to run and will partition the disk to have a small root file system with the remaining disk allocated to /OVS, where the guest VMs, shared disk, templates, and ISO install files are stored.

If you are not intending to use Oracle VM Manager, you are not constrained to using the supplied directory structure; however, we recommend using the logical structure, and if you later decide to use the Oracle VM Manager, the work you have done can be discovered and added to the repository.

NOTE
You do not see /OVS mounted because the actual mount point has a unique repository ID path that is symbolically linked to /OVS.

```
Filesystem              1K-blocks       Used Available Use% Mounted on
/dev/sda2                3050092    1126332   1766324  39% /
/dev/sda1                 101086      45738     50129  48% /boot
tmpfs                     288340          0    288340   0% /dev/shm
/dev/sda3              308262912  192717824 115545088  63%
                                                          /var/ovs/mount/<id>

# ls -ald /OVS
lrwxrwxrwx 1 root root 47 Nov 25 09:28 /OVS -> /var/ovs/mount/<id>
```

Under the /OVS mount point, you see the following directories:

```
drwxr-xr-x 10 root root      3896 Jan 19 07:40 .
drwxrwxrwx  3 root root      4096 Nov 25 09:28 ..
drwxrwxrwx  2 root root      3896 Jan 12 11:36 iso_pool
drwxr-xr-x  2 root root      3896 Nov 25 09:22 lost+found
drwxrwxrwx  3 root root      3896 Nov 25 09:28 .ovs-agent
drwxrwxrwx  2 root root      3896 Nov 25 09:28 publish_pool
drwxrwxrwx  8 root root      3896 Feb  8 11:41 running_pool
drwxrwxrwx  2 root root      3896 Nov 25 09:28 seed_pool
drwxrwxrwx  2 root root      3896 Jan 21 10:46 sharedDisk
```

iso_pool   The iso_pool directory is where the virtualization manager will store install International Organization for Standardization (ISO) images if they are loaded via that tool.

ovs-agent   This directory contains agent data that it uses to manage the VMs when under the control of the Oracle VM Manager. The Agent uses Berkeley database to store configuration information.

publish_pool   Within Oracle VM, it is possible to deploy VM images for use by other users or groups. This process is sometimes called *cloning*. If you choose to make a deployed virtual machine sharable by all users (Public group), the VM is compressed and stored in the publish_pool directory.

running_pool   The running_pool directory stores the actual guest VMs that can run on this server. Each guest VM will exist in its own directory and by default consists of System.img and vm.cfg files. The System.img file stores the guest operating system and the vm.cfg file is used by the hypervisor to know how the guest should be started. Here is an example of a simple vm.cfg file, which we will explore a bit later in the chapter.

```
bootloader = '/usr/bin/pygrub'
disk = ['file:/OVS/running_pool/el5x64VM1/System.img,xvda,w']
memory = '1536'
name = 'el5x64VM1'
on_crash = 'restart'
on_reboot = 'restart'
vcpus = 2
vfb = ['type=vnc,vncunused=1,vnclisten=0.0.0.0,vncpasswd=unsecure']
vif = ['bridge=xenbr0,mac=00:16:3E:7A:C9:43,type=netfront']
vif_other_config = []
```

As defined in the vm.cfg file, the hypervisor knows that when it tries to boot the guest, it needs to take the file /OVS/running_pool/el5x64VM1/System.img and present it to that guest as the device /dev/xvda. The guest will then be allowed to take up 1536MB of memory and will see two CPUs. A single network card has the MAC address 00:16:3E:7A:C9:43, which the guest will see as *eth0* (by default), and its traffic will pass through the local xenbr0, which is a virtual device that can be seen as a network device on Dom-0. Finally, a console window will be available using *vnc* with the password *unsecure*. The host and port used to access that console is dependent on the number of guests running on a server; the port starts at 5900 and increments by 1 for each guest started (for example, serverhostname:5900).

seed_pool   The seed_pool directory stores templates that can be used to set up new guest VMs. Templates normally come with a setup script that will require input of hostname, IP address, and so on. Templates come with fully installed operating system and optionally also application stacks. We will talk more about templates later in this chapter.

sharedDisk   The sharedDisk directory is the default directory for create files that will be shared with multiple VMs. When files are shared with multiple VMs, you add an exclamation point (!) to the access part of the disk line in vm.cfg.

So, a file that only one guest can access for writes would look like this:

```
'file:/OVS/running_pool/el5x64VM1/localdisk10G.img,xvdb,w'
```

And a file that can be written to by multiple guests would look like this:

```
'file:/OVS/shareDisk/el5x64VM1/shareddisk10G,xvdb,w!'
```

NOTE
We are considering a simple single server here that can run multiple guests, so the shared disk is all local. If you want to have VMs on separate servers, you will still need external shared storage.

Oracle VM Manager

Oracle VM Manager is a web-based application written using Oracle Applications Express that by default accesses an Express Edition database. The Manager communicates with agents that run on the hypervisor machines, and agents actually manipulate the state of the guest virtual machines.

Oracle VM Manager Hardware Requirements

Table 2-2 shows the minimum requirements for a machine that will run the Oracle VM Manager.

NOTE
The information in Table 2-2 is from Oracle's published requirements; check this site for any changes: www.oracle.com/technetwork/server-storage/vm/overview/index.html.

Hardware	x86
Operating System	Oracle Enterprise Linux (OEL) 4.5 or later Red Hat Enterprise Linux (RHEL) 4.5 or later
Web Browser	Mozilla Firefox 1.5 or later Microsoft Internet Explorer 6.0 or later
Minimum Swap Space	2GB
Minimum Memory	2GB
Minimum CPU Speed	1.83 GHz
Minimum Disk Space	4GB
Supported Oracle Databases Editions	Oracle Database Express Edition, Standard Edition, Enterprise Edition, Oracle RAC

TABLE 2-2. *Oracle VM Manager Requirements*

Installing Oracle VM Manager

The software can be installed on a standard Linux host or on a virtual machine guest; however, it is not recommended that it be installed on a guest machine that you want to manage. If you intend to install Oracle VM Manager on a virtual machine, you can download a prebuilt template that has the operating system and software preinstalled.

MAA Workshop: *Installing the Oracle VM Manager*

Workshop Notes

For this workshop, the Oracle VM Manager software is being installed on a VM guest itself that was originally built using an operating system template. That virtual machine is managed outside of the manager but it still means the VM can be backed up and restored or moved very simply to other hardware.

Step 1. Download the Oracle VM Manager software from Oracle E-Delivery as a zip file that contains an ISO file, and unzip it in a staging directory:

```
[root]# cd /u01 # This is the directory holding the downloaded file
[root]# unzip  V18419-01.zip
Archive:  V18419-01.zip
  inflating: OracleVM-Manager-2.2.0.iso
```

Step 2. Create a mount directory and mount the ISO file on it:

```
[root]# mkdir /isomount
[root]# mount -o loop,ro /u01/OracleVM-Manager-2.2.0.iso /isomount
```

Step 3. Change to the mounted directory and run the installer. Here are some of the most important lines:

```
[root]# cd /isomount
sh runInstaller.sh
Welcome to Oracle VM Manager 2.2
Please enter the choice: [1|2|3]
1. Install Oracle VM Manager
2. Uninstall Oracle VM Manager
3. Upgrade Oracle VM Manager
```

Choose 1 to install the software. You'll see the following:

```
Starting Oracle VM Manager 2.2 installation ...
Do you want to install a new database or use an existing one? [1|2]
1. Install a new Oracle XE database on localhost
2. Use an existing Oracle database in my network
```

If an Oracle database is already available for your repository, choose 2. Otherwise, choose 1 to install Oracle Express edition and create a new database. You will need to determine a port for HTTP access on the manager's host, the database listener port, and passwords for the SYS and SYSTEM database users. The default ports are normally acceptable.

```
Specify the HTTP port that will be used for Oracle Application Express [8080]:
Specify a port that will be used for the database listener [1521]:

Specify a password to be used for database accounts.  Note that the same
password will be used for SYS and SYSTEM.  Oracle recommends the use of
different passwords for each database account.  This can be done after
initial configuration:
Confirm the password:

Do you want Oracle Database 10g Express Edition to be started on boot (y/n)
[y]:y
To access the Database Home Page go to http://127.0.0.1:8080/apex

Checking the availability of the database ...
Set default database schema to 'OVS'.
Please enter the password for account 'OVS':
```

The OVS schema contains the tables that store the repository information. The installer now moves on to install OC4J, which also requires an admin password and a keystore password, and you need to decide whether you want to use HTTP or HTTPS to access the application:

```
Please enter the password for account 'oc4jadmin':
To access the OC4J Home Page and change the password go to
http://127.0.0.1:8888/em
Deploying application help ... Done
Deploying application ... Done
Please enter the keystore password for the Web Service:
Do you want to use HTTPS access for Oracle VM Manager (Y|n)?n
Configuring OC4J to use HTTP ... Done
```

Finally, enter the SMTP and e-mail account that will be used to forward instructions in case of forgotten passwords:

```
Please enter the password for the default account 'admin':
Configuring SMTP server ...
Please enter the outgoing SMTP mail server(e.g. - mail.abc.com):
Mail server checking, may need some time, please wait ...
Setting the SMTP server to mail.LunarTrax.com ...
Please enter an e-mail address for account 'admin': max@LunarTrax.com
For detailed setup, refer to Oracle VM Manager User's Guide
```

After the installation is complete, the connection details are provided:

```
To access the Oracle VM Manager 2.2 home page go to:
 http://10.148.53.179:8888/OVS
To access the Oracle VM Manager help page go to:
  http://10.148.53.179:8888/help/help
```

Normally, for remote access, you would use the hostname rather than the IP address, though both will work:

```
http://<vm_manager_host>:8888/OVS
```

If you set up Secure Sockets Layer (SSL) on installation, the URL would be as follows:

```
https://<vm_manager_host>:4443/OVS
```

Or, similarly, you can access the Manager from the Oracle VM Manager host using the following:

```
http://127.0.0.1:8888/OVS/ for non SSL
https://127.0.0.1:4443/OVS/ for SSL
```

> **NOTE**
> *If you are trying to access the URL from a remote*
> *machine and the page fails to load, but you are*
> *able to load the page from a browser on the Oracle*
> *VM Manager machine, the problem is probably a*
> *firewall issue. If iptables is running, you can turn it*
> *off to see if that fixes the problem, or you can ensure*
> *that the traffic is allowed through the firewall.*

Step 4. Optionally configure the browser to be able to run a console on the guest. A console button on the Oracle VM Manager GUI allows you to run a console for the guest within the browser; however, if you want to do this, you also need to install some extra software. Depending on the browser you are using, the following RPM Package Manager (RPM) files can be downloaded and installed from http://oss .oracle.com/oraclevm/manager/RPMS:

```
 [root]# rpm -i ovm-console-1.0.0-2.i386.rpm (for x86 browser)
```

or

```
[root]# rpm -i ovm-console-1.0.0-2.x86_64.rpm (for x86-64 browser)
```

If you are not using a Mozilla-based browser, you also need to install TightVNC on the Oracle VM Manager host. The software can be downloaded from http://oss .oracle.com/oraclevm/manager/RPMS/ and is installed using the following:

```
[root]# rpm -ivh tightvnc-java-version.noarch.rpm
```

The guest console can also be accessed by any VNC viewer on external machines.

Using Oracle VM Manager

To use the Oracle VM Manager effectively, you first need to understand a few concepts.

Server Pools

Server pools comprise one or more machines running Oracle VM Server. If more than one machine is in the server pool, those machines must have shared storage for storing the guest VMs. Every server pool has one server pool master, at least one utility server, and at least one VM server. If only one server machine is used, that machine will take on all three roles. When multiple servers are in a pool, the server pool master chooses the server a guest will start on by determining which server has the most currently available resources. Multiple utility servers can be used to spread out the load of managing the guests in the pool.

Servers

A server is a machine with Oracle VM Server and Agent installed. Servers can be configured, started, stopped, and removed by the Oracle VM Manager.

Resources

Resources are used by Oracle VM Manager to create virtual machines. They comprise the following:

- **Virtual machine templates**   Preconfigured system images that require some minor configuration, such as supplying hostname, IP address, and so on, to provision into a running virtual machine.

- **Virtual machine images**   Preconfigured VMs ready to use with no creation or further configuration required.

- **ISO files**   Source operating system install media. These resources can only be used to create hardware virtualized guests.

- **Shared virtual disks**   Created to be used by multiple VMs. Guests that you create to be part of a cluster will use these resources for their shared disk.

Virtual Machines

A virtual machine consists of, at minimum, an operating system that can run as a guest on a virtual machine server. To create a VM, you need a VM server that is part of a server pool and either an ISO file with the operating system install media or an appropriate Oracle VM template.

To access the Oracle VM Manager, point your browser to the URL stated at the install output. If you set up non-SSL, this is normally http://vm-manager-host:8888/OVS; however, if you use SSL, the URL should be https://vm-manager-host:4443/OVS.

MAA Workshop: *Creating a Virtual Machine with the Oracle VM Manager*

Workshop Notes

The Oracle VM Server software is installed on machine ratvmsrv1, a cheap modern PC that meets the specified hardware requirements and has 8GB of memory, so we can run three guests and the Hypervisor. The Oracle VM Manager machine is also already set up and running, so we can access it through our browser.

Step 1. First, we'll create a server pool and server. Click the Server Pools tab, and then click the Create Pool button to open a screen where you can enter the server pool information. Choose a name and provide the information for the server pool master, utility server, and VM server before you click Next. Make sure that the High Availability Mode box is unchecked. In our case, only one machine performs all those jobs, so you can enter that information. Then click Add.

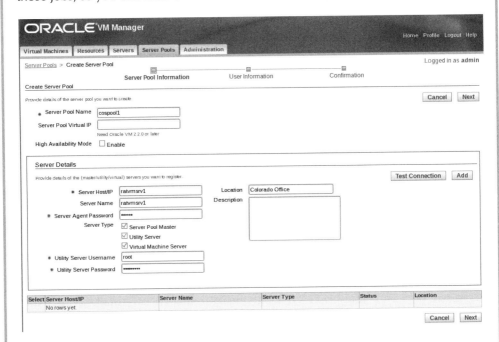

As you can see at the bottom of the next illustration, the server is now added and we can create the pool. Click Next to move on.

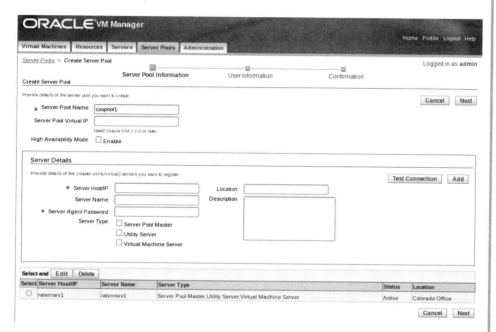

Next, we provide user information. We will create only the admin user, but you can have multiple users with varying levels of authority. Click Next to continue and then confirm you are happy with the setup before creating the pool. The General Information screen appears while the creation process completes in the background. The following shows a completed pool creation.

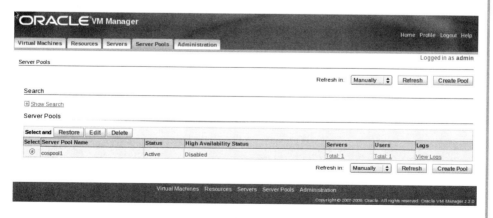

Step 2. Now that we have a server pool and VM server, we can use a precreated template or base operating system install media to create the guest VM. If we were creating a hardware virtualized guest, we could use the install media placed in the ISO pool resource if we had one Oracle RAC requires paravirtualized guests however, so we'd have to use the NFS mount method documented in the Oracle VM Server user's guide. Oracle has created OS templates for us to use, so we can use those to save some effort. The templates can be downloaded from E-Delivery at http://edelivery.oracle.com/linux. For this exercise, we are using Enterprise Linux 5 Update 5. Download the template and place it in the /OVS/seed_pool directory, and then unzip and untar it.

```
[root]# cd /OVS/seed_pool/
[root]# unzip V21107-01.zip
Archive:  V21107-01.zip
  inflating: OVM_EL5U5_X86_64_PVM_10GB.tgz
[root]# tar xzf OVM_EL5U5_X86_64_PVM_10GB.tgz
```

We now have a directory under seed pool called OVM_EL5U5_X86_64_PVM_10GB that contains a System.img file containing the installed guest and a vm .cfg with the configuration information to start the VM. We can now register it with the Oracle VM Manager.

In the Manager, open the Resources tab, and then the Virtual Machine Templates tab and click the Import button. Then choose Select from Server Pool (Discover and Register) and click Next. After you select your server pool on the next screen, the Manager will discover the template—as long as you put it in the right place. Then you can select the template you want, as shown in the following illustration. The password for root in these templates is *ovsroot*.

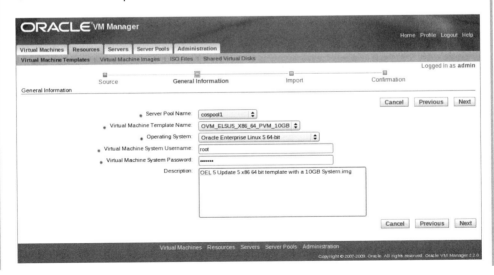

Click Next and confirm the import on the next screen. The template will start to import. A completed import is shown in the following illustration; notice that it shows a status of *Pending*. This is because any user can import templates, but the administrator must approve them before they can be used to create a VM. Other users have not been mentioned here because we are working as the admin for our test system.

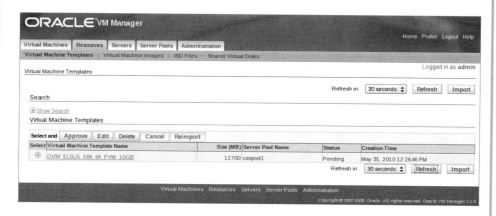

The admin user (that's us in this case) can then approve the template by clicking Approve and then confirming on the following page. Once complete, the template status will appear as *Active*.

Step 3.   We can use our template to create the virtual machine. On the Virtual Machines tab, click Create Virtual Machine. The next screen, shown in the following illustration, offers choices for creating a virtual machine. Choose Create Virtual Machine Based on a Virtual Machine Template.

Next, select the server pool; we set up only one, so we can move on to the next screen and select the Oracle VM template to use. We have only one template, so click Next to move on.

Next, choose the name and console password for this guest, as shown in the following illustration. Remember that you can access the console from the Manager screen itself (if you installed the extra software), or you can use a VNC connection to reach the console. The password you enter here will let you access the console via VNC. By default, you get one virtual network interface, which will be eth0 on the guest, but you can add more now (as you will need a private interface for Oracle RAC) or do this later.

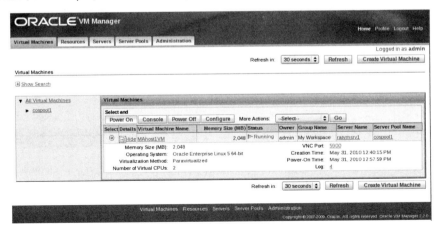

On the next page, view all the details to make sure you made the right entries and then click Confirm. The VM will create in the background, and you can refresh the main VM page to see when it completes. Initially it will be powered off (shut down), so you need to click Power On. The next screen shows the new VM powered on and in running state, which means we can connect to the guest machines console using a VNC viewer connecting to the VM server machine at the port shown on the screen (for example, ratvmsrv1:5900).

Step 4.   Now connect to the VM console to configure the network settings; by default, the system uses the Dynamic Host Configuration Protocol (DHCP), and we have no idea what IP will have been assigned. The template configuration should normally run by default on first startup and be accessible in the console accessed from the Oracle VM Manager screen; however, if this does not happen or you cannot reach that console, the process can be started manually from the VNC console, as follows:

```
[root]#  /usr/sbin/oraclevm-template –enable
Template configuration enabled.
[root]#  /usr/sbin/oraclevm-template –config
Regenerating SSH host keys.
Stopping sshd: [  OK  ]
Generating SSH1 RSA host key: [  OK  ]
Generating SSH2 RSA host key: [  OK  ]
Generating SSH2 DSA host key: [  OK  ]
Starting sshd: [  OK  ]
Regenerating up2date uuid.
Setting Oracle validated configuration parameters.
Configuring network interface.
  Network device: eth0
  Hardware address: 00:16:3E:45:12:7B
Do you want to enable dynamic IP configuration (DHCP) (Y|n)? n
Enter static IP address: 10.2.53.204
Enter netmask: [255.0.0.0] 255.255.252.0
Enter gateway: 10.2.52.1
Enter DNS server: 155.2.202.15
Shutting down interface eth0:  [  OK  ]
Shutting down loopback interface:  [  OK  ]

Configuring network settings.
  IP configuration: Static IP address
Bringing up loopback interface:  [  OK  ]
Bringing up interface eth0:  [  OK  ]
Enter hostname (e.g, host.domain.com): [racassur-ipfix01]
Network configuration changed successfully.
  IP configuration: Static IP address
  IP address:       10.2.53.204
  Netmask:          255.255.252.0
  Gateway:          10.2.52.1
  DNS server:       155.2.202.15
  Hostname:         racassur-ipfix01
[root]#  /usr/sbin/oraclevm-template –disable
```

NOTE
You need to disable the template configuration to ensure that it does not run at each boot.

Now one guest VM is running on our VM Server under the management of the Oracle VM Manager. We want a cluster, however, so we need to create more VMs using the same methods described earlier. And we need some shared disks and a second network interface for the private interconnect.

MAA Workshop: *Adding Shared Disks and NICs with the Oracle VM Manager*

Workshop Notes
In this workshop, we will add more resources on the server that can then be used by our guest VMs.

Step 1. We need to add the shared disk resource, so navigate to the Resources and Shared Virtual disk pages and click Create. You could import a shared virtual disk if you already had a shared file created under /OVS/sharedDisk, which can be done like so:

```
[root]# dd if=/dev/zero of=/OVS/sharedDisk/shared10GBfile1 count=10
bs=1G
```

But because we have not done that, we will let the Oracle VM Manager create the disk for us. The following illustration shows the parameters needed to complete this process. In this case, we are working on only one server, but remember that if the server pool includes multiple servers, you need to create these on disks that are accessible from all servers.

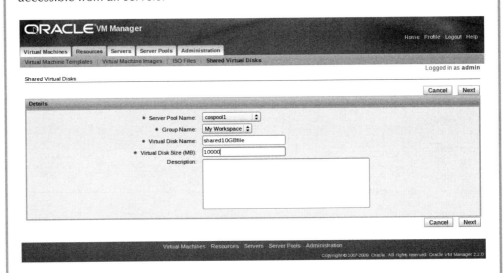

   Click Next and then confirm the options. It might take a few minutes to complete the task if you created a large sharable disk file. Until complete, the shared virtual disk will show as a status of Creating.

Step 2.   Having created the disk resource, we can add it to the VM. From the Virtual Machines page, select the VM and click Configure. As shown in the following illustration, you can configure both the network interface and storage here. Let's configure the network first since the disk is still creating.

   Click the Network tab to see all the current interfaces on the VM, and then click Add. The default interface created is called VIF0, so we will create VIF1. Leave the other parameters at their default settings, as shown in the next illustration; however, if we had multiple physical network cards on the VM server, we could use any of them.

   After you confirm the addition of the network card, the VM configuration will be changed on the VM server; however, the VM will have to be restarted to pick up the change. The vm.cfg line for the network will now look like this:

```
vif = ['bridge=xenbr0,mac=00:16:3E:45:12:7B,type=netfront',
'bridge=xenbr0,mac=00:16:3E:76:F4:42,type=netfront',
]
```

Step 3. Because we need to restart the VM, we can add that shared disk now. Go back to the VM configuration page and click the Storage tab; you'll see the following:

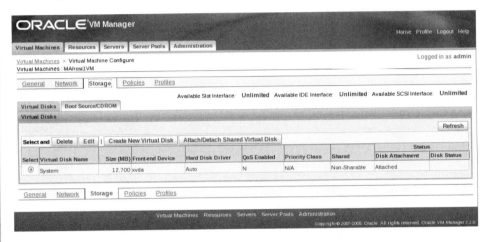

Click Attach/Detach Shared Virtual Disk, and then select the disks you want to add from the list of available disks, as shown next. Then click OK.

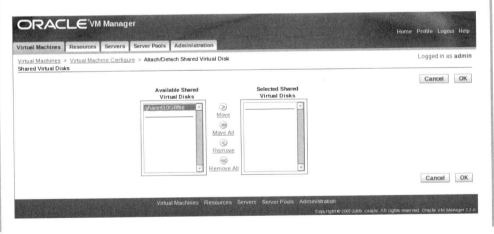

The VM now has two disks attached—one is the System disk and one is the sharable disk:

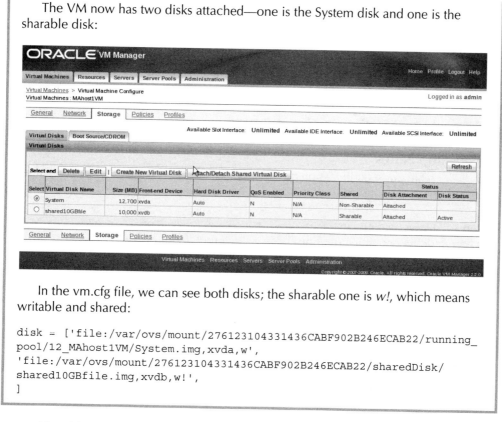

In the vm.cfg file, we can see both disks; the sharable one is *w!*, which means writable and shared:

```
disk = ['file:/var/ovs/mount/276123104331436CABF902B246ECAB22/running_
pool/12_MAhost1VM/System.img,xvda,w',
'file:/var/ovs/mount/276123104331436CABF902B246ECAB22/sharedDisk/
shared10GBfile.img,xvdb,w!',
]
```

After this VM is restarted, it will have access to a shared disk and will have both eth0 and eth1 network cards. The basic 10GB system disk may not be enough for your install requirements, so you might want to add a 20GB local disk to each guest you configure for the database Oracle Home. You will also need to configure the second network card on the guest, because, by default, it will be using DHCP. This VM guest is now ready to be part of an Oracle grid, so long as that grid is just for testing purposes. The setup we have created is fine for testing but would not cut it as a supported production environment, but more on that later in the chapter.

Using Oracle VM Server

You can set up guest VMs, shared disks, templates, and other features without using the Oracle VM Manager. You won't necessarily have to worry about the structures the Manager expects, and you can do everything from the command line. Xen has its own set of commands to create and manage guest VMs, plus you can edit the vm.cfg yourself at any time.

We concentrate on using the Oracle VM Manager to create VMs in this book and do not intend to go too deep into Oracle VM, but it's worth a look at how we can create the same features directly on the VM server to get a VM running from a template.

MAA Workshop: *Creating a VM from a Template Without the Manager*

Workshop Notes
We will create our second VM on the same VM server we used earlier, but this time we will do it manually without the Oracle VM Manager.

Step 1. Download and extract your Oracle VM template from Oracle E-Delivery at http://edelivery.oracle.com/linux. Place the template in the /OVS/seed_pool directory, and then unzip and untar it. Although not strictly required, it's a good idea to store the template in the seed pool and then copy it as needed.

```
  [root]# cd /OVS/seed_pool/
[root]# unzip V21107-01.zip
Archive:  V21107-01.zip
  inflating: OVM_EL5U5_X86_64_PVM_10GB.tgz
[root]# tar xzf OVM_EL5U5_X86_64_PVM_10GB.tgz
```

Step 2. Copy the directory to the running pool, and rename it to the guest name you want:

```
[root]# cp -r OVM_EL5U5_X86_64_PVM_10GB /OVS/running_pool/MAhost2VM
```

Step 3. Generate two virtual MAC addresses to be used in vm.cfg:

```
[root]# export PYTHONPATH=/opt/ovs-agent-2.3
[root]# python -c "from OVSCommons import randomMAC; print randomMAC()"
00:16:3e:74:11:da
[root]# python -c "from OVSCommons import randomMAC; print randomMAC()"
00:16:3e:0d:bd:42
```

Step 4. Create a disk to use for the shared disk (if not created earlier):

```
[root]# dd if=/dev/zero of=/OVS/sharedDisk/shared10GBfile.img bs=1G
count=10
```

Step 5.   Edit the vm.cfg file and correct the path to the files. Then add the network interface details, and change the filename. Remove the uuid and set the VNC console password. The vm.cfg should look something like this:

```
bootloader = '/usr/bin/pygrub'
disk = ['file:/OVS/running_pool/MAhost2VM/System.img,xvda,w',
'file:/OVS/sharedDisk/shared10GBfile.img,xvdb,w!']
memory = '2048'
name = 'MAhost2VM'
on_crash = 'restart'
on_reboot = 'restart'
vcpus = 2
vfb = ['type=vnc,vncunused=1,vnclisten=0.0.0.0,vncpasswd=welcome1']
vif = ['bridge=xenbr0,mac=00:16:3E:74:11:DA',
       'bridge=xenbr0,mac=00:16:3E:0D:BD:42', ]
vif_other_config = []
```

Step 6.   Now start the VM:

```
[root]# xm create /OVS/running_pool/MAhost2VM/vm.cfg
Using config file "/OVS/running_pool/MAhost2VM/vm.cfg".
Started domain MAhost2VM (id=19)
```

Step 7.   Connect to the command line console using this ID. If you don't know the VM ID, try the command **xm list** to see a list of running VMs and their IDs:

```
xm console 19
```

The console will show you the startup, as you would expect from any Linux-based machine console, and will then either offer the network setup screen or a login screen. The root password will by default be *ovsroot*.

Step 8.   You should find that on first boot the network setup screen is presented to the console; if not, it can be run again after login:

```
[root]#  /usr/sbin/oraclevm-template --enable
Template configuration enabled.
[root]#  /usr/sbin/oraclevm-template --config
Regenerating SSH host keys.
Stopping sshd: [  OK  ]
Generating SSH1 RSA host key: [  OK  ]
Generating SSH2 RSA host key: [  OK  ]
Generating SSH2 DSA host key: [  OK  ]
Starting sshd: [  OK  ]
Regenerating up2date uuid.
Setting Oracle validated configuration parameters.
```

```
Configuring network interface.
  Network device: eth0
  Hardware address: 00:16:3E:45:12:7B
Do you want to enable dynamic IP configuration (DHCP) (Y|n)? n
Enter static IP address: 10.2.53.204
Enter netmask: [255.0.0.0] 255.255.252.0
Enter gateway: 10.2.52.1
Enter DNS server: 155.2.202.15
Shutting down interface eth0:  [  OK  ]
Shutting down loopback interface:  [  OK  ]

Configuring network settings.
  IP configuration: Static IP address
Bringing up loopback interface:  [  OK  ]
Bringing up interface eth0:  [  OK  ]
Enter hostname (e.g, host.domain.com): [racassur-ipfix01]
Network configuration changed successfully.
  IP configuration: Static IP address
  IP address:       10.2.53.204
  Netmask:          255.255.252.0
  Gateway:          10.2.52.1
  DNS server:       155.2.202.15
  Hostname:         racassur-ipfix01
[root]#  /usr/sbin/oraclevm-template -disable
```

NOTE
*You need to disable the template configuration to
ensure that it does not run at each boot.*

The VM is now running and ready to use in an Oracle grid for testing—but
what about normal operations? There are **xm** commands that will shut down or in
extreme cases destroy a guest VM but we recommend using **shutdown** or **reboot**
from the guests root user if possible. If the guest is already down, use the **xm create**
command used in the preceding listing to restart it. (You can see a number of **xm**
commands by using **xm help**.)

Multiple VM Servers Using
iSCSI for Shared Discs

You'll remember at the start of the chapter that iSCSI was mentioned. So far, we have
worked with a single VM server and intend to run three nodes directly on there. In
this case, the shared disk is available to the three guests from the local physical disk,
so nothing else is required.

Let's assume for a minute that we wanted to set up a four-node cluster. Our little desktop with only 8GB of RAM is insufficient for that task, so we'd need to expand to two physical VM servers—and to do that, we need external shared disks.

NOTE

The Oracle VM Manager allows two or more servers to be in the same pool only if they have shared disks for the running_pool, because the VMs need to be able to start on any physical machine in the pool.

You can create external shared disks in a test system with iSCSI using a product such as Openfiler, which is free and requires little configuration on the client side. We won't go into Openfiler configuration here; we'll assume that Openfiler is already set up and serving disk devices (iSCSI targets) on the network. In this case, a third desktop computer was used for Openfiler connected to each VM server using a dedicated gigabit switch.

We have two choices: Get the guests to access the shared storage as would occur for a nonvirtual machine, or allow dom-0 to manage the storage and pass it up to the guest as a file system file or a block device. You use **iscsiadm** to discover the iscsi-targets served by Openfiler.

Assuming that the Openfiler machine was set up to serve targets on the interface with address 192.168.1.50, here's the command:

```
[root]# iscsiadm --mode discovery --type sendtargets --portal
192.168.1.50
service iscsi restart
Turning off network shutdown. Starting iSCSI daemon:        [ OK ]
                                                            [ OK ]
Setting up iSCSI targets: Logging in to [iface: default, target:
iqn.2006-01.com.openfiler:tsn.8b538107031c, portal: 192.168.1.50,3260]
Login to [iface: default, target: iqn.2006-01.com.
openfiler:tsn.8b538107031c, portal: 192.168.1.50,3260]: successful
[ OK ]
```

We then can look at the system message log /var/log/messages to see the devices that were discovered:

```
kernel:    Vendor: OPNFILER  Model: VIRTUAL-DISK Rev: 0
kernel:    Type:   Direct-Access ANSI SCSI revision: 04
kernel: SCSI device sdb: 2097152 512-byte hdwr sectors (1074 MB)
kernel: sdb: Write Protect is off
kernel: SCSI device sdb: drive cache: none
kernel: SCSI device sdb: 2097152 512-byte hdwr sectors (1074 MB)
kernel: sdb: Write Protect is off
kernel: SCSI device sdb: drive cache: none
```

```
kernel:  sdb: sdb1
kernel: sd 13:0:0:0: Attached scsi disk sdb
kernel: sd 13:0:0:0: Attached scsi generic sg2 type 0
```

In this case, we see sdb and a partition sdb1, which we can now use as a shared device. If we let the guest VM manage this, the guest can use the device /dev/sdb1 as it would any other shared file. If VM server is used to manage the disks, you'll need to create a file system on it and create a file or pass it directly to the guest as a block device by adding a line such as the following to the disk section of vm.cfg:

```
'phy:/dev/sdb1,xvdb,w!',
```

NOTE
*Here we use **phy:** for a device rather than in earlier examples where we used **file:** for a file system file that is attached to the guest.*

Using this shared disk we can now expand our cluster to more guests on other physical machines.

Supported Oracle VM Configurations for Grid Infrastructure and Oracle RAC

This chapter hasn't spent much time on what Oracle considers "supported use of Oracle VM for Oracle RAC installations." The intention here was to set up a test environment to help you learn the new product before you worry about production, so supportability is not a major concern—but for Oracle it certainly is important.

A lot of research has gone into what should and should not be considered supported when using Oracle VM to ensure that Oracle RAC's strength is not distilled. For a start, you need to have at least two VM servers, because otherwise a single point of failure exists at the hardware level. You also need to have multiple physical network interfaces to isolate public, private, and storage traffic; overcommitting CPUs is allowed a little, but never by more than two times. (For much more information, read the Oracle Technical white paper, Oracle Real Application Clusters in Oracle VM Environments at www.oracle.com/technetwork/database/clustering/oracle-rac-in-oracle-vm-environment-131948.pdf.)

Using Prebuilt Oracle RAC Templates

You can actually use Oracle VM templates to build a two or more–node cluster running grid infrastructure and Oracle RAC RDBMS in about 30 minutes (depending on machine and network speed) with very little interaction. I probably should have left that statement until after Chapter 5, but I know that like Max, you want to understand how things work rather than just have them work. Templates are available from Oracle E-Delivery for Grid Infrastructure and Oracle RAC 11.2.0.1, and through My Oracle Support for 11.2.0.2. These templates are simply placed in the seed_pool, imported into the Oracle VM Manager and used to create VMs. Then, after a short interview process on first startup, it will completely handle configuring your cluster. What's more, the templates come with scripts to deconfigure the cluster and set it back to its original state, add nodes, and perform other tasks. We won't go into these templates any further, but you can find templates for quick testing setups and production systems, plus more information at this web site: www.oracle.com/technetwork/database/clustering/overview/rac-template-11grel2-166623.html.

Summary

You've seen how Oracle VM can be used to set up virtual hosts to be included in a cluster and how this is ideal for test setups. Even better is that by copying just a couple of files, you can create a machine backup that can be restored in minutes. Oracle VM is much more than this because it can be used for protecting single-instance Oracle RDBMS as well as nodes of a cluster.

Oracle VM can be a complementing technology to grid infrastructure and Oracle RAC. It allows you to move guest nodes to different physical hardware when you need to perform maintenance, and it allows for consolidation of multiple machines to one, but still with controls in place to ensure proper sharing of resources. You'll learn how grid infrastructure works in Chapter 3.

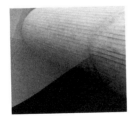

CHAPTER
3

Grid Infrastructure

ax liked the idea of having a template to use to create his clusters quickly and with little configuration, but understands that you need to know how things work when things go wrong. In this chapter, we will concentrate on the Oracle Clusterware side of grid infrastructure, explaining the new concepts, architecture, and hopefully clearing up some of the more challenging parts of the changes made in this release. Not much practical in here for Max to get his hands dirty with, but Chapter 4 provides more hands-on install requirements and an installation or upgrade guide. Chapter 5 covers Automatic Storage Management (ASM) and the ASM Cluster File System (ACFS), so there are plenty of workshops to review once the theory is understood.

Let's define the purpose of grid infrastructure. Oracle Real Application Clusters (Oracle RAC) was the underpinning of the Oracle Database Grid. Oracle RAC came into its own in Oracle9*i*, realizing the potential of Oracle Parallel Server (OPS) by making applications truly scalable, without requiring modifications. The central idea behind Oracle RAC was the same as the central idea behind grid computing: Plug in nodes as needed to handle the additional workload, or remove nodes and move them elsewhere when the situation warrants.

Oracle Database 10*g* took that to the next level by simplifying the process of adding and removing nodes and increasing the number of nodes you can include in an Oracle RAC cluster. Oracle went even further by providing an end-to-end clustering solution on all supported platforms, as well as providing its own Cluster File System (OCFS) on some platforms and a Volume Management solution for database files, with ASM.

Oracle 11*g* Release 2 has improved performance and made clustering and Oracle RAC databases easier to manage. This has been achieved by rewriting the Cluster Ready Services (CRS) stack to allow voting and Oracle Cluster Registry (OCR) files to exist in ASM, providing a policy-driven engine for resource management and supplying a cluster file system that sits on top of ASM, removing the need for any third-party cluster file system. ASM has been moved to the same Oracle Home as the CRS software, and the combination of the two is now called Grid Infrastructure. This chapter will explain the concepts behind grid infrastructure and what has changed from previous versions.

Cluster Ready Services

Oracle Database 10g introduced Cluster Ready Services (CRS), which was the logical next step in the evolution of the clusterware provided by Oracle. CRS is provided to cluster together nodes on any supported operating system, whether Linux, Solaris, AIX, Windows or HP/UX, or another system.

It is possible to use CRS instead of the OS vendor clusterware or third-party clusterware on any of these platforms. It is also possible to use CRS alongside third-party or operating system clusterware: if the maximum availability (MA) DBA chooses to stick with the vendor-provided or third-party clusterware, CRS can be used to integrate Oracle clustering with the existing clusterware, allowing the Oracle RDBMS to also communicate and work correctly with the vendor clusterware. This is done by ensuring that the third-party clusterware is installed before installing Oracle clusterware. All combinations of third-party clusterware may not be supported, so it is a good idea to check the certification site at support .oracle.com to confirm. Assuming the combination of third-party clusterware and Oracle clusterware is supported, a file usually called libskgxn.so (extention may be .a on some O/S's) will be created in the /opt/ORCLcluster/ directory by the third-party clusterware installation either automatically or via manual steps.

It is important to note that Oracle does not support adding third-party clusterware after Oracle Clusterware has been installed. If third-party clusterware is absolutely required, then it requires Oracle clusterware to be re-installed. Any other workaround can cause problems and is not supported by Oracle.

CRS is supported to run Oracle RAC with the Standard Edition of Oracle, although some limitations and requirements apply that are documented in the install guide.

CRS Concepts

Some of the 10g and 11g Release 1 concepts remain; however, a lot of new features are included and some changes were made in Release 2. Let's take a look at these before we discuss the architecture.

Voting Disk/File

The voting disk is used by the Oracle cluster synchronization services daemon (ocssd) to help determine and save the current state of nodes within the cluster. Each node should send a network heartbeat at a predetermined interval so that the other nodes know which ones are alive. If one or more nodes are determined to be missing heartbeats, you have to fence them from the cluster to avoid corruption due to a split brain (subclusters that can make unsynchronized writes to disk). Each node will send one heartbeat per second via network and write one heartbeat per voting disk per second. If a particular node does not write its heartbeat via network or voting disk until misscount seconds, the node is deemed to have problems. The rest of the nodes initiate a reconfiguration which is essentially a method to determine which nodes are still able to communicate with each other. Once the reconfiguration is completed, the node which was not heartbeating is sent a poison packet via network and disk. When a problem is determined with the heartbeats, each node votes on cluster membership using the voting disk, and that vote determines which nodes can survive or be evicted.

Basically, each node declares with which other nodes it can and cannot communicate, and from this we can determine the surviving cluster member set. This is a very high level explanation and there are multiple processes involved that ensure that we cover most scenarios. In an equal node cluster, the sub-cluster containing the lowest number node normally survives, and in a larger cluster, the subset with the most members should survive. In previous releases, the voting file could be on a shared cluster file system such as OCFS or in a raw partition. Oracle Database 11*g* Release 2 has made it possible to use ASM to store the voting file and deprecated the raw option for new installs. Systems that upgrade can leave their voting file on raw, but you should move away from raw before it is fully desupported. ASM is the primary choice for voting files in 11*g* Release 2.

If you're using a cluster file system to store the voting file, then for maximum availability you should configure 3 or 5 copies, though the limit is actually 15. You can use third-party mirroring or maintain 3 copies manually within CRS, and these copies need to be stored on separate disks with separate access paths to ensure no single point of failure.

If you use ASM to store the voting file, you have no direct control on the number of files that are actually created, because ASM will mirror based on the number of failure groups configured. A failure group can be configured in ASM to logically split up disks that would not be affected by a single point of failure. For example, disks that are accessed through separate controllers could be in different failure groups so that a single controller failure will not take out access to both disks.

Following are the general rules for voting files on ASM:

- **External redundancy**   Only one voting file will be used.

- **Normal redundancy**   Three voting file copies will exist but only if at least three failure groups exist in the disk group.

- **High redundancy**   Five voting file copies will exist but only if five failure groups exist in the disk group.

You must have at least three failure groups for normal redundancy disk groups and five failure groups for high redundancy disk groups before trying to place a voting file in the disk group. If you do not meet that requirement, you will receive the following errors when trying to move the voting file to ASM:

```
[root]# /u01/app/11.2.0/grid/bin/crsctl replace votedisk +DG2FG
Failed to create voting files on disk group DG2FG.
Change to configuration failed, but was successfully rolled back.
CRS-4000: Command Replace failed, or completed with errors.
```

If you look at the ASM trace files, you will see that disks in the first two failure groups are added fine, but it fails because there is no third failure group:

```
NOTE: Voting File refresh pending for group 2/0x8232f88c (DG2FG)
NOTE: Attempting voting file creation in diskgroup DG2FG
NOTE: voting file allocation on grp 2 disk DG2FG_0000
```

```
NOTE: voting file allocation on grp 2 disk DG2FG_0001
ERROR: Voting file allocation failed for group DG2FG
Errors in file
/u01/app/oracle/diag/asm/+asm/+ASM1/trace/+ASM1_ora_22552.trc:
ORA-15273: Could not create the required number of voting files.
NOTE: Voting file relocation is required in diskgroup DG2FG
NOTE: Attempting voting file relocation on diskgroup DG2FG
NOTE: voting file deletion on grp 2 disk DG2FG_0000
NOTE: voting file deletion on grp 2 disk DG2FG_0001
```

The error is high level and should have another error reported with the detail of the exact cause, such as this:

```
[oracle]$ oerr ORA 15274
15274, 00000, "Not enough failgroups (%s) to create voting files"
// *Cause:  The number of failgroups required for this redundancy were
//          not present in the diskgroup to create voting files.
// *Action: Retry the operation after creating new failgroup(s).
```

You must have an odd number of voting files because you must guarantee that an intersect remains in the voting files that each node is accessing when access to one file is lost. If you have only two files and a node loses access to it, you cannot guarantee which file the other node can access, if any. If you have three voting files and lose access to one, you know that even if the other node loses access to one, both nodes will be accessing at least one common file. So with three voting files, you can tolerate loss of access to one file, but a loss of access to two files will mean a cluster reconfiguration has to happen.

It's also worth noting that in Oracle Database 11*g* Release 2, the voting file in conjunction with the local registry and the Grid Plug and Play (GPnP) profile holds all the information required to form a cluster, and as such it does not depend on the OCR for cluster information, although OCR is required to manage cluster resources run out of Cluster Ready Services Daemon (CRSD).

You'd use this command to check which voting files are configured:

```
[root]# /u01/app/11.2.0/grid/bin/crsctl query css votedisk
##   STATE    File Universal Id                  File Name Disk group
--   -----    ----------------                  --------- ---------
 1. ONLINE   432bda713c544fcabf2eac58a476f2a5 (/dev/xvdb1) [DATA]
Located 1 voting disk(s).
```

You can see that this is an ASM located file using the +DATA disk group, which uses the disk partition /dev/xvdb1. To move voting files into or out of ASM in 11*g* Release 2, you'd use **crsctl replace votedisk**:

```
[root]# crsctl replace votedisk +NEWDG
```

This command will take any existing voting files and move them to be in the +NEWDG disk group.

The following command will take the voting file out of ASM and create three mirrors on shared disk storage:

```
[root]# crsctl replace votedisk /shared1/vfile1 /shared2/vfile2 /
shared3/vfile3
```

If you need to add one or more non-ASM voting files, you'd use the following:

```
[root]# crsctl add css votedisk /shared4/vfile4 /shared5/vfile5
```

Finally, to remove a non ASM voting file, use the following:

```
[root]# crsctl delete css votedisk <UID>
```

The UID is simply the Universal ID obtained by using **crsctl query css votedisk**, but remember that we cannot delete ASM stored files. The only way to change the storage of voting files in ASM is to change redundancy or failure groups in the disk group the voting file uses.

NOTE
*In Oracle Database 11*g *Release 2, manual backup of the voting disk is no longer required as the data is backed up automatically along with the backup of the OCR.*

Finally, the voting disks are actually stored on individual ASM disks (as opposed to a file in a disk group) within a disk group. Cluster Synchronization Services daemon (CSSD) directly accesses the ASM disks that contain the voting disks. This functionality is what allows CSS to start prior to ASM.

```
## STATE    File Universal Id                 File Name Disk group
-- -----    -----------------                 --------- ---------
 1. ONLINE  9bdaa2686ae14fccbf7c3656f4a20299  (ORCL:ASM_OCR_VD1)  [OCR_VD]
 2. ONLINE  14fb835a34754fb3bf5ba01a268daeac  (ORCL:ASM_OCR_VD2)  [OCR_VD]
 3. ONLINE  992c00ecbbe74fabbfe99d43e2b9cd54  (ORCL:ASM_OCR_VD3)  [OCR_VD]
```

From this output, you can see that there are three voting disks on three separate disks within the OCR_VD disk group. Within the disk header of these three ASM disks are markers that define the starting Allocation Unit (AU) (vfstart) and ending AU (vfend) for the voting disk. You can pull them with **kfed**, and if the markers are 0, the disk does not contain a voting disk. On startup, Cluster Synchronization Services (CSS) will scan all ASM disks (using the ASM discovery string from the GPnP profile) for these markers; once found, we use them without any direct relationship to an ASM instance.

Oracle Cluster Registry (OCR)

The OCR holds the metadata and wallets for all the resources the clusterware manages. The OCR is required to manage all the resources that come under the CRSD stack and its agents, as opposed to all resources in the cluster as it did in previous releases. Oracle Database 11*g* Release 2 includes the Oracle Local Registry (OLR), which will be covered later in this chapter.

Note that the OCR may still hold information about local resources, but it is not required to be accessible to join the cluster because that information is held in the OLR and GPnP profile (for example, the cluster interconnect information). The metadata for a resource includes information the agent process needs to know about how to create or start a resource, how to check that resource's status, and how to stop the resource. Finally, the metadata tells us what other resources need to be started or stopped when our resource changes its state, which is known as a dependency. A good example of a dependency would occur when a node listener requires its node virtual IP (VIP) to be available on a specific node before it can start.

At least one OCR must exist, but it is possible to have up to five copies. The OCR can also be stored in ASM with 11*g* Release 2, but unlike voting files, you can have an OCR file in each disk group and a mix of ASM and cluster file system copies can be stored. If you upgrade to 11*g* Release 2, OCR files stored on raw devices are also supported, but you should consider moving away from raw as soon as possible. The location of the OCR files is maintained in /etc/oracle/ocr.loc on Linux systems:

```
[root]# cat /etc/oracle/ocr.loc
ocrconfig_loc=/dev/xvdb1
ocrmirrorconfig_loc=+DATA
ocrconfig_loc3=+DATA2
```

To check on the status of OCR files, you can use the **ocrcheck** command:

```
[root]# /u01/app/grid/11.2.0/bin/ocrcheck
Status of Oracle Cluster Registry is as follows :
         Version                  :          3
         Total space (kbytes)     :     493728
         Used space (kbytes)      :       7780
         Available space (kbytes) :     485948
         ID                       :  584982144
         Device/File Name         : /dev/xvdb1
                                    Device/File integrity check succeeded
         Device/File Name         :     +DATA
                                    Device/File integrity check succeeded
         Device/File Name         :     +DATA2
                                    Device/File integrity check succeeded
                                    Device/File not configured
                                    Device/File not configured
         Cluster registry integrity check succeeded
         Logical corruption check succeeded
```

As you can see, five slots are available for OCR files, but only three are used. One is a raw block device, and the ASM disk groups +DATA and +DATA2 have one each. It is worth noting that a logical check of the OCR will only be executed when running ocrcheck as a privileged user. To add/delete/replace OCR files, you use the **ocrconfig** command:

```
[root]# /u01/app/grid/11.2.0/bin/ocrconfig -delete +DATA
```

That removes the OCR copy from the +DATA disk group. We can add it back with the **–add** option:

```
[root]# /u01/app/grid/11.2.0/bin/ocrconfig -add +DATA
```

A **replace** command replaces one OCR file location with a different one:

```
[root]# /u01/app/11.2.0/grid/bin/ocrconfig -replace +DATA2 -replacement
+DATA3
```

NOTE
If there's only one OCR file, you must add a second file and then delete the first rather than use the **replace** *command.*

The OCR is backed up by the clusterware every four hours on at least one of the nodes in the cluster to the location GI_HOME/cdata/<cluster name>, where GI_HOME is the clusterware install directory. In previous releases, the backup may only be on one node, but in Oracle Database 11*g* Release 2 the backup is spread out on different nodes. The last three four-hour backups are kept, along with one that is a day old and one that is a week old. The backups available with the node on which they are stored can be viewed using the **ocrconfig –showbackup** command by any user with access privileges:

```
[grid]$ /u01/app/11.2.0/grid/bin/ocrconfig -showbackup
racassur-ipfix01    2010/07/13 23:34:35
        /u01/app/11.2.0/grid/cdata/ratclu2/backup00.ocr
racassur-ipfix01    2010/07/13 19:34:34
        /u01/app/11.2.0/grid/cdata/ratclu2/backup01.ocr
racassur-ipfix01    2010/07/13 15:34:34
        /u01/app/11.2.0/grid/cdata/ratclu2/backup02.ocr
racassur-ipfix01    2010/07/12 07:34:30
        /u01/app/11.2.0/grid/cdata/ratclu2/day.ocr
racassur-ipfix01    2010/07/12 07:34:30
        /u01/app/11.2.0/grid/cdata/ratclu2/week.ocr
```

Only a few of the options for the preceding commands have been mentioned, but the full syntax is available in Oracle's "Clusterware Administration and Deployment Guide," or you can simply add the **-h** flag to see the available help.

Finally, when OCR is stored in ASM, a dependency in the local registry causes the ASM instance to be started, and disk groups containing the OCR are mounted before the CRSD can be started. This is because the CRSD requires OCR access. If the ASM instance needs to be shut down, the whole stack must be shut down using **crsctl stop crs**. An attempt to shut down an ASM instance, and hence offline a disk group containing OCR, will fail with "ORA-15097: cannot SHUTDOWN ASM instance with connected client." Do not forcefully kill the ASM instance if you're using it for OCR file storage.

Oracle Local Registry (OLR)

As its name suggests, the OLR holds metadata for the local node and, in conjunction with the GPnP profile, has all the information required initially to join the node to the cluster. The OLR is managed by the HA services daemon (OHASD) that also manages the low-level processes required to allow a node to join a cluster. None of the OLR data is shared across the cluster, but the file format is the same as the OCR and as such you can use all of the same **ocr*** commands as the root user to access OLR information—just add the **–local** flag.

Only one OLR is configured for each node and its default location is $GI_HOME/cdata/<hostname>.olr. This location can be confirmed by looking at the /etc/oracle/olr.loc file, as shown:

```
[root]# cat /etc/oracle/olr.loc
olrconfig_loc=/u01/app/11.2.0/grid/cdata/racassur-ipfix01.olr
crs_home=/u01/app/11.2.0/grid
```

You can also use **ocrcheck** with the **–local** flag:

```
[root@racassur-ipfix01 ~]# /u01/app/11.2.0/grid/bin/ocrcheck -local
Status of Oracle Local Registry is as follows :
         Version                  :          3
         Total space (kbytes)     :     262120
         Used space (kbytes)      :       2204
         Available space (kbytes) :     259916
         ID                       : 1782266269
         Device/File Name         : /u01/app/11.2.0/grid/cdata/racassur-
ipfix01.olr

                            Device/File integrity check succeeded

         Local registry integrity check succeeded
         Logical corruption check succeeded
```

The OLR is backed up automatically only after initial installation or upgrade to the $GI_HOME/cdata/<hostname> directory, but you can back up your OLR using the **ocrconfig –local –manualbackup** command as the root user:

```
[root]# /u01/app/11.2.0/grid/bin/ocrconfig -local –manualbackup
racassur-ipfix01     2010/06/15 01:06:05     /u01/app/11.2.0/grid/cdata/
racassur-ipfix01/backup_20100615_010605.olr
racassur-ipfix01     2010/06/12 03:20:16     /u01/app/11.2.0/grid/cdata/
racassur-ipfix01/backup_20100612_032016.olr
```

NOTE
This should be done after moving OCR either into or out of ASM.

Grid Naming Service (GNS)

The Grid Naming Service is an optional feature that is completely new to Oracle Database 11*g* Release 2 and significantly simplifies the network administration for your cluster. It lets you use Dynamic Host Configuration Protocol (DHCP) for your node VIPS and Single Client Access Name (SCAN) name IPs, which are covered shortly.

If you decide not to use GNS, the network requirements are as follows on the cluster's public network:

- Static IP address for each hostname

- Static IP address for each host's VIP

- SCAN name that resolves to three static IP addresses

This means you will need to have at least two static IP addresses assigned for each node that is in the cluster and a SCAN name that has three IP addresses allocated to it. For a three node cluster, there are at least three public IPs, three node VIPs, and three scan IPs, which is 9 IPs. If you use GNS, the network requirements are as follows on the cluster's public network:

- Static IP address for each hostname

- Static IP address for GNS VIP

GNS saves you more than half the required static IP addresses for your cluster; for a three node cluster, there are three public IPs and one GNS VIP, which is 4 IPs. GNS in conjunction with DHCP handles all the remaining cluster IP requirements dynamically.

NOTE
You can use DHCP for your public hosts, but having a static hostname address makes for easier connection outside of the clusterware and easier installation.

To use GNS, you will need to have DHCP and Domain Name System (DNS) servers available on your network. First, a static IP address must be allocated to your GNS VIP. The GNS VIP is the endpoint used by GNS to listen for name-resolution requests and will always be available in the cluster when the cluster is up. The GNS agent will handle restart and relocation as required. Once a GNS VIP is allocated, a subdomain must be created on your network, and DNS has to be configured to redirect any name resolution requests for that subdomain to the GNS VIP on port 53. Once this is done, GNS can be selected at install or upgrade time, as shown in Figure 3-1.

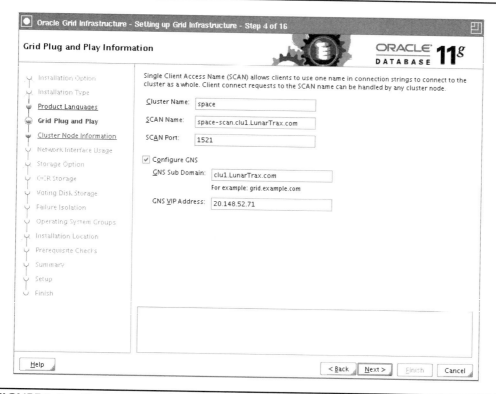

FIGURE 3-1. *Options entered to allow for GNS selection on the installer screen*

Figure 3-1 shows all of the information required by the installer to use GNS:

■ The cluster name, which should be unique across the organization.

■ The SCAN name that defaults to clustername-scan.<gns subdomain>.

■ SCAN Port is the port that the SCAN Listener will listen on and can be the same as node listener ports because they are configured on a different virtual interface.

■ GNS subdomain created within the corporate domain.

■ GNS VIP, which is a statically allocated IP set up in DNS to receive the redirect for resolution of hostnames in our cluster's subdomain.

After installation, GNS will listen on the GNS VIP and resolve any requests directed to it from the corporate DNS. It can do this as it registers the names and IP address received from DHCP when the SCAN or node VIPs start in the OCR. The node VIPs will be named hostname-vip.<gns subdomain>, but for ease of configuration, all clients should simply connect to the scan name.

Single Client Access Name and Its Listener
The SCAN has been added to the Grid Infrastructure setups to give a single point of access for clients to the cluster. In previous releases, whenever a node was added to the cluster, DBAs needed to somehow propagate the new hostname entries in the appropriate tnsnames.ora files on the client side. Oracle Database 11*g* Release 2 solves this using SCAN. No matter how many nodes are added or removed, the connection list (just one entry) remains the same. So how does it work?

SCAN can either be statically registered in the corporate DNS or allocated by GNS if GNS is configured. If you are using a manual network configuration with no GNS, your network administrator needs to define a hostname that resolves to three IP addresses returned by DNS in a round-robin manner. The default naming for a SCAN is *clustername-scan* and an **nslookup** for the SCAN would look something like this:

```
[root]# nslookup cluster1-scan
Server:         101.35.249.52
Address:        101.35.249.52#53

Name:    cluster1-scan.mycompany.com
Address: 20.148.52.248
Name:    cluster1-scan.mycompany.com
Address: 20.148.52.249
Name:    cluster-scan.mycompany.com
Address: 20.148.53.200
```

Note that the installer will check the resolution of the scan at install time and will not proceed until it is set up correctly. It is also possible to set up SCAN not in DNS but in /etc/hosts. If that is done, however, every client has to set up manually, and I strongly recommend staying away from that effort, but My Oracle Support Note:887522.1 is available if you need to know more. Even in a test environment, you can set up your own DNS and DHCP server, which would be the far better way to go.

If you are using GNS, the SCAN will be set up when the clusterware stack starts and GNS is running. The IP addresses will be dynamic, but that does not matter to you, because you will access the cluster via the SCAN and GNS will resolve that name to an IP address at connect time. A non-GNS SCAN should resolve through DNS to three IP addresses, and when you install the clusterware that name is checked and the IP addresses determined.

So whichever way the SCAN is set up, when the clusterware starts, CRS will plumb a virtual interface on each of the three SCAN IP addresses. Where they are plumbed is determined using a dispersion rule, which means in a three-node cluster with clusterware up on all three, each node should get one SCAN IP. In a two-node cluster, you would expect to see two SCAN IPs on one node and one on the other.

NOTE
You cannot manually force a particular SCAN IP to be located on a particular host.

A SCAN listener will start under each SCAN IP and listen on port 1521 (chosen during install) by default. The SCAN listener will always be on the same node as its corresponding SCAN IP.

Three SCAN IPs (assuming three IP addresses registered) and three SCAN listeners will be up in the cluster even if only one node is up with the clusterware active. This is because SCAN listeners are not like node listeners; they simply reroute connections so they do not need an instance to be available beneath them to make a database connection. If you have more than three nodes, you will still get only three SCAN listeners. You may wonder why three and not some other arbitrary number like two or six was chosen. Three SCAN listeners was determined to be sufficient to handle large volumes of client connections, and remain highly available when listeners fail or are relocated. Of course, having more than three SCAN would be fine, but it is a waste of valuable IPs.

Clients should normally attempt to connect to the SCAN. The client's DNS/GNS server will resolve that name to one of the three possible host IP addresses. The client will then attach to the SCAN listener at that IP address and port 1521 by default (specified by the original connect string). When the SCAN listener receives the connection, it will simply redirect the client to a node VIP and port where it expects to find the node listener. It is still the node VIP that makes the final connection, and as such clients can bypass SCAN and connect to the node VIP directly as they would have in the past should their application require this.

The SCAN listener determines which node to redirect the connection to based on load statistics and what services an instance serves. Database instances now register their services and load to the scan listeners so that incoming client service requests can be directed to the least loaded node that can provide the requested service. Databases that are created new in 11.2 will register only with SCAN, but upgraded databases will continue to register with SCAN and node listeners.

You can view the SCAN, SCAN listener, and listener configuration using **srvctl** from the Grid Infrastructure (GI) home as the GI home owner. Here, the three SCAN IPs were set up in the DNS; if GNS was used, you would see a similar output, but the SCAN name would also show a fully qualified domain name to ensure that it resolves to our subdomain.

```
[grid]$ /u01/app/11.2.0/grid/bin/srvctl config scan
SCAN name: space-scan, Network: 1/20.148.52.0/255.255.252.0/eth0
SCAN VIP name: scan1, IP: /space-scan.us.oracle.com/20.148.53.201
SCAN VIP name: scan2, IP: /space-scan.us.oracle.com/20.148.53.202
SCAN VIP name: scan3, IP: /space-scan.us.oracle.com/20.148.53.203
```

The config for the scan_listener simply shows us the three listeners and what port they are listening on:

```
[grid]$ /u01/app/11.2.0/grid/bin/srvctl config scan_listener
SCAN Listener LISTENER_SCAN1 exists. Port: TCP:1521
SCAN Listener LISTENER_SCAN2 exists. Port: TCP:1521
SCAN Listener LISTENER_SCAN3 exists. Port: TCP:1521
```

Finally, the listener shows us the network, owner, and HOME from which it is running:

```
[grid]$ /u01/app/11.2.0/grid/bin/srvctl config listener
Name: LISTENER
Network: 1, Owner: grid
Home: <CRS home>
End points: TCP:1521
```

Many of the attributes of these resources can be changed using the **srvctl modify** command:

```
[root]# /u01/app/11.2.0/grid/bin/srvctl modify scan -n space-scan
```

The scan name supplied can either be a new name, or you can provide the existing name. Either way, it will check to which IPs this address now resolves and then adjust the scan configuration accordingly. You would do this after making changes to DNS or /etc/hosts for the scan name resolution. This should be done only with due consideration of the consequences. SCAN listener and listener have more configurable attributes; to see the configurable attributes, you can use the following commands:

```
[root]# /u01/app/11.2.0/grid/bin/srvctl modify scan_listener -h
[root]# /u01/app/11.2.0/grid/bin/srvctl modify listener -h
```

If you use **GI_HOME/bin/srvctl -h**, you can see all the **srvctl** command options. They are also documented in the "Clusterware Administration and Deployment Guide."

Virtual IP Addresses

Oracle's grid infrastructure takes advantage of the concept of Virtual IP Addresses (VIPs) to enable a faster failover in the event of a failure of a node. Thus, each node will have not only its own host IP address, but a VIP address will also be assigned to the node either statically or through GNS. The listener on each node will actually be listening on the VIP, and client connections are meant to come in on the VIP, either directly or via SCAN listeners, as mentioned earlier. Should the node fail, the VIP will actually failover and come online on one of the other nodes in the cluster.

Note that the purpose of the IP address failover is not so that clients can continue to connect to the database using that VIP on the other node. The purpose of the IP address failover is to reduce the time it takes for the client to recognize that a node is down. If the IP has failed over and is actually responding from the other node, the client will immediately get a response back when making a connection on that VIP. However, the response will not be a successful connection, but rather a service access failure from the listener indicating that although the IP is active, no instance providing the required service is available at that address. The client can then immediately try to connect to another address in the address list. Hopefully, this time we can successfully connect to a VIP that is actually assigned to one of the existing/functioning nodes in the cluster. This is referred to as *rapid connect-time failover*.

Cluster Time Synchronization Services

Historically, a number of problems have occurred with false evictions/reboots caused by time synchronization among nodes in the cluster. Because of the way the clusterware detect hangs, sudden large movements in time could make it falsely believe a significant hang had occurred causing node fencing. Of course, it is important to keep the same time across all nodes in the cluster, but using a feature such as network time protocol (ntp) left you open to such large time changes without specific ntp parameters being used when starting. In Oracle Database 11*g* Release 2, the Cluster Time Synchronization Services daemon (CTSSD) can take care of this for you.

If CTSSD determines that ntp is running on or configured on all nodes of the cluster, it will run in an observer mode and only log to the clusterware alert log information about time mismatch.

If CTSSD determines that ntp is not running or configured on any one node of the cluster, it will run in active mode and will synchronize the system clocks on all nodes to the master node. This can occur in two ways:

■ When a node joins the cluster, if the node time is out of sync but within a certain limit, the clocks will be adjusted in very small units in a stepping manner until they are back in sync. If the time is outside the limit for time-stepping, the node will not be allowed to join the cluster and a message will be written to the clusterware alert log.

■ During normal running, if nodes become out of line with the master, the system clock will be slowed down or speeded up to regain synchronization. This is known as *clock slewing.*

NOTE
The system clock will never be set back in time by the CTSSD.

Moving CTSSD from observer to active mode simply requires the removal of ntp from all nodes in the cluster, as the CTSSD will detect this and change its mode. The reverse situation is also true, so configuration of ntp on the cluster will cause CTSSD to become an observer again.

Server Pools and Policy-Based Cluster Management

In this release, you can either have your resources managed traditionally, which means you determine what runs where, or you can use server pools to manage where your resources run. A server pool is basically a logical collection of servers in the cluster—in theory, it could be one, all, or none of the servers, but it is a collection all the same. Once you have the server pools set up, you allocate some rules or policies to the pool that determine how many servers should be in the pool at any one time:

■ **Min Servers**   The minimum number of servers allowed to be running in the pool

■ **Max Servers**   The maximum number of servers allowed to be running in the pool

■ **Importance**   How important are the resources that run in this pool, as opposed to the resources in other pools

The first two policies should be self explanatory, but the third takes a bit of careful consideration and may affect the other two also. Here's an example:

Server Pool 1 sp1 has min 3 max 6 and importance 2.

Server Pool 2 sp2 has min 2 max 8 and importance 3.

Seven servers are currently available for use in either pool.

NOTE
A server can be ACTIVE in only one top level pool at a time but can be available for use in multiple pools. Top-level server pools can have subpools that can be set up to be exclusive from other subpools under the same parent. This allows for greater granularity of what resources can run concurrently on a specific server.

In this example, we are not considering subpools; first, two servers to start up in the cluster would be assigned to meet sp2's minimum, even though sp1 has no servers, because sp2 has a higher importance. The next three servers to start would be assigned to sp1 so as to meet its minimum. The last two to be started would be assigned to sp2 because of its higher importance, and that would be true until sp2 hits its max.

So what would happen if the resources running on sp2 needed more horsepower to meet their required service levels? If you increase the minimum servers on sp2, it would shut down the resources on one of sp1's servers and move that server to sp2, even if sp1 would then be below its minimum, as sp2 has higher importance.

As you can see, setting these policy attributes correctly is critical: consider the scenario in which only two nodes are available; then sp1 would have no servers, and that probably means a service is down somewhere.

Initially, just two server pools are created and they are Free and Generic, and these can be seen by issuing the **srvctl config svrpool** command for server pools containing Oracle RAC databases:

```
[grid]$ /u01/app/11.2.0/grid/bin/srvctl config srvpool
Server pool name: Free
Importance: 0, Min: 0, Max: -1
Candidate server names:
Server pool name: Generic
Importance: 0, Min: 0, Max: -1
Candidate server names:
```

You can use **crsctl status serverpool** for all other server pools:

```
[root]# /u01/app/11.2.0/grid/bin/crsctl status serverpool
NAME=Free
ACTIVE_SERVERS=racassur-ipfix01 racassur-ipfix02
NAME=Generic
ACTIVE_SERVERS=
```

The *free pool* is a collection of all servers that are in the cluster but are not currently assigned to an active server pool. The *generic pool* has all the servers that for one reason or another cannot be in a dynamic pool, such as those running older versions of the RDBMS, as well as those Oracle 11*g* Release 2 databases specifically configured as administrator managed.

NOTE
In the preceding example, you can see that our servers are allocated to the free pool for non-Oracle RAC RDBMS servers, because no RDBMS software has been installed yet on those servers.

As you saw earlier, we view and manage all server pools for Oracle RAC databases with the **srvctl** commands and all other server pools with **crsctl**.

Role-Separated Management

Role-separated management for the cluster is simply a way to control the administrative access to server pools within the cluster. In the database, this access control occurs in a different way, because it is done at an OS group level, but here access information is stored in the OCR on a per-user basis. After installation, all users have the admin privilege, and as such no role separation is in place. The only users who can actually change this are root and the GI owner, because they are considered permanent administrators. Role separation means that different users can have access to manage different server pools, databases, and applications within the same cluster without affecting the other server pools.

Node Number Pinning and Leases

Prior to Oracle Database 11*g* Release 2, node numbers were static and assigned at the time of install or node addition to the cluster. This static node number was then used in a number of ways to define certain resources uniquely, such as databases and ASM instances. In this release, node numbers are not static but are leased in a similar way to a DHCP IP addresses. If an unpinned node is down for more than a week, it will effectively be removed from the cluster and will not be reported by the **olsnodes** command. Another node can obtain a lease on its number after that lease has expired. This was an important step in breaking the link between a node and what runs on it, to make policy-based server management work as it does.

This is not really anything a user needs to be concerned about when the managed databases are also Oracle 11*g* Release 2, and the only thing the average user may see are instances of a certain name starting up on various servers over time, as instances are not directly linked to hosts anymore. For example, MyDB databases may have instance mydb1 start on myhost1 for some time, because it has the lease for node number one, but you may find that instance mydb1 starts on myhost5 if myhost5 obtains the lease for node number one in the future.

If you are running pre-Oracle 11*g* Release 2, databases, or you add such to Grid Infrastructure control, those versions cannot tolerate this dynamic node number assignment, so you will need to pin the node number for hosts running previous versions of software. A pinned node never loses its lease on a node number. The **crsctl css pin** command is used to pin a node to its current node number:

```
[root]# /u01/app/11.2.0/grid/bin/crsctl pin css -n racassur-ipfix01
CRS-4664: Node racassur-ipfix01 successfully pinned.
```

You can see the status of nodes using the **olsnodes** command:

```
[root]# /u01/app/11.2.0/grid/bin/olsnodes -t
racassur-ipfix01        Pinned
racassur-ipfix02        Unpinned
```

And to unpin the node, use **crsctl unpin css**:

```
[root]# /u01/app/11.2.0/grid/bin/crsctl unpin css -n racassur-ipfix01
CRS-4667: Node racassur-ipfix01 successfully unpinned.
```

NOTE
It is impossible to assign a node number to a node; you can only pin it to its current node number. Also, the Grid Infrastructure upgrade will pin nodes automatically when it detects an older version of the RDBMS under its control.

Agents

In previous releases, resources were managed by scripts. When CRS wanted to start stop or check a resource, it called a script that would do that. Oracle Database 11*g* Release 2 includes multithreaded daemons for each user who is managing resources; these daemons are called *agents*. The agents are highly available as they are spawned through Oracle High Availability Services daemon (OHASD) and CRSD and can manage multiple resources. Agents implement a common framework that can handle C, C++, and Script plug-ins, and as such they can be used to manage all of your resources with custom code.

The base agents are orarootagent, oraagent, and script agent, and the log files can be found at $GI_HOME/log/<hostname>/agent/{ohasd|crsd}/<agentname>_<owner>/<agentname>_<owner>.log. For example, here's an agent log file for ora .crsd, managed by OHASD, owned by root user, and its agent name is orarootagent: $GI_HOME/log/<hostname>/agent/ohasd/orarootagent_root/orarootagent_root.log.

The same agent log file can have log messages for more than one resource, if those resources are managed by the same daemon, use the same agent, and have the same owner.

Integrating Intelligent Platform Management Interface (IPMI)

We have talked a little about evicting nodes from a cluster when they are not responsive—perhaps because they went down, they are running extremely slowly, they cannot ping on the network, cannot write a disk heartbeat, or they may be completely hung. It is one thing to tell a node to die, but making sure it does is something else. If a node is truly hung, it cannot evict itself, and this is where IPMI comes into play.

IPMI is an industry standard. For the clusterware to use IPMI, all servers in the cluster must have a Baseboard Management Controller (BMC) running firmware that's compatible with IPMI version1.5, which supports IPMI over a local area network (LAN). More simply put, a supported controller must be on the server that allows us to restart the server across the network from a healthy node when for all other purposes it is hung. The node kill via IPMI is the last escalation in the member kill process and will ensure that cluster integrity is maintained no matter the state of the remote node. IPMI can be set up (assuming you have the right hardware) at installation time or manually using **crsctl**.

CRS Architecture

So far in this chapter, we have looked at the most important aspects that have changed in CRS and that you need to know to make installation and configuration decisions. Now we will quickly cover the way the software hangs together in this new release.

In 10*g*, CRS consisted of three major components, as shown in Figure 3-2. These components manifested themselves as daemons, which ran out of inittab on Linux/ Unix, or as services on Windows. The three daemons were the Oracle Cluster Synchronization Services daemon (CSSD); Cluster Ready Services daemon (CRSD), which is the main engine for maintaining availability of resources; and Event Manager

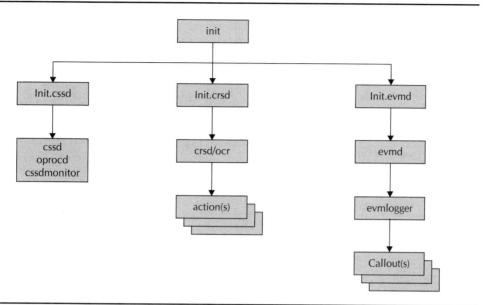

FIGURE 3-2. *Oracle 10g and 11g Release 1 CRS processes*

daemon (EVMD). Of these three components, CSSD and EVMD ran as user oracle, while CRSD ran as root. The CSSD was responsible for cluster synchronization, cluster membership, and group membership; EVMD handled event messaging for the processes; and CRSD managed the resources. Resource management such as start, stop, and monitor was done using scripts and processes that came under the RACG label. An example would be racgimon, which monitored the status of database instances.

In Oracle 11*g* Release 1, the init-managed stack remained; however, as you see in Figure 3-3, the Oracle 11*g* Release 2 startup and process stacks have completely changed. The CRS stack has effectively been split into two stacks, with the Oracle High Availability Services daemon (OHASD) handling the low-level processes and the Cluster Ready Services daemon (CRSD) handling the higher level resources such as database instances. These two stacks no longer use the old RACG framework but have a new agent framework to manage their availability, and now the concept of a local registry (OLR) is managed by OHASD as well as the Cluster Registry (OCR) which is managed by CRSD.

In the next few pages, we will look at the processes that make up the OHASD and CRSD stacks and discuss what they do and how they are started, plus where to find the logs should something go wrong.

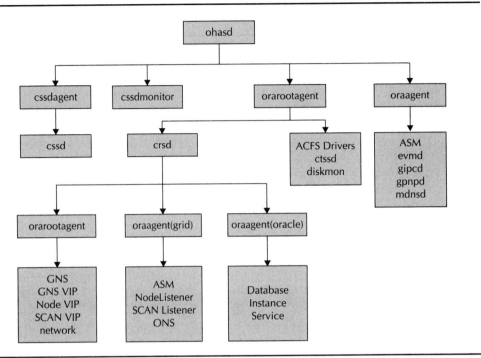

FIGURE 3-3. *Oracle 11g Release 2 GI processes*

Oracle HA Services Daemon

The OHASD process underpins the rest of the stack and determines what state it should be in from the flags contained in files under (for Linux) /etc/oracle/scls_scr/<hostname>. These flags are maintained by the software and should not be manually edited unless you're advised to do so by Oracle support. The OHASD process also uses a named pipe in the /var/tmp/.oracle directory, which is the same directory other cluster processes use for sockets, and as such you should never clean up that directory in a running cluster. Init is still the entry point for this daemon, and after a successful install, you would expect to see the following line in your /etc/inittab file:

```
h1:35:respawn:/etc/init.d/init.ohasd run >/dev/null 2>&1 </dev/null
```

This means that at run levels 3 and 5, this process should be running, and if it fails it should be respawned, but you should note that if the process keeps failing on respawn, init will give up. This script can do two things: It will sync up the required state of OHASD on reboot by setting the flags mentioned previously, or if the actual OHASD process fails, it will restart it.

A Quick Note on init and runlevel Change

You might be thinking that it appears that OHASD will not be started on boot, but this is not actually the case. When we enter different run levels, the scripts starting with the letter *S* in the /etc/rc<level>.d directory get called on entry with a **start** argument, and the scripts starting with the letter *K* in the /etc/rc<level>.d directory get called on exit with a **stop** argument. The number after the first letter determines in which order *rc* runs these scripts. The scripts are not normally physically placed in those directories, however; instead, all scripts can take a **start** or **stop** argument and are placed in /etc/init.d directory with symbolic links made in the /etc/rc<level>.d directories. If you are on Linux, then the rc script is /etc/rc, where as Solaris has a script for each level, such as /etc/rc0, /etc/rc1, and so on.

Another OHASD script, /etc/init.d/ohasd, accepts the **start** and **stop** arguments, and this is the one that gets called by *rc* when we enter run levels 3 and 5 to actually start or stop the OHASD process. Here you can see the different symbolic links to the same script file depending on which run level we would be going to:

```
[grid rc3.d]$ ls -al *hasd*
lrwxrwxrwx 1 root root 17 Nov 10  2009 S96ohasd -> /etc/init.d/ohasd
grid rc3.d]$ cd ../rc1.d
[grid rc1.d]$ ls -al *hasd*
lrwxrwxrwx 1 root root 17 Nov 10  2009 K19ohasd -> /etc/init.d/ohasd
```

The simplest way to consider this startup is that the *inittab*-based script sets it up to run and the *rc*-based script actually starts or stops it. This is true for the automatic startup and shutdown, on boot at least. We would always expect to see this process from a **ps** even when the stack is not up:

```
/bin/sh /etc/init.d/init.ohasd run
```

You can manually disable the automatic startup of OHASD with this,

```
[root]# crsctl disable crs
```

and then re-enable it with this:

```
[root]# crsctl enable crs
```

Both these commands set the flags mentioned earlier.

The following commands can be used to stop and start the stack manually and must be run as the root user. To start a previously stopped CRS stack, use this:

```
[root]# /u01/app/grid/bin/crsctl start crs
CRS-4123: Oracle High Availability Services has been started.
```

Notice that we don't get much feedback from this command. It says it is started, but it has actually just initiated a start, and we have to look elsewhere to see if the resources started correctly.

To stop the CRS stack, you use this:

```
[root]# /u01/app/grid/bin/crsctl stop crs
CRS-2791: Starting shutdown of Oracle High Availability Services-managed
Resources on 'server1'
CRS-2673: Attempting to stop 'ora.crsd' on 'server1'
CRS-2790: Starting shutdown of Cluster Ready Services-managed resources
on 'server1'
. . . . All crsd managed resources are stopped first.. We will look at
these later.
CRS-2792: Shutdown of Cluster Ready Services-managed resources on
'server1' has completed
CRS-2677: Stop of 'ora.crsd' on 'server1' succeeded
. . . . Now we are going to stop the ohasd managed resources
CRS-2673: Attempting to stop 'ora.asm' on 'server1'
CRS-2673: Attempting to stop 'ora.cssdmonitor' on 'server1'
CRS-2673: Attempting to stop 'ora.ctssd' on 'server1'
CRS-2673: Attempting to stop 'ora.evmd' on 'server1'
CRS-2673: Attempting to stop 'ora.drivers.acfs' on 'server1'
CRS-2673: Attempting to stop 'ora.mdnsd' on 'server1'
CRS-2677: Stop of 'ora.cssdmonitor' on 'server1' succeeded
CRS-2677: Stop of 'ora.mdnsd' on 'server1' succeeded
CRS-2677: Stop of 'ora.ctssd' on 'server1' succeeded
CRS-2677: Stop of 'ora.evmd' on 'server1' succeeded
CRS-2677: Stop of 'ora.drivers.acfs' on 'server1' succeeded
CRS-2677: Stop of 'ora.asm' on 'server1' succeeded
CRS-2673: Attempting to stop 'ora.cssd' on 'server1'
CRS-2677: Stop of 'ora.cssd' on 'server1' succeeded
CRS-2673: Attempting to stop 'ora.gpnpd' on 'server1'
CRS-2673: Attempting to stop 'ora.diskmon' on 'server1'
CRS-2677: Stop of 'ora.gpnpd' on 'server1' succeeded
CRS-2673: Attempting to stop 'ora.gipcd' on 'server1'
CRS-2677: Stop of 'ora.diskmon' on 'server1' succeeded
CRS-2677: Stop of 'ora.gipcd' on 'server1' succeeded
CRS-2793: Shutdown of Oracle High Availability Services-managed
resources on 'server1' has completedCRS-4133: Oracle High Availability
Services has been stopped.
```

From the **stop** command output, you can see all the resources that are managed by the HASD—that is, those that stopped after CRSD went down. These resources in the main correspond to processes running when the stack is up, and as you saw in Figure 3-2, these are managed by agent processes started by OHASD. Note that as long as OHASD is running on a node, it can send or respond to the following cluster wide commands:

- **crsctl start cluster –all**

- **crsctl stop cluster –all**

- **crsctl check cluster –all**

NOTE
*Without the –all flag, only the local node is affected.
There is also a –n flag to specify which nodes should
be started/stopped or checked.*

OHASD oraagent

The OHASD oraagent is an agent that runs as the GI home owner and manages (start/stop/check) the ora.asm, ora.evmd, ora.mdnsd, ora.gpnpd, and ora.gipcd resources. All these processes will run as the GI home owner.

EVMD   The Event Monitor Daemon both subscribes to and publishes events to processes within the node. Events such as "database instance down" will be received by the event monitor and passed on to any process that has subscribed to that event so that they can take required action. It is possible to see the events EVMD is processing by using the **evmwatch** command to detect the events and piping them into **evmshow** for formatting and output. Here's an example:

```
[grid]$ $GI_HOME/bin/evmwatch | $GI_HOME/bin/evmshow
```

The EVMD also spawns an evmlogger process. The EVMD process writes its trace to $GI_HOME/log/<hostname>/evmd/evmd.log.

MDNSD   Multicast Domain Name Services daemon is used by OHASD and Grid Plug and Play daemon (GPnPD) as a service registry, and for resource discovery as well as responding to DNS requests with Grid Naming Service daemon (GNSD). The MDNSD process writes its trace to GI_HOME/log/<hostname>/mdnsd/mdnsd.log.

GPNPD   Grid Plug and Play daemon is new in Oracle Database 11*g* Release 2 and is intended to ensure synchronization of the GPnP profile across the nodes in the cluster. The profile is an XML file that is stored locally on each node and has the most basic information required for a node to join the cluster. The full path to the file is $GI_HOME/gpnp/profiles/peer/profile.xml. The GPnPD process writes to the trace file $GI_HOME/log/<hostname>/gpnpd/gpnpd.log.

GIPCD In previous releases, the clusterware used TNS for its communications, which is the same stack used by the RDBMS for its client communications. In 11*g* Release 2, Oracle has written new code for cluster communications called grid IPC and the Grid Inter Process Communications daemon (GIPCD). Grid IPC supports multiple communications types such as User Datagram Protocol (UDP), Inter Process Communications (IPC), Transaction Control Protocol (TCP), and Grid IPC itself. GIPCD itself is a helper daemon for that, but is redundant in 11.2.0.1. GIPCD handles redundant interconnect management within Oracle clusterware from 11.2.0.2 onward. The GIPCD process writes to the trace file $GI_HOME/log/<hostname>/gipcd/gipcd.log.

ASM Automatic Storage Management must be started before CRSD can start if the OCR is stored within ASM, so OHASD is now in charge of starting/stopping and monitoring the ASM instance. The ASM trace files by default can be found under the grid owners $ORACLE_BASE/diag/asm directory. This can be changed using the ASM instances **diagnostic_destination** parameter.

OHASD orarootagent
The OHASD root agent is an agent that runs as the root user and manages (start/stop/check) for ora.crsd, ora.ctssd, ora.drivers.acfs, and diskmon resources. All these processes will run as the root user.

ora.ctssd This process handles time synchronization across the cluster that was discussed earlier in the chapter. The CTSSD process writes to the trace file $GI_HOME/log/<hostname>/ctssd/octssd.log.

ora.drivers.acfs This resource ensures that the drivers are loaded to allow ACFS to be used if configured on the node. The drivers are discussed more in Chapter 4 and write their trace to the system log file and console.

diskmon The diskmon process is only active and used on Oracle Exadata systems.

CRSD The CRSD spawns agents to manage application-level resources such as database instances and is covered in more detail later in this chapter.

OHASD cssdagent and cssdmonitor
The cssdagent starts, stops, and checks the CSSD (OCSSD process), and the cssdmonitor actually monitors the cssdagent. On top of this, both agents have taken on the work previously done by the oprocd and oclsomon processes. Both these processes and the OCSSD run in real time to ensure that they get scheduled, because a scheduling delay will be seen as a hang and requires the node to be fenced.

These processes write their trace to the files $GI_HOME/log/<hostname>/agent/ohasd/oracssdagent_root/agent/ohasd/oracssdagent_root.log and $GI_HOME/log/<hostname>/agent/ohasd/oracssdmonitor_root/ oracssdmonitor_root.log.

NOTE
From Oracle 11g Release 1 forward, it is no longer required to configure the Linux fencing mechanism known as the hangcheck-timer.

CSSD is the foundation of the cluster as it manages and distributes configuration and membership information. If CSSD does not start properly, the node cannot become part of the cluster. It controls which nodes are members by monitoring cluster health through network heartbeats to other CSSD processes in the cluster and disk heartbeats to the voting disk. It also mediates on votes and notifies all registered processes of any node membership changes such as a node joining or leaving the cluster. The CSSD process writes its trace to $GI_HOME/log/<hostname>/cssd/ocssd.log.

Cluster Ready Services Daemon (CRSD)

The CRSD is primarily responsible for maintaining the availability of application resources, such as database instances. CRSD is responsible for starting and stopping these resources, relocating them when required to another node in the event of failure, and maintaining the resource profiles in the Oracle Cluster Registry (OCR). In addition, CRSD is responsible for overseeing the caching of the OCR for faster access and also backing up the OCR. The CRSD process itself writes its trace to $GI_HOME/log/<hostname>/crsd/crsd.log.

CRSD oraagent

CRSD's oraagent manages (start/stop/check/clean) many resources, including all database, instance, service, and diskgroup resources; node listeners; SCAN listeners; and the Oracle Notification Service (ONS). If the GI owner is different from the RDBMS home owner, you would have two oraagents, each running as one of the installation owners. The database and service resources would be managed by the RDBMS home owner and other resources by the GI home owner. CRSDs oraagent for grid username processes writes it trace to $GI_HOME/log/<hostname>/agent/crsd/oraagent_grid/oraagent_grid.log.

CRSD orarootagent

CRSD's rootagent manages (start/stop/check/clean) GNS and its VIP, node VIP, SCAN VIP, and the network resources. CRSDs orarootagent process writes its trace to $GI_HOME/log/<hostname>/agent/crsd/orarootagent_root/orarootagent_root.log.

CRSD scriptagent

The script agent is the entry point for third-party/custom resource management using the Agent Framework APIs, though some resources are managed by this agent from the default install. There will be one script agent for each user that registers resources for management in this way. The script agent for the grid user writes its trace to $GI_HOME/log/<hostname>/agent/crsd/scriptagent_grid/scriptagent_grid.log.

Clusterware Trace Files

As we have gone through the processes so far, we have mentioned where the processes write their trace files, but I would like to spend a few lines talking about the logs that are included in Oracle 11*g* Release 2. In Oracle 11*g* Release 1, RDBMS instances, listeners, and so on, moved to using the Automatic Diagnostic Repository (ADR). The default repository home location is the ORACLE_BASE/diag directory, and the various process types have directories under that, such as asm, rdbms, and tnslsnr. When an error occurs, the ADR framework creates an incident and gives you the option of packaging up that incident using the ADR Command Interpreter (ADRCI) to send to Oracle Support.

Although I will not go into ADR here, because ASM is now under our GI home and may be a critical part of the clusterware, you need to know where to go for troubleshooting. The clusterware has not as yet followed the ADR model; however, the tracing has evolved significantly since 10*g* Release 1. Most of the trace files are fairly low level and for use by Oracle Support to diagnose problems—only the cluster alert log is meant for user consumption in the same way as the RDBMS alert log is.

It is, of course, never a bad thing to look at the traces to get an understanding of what is going on so long as you don't get paranoid about the contents and log Support Requests for every line that does not look right. (I guess I'm saying don't go looking too hard for problems in these logs because many of the messages look like a problem but are quite normal.) The cluster alert log is a good one to look at to look for problems. The cluster alert log is found at $GI_HOME/log/<hostname>alert<hostname>.log and included only the top-level information such as startups, shutdowns, Cluster Verification Utility (CVU) checks, evictions, and reconfigurations due to eviction or shutdown of other nodes, as well as actual problems encountered by other processes. Even some of these reported problems may not be of concern—for example, errors from processes on startup may occur simply because they need resources that are not yet online. Having said that, you may find it helpful to check out these logs.

Here is an example of a message in the cluster alert log:

```
2010-09-22 02:35:11.474
[/u01/app/11.2.0/grid/bin/oraagent.bin(4696)]CRS-5016:
Process /u01/app/11.2.0/grid/bin/lsnrctl" spawned by agent
/u01/app/11.2.0/grid/bin/oraagent.bin" for action "check" failed: details
at"(:CLSN00010:)" in "/u01/app/11.2.0/grid/log/racassur-
pfix01/agent/crsd/oraagent_grid/oraagent_grid.log"
```

You can see that CRSD's oraagent tries to do a check on the listener using the **lsnrctl** command and it failed. Let's take a look at the file mentioned to see what happened. (I show only the more interesting lines and remove the date and time stamps.)

NOTE
If you do not find the timestamp you expect in the file, check the other files in the directory, because the log files are aged out when they reach a certain size, so there can be up to ten old versions of the file named (in this case) oraagent_grid.l01 to l10.

```
[ora.LISTENER_SCAN3.lsnr][1579252032] {1:63693:62933} [check] lsnrctl
status LISTENER_SCAN3
[ora.LISTENER_SCAN3.lsnr][1579252032] {1:63693:62933} [check]
(:CLSN00010:)Connecting to (DESCRIPTION=(ADDRESS=(PROTOCOL=IPC)
(KEY=LISTENER_SCAN3)))
[ora.LISTENER_SCAN3.lsnr][1579252032] {1:63693:62933} [check]
(:CLSN00010:)TNS-12541: TNS:no listener
[ora.LISTENER_SCAN3.lsnr][1579252032] {1:63693:62933} [check]
(:CLSN00010:) TNS-12560: TNS:protocol adapter error
[ora.LISTENER_SCAN3.lsnr][1579252032] {1:63693:62933} [check]
(:CLSN00010:)  TNS-00511: No listener
[ora.LISTENER_SCAN3.lsnr][1579252032] {1:63693:62933} [check]
(:CLSN00010:)   Linux Error: 2: No such file or directory
```

These errors show that the listener was down when the check ran, but the trace file also shows that, just before this, a stop for that listener was called, so it is expected it would be down.

```
2010-09-22 02:35:11.365: [    AGFW][1646369088] {1:63693:62933} Com-
mand: stop for resource: ora.LISTENER_SCAN3.lsnr 1 1 completed with
status: SUCCESS
```

Nothing to worry about there, so long as the listener can be restarted when needed.

If you do happen to find a real problem that requires the help of Oracle Support, you can zip all the required trace files using $GI_HOME/bin/diagcollection.sh, which is a wrapper for diagcollection.pl. It can collect ADR incident data, Cluster Health Monitor O/S data, as well as clusterware trace files:

```
[root]# /u01/app/11.2.0/grid/bin/diagcollection.sh -h
Production Copyright 2004, 2010, Oracle.  All rights reserved
Cluster Ready Services (CRS) diagnostic collection tool
diagcollection
```

```
--collect
 [--crs] For collecting crs diag information
 [--adr] For collecting diag information for ADR; specify ADR location
 [--chmos] For collecting Cluster Health Monitor (OS) data
 [--all] Default.For collecting all diag information.
 [--core] UNIX only. Package core files with CRS data
 [--afterdate] UNIX only. Collects archives from the specified
Date. Specify in mm/dd/yyyy format
 [--aftertime] Supported with -adr option. Collects archives after the
specified time. Specify in YYYYMMDDHHMISS24 format
 [--beforetime] Supported with -adr option. Collects archives before
the specified date. Specify in YYYYMMDDHHMISS24 format
 [--crshome] Argument that specifies the CRS Home location
 [--incidenttime] Collects Cluster Health Monitor (OS) data from the
specified time.  Specify in MM/DD/YYYY24HH:MM:SS format
    If not specified, Cluster Health Monitor (OS) data generated in the
past 24 hours are collected
 [--incidentduration] Collects Cluster Health Monitor (OS) data for the
duration after the specified time.  Specify in HH:MM format.
    If not specified, all Cluster Health Monitor (OS) data after inci-
denttime are collected
```

NOTE
*For 11.2.0.1, check the valid arguments with the **–h***
flags as the arguments shown in this example are the
11.2.0.2 options.

Summary

The entire GI stack has gone through a massive rewrite in the Oracle Database 11*g* Release 2. The agent framework provides a much more scalable solution to resource management and provides a more flexible API to integrate non–Oracle resources into clusterware management. ASM has moved under the same home as the clusterware to allow ASM to be managed more easily by storage administrators instead of DBAs, and the whole startup has been rewritten. Many of these changes were driven by clients' requirement to more easily add and remove servers from the cluster and to provision those servers to different services dependent on load and changing user requirements. The introduction of Quality of Service in 11.2.0.2 takes this ability to the next level by automatically moving resources as required by service levels.

Remember that 11.2.0.2 is still a patchset release and will be available only to those with the rights to get patches from Oracle. If you do not have those rights, you will be able to install and use only 11.2.0.1 for testing and learning. Chapter 4 will deal with GI installation and configuration.

CHAPTER
4

Grid Infrastructure Installation and Configuration

n this chapter, we'll catch up with Max who, back in Chapter 2, set up a test cluster using Oracle VM. Now that Max knows the concepts behind Grid Infrastructure (GI) Cluster Ready Services (CRS) and much of what needs to be configured to install the cluster, he's ready to get his hands dirty.

First, we'll cover at a more practical level the requirements to set up our nodes to install GI, which includes the best practices for setting up the environment, such as Oracle homes, shared clusterware files (Oracle Cluster Registry [OCR] and voting files), the use of Automatic Storage Management Cluster File System (ACFS), and patching. After that, we'll talk about installation and upgrade, step-by-step, covering the most interesting and/or possible problem areas.

GI Installation Choices and Requirements

Before installing the software, you need to make a number of installation decisions and set up the system to support those decisions. Some configuration decisions you might need to consider are whether to use Grid Naming Service (GNS) or static IPs, whether to use ASM for voting and/or OCR files, and whether to install locally on a node or use a shared home. Other simple requirements include two physical network interfaces for public and private networks. We will quickly discuss these installation options before moving onto the installation itself.

Shared GI Home vs. Local GI Home

Each node in a cluster needs Oracle software to access the Oracle Real Application Clusters (Oracle RAC) database. This brings up the question of whether the software should be located on shared drives (shared Oracle home) or on local drives on each node (local Oracle home). For the GI home, the argument is pretty clear. Even though having a shared home is easier to maintain for patching and requires a little less setup and space for larger clusters, it makes it impossible to patch or upgrade the home without taking a complete cluster outage. Any failure with accessing that shared disk, whether physical access or corruption, will cause a cluster outage because it is a single point of failure. The recommendation here is to use local disk for placement of GI home; it is not supported to have a GI home on any cluster file system. It is possible to use Network File System (NFS) with Network Attached Storage (NAS), but it is highly recommended to use local disks.

Separate Users for GI Home and DB Home

Almost all enterprises today have implemented role separation for their IT systems. A system administrator looks after your OS, the network administrator keeps the network working, the storage administrator provides storage space, and the DBA has to keep the database up and meeting service level agreements (SLAs). So who should manage the GI? Traditionally, because it is an Oracle product, it was assigned to the DBA; on the other hand, ASM handles storage and some might consider allocating it to the system administrator since various clusterware administration tasks require root access. In Oracle 10*g*, you could install CRS as one user and the RDBMS as a different user for a level of separation; however, ASM could exist in the RDBMS home. ASM also was predominantly managed using SQL instructions, and as such was still considered built primarily for DBAs. Oracle 11*g* introduced role-separated management, and ASM provides an approach using operating system groups to split ASM management away from the DBA; this is known as *job role separation*. With this separation, the new ASM Configuration Assistant (ASMCA) GUI, and command line tool asmcmd, it is now truly built for storage and system administrators.

Because of this alignment of ASM with the clusterware, even if you do not plan to use role-separated management, the recommendation is to have separate owners for GI home and RDBMS home. If you are a DBA in a job role separation environment, now is a good time to become best friends with your system and storage admins. In this book, we will use job role separation, in which the grid user will own the GI software stack and the oracle user will own the RDBMS software stack.

Shared Storage Choices for Clusterware Files

Oracle provides three possible configuration options to be used for storage of the voting and OCR files: ASM, clustered file system, and NAS. ASM is available on all platforms and is recommended for voting and OCR files, as well as Oracle Real Application Clusters (Oracle RAC) database files. In addition, Oracle offers its own cluster file system on both Linux (OCFS2) and Windows (OCFS). Other vendors also offer cluster file systems for various platforms. These third-party clustered file systems must be certification tested by the vendor and approved by Oracle. Certification details are not covered in this book but are available through Oracle Support. If you are using a Linux or Unix platform you have a third option, which is to use NFS mounts via a network attached storage device (that is, network appliance or other storage vendor whose NFS solution certified by Oracle) for storage of the shared database and CRS files.

Support for the OCR and voting disks on raw or block devices is fully supported in upgrade situations. In fact, when performing the upgrade, you are not provided with the option to move these files off raw or block devices. That being said, after successfully upgrading to Oracle Database 11*g* Release 2, you should give serious consideration to moving these files to one of the natively supported storage options.

Shared Everything Disk Storage

One thing all storage options discussed so far share in common is that they all involve disks that are accessible from multiple nodes, simultaneously. This is often referred to as a "shared everything architecture," referring to all disks as being shared. Some cluster and database vendors use a different architecture—that is, a "shared nothing architecture," in which a disk can be accessed only by one node at a time. If a node accessing a disk goes down, that disk must be failed over to another, surviving node. The advantage with Oracle's shared everything architecture is that any node can access the data needed on any disk at any given time. It is not necessary to go through one specific node to get to the disks. Oracle requires that voting and OCR files, control files, all online redo logs, and all database files be stored on the shared drives, and these files are therefore accessible from all nodes in the cluster. In addition, certain files, such as archived redo logs, the system parameter file, and flashback logs can be, or more correctly—should be—stored on the shared drives (more on this in the upcoming chapters).

Automatic Storage Management

ASM removes the complexity of using block and raw devices, while still offering the advantage of speed that these devices provide. In Oracle Database 11g Release 2, ASM management can be achieved through the asmca GUI, asmcmd, as well as SQL*Plus—all of which require a connection to the ASM instance.

At a high level, ASM natively supports shared storage for database archive logs, flashback logs, database files, RMAN backups, Oracle Data Guard Broker configuration files, and server parameter files (SPFILEs). When using ASM as your shared storage option, you are provided benefits such as striping, mirroring, online storage reconfiguration and dynamic rebalancing, managed file creation, and deletion.

Enough of the "old features"—let's discuss some new features. As mentioned in our discussion about clusterware file storage options, Oracle 11g Release 2 introduces the ability to store voting and OCR files within ASM alongside of the RDBMS files that it has supported in previous releases. New features ASM Dynamic Volume Manager (ADVM) and ASM Cluster File System (ACFS) make GI 11g Release 2 a complete clusterware solution able to compete against the likes of Veritas, Serviceguard, and others. Basically with these features, you can carve out a logical volume from an ASM disk group, present that volume to the OS, and create an ACFS file system on that volume. This allows for support of shared RDBMS homes as well as storage of any file type that is not natively supported within an ASM disk group.

All these features can make Oracle ASM your preferred storage option, because it provides performance similar to raw devices with management options as easy as those for a file system. Chapter 5 is devoted entirely to ASM.

Oracle Cluster File System (OCFS)

As mentioned, Oracle provides a general-purpose Cluster File System (CFS) for both Windows and Linux platforms, which can be used for voting disks, OCR files, and RDBMS-related files. Note that OCFS is the Windows product, while OCFS2 is for the Linux platform and is open source, which OCFS is not. The obvious advantage of the CFS is that it simplifies the management of the shared files by allowing a directory structure and by allowing multiple files to be stored on a single shared disk/partition. In addition, on some platforms, the CFS can also be used as a shared location for the installation of the Oracle binaries for the RDBMS. Keep in mind, however, that the maintenance and single point of failure issues associated with shared homes.

NFS Mounts

On most Linux and Unix platforms, it is also possible to have the shared device for the data files be on an NFS mount, using a certified network-attached storage vendor. This requires that all nodes have network access to the device and have the same NFS mount point. The advantage is that it does also allow file system management, easing the complexity. The disadvantage is that network latency introduced into the file I/O equation can slow down performance, depending on the speed of your network and the cards.

Raw/Block Devices

From Oracle Database 11*g* Release 2 onward, the Oracle installer and Database Configuration Assistant (DBCA) will no longer support raw/block devices for database files. In addition, raw/block device support for storing the OCR and voting disks for new installs no longer exists.

Networking Requirements for CRS and Oracle RAC

To configure an Oracle RAC environment, you must have two network cards in each node at a minimum: one network card to be used for client communication on the public network and the other to be used for private cluster communication. You can choose to use statically allocated IP addresses for cluster resources or, as discussed in Chapter 3, use Grid Naming Service (GNS) for your node virtual IP (VIP) and SCAN addresses. Either way, you must first configure the /etc/hosts file on *each* node to have a unique name for the private nodes. The public node names must be resolvable through your Domain Name System (DNS) server or /etc/hosts on all cluster nodes. Even with DNS resolution, it is normal to have the public hostname and address resolvable in /etc/hosts as well. Ideally, these names should be easily identifiable hostnames for public and private—such as node1, node1_private, node2, node2_private, and so on. If you chose to use statically allocated IP addresses for VIPs, those must also be resolvable through DNS or /etc/hosts on all cluster nodes. The default naming convention for VIPs is

<hostname>-vip. The SCAN name must be resolvable from DNS to three static IP addresses (*not* configured in /etc/hosts) if GNS is not used. If GNS is enabled, DNS and DHCP servers are required, as discussed in Chapter 3. The VIP addresses and SCAN IP addresses will be requested from the Dynamic Host Configuration Protocol (DHCP) and registered in GNS.

Although it is possible in a two-node cluster to have the private network consist of a simple crossover cable, this is not recommended (or supported), because some network interface cards (NICs) and drivers require media sensing, which is not available without connectivity to a switch. For example, if one node is powered down, the card for the interconnect on the surviving node is disabled, because no more activity is being sensed across the interconnect. This can lead to errors on the surviving node.

The best solution is to have a dedicated switch between the nodes, which means constant activity is occurring on the card (coming from the switch), even when the other node is down. Of course, this also allows for expansion of your cluster to more than two nodes. The other consideration for production environments is that the switch and the cards for the interconnect should be capable of handling all the Cache Fusion traffic and other messaging traffic across the interconnect—therefore, you want this network to be a high-speed, low latency network (1Gb Ethernet or faster).

Network Interface Bonding

Network interface bonding is simply a way to join two or more interfaces together to provide interface redundancy and/or improved bandwidth. The application sees only one logical interface (the bonded interface), and the actual send and receive traffic is handled by one or more members of the bonded interface (depending on the bonding configuration). In previous versions, third-party bonding was the only supported way to use more than one network card, but beginning with 11.2.0.2, the clusterware provides a way to use more than one interface for the private interconnect.

Hardware Requirements

Each node in the cluster must satisfy some minimum hardware requirements before the installation can begin.

Chip Architecture

A processor type (CPU) that is certified with the version of the Oracle software being installed must be used. All servers that will be used in the cluster have the same chip architecture—for example, all 32-bit processors or all 64-bit processors, all SPARC processors, or all x86 processors. Oracle does allow cluster nodes of different sizes within the cluster so long as they are running on similar architecture. The rule of thumb is that if you install the same exact release of GI on all the machines, they should be clusterable. It is, of course, another job to ensure correct workload placement.

Physical Memory

The amount of physical memory required is dependent on what each node of the cluster will be doing; however, the following offers some guidelines to the minimum requirement to complete an installation:

- **Cluster node with GI only**   At least 1.5GB of RAM

- **Cluster node with GI and RDBMS**   At least 2.5GB of RAM

To check the amount of physical memory on Linux, you can use the following command:

```
[root]# grep MemTotal /proc/meminfo
MemTotal:       2097152 kB
```

This node has only 2GB of memory, which is fine for a GI only install.

NOTE
In a test environment, you can start GI and Oracle RAC with less memory than the guidelines suggest; however, your performance will likely suffer and other problems may occur due to memory starvation.

Swap Space

The amount of swap space that is recommended depends on the amount of physical memory on the cluster node, as shown in the following:

- **Up to 2GB of RAM**   1.5 × Physical memory of swap

- **2GB to 16GB of RAM**   Swap space equal to physical memory

- **Over 16GB of RAM**   16GB of swap space

To check on the amount of swap configured on your Linux system, use the following command:

```
[root@racassur1-node3 ~]# /sbin/swapon -s
Filename                    Type            Size     Used    Priority
/dev/xvda3                  partition       2104504 0        -1
```

Disk Space

The disk space requirements vary, depending on what decisions you make as far as voting/OCR placement and use of shared homes, however the following provides a set of guidelines for installation. Note that only one disk group is considered here and as such only one OCR file exists, as discussed in Chapter 3.

- **Temporary space**   >= 1GB in /tmp on all nodes

- **GI home**   10GB – Oracle states 5.5GB, however patch backups and log files can take up significant space.

- **RDBMS home**   5GB

- **ASM voting/OCR external redundancy**   600MB (300MB for each file)

- **ASM voting/OCR normal redundancy**   1.5GB (900MB for voting, 600MB for OCR) in three failure groups with three separate disks

- **ASM voting/OCR high redundancy**   2.4GB (1500MB for voting, 900MB for OCR) in five failure groups with five separate disks

- **CFS Voting/OCR**   300MB for each file configured

NOTE
The disk space required for your database depends on placement type and the size of the data in that database, so we have not tried to cover that here. In sizing your database, however, you should consider disk group redundancy if you're using ASM and also the size of any Fast Recovery Area (aka Flash Recovery Area).

Kernel Parameters
The Cluster Verification Utility (CVU) can be used to check the required kernel parameter settings and provides a fixup script to correct these as the root user.

Operating System Packages
The OS packages required depend on the operating system type and version. Requirements for all supported platforms can be found in the My Oracle Support Note# 169706.1 as well as the installation guide for that platform. The CVU can check these for you prior to installation, and we'll talk about that next.

Cluster Verification Utility
Setting up your Oracle RAC environment is a process that requires multiple steps. Hardware and OS, cluster file system, clusterware, and the database have to be

installed sequentially. All the stages require important components that are necessary for the success of your installation. Oracle provides you with a utility that verifies all the important components that are needed at the different stages of your Oracle RAC installation.

CVU is better known by the name of its command line tool: cluvfy. CVU provides prechecks and postchecks for each stage of installation. The prechecks ensure that your system has met prerequisites before a particular stage. The postchecks confirm that all the activities for the certain stage are correctly completed. It also checks for components such as SCAN or OCR so you can evaluate their configuration or integrity. The CVU not only checks that all parameters meet the requirements, but for some parameters it also generates a script that will fix them for you. The CVU is integrated in the Oracle Universal Installer (OUI), but you can run it from the command line whenever you want to check whether you are ready to go to the next stage or to confirm that a stage has completed successfully.

It is recommend that you run CVU before and after every configuration step. To run the CVU prior to install, you will find it in the /Disk1 directory on the installation media or download:

```
[grid]$ sh runcluvfy.sh -help
USAGE:
runcluvfy [-help]
runcluvfy stage {-list|-help}
runcluvfy stage {-pre|-post} <stage-name> <stage-specific options>
               [-verbose]
runcluvfy comp  {-list|-help}
runcluvfy comp  <component-name> <component-specific options>  [-verbose]
```

After install, you will find CVU in the GI_HOME/bin directory as *cluvfy*.

MAA Workshop: *Prepare a Linux/Oracle RAC Cluster*

Workshop Notes

The first part of the workshop will walk you through the node preparation steps for a test environment on Oracle Enterprise Linux. For this test setup, we will configure a two-node Oracle RAC cluster running Oracle Enterprise Linux 5 running as Oracle VM guests on a single server. Although you can choose from among several storage options for setting up a test environment, including shared SCSI devices, NFS, and so forth, we have chosen to use Oracle VM (OVM) shared disks for this workshop. Remember that OVM has specific requirements to be supported for use by GI and Oracle RAC, as noted in Chapter 2. The configuration used here with multiple guests for the same cluster being run on one physical machine is not supported for production systems. We demonstrate it here because it affords a low-cost means of testing the functionality and concepts of Oracle RAC, using hardware that is readily affordable and accessible for just about anyone. If we were running for political office, our platform would call for a chicken in every pot, two cars in every garage, and a test cluster under the desk of every DBA. We are not in political office, so we had to configure a two-node Oracle RAC cluster using hardware that cost less than $1000—times are tight after all. Although you do not have to do it so cheaply, this also demonstrates how Oracle RAC can be used to turn low-cost commodity hardware into a highly available system.

The assumption here is that we have configured our guest VMs as per Chapter 2 and have Oracle Enterprise Linux up and running on both guests. Our SCAN has been allocated by the network administrators. For completeness, we will cover all the manual actions required, but will note where you could shortcut the process by using the CVU, Secure Shell (SSH) setup scripts, or the OUI in some places. We will note those and mention what would be different if you had chosen GNS.

Step 1. Create OS groups to be used for our grid and Oracle users by entering these commands as the root user:

```
#/usr/sbin/groupadd -g 501 oinstall
#/usr/sbin/groupadd -g 502 dba
#/usr/sbin/groupadd -g 504 asmadmin
#/usr/sbin/groupadd -g 506 asmdba
#/usr/sbin/groupadd -g 507 asmoper
```

> **NOTE**
> *If you are not using role separation and Grid/RDBMS is to be installed as the same user, then only the oinstall and dba groups are actually required as the sysasm privilege will be given to the dba group.*

Step 2. Create the users that will own the Oracle software using these commands:

```
#/usr/sbin/useradd -u 501 -g oinstall -G asmadmin,asmdba,asmoper grid
#/usr/sbin/useradd -u 502 -g oinstall -G dba,asmdba oracle
```

> **NOTE**
> *Again, only one user is needed if no role separation exists. Also see that only **grid** has the asmadmin group that will be given the sysasm privilege. The asmdba group will be given the asmdba privilege to allow it to use ASM for file storage.*

Step 3. Set the password for the oracle and grid accounts using the **passwd** command so that it is the same for all nodes across the cluster.

Step 4. Repeat steps 1 through 3 on each node in your cluster.

Step 5. Add lines to the /etc/hosts file on each node, specifying the public IP, VIP, and private addresses. Configure the /etc/hosts file so that it is similar to the following example:

```
#eth0 - PUBLIC
172.0.2.100 racassur-ipfix01.example.com racassur-ipfix01
172.0.2.101 racassur-ipfix02.example.com racassur-ipfix02
#VIP
172.0.2.102 racassur-ipfix01-vip.example.com racassur-ipfix01-vip
172.0.2.103 racassur-ipfix02-vip.example.com racassur-ipfix02-vip
#eth1 - PRIVATE
192.168.1.101 racassur-ipfix01-priv
192.168.1.101 racassur-ipfix02-priv
```

> **NOTE**
> *If you are using GNS, only the public and private hostnames will need to be set up in /etc/hosts.*

Step 6. Deactivate Network Time Protocol daemon (NTPD) on all nodes in the cluster using the following commands as the root user:

```
[root]# /sbin/service ntpd stop
[root]# chkconfig ntpd off
[root]# rm /etc/ntp.conf
[root]# rm /var/run/ntpd.pid
```

This will make Cluster Time Synchronization Server daemon (CTSSD) run in active mode, handling cluster time synchronization. Alternatively, you can ensure that the date and time settings on all nodes are set as closely as possible and set up NTPD with the **–x** option that allows CTSSD to run in observer mode.

Step 7. Configure SSH user equivalency as the grid user to allow for remote commands and copying to be completed by the installer. The OUI can set up SSH for you, and we'll cover a script for this as well, but we will go through the manual method here if you encounter problems with the other methods:

```
[grid@racassur-ipfix01]$ cd ~
[grid@racassur-ipfix01]$ mkdir ~/.ssh
[grid@racassur-ipfix01]$ chmod 700 ~/.ssh
```

```
[grid@racassur-ipfix01]$ /usr/bin/ssh-keygen -t dsa
Generating public/private dsa key pair.
Enter file in which to save the key (/home/grid/.ssh/id_dsa):
Enter passphrase (empty for no passphrase):
Enter same passphrase again:
Your identification has been saved in /home/grid/.ssh/id_dsa.
Your public key has been saved in /home/grid/.ssh/id_dsa.pub.
```

Repeat the process of generating the key on node 2 by running **ssh-keygen -t dsa** as user grid on node 2. Back on node 1, write out the contents of id_dsa.pub to the authorized_keys file and copy that to node 2:

```
[grid@racassur-ipfix01]$ cd .ssh
[grid@racassur-ipfix01]$ cat id_dsa.pub > authorized_keys
[grid@racassur-ipfix01]$ scp authorized_keys racassur-ipfix02:/home/
grid/.ssh/
```

> **NOTE**
> *You will be prompted to accept a Digital Signature Algorithm (DSA) key and add the node to known hosts. You must answer yes. Then you will provide the grid user's password. Next, you need to SSH to node 2 and go to the .ssh directory.*

```
[grid@racassur-ipfix01]$ ssh racassur-ipfix02
[grid@racassur-ipfix02]$ cd .ssh
```

Append the information from id_dsa.pub on into the authorized_keys file as follows:

```
[grid@racassur-ipfix02]$ cat id_dsa.pub >> authorized_keys
```

Node racassur-ipfix02 now has an authorized_keys file that will allow the grid user from either node to do an SSH to node 2. Copy this file back over to node 1 now, replacing the original authorized_keys file on that node:

```
[grid@racassur-ipfix02]$ scp authorized_keys racassur-ipfix01:/home/
grid/.ssh/
```

Test the user equivalence setup from each node via a command such as this:

```
[grid@racassur-ipfix01]$ hostname
racassur-ipfix01
[grid@racassur-ipfix01]$ ssh racassur-ipfix02 hostname
racassur-ipfix02
```

NOTE
If anything (such as a login banner) is returned to the screen other than the hostname, then SSH may not work for the CVU or the installer.

Alternatively, as stated at the start of this step, you can use the installer to set up SSH. Simply start the OUI and go through the install screens to allow it to set up SSH for you; then cancel the install. (See the section for the actual GI installation later in the chapter to see how to do this.) Alternatively, use the SSH setup script provided in the OUI directory. Here is an example for the grid user:

```
_$GI_HOME/oui/sshsetup/sshUserSetup.sh -user grid -hosts "racassur-
ipfix01 racassur-ipfix02" -advanced -noPromptPassphrase
```

Step 8. As the root user, add the following kernel parameter settings to /etc/sysctl .conf. If any of the parameters are already in the /etc/sysctl.conf file, the higher of the two values should be used:

```
kernel.shmmni = 4096
kernel.sem = 250 32000 100 128
fs.file-max = 6553600
net.ipv4.ip_local_port_range = 9000 65500
net.core.rmem_default = 262144
net.core.rmem_max = 4194304
net.core.wmem_default = 262144
net.core.wmem_max = 1048576
```

NOTE
These settings are required to install the GI correctly, but they do not take into account resources required for running database instances or other applications. As a post installation task, you should tune the semaphore parameters to meet any needs beyond GI. You might also consider implementing huge pages, which is again not a requirement for GI but may help performance for the RDBMS.

Step 9. Run the following as the root user to allow the new kernel parameters to be put in place:

```
[root]#/sbin/sysctl -p
```

Step 10. Repeat steps 7 and 8 on all cluster nodes.

Step 11.   Add the following lines to the /etc/security/limits.conf file:

```
grid soft nproc 2047
grid hard nproc 16384
grid soft nofile 1024
grid hard nofile 65536
oracle soft nproc 2047
oracle hard nproc 16384
oracle soft nofile 1024
oracle hard nofile 65536
```

Step 12.   Add or edit the following line in the /etc/pam.d/login file, if it does not already exist:

```
session required pam_limits.so
```

Step 13.   Make the following changes to the default shell startup file. Add the following lines to the /etc/profile file:

```
if [ $USER = "oracle" ] || [ $USER = "grid" ]; then
if [ $SHELL = "/bin/ksh" ]; then
ulimit -p 16384
ulimit -n 65536
else
ulimit -u 16384 -n 65536
fi
umask 022
fi
```

For the C shell (csh or tcsh), add the following lines to the /etc/csh.login file:

```
if ( $USER = "oracle" || $USER = "grid" ) then
limit maxproc 16384
limit descriptors 65536
endif
```

Step 14.   Repeat steps 11 to 13 on all other nodes in the cluster.

Step 15.   To create the GI home directory, enter the following commands as the root user:

```
[root]# mkdir -p /u01/11.2.0/grid
[root]# # chown -R grid:oinstall /u01/11.2.0/grid
[root]# # chmod -R 775 /u01/11.2.0/grid
```

Step 16.   To create the Oracle base directory, enter the following commands as the root user. Each installation owner should have its own Oracle base.

```
[root]# # mkdir -p /u01/app/grid.
[root]# # chown -R grid:oinstall /u01/app/grid
[root]# # chmod -R 775 /u01/app/grid
```

> **NOTE**
> *The GI home should not be under an Oracle base directory, and should not exist within another Oracle home. During installation, the path to the GI home is changed to be owned by root, and this can cause permission errors for other installations.*

Step 17.   If you are using GNS, ensure your /etc/resolv.conf is set up to search the domain in which your cluster will exist and can reach the required DNS server, as shown here:

```
[root]# cat /etc/resolv.conf
options attempts: 2
options timeout: 1
search LunarTrax.com clu1.LunarTrax.com
nameserver 140.25.249.12
nameserver 148.22.202.16
```

Step 18.   Stage the required Oracle software onto a local drive on node 1 of your cluster. For the RDBMS software, download the following from Oracle Technology Network (OTN): Oracle Database 11*g* Release 2 (11.2.0.1.0) for Linux.
     For the GI (clusterware and ASM) software, download the following: Oracle Database 11*g* Release 2 Grid Infrastructure (11.2.0.1.0) for Linux.

> **NOTE**
> *Ensure that you use only 32-bit versions of the Oracle software on a 32-bit OS and 64-bit versions of the Oracle software on a 64-bit OS.*

Workshop Notes

The second part of the workshop will walk you through the preparation steps for the shared storage. Two 10GB files were attached to the VMs for shared storage through devices xvdb and xvdd. Table 4-1 shows the storage layout for this implementation.

Block Device	ASMLib Name	Size	Comments
/dev/xvdb1	None—not configured through ASMLib	10GB	ASM disk group for OCR, voting disks, and database when installed
/dev/xvde1	ACFSDG	10GB	ASM disk group for ACFS

TABLE 4-1. *Storage Layout*

> **NOTE**
> *It is recommended that you use ASMLib for all the disks going into ASM, but we have left /dev/xvde out of ASMLib to show you how to set up udev for these devices and discover them at install time.*

Step 1. Once the Logical Unit Numbers (LUNs) have been presented to *all* servers in the cluster, partition the LUNs from one node only and run fdisk to create a single whole-disk partition to be used as an ASM disk. There are different requirements depending on OS and storage choice as to where to start the first partition for correct LUN alignment. In this case, we will start our first partition 1MB into the disk to ensure proper alignment for 1MB stripe size; however, a larger offset may be advisable depending on the stripe size being used. The general rule is that you must offset using a power of 2 bytes up to the maximum stripe size you need. Note that this is not required on Linux, but correct LUN alignment can improve your disk access times.

The following example for /dev/xvde starts the partition at sector 2048 due to a sector size of 512 bytes:

```
[root]# fdisk /dev/xvde
Command (m for help): p    -- p is to print the partition table
Disk /dev/xvde: 10.7 GB, 10737418240 bytes
255 heads, 63 sectors/track, 1305 cylinders
Units = cylinders of 16065 * 512 = 8225280 bytes

    Device Boot      Start         End      Blocks   Id  System

Command (m for help): u
Changing display/entry units to sectors

Command (m for help): n
Command action
   e   extended
```

```
   p   primary partition (1-4)
p
Partition number (1-4): 1
First sector (63-20479999, default 63): 2048
Last sector or +size or +sizeM or +sizeK (2048-20479999, default
20479999):
Using default value 20479999

Command (m for help): p

Disk /dev/xvde: 10.4 GB, 10485760000 bytes
255 heads, 63 sectors/track, 1274 cylinders, total 20480000 sectors
Units = sectors of 1 * 512 = 512 bytes

    Device Boot      Start         End      Blocks   Id  System
/dev/xvde1            2048    20479999    10238976   83  Linux

Command (m for help): w
The partition table has been altered!

Calling ioctl() to re-read partition table.
Syncing disks.
```

Step 2.   Load the updated block device partition tables by running the following on *all* servers participating in the cluster:

```
[root]#/sbin/partprobe
```

Step 3.   ASMLib is highly recommended for those systems that will be using ASM for shared storage within the cluster due to the performance and manageability benefits that it provides. ASMLib automatically provides LUN persistence, so when using ASMLib, you don't need to configure LUN persistence manually for the ASM devices on the system (and this feature alone makes ASMLib worth using). Perform the following steps to install and configure ASMLib on the cluster nodes.

1.   Download the following packages from the ASMLib OTN page. If you are an Enterprise Linux customer, you can obtain the software through the Unbreakable Linux network. The ASMLib kernel driver *must* match the kernel revision number of your system, which can be identified by running the **uname -r** command:

```
[root]# uname -r
2.6.18-194.0.0.0.3.el5xen
```

2. Download the set of RPMs that pertain to your platform architecture; in our case, this is x86_64, and notice the oracleasm itself is for the Xen kernel version.

```
oracleasm-support-2.1.3-1.el5x86_64.rpm
oracleasmlib-2.0.4-1.el5.x86_64.rpm
oracleasm-2.6.18-194.0.0.0.3.el5xen-2.0.5-1.el5.x86_64.rpm
```

3. Install the RPMs by running the following as the root user:

```
[root]# rpm -ivh oracleasm-support-2.1.3-1.el5x86_64.rpm \
oracleasmlib-2.0.4-1.el5.x86_64.rpm \
oracleasm-2.6.18-194.0.0.0.3.el5xen-2.0.5-1.el5.x86_64.rpm
```

4. Configure ASMLib by running the following as the root user:

```
[root]#/usr/sbin/oracleasm configure -i
Configuring the Oracle ASM library driver.
This will configure the on-boot properties of the Oracle ASM
library driver. The following questions will determine whether
the driver is loaded on boot and what permissions it will have.
The current values will be shown in brackets ('[]'). Hitting
<ENTER> without typing an answer will keep that current value.
Ctrl-C will abort.
Default user to own the driver interface []: grid
Default group to own the driver interface []: asmadmin
Start Oracle ASM library driver on boot (y/n) [n]: y
Scan for Oracle ASM disks on boot (y/n) [y]: y
Writing Oracle ASM library driver configuration: done
Initializing the Oracle ASMLib driver: [ OK ]
Scanning the system for Oracle ASMLib disks: [ OK ]
```

5. Repeat the steps to install and configure ASMLib on all cluster nodes.

Step 4. Start oracleasm using the following command on all nodes:

```
[root]# /etc/init.d/oracleasm start
Initializing the Oracle ASMLib driver:                    [  OK  ]
Scanning the system for Oracle ASMLib disks:              [  OK  ]
```

Step 5. As the root user, use oracleasm to create ASM disks using the following syntax:

```
# /usr/sbin/oracleasm createdisk disk_name device_partition_name
```

In this command, **disk_name** is the name you choose for the ASM disk. The name you choose must contain only ASCII capital letters, numbers, or underscores;

the disk name must also start with a letter—for example, DISK1 or VOL1, or RAC_
FILE1. The name of the disk partition to mark as an ASM disk is the device_
partition_name. Here's an example:

```
[root]# /usr/sbin/oracleasm createdisk ACFSDG /dev/xvde1
```

Repeat this for each disk that will be used by Oracle ASM. After you have
created all the ASM disks for your cluster, use the **listdisks** command to verify their
availability:

```
[root]# /usr/sbin/oracleasm listdisks
ACFSDG
```

Step 6. On all the other nodes in the cluster, use the **scandisks** command as the
root user to pick up the newly created ASM disks. You do not need to create the
ASM disks on each node, only on one node in the cluster.

```
[root]# /usr/sbin/oracleasm scandisks
Scanning system for ASM disks [ OK ]
```

After scanning for ASM disks, display the available ASM disks on each node to
verify their availability:

```
# /usr/sbin/oracleasm listdisks
ACFSDG
```

Step 7. Because we have left /dev/xvdb1 out of ASMLIB management (specifically
to allow us to look at this), that device needs to be set up in udev to ensure
persistence of permissions. To do this, we have to create/edit a udev rules file that
udev will read on startup to set the correct permissions on the devices we want to
use for ASM. In our simple setup here using Oracle VM, the disks are always given
the same device name, as we have specified it in the vm.cfg, which makes the
entries simple to add:

```
[root]# cat /etc/udev/rules.d/99-oracle.rules
# Setting Up Permissions for the Oracle Devices
# Example of using a range of devices
#KERNEL=="xvd[a-e]1", OWNER="grid", GROUP="asmadmin", MODE="660"
# ASM device 10GB
KERNEL=="xvdb1", OWNER="grid", GROUP="asmadmin", MODE="660"
# ASM devices for ACFS # commented out as ASMlib managed
#KERNEL=="xvde1", OWNER="grid", GROUP="oinstall", MODE="660"
```

Normally on Linux, we cannot guarantee what device a disk will get, and as
such we need to get the scsi-id of the device and use that to make the entry in the

rules file. First, we need to ensure that the /etc/scsi_id.config file has the line **options=–g** because without that, the scsi_id command will not return a value.

```
[root]# cat > /etc/scsi_id.config
vendor="ATA",options=-p 0x80
options=-g
```

Then we can get the scsi_id for the device (note we use /block/sdb) using:

```
[root]#/sbin/scsi_id -g -u -s /block/sdb
3500507671dc0322d
```

Now add the udev rules entry for all partitions on this disk:

```
KERNEL=="sdb*", BUS=="scsi", PROGRAM=="/sbin/scsi_id",
RESULT=="3500507671dc0322d", OWNER="grid", GROUP="asmadmin",
MODE="0660"
```

Here's the simple command to get all the scsi_id's for attached disks on Linux:

```
for i in 'cat /proc/partitions | awk {'print $4'} |grep sd';
do echo "### $i: 'scsi_id -g -u -s /block/$i'";
done
```

> **NOTE**
> *From 11.2.0.2, the CVU will check udev rules for disks not in ASMLib. To avoid potential false error reporting problems, ensure that the parameter ordering is as shown previously (additional parameters would go after this) and that the parameter names are in uppercase. Also ensure there are no commented out rules for the same devices we have valid rules for. All of these things can cause CVU to report a problem with udev rules.*

Then restart udev:

```
[root]# /sbin/udevcontrol reload_rules
[root]# /sbin/start_udev
```

You should see the permissions set as requested on the device file:

```
[root]# ls -al /dev/xvdb*
brw-r----- 1 root disk     202, 16 Jun 15 14:08 /dev/xvdb
brw-rw---- 1 grid asmadmin 202, 17 Jun 23 09:10 /dev/xvdb1
```

Note that if we had used ASMLib for all our disks, this step would not be required, but we left /dev/xvde1 out of ASMLib so this process can be shown.

Workshop Notes

At this point, the machine should be ready to do the install; however, just to be sure, now would be a good time to run the CVU as the grid user:

```
[]$./runcluvfy.sh stage -pre crsinst -n racassur-ipfix01,racassur-ipfix02
-r 11gR2 -asm -asmgrp asmadmin -asmdev /dev/xvdb1,/dev/xvde1 –fixup –verbose
```

NOTE
The output is way too verbose to include here, but it will tell you anything you need to fix and even provide a fixup script for those things that can be fixed by a simple command. Of course, you could have done this earlier rather than setting those kernel parameters manually, but there is benefit in understanding that part, which is why it was included. For your next install, you should use the tools (OUI, CVU) and see how much easier it is.

Grid Infrastructure Install

During the node preparation, we created the OS user called *grid* to be the GI software owner. As the grid user on the first node, we will now install GI for the cluster. The OUI uses SSH to copy the binary files from this node to the other nodes during the installation. OUI can configure SSH for you during installation, and we will make use of that option for demonstration purposes.

Before we start the OUI, we need to ensure that an X display or VNC can be started on our terminal. A simple test would be to run **xclock** in the session from which we want to install to ensure that the clock appears successfully. If it does not, we should check your DISPLAY environment setting and check that non-root users can make a connection to the X server. This requires us to log into the machine on which the installer will run and execute **xhost +**.

Now we log in as the grid user and change to the directory where we staged the GI software. The following command starts the OUI:

```
[grid]$./runInstaller
```

On the screen shown in Figure 4-1, we select Install And Configure Grid Infrastructure For A Cluster. Another option, Install And Configure Grid Infrastructure For A Standalone Server, lets us install GI on a single-server system to support a single-instance database and applications. The Upgrade option should automatically be selected if a previous version of the clusterware is detected. We can also do a software only install in a new home and configure it for use later.

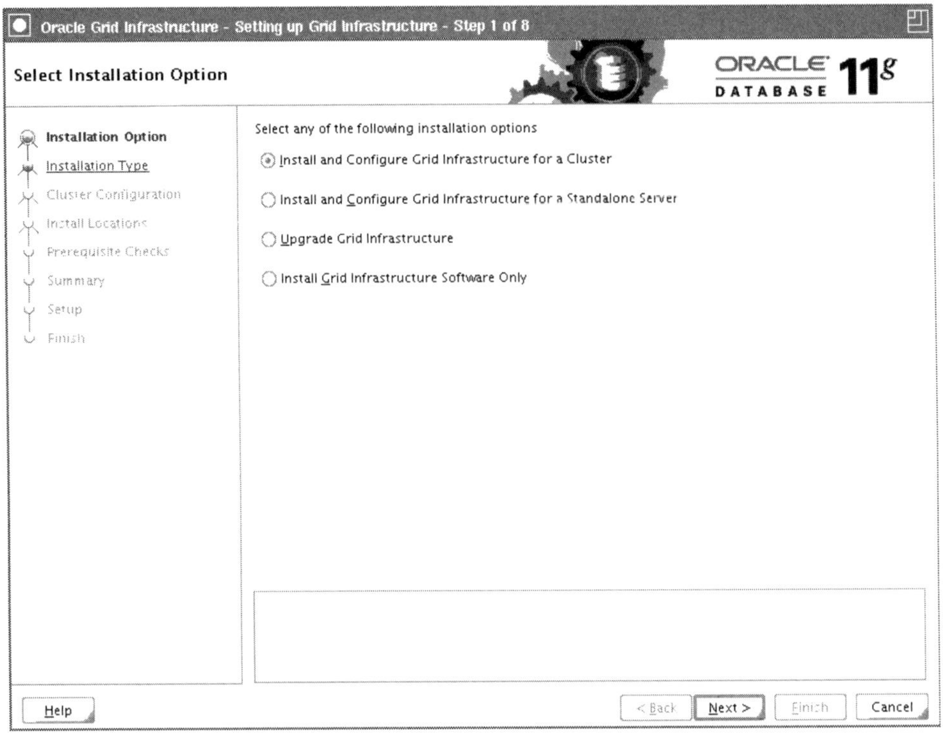

FIGURE 4-1. *Install options*

After selecting Install And Configure Grid Infrastructure For A Cluster, another screen appears that allows us to choose a Typical (minimal configuration setup) or Advanced Installation type of installation. We choose Advanced because that shows how to configure each component of GI.

The next screen is Language Selection (not shown), English in our case. We click Next to open the Grid Plug and Play Screen. This screen asks for a Unique Cluster name, SCAN Name, and Port, and the remaining options on the Screen are optional.

Figure 4-2 shows us a typical setup for manual configuration without GNS selected. Keep in mind that as a prerequisite, the SCAN name must resolve to at least one IP address through DNS, or /etc/hosts, though we strongly recommend

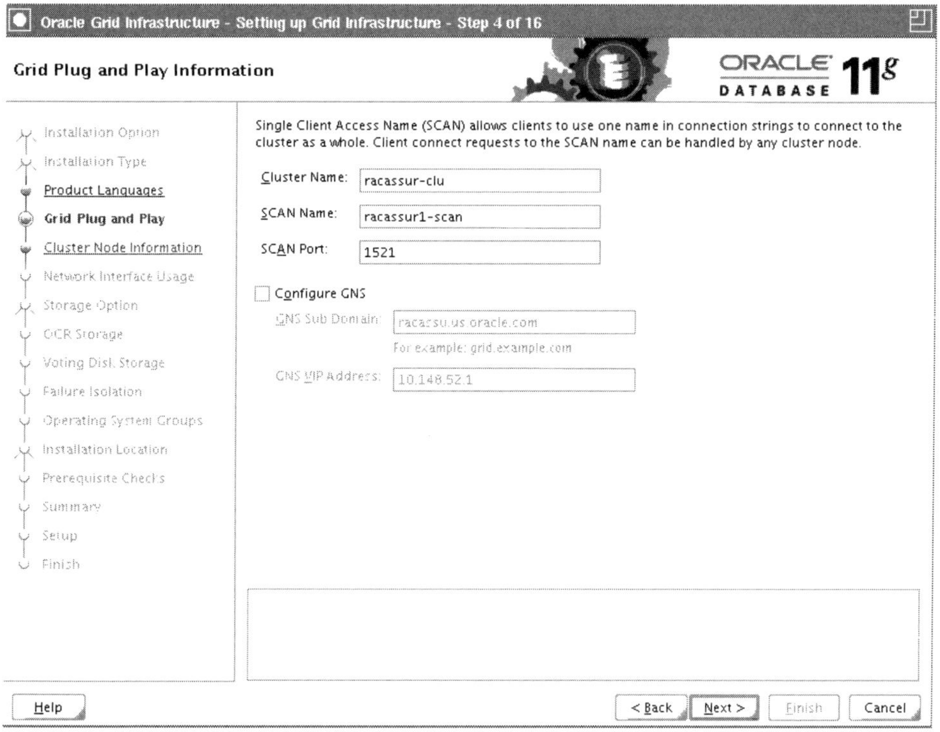

FIGURE 4-2. *Grid Plug and Play—no GNS*

using three IPs even for test systems. This requirement will be validated by the OUI upon clicking Next (assuming this is a non-GNS setup).

If we select the GNS option, we must populate the GNS subdomain and GNS VIP fields just below the checkbox, as shown in Figure 4-3. Here we can see LunarTrax has been set up to use GNS. The cluster named space is going to be accessible through the clu1.LunarTrax.com subdomain, and the SCAN name will be the default which is determined from the other choices. The GNS VIP address has been set up in the DNS to resolve names in the subdomain—for example, if a client requests to connect to space-scan.clu1.lunarTrax.com, then first it will go to the corporate DNS. The Corporate DNS will see clu1.LunarTrax.com and will know to reroute all requests to the GNS VIP for that subdomain.

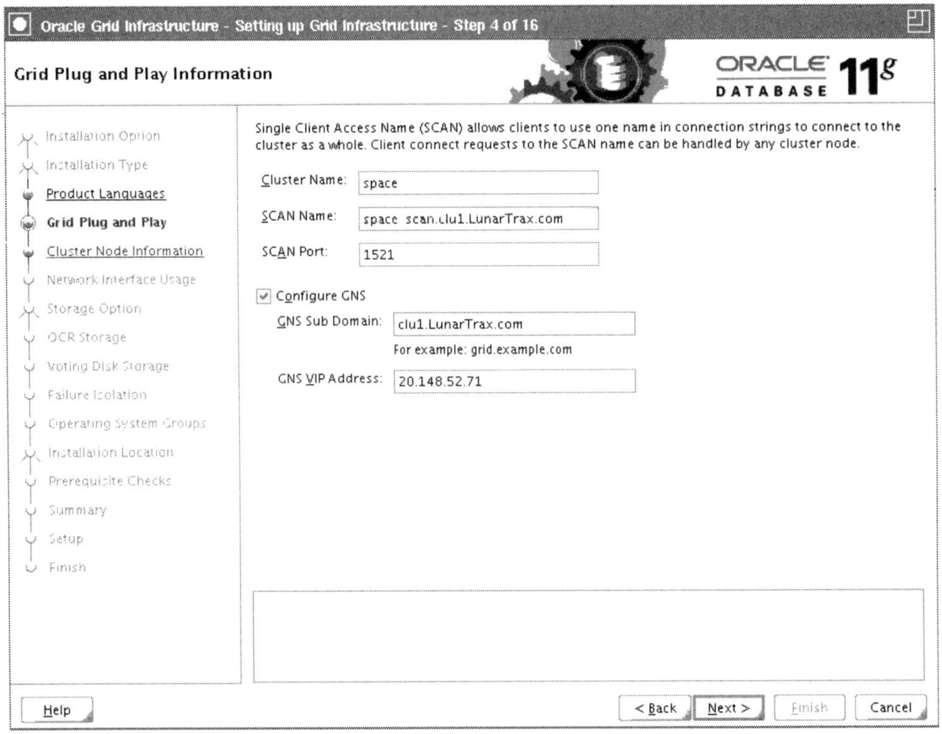

FIGURE 4-3. *Grid Plug and Play—with GNS*

On the next screen, shown in Figure 4-4, we tell the installer about the nodes that we want to use for install in our cluster. The local host should be discovered, but we will have to add all other nodes, as shown in the figure. We may have to edit entries if the default VIP name determined from the host is not correct. It is also possible to use a configuration file containing this information for all hosts in the cluster to ease the burden of host entries for large clusters. If we had chosen to use GNS, only the Hostname would be entered and the Virtual IP Name would show AUTO.

If we had not configured passwordless SSH connectivity (we did demonstrate this as a prerequisite), we'd click the SSH Connectivity button to configure passwordless

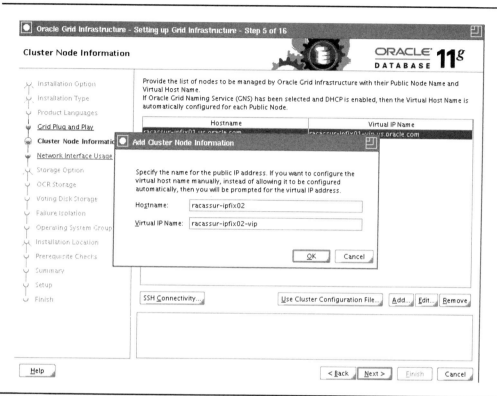

FIGURE 4-4. *Cluster node information*

SSH connectivity between the cluster nodes for the grid user. As Figure 4-5 shows, clicking SSH Connectivity reveals fields to enter the OS username and password. We should not be selecting a shared home for GI HOME. If we already had configured passwordless SSH connectivity as part of the installation prerequisite steps, we'd click the Test button to ensure proper functionality.

NOTE
The Installer will not let us past this page unless SSH is correctly configured.

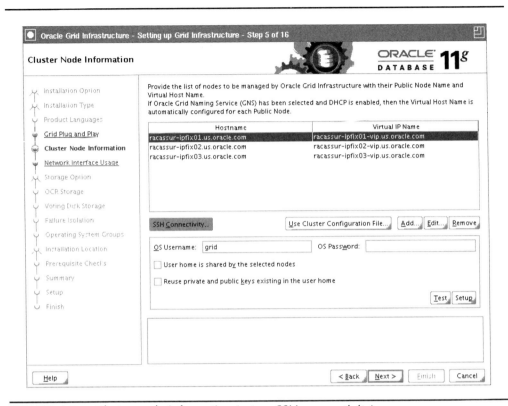

FIGURE 4-5. *Cluster node information (set up SSH connectivity)*

After SSH is confirmed, the Specify Network Interface Usage screen shown in Figure 4-6 appears. Here we can ensure that the correct network is being used for IPC traffic (that is, the interconnect) by choosing that network as Private and the other as Public. If we have additional network cards that we do not want to be used for the Oracle RAC configuration, we simply leave the default of Do Not Use for those particular subnets. We can select multiple interfaces for the private interconnect, and these will be used for load balancing in 11.2.0.1 but not failover, so be aware that a failure in any of the connections may cause an eviction.

In 11.2.0.2, the new High Availability (HA) IP facility is active, and multiple interface selection will support load balancing and failover. We can select more than four interfaces for private interconnect but only up to four will be used at one time. If an interface fails, one of those spare interfaces will be brought online.

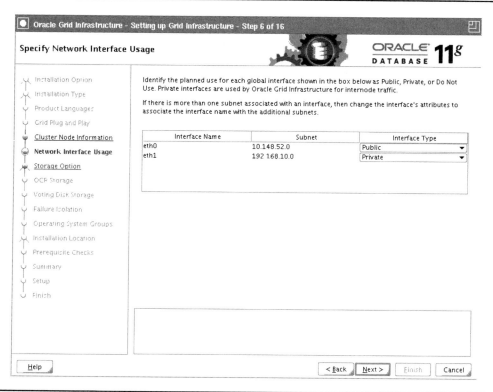

FIGURE 4-6. *Specifying network interface usage*

Virtual IPs will be started on the private interfaces so that they can be relocated to other interfaces on failure. Also note that by default in 11.2.0.2, the interconnect has to support multicast. If cluster nodes cannot multicast using address 230.0.1.0 on the private network, and cannot be reconfigured to do so, then you will need to contact Oracle Support to get a patch before installing or upgrading to 11.2.0.2. The patch will cause the clusterware to multicast also using 224.0.0.251, which is likely to work.

After specifying network usage on the next screen, we are asked to use either ASM or a shared file system (not shown). As stated earlier, we will use ASM to store OCR and voting disk in our main DATA disk group. Having selected ASM and clicked next, the Create an ASM Disk Group screen is displayed, as shown in Figure 4-7. We type a name for the disk group and select the disk we created. The disk we configured for use in this demonstration was actually a block device managed by udev, and as such

Oracle Grid Infrastructure - Setting up Grid Infrastructure - Step 8 of 15

Create ASM Disk Group

ORACLE DATABASE 11*g*

Installation Option
Installation Type
Product Languages
Grid Plug and Play
Cluster Node Information
Network Interface Usage
Storage Option
Create ASM Disk Group
ASM Password
Operating System Groups
Installation Location
Prerequisite Checks
Summary
Setup
Finish

Select Disk Group Characteristics and select disks

Disk Group Name   DATA

Redundancy   ○ High   ◉ Normal   ○ External

Add Disks

◉ Candidate Disks   ○ All Disks

	Disk Path	Size (in MB)	Status
☐ /dev/xvdb1		9993	Candidate

Change Discovery Path

Help   < Back   Next >   Finish   Cancel

FIGURE 4-7. *ASM diskgroup setup*

this screen would show no disks to add to the disk group initially. The reason is because the default discovery path (where ASM goes to find disks) is ORCL:*, which is specifically what you get from ASMLib disks. Seeing as our disk is a block device, we have to tell ASM to look at accessible block devices in its discovery path. If we click Change Discovery Path and change it to /dev/xvd*, it should discover the disk we set up previously.

NOTE
The number of voting disks that will be created depend on the redundancy level we specify: External will create one voting disk; Normal will create three voting disks; and High will create five voting disks, assuming failure groups are set up as stated earlier.

On the next screen (not shown), we specify either separate passwords for sysasm and asmsnmp access or choose a single password for both. Once finished, we click Next to display the Intelligent Platform Management Interface (IPMI) screen. We did discuss IPMI in Chapter 3, however here we must choose the Do Not Use option because we do not have the required hardware for IPMI in our cluster. Of course, if you do have IPMI set up then you would enter the address here.

The screen shown in Figure 4-8 allows us to specify different operating system groups for the management of ASM, also known a job role–separated management. You may remember that we created the groups at the start of the workshop. Operating system users must be part of the asmdba group to use ASM for storage. ASM Operator will allow simple startup/shutdown type operations. The ASM Administrator has full access to manage all ASM objects.

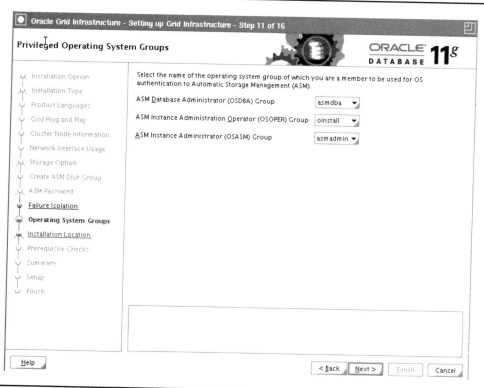

FIGURE 4-8. *Setting up groups for job role separation*

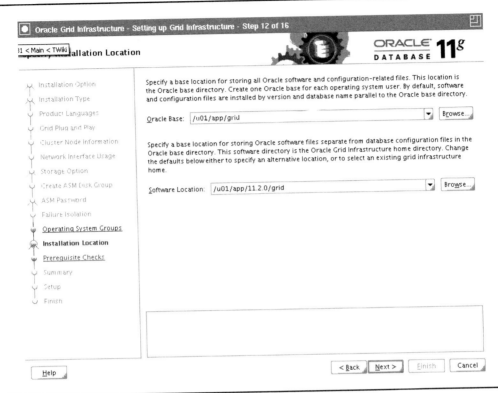

FIGURE 4-9. *Specify Oracle base and home directories*

On the next screen, we specify the locations for ORACLE_BASE and ORACLE_HOME. These directories were created earlier in our workshop. It is worth noting again, as shown in Figure 4-9, that each installation user should have its own base directory.

In the next screen (not shown), we set the directory for the Oracle Inventory that holds information for all the Oracle products installed on this machine. It should show the oinstall group for the oraInventory group name. Each user who wants to install or manage Oracle software needs to be a member of the Oinstall group. The inventory should not be placed in an Oracle home.

Now the OUI will call **cluvfy** to perform setup checks and displays the screen shown in Figure 4-10. Ideally, we would like to have every check performed succeed, but that would show nothing on the screen as it shows only failures. By design, some failures have occurred and the screen in Figure 4-10 shows a mixture of Fixable and Not Fixable failures. The Not Fixable failures must either be fixed outside the installer and then checked again or ignored by checking the Ignore All checkbox. Use the Ignore All checkbox wisely because ignoring certain checks may result in a failed installation. If we have fixable failures, we click Fix and Check Again.

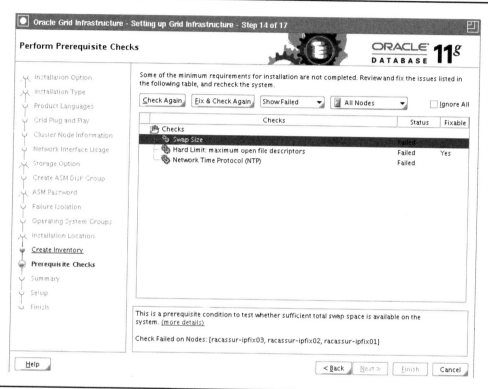

FIGURE 4-10. *Setup check by installer showing failures*

NOTE
In 11.2.0.2, you may see failures in a new check—Device Checks for ASM. These may be due to problems parsing the udev rules files, as mentioned in step 7 of the second section in the preparing workshop, but even if that is right, you may see "Unable to determine the sharedness of /dev/xvdb on nodes" and/or "PRVF-5149 : WARNING: Storage '/dev/xvdb1' is not shared on all nodes." If you see this error and can confirm the device is correctly set up and shared across the nodes, this can be ignored.

Figure 4-11 shows a screen asking us to run a fixup script on each node as root. The installer just generated this script to fix the parameter failure we saw

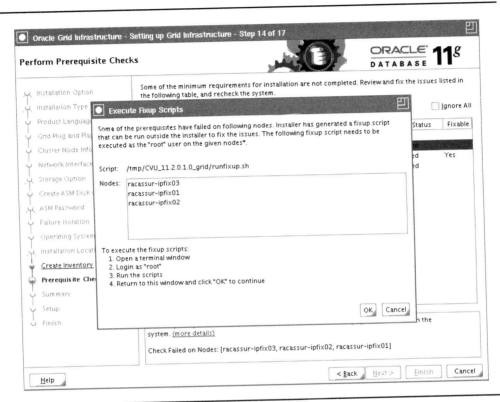

FIGURE 4-11. *Fixup scripts*

in Figure 4-10. After having run the scripts successfully, we click OK and the installer will rerun the checks.

Our corrected failure is no longer displayed, so we can click Ignore All for the others because this is a test system. Clicking Next takes us to the last confirmation screen, which we should check over. Clicking Next starts the installation. The software will be installed locally and then pushed to the remote systems before root scripts have to be run to configure the cluster. The root script request screen, shown in Figure 4-12, shows the scripts that need to be run on all nodes as root.

NOTE
The screen in Figure 4-12 states that the root script must be run to completion on the local node first, but after that it can be run in parallel on all remaining nodes. That will be slightly different for an upgrade, but we'll get to that shortly.

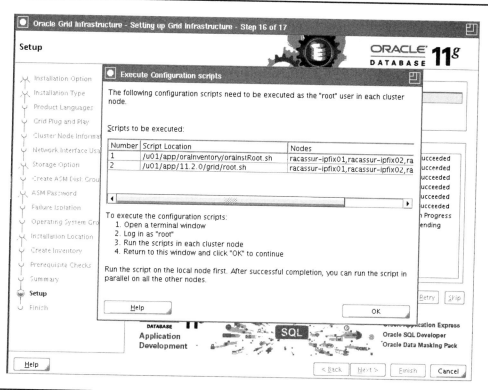

FIGURE 4-12. *Root scripts that require running*

The root script does the entire configuration for this node of the cluster using parameters determined by the installer's interview process. It also does some configuration to be used by new nodes that join, such as setting up the Grid Plug and Play (GPnP) profile with the most basic information required by new nodes to join the cluster.

The following is a snippet of output of root.sh on the first node that is run, with some notes to confirm what is happening:

```
[root]# /u01/app/11.2.0/grid/root.sh
Running Oracle 11g root.sh script...
The following environment variables are set as:
    ORACLE_OWNER= grid
    ORACLE_HOME=  /u01/app/11.2.0/grid
Enter the full pathname of the local bin directory: [/usr/local/bin]:
```

This first section has not changed for many releases, where the oraenv, dbhome, and coraenv are copied to the /usr/local/bin directory and the oratab is created. The next part of the execution of the script is where the rubber meets the road. First, all the local setup is done, which includes setting up the GPnP profile and checking that the OCR and OLR location files exist and are valid. Once that is done, the init .ohasd and ohasd scripts are copied to /etc/init.d and the symbolic links are made to the rc directories. Once that is done, OHASD is started.

```
Finished running generic part of root.sh script.
Now product-specific root actions will be performed.
2010-07-25 16:21:02: Parsing the host name
2010-07-25 16:21:02: Checking for super user privileges
2010-07-25 16:21:02: User has super user privileges
Using configuration parameter file:
u01/app/11.2.0/grid/crs/install/crsconfig_params
LOCAL ADD MODE
Creating OCR keys for user 'root', privgrp 'root'..
Operation successful.
Adding daemon to inittab
CRS-4123: Oracle High Availability Services has been started.
ohasd is starting
```

Starting OHASD starts a number of resources through their agents, and we see all of OHASD's stack except Cluster Ready Services daemon (CRSD) start initially. The Cluster Synchronization Services daemon (CSSD) will try to start in exclusive mode at this time, and if it detects another active node in the cluster it will fail to start and will restart in cluster mode. Since we are running this first node on its own, we shouldn't have any problems. Once ASM is up, the +DATA disk group is created as CRSD needs that for the storage of the OCR file. You can see that after that is done, CRSD will start and store the required OCR keys. The voting disk location will also be set at this point and the GPnP profile will be sent to other known nodes in the cluster.

```
CRS-2672: Attempting to start 'ora.gipcd' on 'racassur-ipfix01'
CRS-2672: Attempting to start 'ora.mdnsd' on 'racassur-ipfix01'
--- Cutting out a few lines here..
CRS-2672: Attempting to start 'ora.ctssd' on 'racassur-ipfix01'
CRS-2676: Start of 'ora.ctssd' on 'racassur-ipfix01' succeeded

ASM created and started successfully.
DiskGroup DATA created successfully.
clscfg: -install mode specified
Successfully accumulated necessary OCR keys.
Creating OCR keys for user 'root', privgrp 'root'..
Operation successful.
```

```
CRS-2672: Attempting to start 'ora.crsd' on 'racassur-ipfix01'
CRS-2676: Start of 'ora.crsd' on 'racassur-ipfix01' succeeded
Successful addition of voting disk 83475c179f3a4f25bf747cd93117d639.
Successfully replaced voting disk group with +DATA.
CRS-4266: Voting file(s) successfully replaced
## STATE    File Universal Id                    File Name Disk group
-- -----    -----------------                    --------- ---------
 1. ONLINE  83475c179f3a4f25bf747cd93117d639 (/dev/xvdb1) [DATA]
Located 1 voting disk(s).
```

Now the whole stack should restart with CSSD in cluster mode, and a normal startup will occur. Once the last of the resources are started, basic housekeeping operations such as backing up the OLR and registering the home and its contents with the Oracle inventory are performed.

```
CRS-2672: Attempting to start 'ora.registry.acfs' on 'racassur-ipfix01'
CRS-2676: Start of 'ora.registry.acfs' on 'racassur-ipfix01' succeeded

racassur-ipfix01 2010/07/25 16:32:24
/u01/app/11.2.0/grid/cdata/racassur-ipfix01/backup_20100725_163224.olr
Preparing packages for installation...
cvuqdisk-1.0.7-1
Configure Oracle Grid Infrastructure for a Cluster ... succeeded
Updating inventory properties for clusterware
Starting Oracle Universal Installer...

Checking swap space: must be greater than 500 MB.   Actual 2030 MB
Passed
The inventory pointer is located at /etc/oraInst.loc
The inventory is located at /u01/app/oraInventory
'UpdateNodeList' was successful.
```

As stated earlier, the first node to run the root.sh script must do it on its own, because there are some tasks only the first node does for setup. The second node's root.sh output would look very similar; however, we would expect that node to try to start CSS in exclusive mode and fail as node 1 is up. It will immediately restart in cluster mode and not try to do some of the configuration as seen here in an extract from node 2's root.sh output.

```
ohasd is starting
CRS-4402: The CSS daemon was started in exclusive mode but found
an active CSS daemon on node racassur-ipfix01, number 1, and is
terminating
CRS-2673: Attempting to stop 'ora.cssdmonitor' on 'racassur-ipfix02'
CRS-2677: Stop of 'ora.cssdmonitor' on 'racassur-ipfix02' succeeded
CRS-2673: Attempting to stop 'ora.gpnpd' on 'racassur-ipfix02'
```

```
CRS-2677: Stop of 'ora.gpnpd' on 'racassur-ipfix02' succeeded
CRS-2673: Attempting to stop 'ora.gipcd' on 'racassur-ipfix02'
CRS-2677: Stop of 'ora.gipcd' on 'racassur-ipfix02' succeeded
CRS-2673: Attempting to stop 'ora.mdnsd' on 'racassur-ipfix02'
CRS-2677: Stop of 'ora.mdnsd' on 'racassur-ipfix02' succeeded
An active cluster was found during exclusive startup, restarting to
join the cluster
CRS-2672: Attempting to start 'ora.mdnsd' on 'racassur-ipfix02'
CRS-2676: Start of 'ora.mdnsd' on 'racassur-ipfix02' succeeded
```

If root.sh has worked fine on all nodes, we can click OK on the root script request screen and the installer will continue with the remaining required configuration, as shown in Figure 4-13. Once those are completed, our clusterware should be fully functional just waiting to manage those highly available applications (in our case, Oracle RAC).

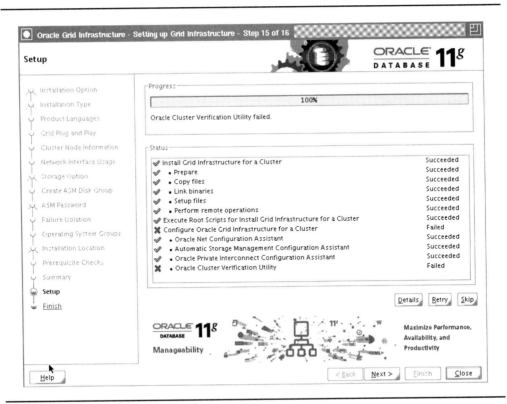

FIGURE 4-13. *Installation completion*

NOTE
Figure 4-13 shows that Configure Oracle Grid Infrastructure for a Cluster failed. The screen shows us what part of the configuration failed and it appears that was cluster verification. Remember that we ignored a couple of failures earlier on the CVU screen? Those will cause CVU to fail again here, so they can be ignored and we can click Next to finish the install.

A number of ways can be used to confirm a successful installation on all nodes, but the following command will test the status of the clusterware on all nodes:

```
[grid]$ /u01/app/11.2.0/grid/bin/crsctl check cluster -all
**************************************************************
racassur-ipfix01:
CRS-4537: Cluster Ready Services is online
CRS-4529: Cluster Synchronization Services is online
CRS-4533: Event Manager is online
**************************************************************
racassur-ipfix02:
CRS-4537: Cluster Ready Services is online
CRS-4529: Cluster Synchronization Services is online
CRS-4533: Event Manager is online
**************************************************************
```

In addition, the following command can be used to check the status of the resources created, though only a couple are shown here:

```
[grid@racassur-ipfix01 Disk1]$ /u01/app/11.2.0/grid/bin/crsctl status
resource -t
--------------------------------------------------------------------
NAME          TARGET  STATE       SERVER              STATE_DETAILS
--------------------------------------------------------------------
ora.DATA.dg
              ONLINE  ONLINE      racassur-ipfix01
              ONLINE  ONLINE      racassur-ipfix02
ora.asm
              ONLINE  ONLINE      racassur-ipfix01        Started
              ONLINE  ONLINE      racassur-ipfix02        Started
```

NOTE
*Anyone accustomed to working with CRS may be familiar in previous releases with using **crs_*** commands such as **crs_stat**. The **crs_*** commands have been deprecated in 11.2 and as such **crsctl status resource** is the way to see your resource status now, with the **–t** flag providing a tabular response.*

Troubleshooting a GI Installation

As you have seen, the installation procedure involves a few major stages: the initial OUI stage, the root.sh stage, and the assistants stage. Let's look at the files they produce that help us know what, if anything, may have gone wrong.

Oracle Universal Installer Stage

The installer writes to the oraInventory directory specified as part of the install process. The log file has a name similar to the one shown here:

```
[grid]$ ls /u01/app/oraInventory/logs/inst*
/u01/app/oraInventory/logs/installActions2010-07-16_10-54-18AM.log
```

The installer initially stages its files and logs in /tmp until the permanent oraInventory directory is created, so early install errors may be found in that staging area. It is also possible to run the installer in debug mode, which will show everything it is doing and will generally pinpoint exactly where an issue occurs. This verbose output is displayed to stdout (your terminal), and it is a good idea to capture terminal output as shown:

```
[grid]$ script /tmp/installlog
Script started, file is /tmp/installlog
[grid]$ ./runInstaller -debug
---- Output from Installer too verbose to show.
[grid]$ exit
exit
Script done, file is /tmp/installlog
```

NOTE
The most common problem we have seen when installing is shown as the installer hanging at around 65 percent completion when copying to remote nodes. This is normally caused by forgetting to disable SELinux and Linux firewall (iptables) before doing the install, as that causes the copy to fail and the Installer does not pick up the failure.

root.sh Stage

As you saw previously, the root.sh writes some basic information to the terminal to show what it is doing. The full text and any errors reported would be found in $GI_HOME/cfgtoollogs/crsconfig/rootcrs_<hostname>.log. That should be the first place you look when a problem occurs with root.sh. The rootcrs log may simply point you to an area where the problem occurred and you can then dig deeper using the clusterware alert log, agent, and process logs mentioned in Chapter 3. These cluster logs are found in $GI_HOME/log/<hostname>/.

If the problem occurs in ASM, the trace files for the instance will be found in $GI_BASE/diag/asm/+asm/<asm instance>/trace.

Assistants Stage

The configuration assistants such as asmca and netca will write trace to the following directory: $GI_BASE/cfgtoollogs.

Recovering from Failure in root.sh

When root.sh fails, it is possible to clean up and rerun it once the problem has been resolved. The command to deconfigure CRS on the local node is

 [root]# /u01/app/11.2.0/grid/crs/install/rootcrs.pl -deconfig

NOTE
*The **–force** flag may be required if the CRS stack is not started.*

This will stop any processes running and then clean up the rc.* and init.d directories, but it will not clear any data from devices that may have been written to for voting and OCR files, which you would of course do only on the last node in the cluster. The rootcrs.pl has a **-lastnode** flag that is used specifically for clearing these files:

[root]# /u01/app/11.2.0/grid/crs/install/rootcrs.pl –deconfig -lastnode

If all else fails and you still need to clear the voting and OCR files, then after ensuring that clusterware is down on all nodes, you can either remove them if they are on a shared file system or write zeros to the start of the device for block devices in ASM:

[root]# dd if=/dev/zero of=/dev/xvdb1 count=100 bs=1M

NOTE
*Take great care that you have the right device. You need to clear the disk header, because this operation is not easily reversible. Also, if this device is in ASMLib, after doing **dd**, you will have to re-create the disk using **oracleasm**.*

Once the deconfigure is complete and problems are resolved, the root.sh can be rerun on this node.

Adding and Removing Nodes from a Cluster

Changing the makeup of the cluster is much simplified in Oracle Database 11g Release 2 due to GPnP, but a number of tasks are still required to be completed manually. Oracle recommends using the cloning process, which has not been covered here, to clone clusters, but the approach below is still the best way to add and remove single nodes.

Adding a Node

Only one command is needed to add a node to the cluster, but that node must meet all the prerequisites that were covered earlier for a new install. These include OS installed, kernel parameters set up, SSH configured, and shared storage accessible. It is possible to use CVU on the currently running nodes to ensure that the new node is configured correctly for installation and even get a fixup script for anything you may have missed.

```
[grid]$ cd /u01/app/11.2.0/grid/bin
[grid]$ ./cluvfy stage -pre nodeadd -n racassur-ipfix03 -fixup -verbose
```

After you are certain that the new node is configured correctly, it can be added to the cluster. The command **addNode** takes up to two parameters depending on whether you use GNS or not. If GNS is used, only the new hostname is required (static resolvable by DNS or at least /etc/hosts):

```
[grid]$ cd /u01/app/11.2.0/grid/oui/bin/
[grid]$ ./addNode.sh -silent "CLUSTER_NEW_NODES={racassur-ipfix03}"
```

NOTE
You have to cd to the oui/bin directory. Also, this command does not work on 11.2.0.1, despite being the documented way for GNS. The error is "SEVERE: Number of new nodes being added are not equal to number of new virtual nodes. Silent install cannot continue." This is due to a bug, so we are leaving it here as it should be fixed eventually. Use the non-GNS command even in a GNS environment, and the node will be added just fine with GNS set up correctly.

If you are not using GNS, the hostname and VIP hostname are required (both static resolvable by DNS or at least /etc/hosts):

```
[grid]$ cd /u01/app/11.2.0/grid/oui/bin/
[grid]$ ./addNode.sh -silent "CLUSTER_NEW_NODES={racassur-ipfix03}"
"CLUSTER_NEW_VIRTUAL_HOSTNAMES={racassur-ipfix03-vip}"
```

Notice that this command uses the **-silent** option, which means you will not get an installer screen; however, you will get some progress written to the terminal. With 11.2, the graphical OUI addNode interface has been removed, hence the need for **-silent**. If the prompt returns with no output, it is likely that a CVU check has failed as the addNode is by default very picky about this, but it does not tell you why. Of course, we ran **cluvfy** to check that everything was right, so unless you ignored those errors, this would not happen. If you did happen to ignore those errors, you will need to fix them now or set IGNORE_PREADDNODE_CHECKS to Y in your environment. You should only do this if you are certain that the verification failures would not cause an actual failure.

```
[grid]$ cd /u01/app/11.2.0/grid/oui/bin/
[grid]$ export IGNORE_PREADDNODE_CHECKS=Y
[grid]$ ./addNode.sh -silent "CLUSTER_NEW_NODES={racassur-ipfix03}
CLUSTER_NEW_VIRTUAL_HOSTNAMES={racassur-ipfix03-vip}"
```

NOTE
The addNode may be run from any existing cluster member.

On completion of the addNode, you will be told to run the root scripts on the new node:

```
[root]# /u01/app/oraInventory/orainstRoot.sh
[root]# /u01/app/11.2.0/grid/root.sh
```

The clusterware will configure and start on the new node. You can use **cluvfy** once again to ensure that the operation was successful:

```
[grid]$ cd /u01/app/11.2.0/grid/bin
[grid]$ ./cluvfy stage post nodeadd -n racassur-ipfix03 -verbose
```

Deleting a Node

The tasks required to delete a node from the cluster depend partly on how it was added and whether the node to be removed its still active. You might remember that nodes only lease node numbers now and if they are down for long enough, they will be effectively removed from the cluster anyway. In the following workshop, we will go through the steps required to delete a node.

MAA Workshop: *Delete a Node from a Cluster*

Workshop Notes

We added the node racassur-ipfix03 to the cluster in the preceding section by example, so now we will use a workshop to see how that can be deleted from the cluster and mention differences. The cluster as it stands is not using GNS.

Step 1. Check for the active nodes in the cluster:

```
[grid]$ /u01/app/11.2.0/grid/bin/olsnodes -t -s
racassur-ipfix01        Active  Unpinned
racassur-ipfix02        Active  Unpinned
racassur-ipfix03        Active  Unpinned
```

We can see that all nodes are active and unpinned in this example. If racassur-ipfix03 was pinned and active, then once all applications are shut down on the node it should be unpinned using **crsctl unpin css –n racassur-ipfix03**.

Step 2. If the node to be removed is accessible, adjust the local inventory so that it knows about the local node only. This is a workaround for bug 8981501, where the deinstall tries to deinstall all nodes even when the **–local** flag is used.

```
[grid]$ cd /u01/app/11.2.0/grid/oui/bin/
[grid]$ ./runInstaller -updateNodeList ORACLE_HOME=/u01/app/11.2.0/grid
CLUSTER_NODES=racassur-ipfix03 CRS=TRUE -silent -local
```

Step 3a. This step is for a non-shared GI home on an accessible node. If you have a shared GI home on an accessible node use steps 3b and 3c. If the node is not accessible use step 3d.

```
[grid]$ cd /u01/app/11.2.0/grid/deinstall/
[grid]$ ./deinstall -local
```

The tool will ask what listeners need to be removed, which by default is the node VIP listener LISTENER for this node. It will then ask you to run a script on the node to be removed, and that script does the deconfig. After that script completes, the tool will clean up the local node.

Step 3b. Deconfigure the clusterware on the node to be removed:

```
[root]# cd /u01/app/11.2.0/grid/crs/install
[root]# ./rootcrl.pl -deconfig -force
```

Step 3c.   Update the inventory to detach this node from the shared GI home:

```
[grid]$ cd /u01/app/11.2.0/grid/oui/bin/
[grid]$ ./runInstaller -detachHome ORACLE_HOME=/u01/app/11.2.0/grid
-silent -local
```

Step 3d.   If the node to be removed is not accessible, remove its VIP on one of the other nodes in the cluster:

```
[root]# /u01/app/11.2.0/grid/srvctl stop vip -i racassur-ipfix03 -f
[root]# /u01/app/11.2.0/grid/srvctl remove vip -i racassur-ipfix03 -f
```

Step 4.   Delete the node from the cluster from any of the other nodes in the cluster:

```
[root]# /u01/app/11.2.0/grid/bin/crsctl delete node -n racassur-ipfix03
```

Step 5.   Update the installer inventory on one of the remaining nodes with the list of nodes remaining in the cluster:

```
[grid]$ cd /u01/app/11.2.0/grid/oui/bin
[grid]$ ./runInstaller -updateNodeList ORACLE_HOME=/u01/app/11.2.0/
grid/ CLUSTER_NODES=racassur-ipfix01,racassur-ipfix02 CRS=TRUE
```

Step 6.   Run the CVU to confirm successful removal:

```
[grid]$ /u01/app/11.2.0/grid/bin/cluvfy stage -post nodedel -n racassur-
ipfix03
```

Upgrading to GI

Upgrading to GI has the same requirements for a cluster node as a new install, so you will need to get a SCAN IP, and make sure the kernel parameters and O/S packages meet the new requirements. You should refer back to the Prepare a Linux/ Oracle RAC Cluster workshop earlier in this chapter for all requirements. The only exception to this is that your existing raw devices can be used for OCR and voting files. An upgrade to GI installs your software into a completely new home, and this is known as an out-of-place upgrade. This allows for the current software to run until the rootupgrade.sh (similar to root.sh) is run on the local node. The upgrade can also be done in a rolling manner such that Oracle Database 11*g* Release 2 GI can be running on one node while a previous version is running on other nodes. This is achieved because 11*g* Release 2 will run as though it were an old version until such time as all nodes in the cluster are upgraded. Then and only then will the CRS active version be set to 11.2 and the cluster software assume its new version.

NOTE
This functionality is provided to allow rolling upgrade, and different versions of the clusterware should not be running in the cluster for more than a short time. In addition, the GI software must be installed by the same user who owns the previous version CRS software.

Things to Note for ASM

If you have ASM, then ASM versions prior to 11.1.0.6 cannot be rolling upgraded—which means although you can do a rolling upgrade with the clusterware stack, at some point all ASM instances (pre 11.1) must be down to upgrade ASM to Oracle Database 11g Release 2. It is possible to choose not to upgrade ASM at GI upgrade time, but this is not advisable because 11g Release 2 was built to work with 11g Release 2 ASM. It is better to take the downtime at upgrade instead of having to reschedule it later or encounter a problem and have to shut down in an emergency. Of course, any databases using ASM will be down while ASM is unavailable.

NOTE
For an 11.1.0.6 ASM home to be rolling upgraded to 11g Release 2, the patch for bug 6872001 must have been applied to that home.

Upgrade Paths

The upgrade paths available for Oracle Clusterware are shown in Table 4-2.

The Actual Upgrade

The upgrade is completed using the normal installer, and rather than go through the screens again, we will mention a few important points here. The upgrade will involve the same screens that appear in a normal installation.

- CVU should be used prior to upgrade to ensure that **stage –pre crsinst** requirements are met.

- The installer must be run as the same user who owned the clusterware home that we are upgrading from.

- The installer should find existing clusterware installed and select Upgrade on the initial screen. If it does not, stop, because this means there is a problem.

- If the installer finds an existing 11.1 ASM installation, it will warn that upgrading ASM in this session will require that the ASM instance be shut down. You should shut down the database instances it supports.

Version	Description
Pre Oracle 10g Release 1	No Oracle clusterware, so simply install 11.2.0.1; also no ASM, so no upgrade consideration for that.
Oracle 10g Release 1	Clusterware and ASM support direct upgrade from 10.1.0.5, but earlier versions must upgrade to 10.1.0.5 first.
	Clusterware is not rolling upgradable. ASM is not rolling upgradable.
Oracle 10g Release 2	Clusterware and ASM support direct upgrade from 10.2.0.3, but earlier versions must upgrade to 10.2.0.3 or higher first.
	Clusterware is rolling upgradable.
	ASM is not rolling upgradable.
Oracle 11g Release 1	Clusterware and ASM support direct upgrade from 11.1.0.6 and 11.1.0.7. Clusterware is rolling upgradable.
	ASM is rolling upgradable from 11.1.0.6 with patch 6872001.
	ASM is rolling upgradable from 11.1.0.7.

TABLE 4-2. *Upgrade Paths to Oracle 11g Release 2 Grid Infrastructure*

rootupgrade.sh will shut down the stack on this node anyway, so this is more of interest if you cannot rolling upgrade ASM, as per Table 4-2.

■ You do have the option of deselecting the Upgrade Cluster ASM checkbox on the Node Selection Screen when ASM is discovered; however, it is recommended that you upgrade ASM at the time of clusterware upgrade.

■ The script to configure and start GI is rootupgrade.sh, not root.sh.

■ Rootupgrade.sh must be run on the installation node first to completion before it is run on any other nodes. It can then be run on all but the last node in parallel to completion. The last node to be upgraded must again be run on its own. If this is not done correctly, some nodes will need to be deconfigured and rerun in the correct order.

■ After the root scripts are run, asmca will upgrade ASM if that option was chosen. It will shut down all instances and upgrade if the old ASM home is on a shared disk and/or the ASM version is prior to 11.1.0.6. If ASM 11.1.0.6 or 11.1.0.7 is used, it will attempt to do a rolling upgrade of ASM to avoid a complete loss of service.

■ Nodes with pre 11.2.0.1 databases running in the cluster will have their node numbers pinned automatically when upgrading to 11.2.0.1 and will be placed in the generic pool as older versions of ASM and RDBMS software require administrator management.

What's New for 11.2.0.2

Most of the work done for GI in this book was completed using the 11.2.0.1 release, and comments have been made about 11.2.0.2 along the way. In this short section, we will cover in brief the main changes for the CRS part of GI in 11.2.0.2. Remember that 11.2.0.2 is a patchset release and is available only to Oracle customers with a support contract that provides access to patches.

Software Update Before Install or Upgrade   A new installer screen, as shown in Figure 4-14, will allow you to download software updates that include installation prerequisite information, bug fixes, and Oracle patches from My Oracle Support.

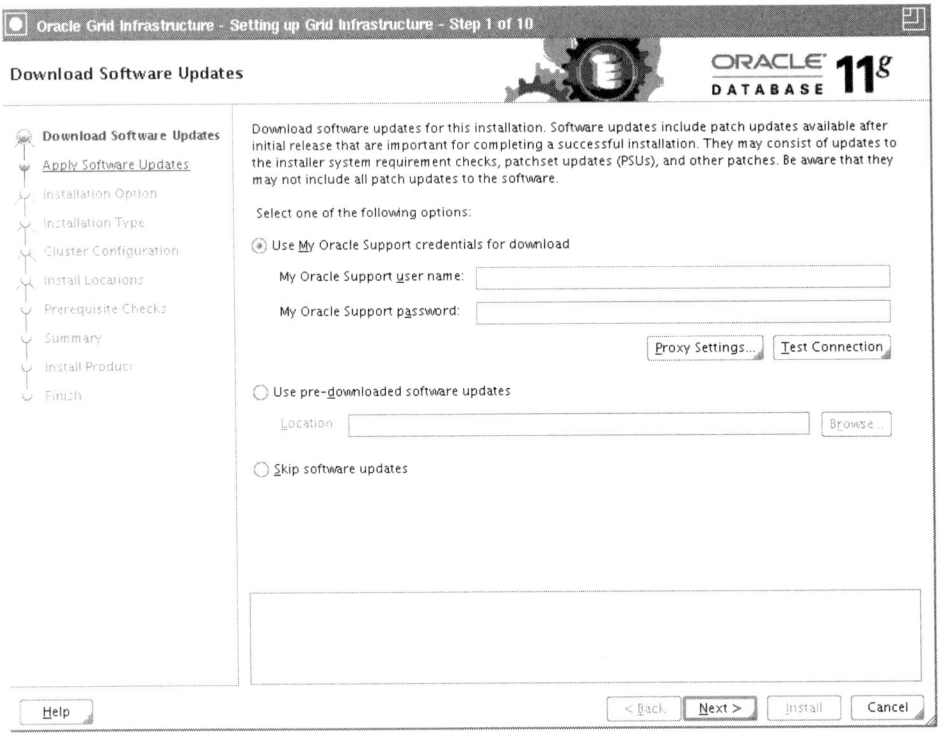

FIGURE 4-14.   *New Download Software screen*

These will be installed as part of the installation or upgrade process. This removes the old requirement of installing and then applying any necessary patches.

Automatic NIC Bonding for Private Networks As mentioned earlier, 11.2.0.2 introduces the ability for the clusterware to automatically bond private interconnect interfaces. In previous releases, this has been done using third-party/OS software. If you have multiple NICs that can be used for private interconnects, you can simply mark them all as private on the network selection screen in the OUI or Configuration Wizard. Up to four NICs will be used at any time for load balancing and failover, and interfaces can be added or removed using the **oifcfg** command. You will see that a VIP is started on each of the active interfaces and this VIP is relocated if any failure occurs.

Cluster Health Monitor The cluster health monitor was previously downloaded from Oracle Technology Network (OTN) and monitored load on the system specifically to help when a hang or system issue would cause a cluster or node outage. This will now be delivered with GI, though the Berkeley Database it uses to store data is to be used only for the monitor. You would have to license Berkeley separately to use it for your applications. OHASD manages a new resource to ensure that the monitor is running and storing the system statistics.

Grid Installation Owner Group Requirements The grid installation owner no longer has to be a member of the group designated for ASMOPER if one has been created.

Out-of-place Install for Patchset Releases The patchset release is now a complete release that can be installed as a new installation or a patch. The software will be installed out of place (in its own separate home) and can be patched easily prior to being applied. This reduces the downtime required to apply a patchset on each node and allows patches to be applied to the patchset before upgrade. The following steps are required to install this as a patchset:

1. Provision local disk space on all cluster nodes for the new GI home (5.5GB at least on Linux). This is on top of the space for the old home.

2. If upgrading from 11.2.0.1, use ASM in a rolling manner; then patches for bugs 9413827 and 9706490 need to be applied to the existing GI home. See MOS Note 1274629.1. For other starting versions, check the README for any prerequisite patches.

3. If you are using udev managed devices, make sure that all the parameter names are in uppercase and the following parameter order is used:

   ```
   KERNEL=="xvdb1", OWNER="grid", GROUP="asmadmin", MODE="660"
   ```

4. Run the OUI and ensure that the upgrade option is chosen.

5. Run rootupgrade.sh when prompted to do so.

Clusterware Configuration Wizard   11.2.0.2 includes a clusterware Configuration Wizard that can be used to configure the cluster after a software-only installation or upgrade. It effectively runs the configuration part of the OUI, which saves you having to edit parameter files before running root.sh, as was previously required.

Automatic CVU Checks   The CVU will run checks at specified intervals to report any problems it sees in the cluster setup. This is a resource managed by CRSD, and you can see/change the check frequency using **srvctl**:

```
[grid]$ /u01/app/11.2.0/grid/bin/srvctl config cvu
CVU is configured to run once every 360 minutes
```

You can also see the CVU checks' output reported to the clusterware alert log.

Summary

Through the practical sessions in this chapter, we have demonstrated both the long and short ways to perform some of the setup tasks and installation of GI. Oracle has significantly shortened the list of required tasks to complete an install so long as you use the tools provided. We make no apologies for showing more than one method. We would not expect to set up SSH by hand ever again, but it is useful to know how to do so. The complexity of the task has also been mostly removed, and with the CVU checks and fixup scripts, there is less chance of not being properly set up for the final install. Things will, of course, still go wrong and the installer does not have a restart ability as yet, although root's deconfig makes a single node failure easy to clean up.

   Having completed the work in this chapter, we have systems set up with GI ready to use to protect Oracle and non-Oracle resources (if you write the plug-ins for third-party software, of course). Some more tuning will be required, depending on what you else you need to run on these nodes, but that is covered in later chapters. For now, you should look at getting your ASM disks provisioned for whatever database, applications, or any third-party files you need to store. If you thought ASM was just for database files, you had better read on.

CHAPTER
5

Oracle Automatic
Storage Management

utomatic Storage Management (ASM) was a new feature in Oracle Database 10*g* Release 1 that revolutionized the way Oracle and the Maximum Availability Architecture (MAA) DBA managed database files. For the Database, ASM combines volume management with the concept of Oracle managed files to allow the MAA DBA to create a database comprising data files that are self-managed, plus the I/O is automatically balanced among available disks. In Oracle Database 11*g* Release 2, ASM has moved out of the database and provides a volume driver to create volumes that utilize ASM disk groups. These can be used to mount standard file systems such as ext3 or the ASM Cluster File System (CFS), which is another new feature. ASM combines the ability to simplify management of files in and out of the database with the ability to self-tune automatically, while providing a level of redundancy and availability that is absolutely imperative for the storage grid.

We discuss ASM in various sections throughout the book, but we will take the time here to discuss the concepts behind ASM, how to implement ASM in your environment, and how to manage ASM and its various features once you are up and running.

ASM Concepts

ASM was created as a volume manager intended specifically for Oracle data files that runs on top of raw or block devices. This file system is kept and maintained by the Oracle kernel, so Oracle knows where file extents are and automatically manages the placement of these extents for maximum performance and availability of your database. You, as the MAA DBA, will not know or care where Oracle is placing extents on disk. Oracle will do all of that management for you through ASM. No third-party volume management software is needed, and no file system is required. ASM manages the data placement and its clients simply make requests to ASM for information on where to go to access that data. The ASM CFS adds the ability to support non-Oracle files still using the same underlying architecture and features inherent in ASM itself.

ASM for Single-Instance Databases

This book is clearly designed for MAA using Grid Infrastructure (GI) and Oracle Real Application Clusters (Oracle RAC) in cluster environments, but ASM is also supported in single-instance environments, and the architecture is much the same in that environment. The only real differences are that only one ASM instance exists, and the disks it manages may not be sharable with other nodes. Because of this, many of the discussions and workshops in this chapter are equally valid in a single-instance setup.

ASM Instances

Traditionally, ASM had its own installation home or shared one with the RDBMS, because the ASM instance is fundamentally an Oracle RDBMS installation with a few flags set to make it a relational ASM metadata management system. ASM is now under the same installation home as the clusterware because of job role management and its ability to store clusterware files, rather than because of any change in its base architecture. In other words, even in Oracle 11*g* Release 2, ASM is still running much the same software as the RDBMS. The implementation of ASM involves the creation of an Oracle instance with **INSTANCE_TYPE=ASM**. This instance does not have an associated database, but is instead used to manage the disks that are accessed by its clients and their metadata.

An ASM instance is never opened or mounted in the way an RDBMS instance is. An ASM instance is started with **nomount**. Mounting an ASM instance involves mounting the disk groups associated with the ASM instance so that the disk groups and files contained in them are then accessible from the ASM clients.

When ASM is started on multiple nodes in the cluster, it manages the shared access to the files across the cluster using a global cache in a similar way to the RDBMS. ASM has a system global area (SGA), background processes, and a parameter file/ server parameter file (PFILE/SPFILE) used to set its startup options, just like an RDBMS instance. By default, in Oracle 11*g* Release 2 the SPFILE for ASM is held within ASM. How clever is that! Not that clever really. If you were the inquisitive type, you could easily work out the fact that the SPFILE location and the ASM disk discovery string are held in the Grid Plug and Play (GPnP) profile. A flag on an ASM disk header indicates whether the SPFILE is located there and in which allocation unit it is located. Given this information, no ASM instance is really required to get the parameters. The code that starts ASM certainly has all the inside knowledge to work it out.

ASM Disks

When the ASM instance starts, and at certain times thereafter, one of the background processes scans all the disk devices that match the ASM disk string. The disk string is determined using the instance parameter **ASM_DISKSTRING**. By default, this parameter is null, and that will mean that ASM will look for disks under ASMLib and /dev/raw/raw* on Linux. If you are using block devices outside of ASMLib, you will need to change this parameter through ASMCMD or SQL*Plus commands. The **ASM_ DISKSTRING** parameter can take multiple paths to look for disks, and any disks from which the ASM user can read the header will be candidates for use within ASM. When reading that header, if we find that a disk is ASMLib managed, the header will show *PROVISIONED,* and if the disk is already part of a disk group, the header will show *MEMBER*; if it was cleanly removed from a disk group, it will show *FORMER*, or will otherwise show *CANDIDATE*.

Here's an example: If you have multiple disk devices in the directory /dev/ and **ASM_DISKSTRING** is set to **/dev/xvd***, you can stop ASM accessing some of these by ensuring that the grid home owner does not have permission to read them. It is, of course, also possible to set the disk string only to discover a single device or ranges of devices. The ASM disk string is set in the ASM SPFILE as well as the GPnP profile. To view the available disks, you can use **asmcmd lsdsk** or a **sqlplus select** from **v$asm_disk**.

NOTE
These tools should prevent you from changing the disk string so that it no longer discovers disks that are used for clusterware files, because that would prevent the stack from being able to start. But you should still be careful when using these tools.

MAA Workshop: *Setting ASM Disk String*

Workshop Notes
In this workshop, we will query the current disk string and show the disks to which we have access. We will then change the string and see how that affects the available disks.

Step 1.   Set the **ORACLE_HOME** and **ORACLE_SID** environment variables and then call the ASMCMD tool:

```
[grid]$ export ORACLE_HOME=/u01/app/11.2.0/grid
[grid]$ export ORACLE_SID=+ASM1
[grid]$ $ORACLE_HOME/bin/asmcmd
ASMCMD>
```

NOTE
*If you see a message stating you are "connected to an idle instance" and your +ASM1 instance is up, the **ORACLE_SID** or **ORACLE_HOME** variable is probably not being set correctly. The **$ORACLE_ HOME** setting in your environment must be exactly the same as the one that was set when the instance was started. This is because Oracle uses those values to map the SGA, and if they aren't the same, you map to a different place and Oracle can't find the started instance. Most commonly the difference is the slash (/) at the end, so look for that.*

Step 2.   Check the current setting for the disk string **dsget** and disks setting that allows us to see **lsdsk**:

```
ASMCMD> dsget
parameter:/dev/xvd*
profile:/dev/xvd*
ASMCMD> lsdsk
Path
/dev/xvdb1
```

NOTE
*The **dsget** command shows the current parameter in memory and the GPnP profile value. The **lsdsk** command has many parameters that let you see all the available information. Use **help lsdsk** within ASMCMD to see all the options.*

Step 3.   Set the disk string to a new value:

```
ASMCMD> dsset '/dev/xvd[a-e]1,ORCL:*'
ASMCMD> dsget
parameter:/dev/xvd[a-e]1, ORCL:*
profile:/dev/xvd[a-e]1,ORCL:*
```

Currently a problem exists with **dsset**, and setting multiple values in the disk string will fail. The bug is fixed in 11.2.0.2 and may be fixed in an 11.2.0.1 Patch Set Update. If **dsset** does not work from ASMCMD, you will need to connect to the ASM instance with **sqlplus** and make the change as shown below:

```
 [grid]$ $ORACLE_HOME/bin/sqlplus / as sysasm
SQL> alter system set asm_diskstring='/dev/xvd[a-e]1','ORCL:*';
System altered.
SQL> show parameter asm_diskstring
NAME                                  TYPE         VALUE
------------------------------------ ----------- -----------------------
asm_diskstring                        string       /dev/xvd[a-e]1, ORCL:*
```

Step 4.
```
Use lsdsk to see which disks are now available to ASM following the
change to the disk string made above: ASMCMD> lsdsk --discovery -p
Group  Disk  Mount_Status Header_Status Mode_Status  State    Path
    1     0   CACHED       MEMBER        ONLINE       NORMAL   /dev/xvdb1
    0     0   CLOSED       PROVISIONED   ONLINE       NORMAL   ORCL:ACFSDG
```

NOTE
*The **lsdsk** command does not reread the disk string and look for new disks by default; instead, it reads cached information, hence the need to use the **--discovery** (two dashes) flag. Note that I have removed a couple of columns for clarity.*

You have seen how disks are discovered, and since you learned how to make disks available to ASM in previous chapters, you should be able to add disks to our system and make ASM see them. Once a disk is visible to ASM, you can add it to a disk group.

ASM Disk Groups

Remember that an ASM instance has no actual database to mount, but instead mounts disk groups. The data for an "ASM database" is the disk metadata that is stored on the disk itself. The ASM instance manages the metadata, and when something changes, the instance writes the changes back out to the disk header. ASM instances know the makeup of disk groups only when all the disks are discovered and their disk headers are read. In ASM, you will create disk groups comprising one or more disks (ASMLib, block device, or Storage Area Network [SAN]). Oracle will use that disk group as the location for creating files and will lay down files by default in 1MB extents across however many disks are available (changing allocation unit and variable extents will be discussed shortly). The more disks that are used within a disk group, the more flexibility you will give Oracle to spread the I/O out among disks, resulting in better performance.

ASM disk groups can be used for all Oracle files, including clusterware files, the SPFILE, the control file, the online redo logs, all data files. In addition, you can use an ASM disk group for your flash recovery area, as a location for all RMAN backups, flashback logs, and archived logs. It can also be used by ASM Dynamic Volume Manager (ADVM) for volume creation that then supports general-purpose file systems and ASM Cluster File System (ACFS).

NOTE
We mentioned that extents are written out by default in 1MB sizes, and this is true for all files except control files and log files. Control files, and prior to 11.2 redo logs and flashback logs use fine-grained striping, by default, which results in extents of 128K, rather than 1MB. This allows large I/Os to be split into smaller chunks and processed by more disks, resulting in better performance for these types of files.

Stripe and Mirror Everything (SAME)

ASM adheres to the *SAME* philosophy, which is handled in ASM by allowing the setting of redundancy levels during the creation of a disk group. Normal redundancy implies that at least two disks are used, because every extent will be written twice, to two different disks, within the disk group. High redundancy implies three-way mirroring, meaning every extent will be written to three separate disks within the disk group.

This mirroring is not the traditional type of mirroring that you may be accustomed to; this is done at the extent level. For example, let's assume that we are mirroring with normal redundancy (two-way mirroring), and that five disks make up a disk group. If we then create a 10MB file on that disk group, the first 1MB allocation unit (AU) may be mirrored across disks 3 and 5, the next 1MB extent may be mirrored across disks 2 and 4, the next extent across disks 1 and 3, and so on. When all is said and done, every extent has been mirrored, but no two disks will contain identical data. If you choose external redundancy when creating a disk group, this is perfectly acceptable, but it implies that all mirroring is handled at the hardware level, and ASM will only maintain a single copy.

By the same token, ASM achieves striping by spreading the extents (which comprise one or more AUs) for a given file across all available disks in a disk group. So, your TEMP tablespace may be 4GB in size, but if you have a disk group with ten disks in it, you will not care how the tablespace is laid out; Oracle with ASM will automatically spread the extents for this file across the disks, seeking to balance out the I/O and avoid hot spots on disk. If Oracle detects that a particular disk is getting too much I/O, it will attempt to read the mirrored copy of an extent from a different disk, if it is available, or it will seek to move extents off of that disk to other, less heavily used disks. The same is true for all files, including redo logs.

Partner Disks

Mirroring is actually performed to what are known as "partner" disks. Within an ASM disk group, any given disk can have a maximum of ten partners. This means that the extents written to a disk can be mirrored to any one of the ten partners defined for that disk. In our simple example, with only five disks, any disk can be the partner of another disk, because we have not exceeded this limit. However, in a disk group with more than ten disks (say, hundreds or even thousands of disks), you need to realize that each disk will be limited in the number of partners that can participate in the mirroring for that disk. This is done intentionally, as limiting the number of partners minimizes the possibility that a double disk failure could lead to data loss—this could happen only if the two disks that fail also happen to be partners. Using high redundancy (triple-mirroring) reduces this likelihood even further. An ASM disk group will theoretically support up to 10,000 disks of up to 2 terabytes (TB) with a single ASM instance spread across as many as 63 disk groups. ASM also supports up to 1 million files in a disk group, with the maximum file size in excess of 128TB with later compatibility settings, though the RDBMS can support only disk files up to 128TB. All this allows for total storage of 20 petabytes without Oracle Exadata, which is not covered here.

Extents and Allocation Units

Extents and AUs are an important concept in ASM that have undergone changes in Oracle 11*g* to improve performance.

Allocation Units   ASM will stripe your data with a one AU stripe size across the disks in the disk group. By default, an AU is 1MB, but in 11*g* it can be specified to be 1, 2, 4, 8, 16, 32, or 64MB (the two largest ones are new). The AU is set on disk group creation and the recommendation for most purposes is to use a 4MB AU, though larger sizes may be useful to applications performing large sequential reads. It is not possible to change the AU for a disk group after creation.

Extents   When an ASM file is created, it requires space for its contents so an initial block of space is allocated for the file, and this is called the *initial extent*. The initial extent for ASM files is one AU. As more data is added to the file, it may fill its initial extent and must be extended so a new extent is added. Excessive extent addition can be an overhead and creates a lot of metadata holding extent information. In 11*g*, variable size extents were added and are used only as files grew large. Table 5-1 shows how the extent size is determined.

> **NOTE**
> *Variable size extents are used automatically if the disk group compatibility is set to a high enough version. We will cover the settings of disk group compatibility next.*

Compatibility

New to 11*g* are the compatible.* disk group attributes. These attributes control what a disk group can be used for and what features can be used. The compatible.asm attribute shows the minimum version of ASM software that can mount this disk group. The compatible.rdbms will ensure that only databases that have their compatibility parameter set to a value at least equal to the compatible.rdbms can access the disk groups. Be careful if you're setting this when older RDBMS versions exist in the cluster

File Extent Range	Extent Size
0–20000	AU size
20000–39990	4 × AU size
40000+	16 × AU size

TABLE 5-1.   *Extent Size Determination*

and may need to use ASM. Also note that a disk group created with ASM Configuration Assistant (ASMCA) will by default have compatible.rdbms set to 11.2, stopping it from being used by older RDBMS versions.

Finally, compatible.advm must be set to 11.2 to allow volumes to be created in the disk group. Table 5-2 shows some of the features that depend on these compatibility settings and the minimum requirements.

NOTE
It is not possible to set any of these values back to a lower setting. If you need to alter a disk group to a lower compatibility setting, you must create a new disk group and move/recover the files from the old disk group into the new one.

Failure Groups

A failure group allows you to take the redundancy of disks to the next level, by creating a group containing disks from multiple controllers. If a controller fails, and all of the disks associated with that controller are inaccessible, other disks within the disk group will still be accessible as long as they are connected to a different controller. By creating a failure group within the disk group, Oracle and ASM will mirror writes to different disks and ensure that those writes are to disks within different failure groups so that the loss of a controller will not impact access to your data. If no failure group is specified when creating a disk group, then all disks are placed in their own failure group.

Feature to be Enabled	compatible.asm	compatible.rdbms	compatible.advm
Larger AU size (32MB, 64MB)	>= 11.1	>= 11.1	n/a
Fast mirror resync	>= 11.1	>= 11.1	n/a
Variable size extents	>= 11.1	>= 11.1	n/a
Intelligent placement	>= 11.2	>= 11.2	n/a
Clusterware files	>= 11.2	n/a	n/a
ASM SPFILE in a disk group	>= 11.2	n/a	n/a
File access control	>= 11.2	>= 11.2	n/a
Volumes in disk groups	>= 11.2	n/a	>= 11.2
New ACFS features	>= 11.2.0.2	n/a	>= 11.2.0.2

TABLE 5-2.   *Minimum compatible.* Settings for New Features*

Storing Voting and Oracle Cluster Registry (OCR) Files

In Oracle Database 11g Release 2, you can store your clusterware files (voting and OCR) within ASM. You can manage these files using the **crsctl** and **ocrconfig** commands. The *quorum failure group* is a special failure group that is specifically for use in holding a copy of the voting file and does not get used for any other data. This group is particularly useful when you would normally just want two failure groups for your data but are forced to create three to meet the requirements for placing voting disks on ASM. This is also useful for stretch clusters that need to have a third voting disk at a site remote to the two main data centers.

Preferred Read Failure Groups

Beginning with Oracle Database 11g Release 1, you have been able to state that a particular failure group is the one you want to read from when possible. You do this by setting the ASM initialization parameter **ASM_PREFERED_READ_FAILURE_GROUPS** to a list of failure groups from which you want this instance to read. This is particularly useful in stretch clusters, where the failure groups are set up to be the local sites disks. It is then possible to use this to read the local mirror copy of the data by default, unless it is inaccessible. Of course, writes have to go to both copies, and if a local read fails, the other copy will be read instead.

Fast Mirror Resync

Another new feature in Oracle Database 11g Release 1 is ASM fast mirror resynchronization. This feature can significantly shorten the time it takes to fix a mirror copy and maintain redundancy following a transient failure such as a cable or power problem. Transient failures are temporary and do not include media type errors. If a disk goes offline, the initialization parameter **DISK_REPAIR_TIME** is used to determine how long we can wait for a disk to be accessible again before it is dropped and requires a complete rebuild. This is achieved by simply logging the required updates and redoing them when the disk comes back online. The default time if the parameter is not set is 3.6 hours, and the only way to change it is with the SQL command **ALTER DISKGROUP**:

```
ALTER DISKGROUP data SET ATTRIBUTE 'disk_repair_time'='5.0h'
```

The setting will be picked up the next time the disk group has a disk go offline, and the time remaining for repair is shown in seconds using the v$asm_disk view repair_timer column.

Rebalancing Operations

ASM allows you to add and remove disks from a disk group on the fly without impacting the overall availability of the disk group itself or of the database. This, again, is one of the precepts of grid computing. ASM handles this by initiating a rebalance operation any time a disk is added or removed. If a disk is removed from the disk group, either due to a failure or excess capacity in the group, the rebalance operation will remirror the extents that had been mirrored to that disk and redistribute the extents among the remaining disks in the group. If a new disk is added to the group, the rebalance will do the same, ensuring that each disk in the group has a relatively equal number of extents.

   Because of the way the allocation units are striped, a rebalance operation requires that only a small percentage of extents be relocated, minimizing the impact of this operation. Nevertheless, you can control the rebalance operation by using the parameter **ASM_POWER_LIMIT**, which is specific to the ASM instance. By default, it is set to 1, which means that any time a disk is added or removed, a rebalance operation will begin using a single slave. By setting this value to 0 for a disk group, you can defer the operation until later (say, overnight), at which time you can set the **ASM_POWER_ LIMIT** to as high as 11 prior to Oracle 11*g* Release 2 and 1024 from Oracle 11*g* Release 2. This will generate that many slave processes to do the work of rebalancing.

NOTE
A rebalance operation runs on only one ASM instance no matter what the power limit, and each instance can handle only one rebalance at a time. Progress of the rebalance can be monitored using the v$asm_operation view.

Disk Group Templates

You can use disk groups templates to specify a number of attributes that are used when creating ASM files such as mirroring, data placement, and striping. When a disk group is created, a set of default templates are associated with it that include all the standard ASM file types such as control files, database files, and so on. You can also define custom templates when you're creating an ASM file. You can even specify to use a template when creating a tablespace from your RDBMS instance by setting the **DB_CREATE_FILE_DEST**. If you had created a custom template with settings ideal for indexes and called it standard index, you could use it as shown:

```
ALTER SYSTEM SET DB_CREATE_FILE_DEST = '+data(standardindex)';
CREATE TABLESPACE INDEX01TBS;
```

   You can create a template with ASMCMD using the **mktmpl** command, as shown here:

```
ASMCMD> mktmpl -G ACFSDG --striping coarse --redundancy mirror --
primary hot --secondary cold acfsdgdeftmpl
```

And you can use **lstmpl** to view the template:

```
ASMCMD> lstmpl acfsdgdeftmpl -l # lstmpl lists template details
Group_Name  Group_Num  Name                 Stripe  Sys  Redund  PriReg  MirrReg
ACFSDG      2          ACFSDGDEFTMPL        COARSE  N    MIRROR  HOT     COLD
```

Use **chtmpl** to make changes to it:

```
ASMCMD> chtmpl -G ACFSDG --secondary hot acfsdgdeftmpl # chtmpl updates it
ASMCMD> lstmpl acfsdgdeftmpl -l
Group_Name  Group_Num  Name                 Stripe  Sys  Redund  PriReg  MirrReg
ACFSDG      2          ACFSDGDEFTMPL        COARSE  N    MIRROR  HOT     HOT
```

And use **rmtmpl** to remove it:

```
ASMCMD> rmtmpl -G ACFSDG acfsdgdeftmpl # rmtmpl deletes the template
```

You can also use SQL directly or ASMCA to manage templates. (ASMCA is covered in the next workshop.) The SQL commands that ASMCMD runs will appear in the ASM instance alert log if you need to view the syntax.

Intelligent Data Placement

Intelligent data placement ensures that your most heavily used or hot data is placed on the fastest part of the disk to access. (You may have noticed the **–primary hot** and **–secondary hot** parameters used in the preceding template example.) In general, the outermost part of the disk will be more quickly accessible, because that part of the disk is spinning faster, and more data can be stored/accessed per revolution. Intelligent data placement lets you specify whether a file's primary and mirror copy is hot or cold, and that information can then be used to determine the placement. Intelligent data placement is most useful when disks are more than 25 percent full and the disk holds data that is accessed at differing rates. If all data is accessed at the same rate, then clearly its placement will make no difference.

If ASM cannot determine the physical makeup of the disk, intelligent data placement will probably not be useful. If, for example, a Logical Unit Number (LUN) is presented to ASM from a storage array, we cannot know which part of the disk is the hot part.

The placement of files in a disk group can be set up or modified using templates or using the SQL command **ALTER DISKGROUP MODIFY FILE**. Changes to an existing file will affect only new extents unless a rebalance occurs.

MAA Workshop: *Creating a Disk Group*

Workshop Notes

For this workshop, we will show how to create an ASM disk group using ASMCMD (steps 1 to 3), how to delete it using ASMCMD (step 4), and how to create it again using ASMCA (steps 5–7). Of course, you can also create disk groups through SQL, but we'll discuss those commands at the end of the workshop. We will also create a template that can be used for files in this disk group to store primary extents on the hot part of the disk (step 8). The disk group we create will have normal redundancy using 2 × 10GB disks that have already been provisioned with ASMLib using the method described in Chapter 4.

Step 1. Confirm that our system can discover the disks that are under ASMLib control:

```
[root]# oracleasm-discover
Using ASMLib from /opt/oracle/extapi/64/asm/orcl/1/libasm.so
[ASM Library - Generic Linux, version 2.0.4 (KABI_V2)]
Discovered disk: ORCL:ACFSDG [20964762 blocks (10733958144 bytes),maxio 64]
Discovered disk: ORCL:ACFSDG2 [20969472 blocks (10736369664 bytes),maxio 64]
```

> **NOTE**
> *If the disks are not under the control of ASMLib, the following instruction still applies, but the external disk device is used instead of the ASMLib disk.*

Step 2. Use the ASMCMD utility to confirm that we can see the disks we want to use for this disk group:

```
[grid]$ export ORACLE_HOME=/u01/app/11.2.0/grid
export ORACLE_SID=+ASM1
[grid]$ $ORACLE_HOME/bin/asmcmd
ASMCMD> lsdsk –candidate
Path
ORCL:ACFSDG
ORCL:ACFSDG2
```

> **NOTE**
> *If the disks you are expecting are not visible, the disk string is incorrect, you do not have permissions to access the disks, or the disks are already being used for something else. If you are using ASMLib and step 1 found the disks, the problem is not a permissions issue.*

Step 3.   Build an XML file to present to ASMCMD for creating the disk group. The **mkdg** (make disk group) command in ASMCMD requires that an XML file be used to pass the required parameters. This can either be a separate file or be written on the command line within parentheses. It is much easier to handle a large command using the configuration file itself, so we use that option here:

```
[grid]$ cat /tmp/acfsdg_mk.xml
<dg name="acfsdg" redundancy="normal">
    <fg name="failgroup1">
        <dsk string="ORCL:ACFSDG" />
    </fg>
    <fg name="failgroup2">
        <dsk string="ORCL:ACFSDG2" />
    </fg>
    <a name="compatible.asm" value="11.2" />
    <a name="compatible.rdbms" value="11.2" />
    <a name="compatible.advm" value="11.2" />
    <a name="au_size" value="4M" />
</dg>
```

Having created the file, we use it to make the disk group:

```
ASMCMD> mkdg /tmp/acfsdg_mk.xml
ASMCMD> lsdg ACFSDG
State     Type    Rebal  Sector  Block      AU   Total_MB   Free_MB
Req_mir_free_MB  Usable_file_MB  Offline_disks  Voting_files  Name
MOUNTED   NORMAL  N         512   4096  4194304     20472     20312
0              10156
```

Step 4.   Drop the ASM disk group:

```
ASMCMD> dropdg ACFSDG
```

> **NOTE**
> *Two flags are used in the **dropdg** command: The **–r** flag will remove all the files that exist in the disk group. The **–f** flag can be used to forcefully remove a disk group that cannot be mounted, which would cause a standard drop to fail.*

Step 5.   Start the ASM configuration tool (ASMCA):

```
export DISPLAY=myvncserver:1
/u01/app/11.2.0/grid/bin/asmca
```

Step 6. When the following screen appears, ensure that we are in the disk groups page and click the Create button at the bottom of the screen:

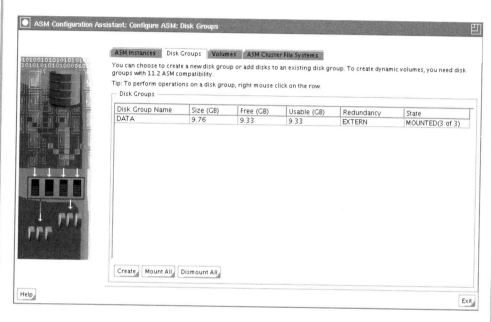

Step 7. On the Create Disk Group page, shown next, provide the disk group name, select the required redundancy, and select the disks to be used for this disk group. To view and change the default attributes, as shown next, click the Advanced option. In this case, we have set the Compatibility and Allocation Unit Size as we did for the ASMCMD creation.

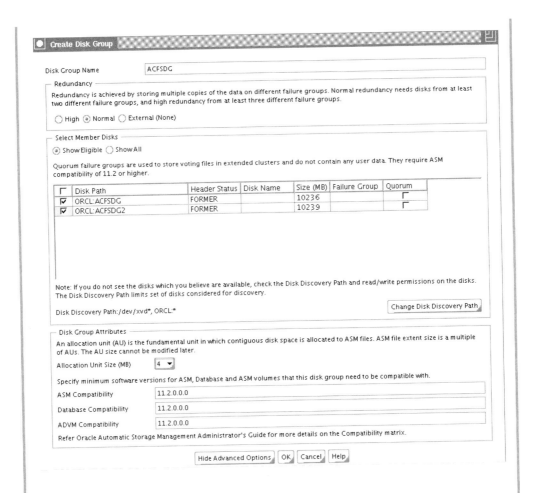

NOTE
Once the creation completes, you can right-click the Disk Group to take actions such as mount, unmount, drop, and edit attributes, as shown in the first illustration for step 8.

Step 8. Create a template for use when creating files in this disk group. We right-click the new disk group and select Manage Templates from the list, as shown next:

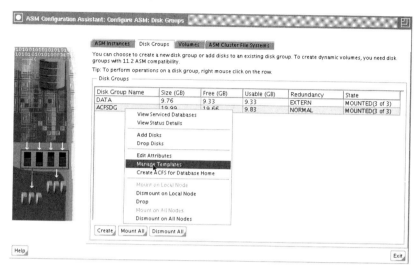

Next, we fill in the required details, as we have here for acfsdgdeftmpl. When we click the Save button, we'll see a success message and then be returned to the same screen.

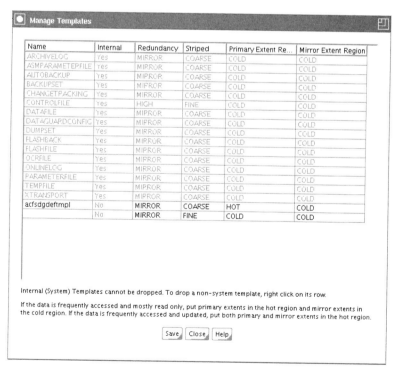

Workshop Notes

ASMCA and ASMCMD are actually front ends to the normal SQL interface, so a quick check of the ASM instance alert log will show us the underlying SQL that was run, and it even tells us which tool was used:

```
SQL> CREATE DISKGROUP ACFSDG NORMAL REDUNDANCY  DISK 'ORCL:ACFSDG'
SIZE 10236M ,'ORCL:ACFSDG2' SIZE 10239M  ATTRIBUTE 'compatible.
asm'='11.2.0.0.0','compatible.rdbms'='11.2.0.0.0',
'compatible.advm'='11.2.0.0.0','au_size'='4M' /* ASMCA */
```

ASM Files, Directories, and Aliases

Any type of file that can be stored in ASM is considered an ASM file. As mentioned, ASM files are a collection of extents within a single disk group. ASM files can be database files, control files, SPFILEs, and so on. ASM automatically assigns names to these files that its clients then use to request information about where the files' data can be found. The files are normally striped using a coarse stripe of one allocation unit; however, some files such as database control files use a fine-grained striping of 128KB.

When an ASM file is created, it gets a fully qualified name that depends on what type of file it is. An example would be an OCR file stored in ASM with this format: +disk_group/cluster_name/OCRFILE/REGISTRY.file_number.incarnation. The fact that this looks very much like a file that exists down a few levels of a directory structure is no coincidence: an ASM directory will be named after the cluster, in the +disk_group directory if ASM is storing the Oracle Cluster Registry (OCR). It is also possible to traverse the directories in ASMCMD exactly as you would any normal file system, as shown here:

```
ASMCMD> ls
ACFSDG/
DATA/
ASMCMD> cd DATA/racass1-cluster/OCRFILE
ASMCMD> ls -l
Type      Redund   Striped  Time            Sys   Name
OCRFILE   UNPROT   COARSE   AUG 25 11:00:00  Y    REGISTRY.255.727858885
```

When you create a tablespace in a database and do not use Oracle managed files, you specify a specific data file name such as this: +DATA/LUNARTRAX/DATAFILE/ROCKET01.DBF. That data filename is not valid for ASM because the filename that is system generated has a file_number and incarnation number. Because of this, aliases exist to link the filename you use to the system-generated file. You can also create your own aliases for ASM files in ASMCMD or by using SQL.

ASM Metadata

As discussed, an ASM instance has no physical storage component associated with it. The ASM instance is purely a logical incarnation in memory. However, an ASM disk group does have physical components that are stored on each ASM disk. When a disk is made part of an ASM disk group, the header of each disk is updated to reflect information, including the disk group name, the physical size of all disks in the group, the allocation unit size, and more. The header also contains information relating specifically to that disk, including the size, the failure group, the disk name, and other information. In addition, virtual metadata (file directory, disk directory, and so on) is stored in ASM files on the disks themselves, using file numbers below 256. For this reason, when a new database is created on an ASM disk group, the system data file will generally be file number 256, and the rest of the files in the database will be numbered upward from there because file number 255 and below are reserved for ASM virtual metadata. The ASM metadata is always mirrored three times for normal and high-redundancy disk groups, but no mirroring is provided for external redundancy.

Using the ASMCMD tool **md_backup**, you can back up the ASM metadata for use in case a disk group has to be rebuilt. In this example, we are backing up the metadata for the DATA disk group and writing to a file in /tmp:

```
ASMCMD> md_backup /tmp/ASMDATADGMD -G DATA
Disk group metadata to be backed up: DATA
Current alias directory path: racass1-cluster/OCRFILE
Current alias directory path: racass1-cluster
Current alias directory path: racass1-cluster/ASMPARAMETERFILE
```

The **md_restore** command can then be used to restore this metadata to a disk group prior to the recovery of any data files stored on it.

ASM Dynamic Volumes

ASM volumes are created within an ASM disk group and are used in conjunction with the volume driver for general purpose or ASM cluster file systems. A volume can take up all or part of a single disk group, but it can exist in only one disk group. However, a disk group can contain many volumes, space permitting. When a volume is created, a device file is created in an ASM directory under the standard devices directory for your operating system. On Linux, this directory is /dev/asm.

Note that in 11.2.0.2, ASM volumes and ACFS are supported on Solaris, AIX, and Windows as well as Linux. Volumes can be managed using ASMCMD commands **volcreate**, **voldelete**, **voldisable**, **volenable**, **volresize**, **volset**, **volstat**, and **volinfo**, through ASMCA, Enterprise Manager, and using SQL commands. From a disk group's perspective, an ASM volume is just another ASM file type, and as such, you can override the default settings for stripe size, redundancy, and intelligent placement when the volume is created. You cannot see this file through ASMCMD using the **ls** command; however, a **select** from **v$asm_file** in SQL on the ASM instance will show files of type ASMVOL and ASMVDRL that exist for each volume. After the volume is created, it will automatically be enabled and will be ready for use by a file system or directly by an application.

ASM Dynamic Volume Manager

The ASM Dynamic Volume Manager (ADVM) is the link between an ASM dynamic volume and the clients that want to utilize that volume—whether that is a file system or an application directly accessing it. ADVM provides a standard interface to those clients to access the dynamic volume device /dev/asm/<vol>-<id>, and as such, it will be used in much the same way as any other volume manager by those clients. You can create ACFS and other file systems on ASM dynamic volumes such as ext3 on Linux.

ADVM relies on ASM, and the driver modules are loaded into the OS when the ora.asm resource starts. An ACFS driver resource, ora.drivers.acfs, is pulled up when ora.asm starts to complete the driver load. The driver's resource is set to be always loaded when GI is running.

You can see the modules using the **lsmod** command on Linux, as shown here:

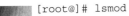

```
[root@]# lsmod
Module              Size  Used by
oracleacfs       1734392  1
oracleadvm        241920  1
oracleoks         295376  2 oracleacfs,oracleadvm
```

NOTE
You may also see the module oracleasm; however, it is for ASMLib and not ADVM or ACFS.

The **oracleoks** is Oracle Kernel Services, which provides driver services to the ACFS (**oracleacfs**) and ADVM (**oracleadvm**) drivers. The ADVM driver provides the block services to the dynamic volume device and the ACFS driver services file and directory requests for ACFS.

MAA Workshop: *Creating an ASM Dynamic Volume*

Workshop Notes

This workshop will show management of an ASM volume through ASMCMD, how to delete the volume using ASMCMD and then re-create it using ASMCA.

Step 1.   Use ASMCMD **volcreate** to create an ASM volume of 5GB:

```
[grid]$ export ORACLE_HOME=/u01/app/11.2.0/grid
export ORACLE_SID=+ASM1
[grid]$ $ORACLE_HOME/bin/asmcmd
ASMCMD> volcreate -G ACFSDG -s 5G --width 128K --column 4 --primary
hot --redundancy high acfsdgvol1
```

Step 2.   Check the volume details using **volinfo**:

```
ASMCMD> volinfo -G ACFSDG acfsdgvol1
Diskgroup Name: ACFSDG
        Volume Name: ACFSDGVOL1
        Volume Device: /dev/asm/acfsdgvol1-49
        State: ENABLED
        Size (MB): 5120
        Resize Unit (MB): 1024
        Redundancy: HIGH
        Stripe Columns: 4
        Stripe Width (K): 128
        Usage:
        Mountpath:
```

> **NOTE**
> *The device name is created under the /dev/
> asm directory with the volume name and an ID
> appended.*

Step 3.   Check that the device has been created at the OS level:

```
[grid]$ ls -al /dev/asm/acfsdgvol1-49
brwxrwx--- 1 root asmadmin 252, 25089 Sep  6 05:25 /dev/asm/acfsdgvol1-49
```

Step 4.   Determine to which disk group and volume the device belongs. Of course we know this, because we just created it, but it's useful to know how to find out later.

```
ASMCMD> volinfo --show_diskgroup /dev/asm/acfsdgvol1-49
acfsdg
ASMCMD> volinfo --show_volume  /dev/asm/acfsdgvol1-49
acfsdgvol1
```

Step 5.   Resize the volume from 5GB to 8GB:

```
ASMCMD> volresize -G ACFSDG -s 8G acfsdgvol1
```

> **NOTE**
> *You cannot resize a volume that already contains an ACFS file system using **volresize**. If an ACFS file system exits on the volume, you must use **acfsutil size** as that will resize both the file system and underlying volume. Also, you will get warning messages when the new size is less than current size stating that corruption may occur. To avoid the message, you can use the –f flag.*

Step 6. Drop the volume using **voldelete**:

```
ASMCMD> voldelete -G ACFSDG acfsdgvol1
```

When you delete a volume, you would expect to see a message similar to this, written to your server console and system messages file:

```
[Oracle ADVM] Volume ACFSDG-ACFSDGVOL1 was disabled.
```

Step 7. Start the ASMCA to create the same volume again:

```
export DISPLAY=myvncserver:1
/u01/app/11.2.0/grid/bin/asmca
```

Step 8. When the Configuration Assistant screen appears, open the Volumes tab and click the Create button near the bottom. Click the Show Advanced Options button to change the redundancy or striping for the volume. By default, they will inherit the disk group redundancy and stripe width of 128K with four columns.

Similar to the following example, enter the required Volume Name, select the disk group and set the size, and then adjust any of the other attributes. Notice that the screen shows Free Space as 19.64GB and Usable Space as 9.82; this is because of the single mirror setting for the disk group, which halves the true free space. If you choose to create a volume with unprotected redundancy (no mirror), you can actually select a size close to the disk group free space.

Note that if you select the full size of 9.82GB for the volume size, you will see the error shown in the following illustration, because in fact the Usable Space shown does not include some overheads. I found that for usable 9.82GB I was able to create a 9GB volume. If I chose unprotected, a 19GB volume could be created.

Step 9.   Resize the volume using ASMCA. Simply go to the Volumes screen in ASMCA and right-click the volume you want to resize. Then select Resize and change the Size field.

> **NOTE**
> *It is impossible to change the redundancy or intelligent placement of a volume once it is created. In addition, ASMCA has no way of setting intelligent placement at creation time.*

Step 10. Check the ASM instance alert log to see what SQL commands could have been used:

```
SQL> /* ASMCMD */alter diskgroup ACFSDG add volume 'acfsdgvol1' size 5G
HIGH stripe_width 128K stripe_columns 4 ATTRIBUTE( HOT)
SQL> /* ASMCMD */alter diskgroup ACFSDG resize volume 'ACFSDGVOL1' size
8192m
SQL> /* ASMCMD */alter diskgroup ACFSDG drop volume 'acfsdgvol1'
```

ASM Cluster File System

The ACFS was first released in GI 11.2.0.1 for Linux only, but in 11.2.0.2, it is available for Solaris, AIX, and Windows. The product has been enhanced in 11.2.0.2 to add replication, tagging, encryption, and realm-based security.

ACFS is a fully Portable Operating System Interface for UNIX (POSIX)-compliant file system that uses ASM dynamic volumes only. ACFS provides synchronized access to various sharable file types such as trace files, database binaries (RDBMS homes), and almost any other files that do not belong in the database. The only files Oracle does not support on ACFS are those that are supported for storage in ASM disk groups directly, such as database redo logs, control files, SPFILEs, and clusterware files (OCR and voting files). It also cannot be used for shared Grid Infrastructure homes, as it would be difficult to start the software from a directory that was not mounted because it needs the software to mount. We are not too keen on shared GI homes for Maximum Availability Architecture (MAA) anyway, so that's not too big a deal.

ACFS is as valid for a single node because it still uses all the ASM features for storage load balancing and ease of management. With ASM's ability to store everything for the database and its new ability to store clusterware files, and ACFS's ability to store shared homes and trace files, third-party file cluster file systems or raw devices are no longer necessary. You could have argued that in 11.2.0.1, with only Linux ACFS available, that OCFS2 was a valid alternative, but with 11.2.0.2 and ACFS for Solaris, Windows, and AIX, you have even less reasons to consider buying a third-party CFS or clusterware. Oracle now provides the whole stack that makes it easier to use and much easier to support.

ACFS for the Database Home

You'll remember that ACFS is not a valid storage option for the GI home, but it can be used for database homes, whether shared or not. Oracle recommends that ACFSs be mounted directly under an ORACLE_BASE/acfsmounts directory, but the ORACLE_ BASE itself should not be on ACFS. This configuration could comprise one or many ACFSs allocated for each home. As such, an ORACLE_HOME of ORACLE_BASE/ acfsmounts/dbhome would exist on a single ACFS. It also may be beneficial to have the diagnostic destination for trace files on a shared file system, so the directory ORACLE_ BASE/diag could be mounted on its own ACFS file system, and this would allow all the nodes trace files to be accessed from one node without requiring NFS mounting.

When an ACFS is created for use as a database home, a Cluster Ready Services (CRS) resource is created that can be managed using the **srvctl** command line interface. Any resource that requires that file system to be mounted to run, such as the database itself, will have dependencies on the file system, so a start of the database will mount the file system if it is not already mounted. If an ACFS is created for use as a database home, it must not be added to the ACFS mount registry, because that is only for file systems that are outside CRS management.

NOTE
We will discuss the ACFS mount registry a bit later in this chapter; for now, you should understand the difference between CRS-managed file systems and those under the control of the ACFS mount registry.

MAA Workshop: *Creating an ACFS for DB Home*

Workshop Notes
In this workshop, we will create an ACFS that can be used for an RDBMS home. Note that the installer will check that the file system is correctly set up before using it for an RDBMS home. Steps 1 to 5 cover how to create the file system using the command line. Step 6 shows you how to remove the file system from CRS control, and steps 7 to 10 show you how to create a file system using the ASM Configuration Assistant (ASMCA).

Step 1. Create the mount point directory on all nodes of the cluster:

```
[root]# mkdir -p /u02/app/oracle/acfsdbhome1
[root]# chown grid:oinstall /u02/app/oracle/
[root]# chown grid:oinstall /u02/app/oracle/acfsdbhome1/
```

> **NOTE**
> *You can leave this to the **srvctl add filesystem**
> command in step 3 if you prefer.*

Step 2. Make the file system on the ASM dynamic volume device:

```
[root]# mkfs -t acfs /dev/asm/acfsdgvol1-49
mkfs.acfs: version                 = 11.2.0.2.0
mkfs.acfs: on-disk version         = 39.0
mkfs.acfs: volume                  = /dev/asm/acfsdgvol1-49
mkfs.acfs: volume size             = 7516192768
mkfs.acfs: Format complete.
```

Step 3. Add the new file system to CRS using **srvctl**:

```
[root]# $GI_HOME/bin/srvctl add filesystem -d /dev/asm/acfsdgvol1-49 -v
acfsdgvol1 -g ACFSDG -m /u02/app/oracle/acfsdbhome1
```

Step 4. Start the resource to get it mounted on all nodes:

```
[grid]$ $GI_HOME/bin/srvctl start filesystem -d /dev/asm/acfsdgvol1-49
PRCR-1079 : Failed to start resource ora.acfsdg.acfsdgvol1.acfs
CRS-0245:  User doesn't have enough privilege to perform the operation
```

Note that I intentionally included that error to show that, by default, the root user is
the only user with the privilege to mount the file system. The user here is grid (the GI
software owner). If I had wanted the grid user to be able to start the resource, I could
have used the **–u** flag with **srvctl add filesystem**, which is the default behavior. But
let's try again as root for now:

```
[root]# $GI_HOME/bin/srvctl start filesystem -d /dev/asm/acfsdgvol1-49
```

When an ACFS is mounted for the first time, we get interesting messages written
to the console and system logs that show us what is happening in the volume
manager at that time:

```
[Oracle OKS] Cluster Membership change - Current  incarn 0x5
[Oracle OKS] Nodes in cluster:
[Oracle OKS]   Node 1 (IP 0xa9fe2e80) Node 2 (IP 0xa9fe1b96)
[Oracle OKS] Node count 2, Local node number 1
[Oracle ADVM] Cluster reconfiguration started.
[Oracle ADVM] Cluster reconfiguration completed.
[Oracle OKS] Cluster Membership change setup complete
[Oracle OKS] Cluster Membership change - Current  incarn 0x6
[Oracle OKS] Nodes in cluster:
[Oracle OKS] Node 1 (IP 0xa9fe2e80) Node 2 (IP 0xa9fe1b96) Node 3 (IP
xa9fe085d) [Oracle OKS]
```

```
[Oracle OKS] Node count 3, Local node number 1
[Oracle ADVM] Cluster reconfiguration started.
[Oracle ADVM] Cluster reconfiguration completed.
[Oracle OKS] Cluster Membership change setup complete
```

These messages show us that as the resource is started on each node, the OKS and ADVM drivers realize that clusterwide resources need to be managed, so they have to reconfigure for each node join.

> **NOTE**
> *If you directly unmount the file system from the OS, this will not be prevented and it will not be automatically remounted. Start the resource on that node again to mount the file system.*

Step 5. Check that the file system is mounted on all nodes using **df –k**, and then check the file system resource in CRS:

```
[grid]$ $GI_HOME/bin/crsctl status resource ora.acfsdg.acfsdgvol1.acfs
NAME=ora.acfsdg.acfsdgvol1.acfs
TYPE=ora.acfs.type
TARGET=ONLINE                    , ONLINE                    , ONLINE
STATE=ONLINE on racassur-ipfix01, ONLINE on racassur-ipfix02, ONLINE on
racassur-ipfix03
```

Step 6. Now remove the file system from CRS control to re-create it using ASMCA:

```
[root]# $GI_HOME/bin/srvctl stop filesystem -d /dev/asm/acfsdgvol1-49
[root]# $GI_HOME/bin/srvctl remove filesystem -d /dev/asm/acfsdgvol1-49
```

> **NOTE**
> *These commands are both run as root; however, if we had used the **-u grid** flag to create the resource in step 3, the grid user would be able to stop the resource but not remove it. We have also removed the resource from CRS, but the file system is still made on the volume until the volume is removed or the file system is removed using **acfsutil rmfs**.*

Step 7. Start the ASM Configuration Assistant to re-create the same volume:

```
export DISPLAY=myvncserver:1
/u01/app/11.2.0/grid/bin/asmca
```

Step 8. When the Configuration Assistant screen appears, choose the ASM Cluster File Systems tab and click the Create button. You will see the following screen:

You can select a previously created volume, as in our case, or select Create Volume to bring up the volume creation screen shown in the preceding workshop. In this case, we simply fill in the form using a previously created volume. If you want to see what ASMCA does to create the file system, click Show Command, but do not be too surprised if you see basically what appears in steps 2 to 6. After you click OK, the **mkfs** command is run for you (the asmadmin group has write privileges on the volume device so it can do this), but it then presents a script that must be run as root on the node from which ASMCA is running, as shown next:

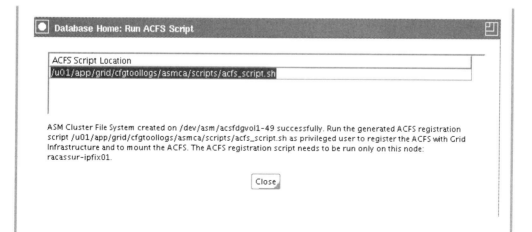

Step 9.   Run the script as root to register and mount the file system. The script does the work to create the file system resource and start it on all nodes:

```
#!/bin/sh
/u01/app/11.2.0/grid/bin/srvctl add filesystem -d /dev/asm/acsfdgvol1-
49 -g ACFSDG -v ACSFDGVOL1 -m /u02/app/oracle/acfsdbhome1 -u grid
if [ $? = "0" -o $? = "2" ]; then
  /u01/app/11.2.0/grid/bin/srvctl start filesystem -d /dev/asm/
acsfdgvol1-49
    if [ $? = "0" ]; then
       chown grid:oinstall /u02/app/oracle/acfsdbhome1
       chmod 775 /u02/app/oracle/acfsdbhome1
 /u01/app/11.2.0/grid/bin/srvctl status filesystem -d /dev/asm/
acsfdgvol1-49
       exit 0
    fi
 /u01/app/11.2.0/grid/bin/srvctl status filesystem -d /dev/asm/
acsfdgvol1-49
fi
```

Now we have an ACFS that can be used to create a shared RDBMS home. When that home is installed, the resources that run out of it will have dependencies on this file system to ensure that the resource starts when required, which in this case means it gets mounted.

ACFS for a General Purpose File System

You may have worked out from the preceding section that an ACFS for shared Oracle home use is just an ACFS under CRS control—so what about an ACFS for general purposes? Once you create an ACFS file system with **mkfs**, it can be used in exactly the same way as any POSIX-compliant file system. You could say that it needs no further action or management other than to mount it and go. The only slight problem with that, however, is when it comes to mounting it automatically at boot time. The file system requires ASM to be up, the underlying disk groups to be mounted, and the ADVM drivers to be loaded, so we need to have something that ensures that all this is true before the mount occurs. The ACFS mount registry is the tool for this; it is managed using the **acfsutil** command.

The general purpose ACFS can be used for anything, but it's ideal for the following:

- **Diagnostic destination** If you've used versions 11.1 and 11.2, you may know this feature as the Automatic Diagnostic Repository (ADR), but beginning in 10.2 RDBMSs, you can as easily mount your ORACLE_HOME/admin directory or wherever your bdump, udump, and cdump directories exist. Not only is it a good idea to have all the instance's trace files in a common store to be viewed from a single node in the cluster, but having a separate file system for trace files can help with file space management. Although the GI home cannot be on the ACFS, the ASM diagnostic destination can be. Be careful that you don't fill the file system, however, because that can cause clusterwide problems.

- **External database files and directories** Having a shared file system for BFile data types and external directories ensures that the files are available no matter what instance you are running on.

- **Applications** Many applications require that common store be used for documents and reports. If the application lives on a middle tier, either GI must be installed on those cluster nodes or exiting ACFSs can be exported using NFS and mounted on those mid-tier servers.

ACFS Mount Registry

The ACFS mount registry can be compared to the /etc/fstab on Linux because it stores information about file systems that require mounting at boot time. One major difference between the registry and fstab is that the registry manages the mounts across the cluster and communicates with CRS to ensure that the required resources are started before mounting. The mount registry is managed using the **acfsutil** command, and all general purpose file systems should be registered with the mount registry. You must not, however, register CRS-managed ACFSs with the mount registry; it is one or the other, but never both.

MAA Workshop: *Creating a General Purpose ACFS*

Workshop Notes

We will now create a general purpose ACFS using the ASM dynamic volume created earlier. Steps 1 to 5 show you how to create the file system and register it using the command line. Step 6 covers how to remove the file system from the registry and steps 7 to 10 show creating the file system using the ASMCA. For good measure, we will resize the file system in step 11.

Step 1.   Create the mount point directory on all nodes of the cluster:

```
[root]# mkdir -p /u02/app/oracle/diag
[root]# chown grid:oinstall /u02/app/oracle/
[root]# chown grid:oinstall /u02/app/oracle/diag/
```

Step 2.   Make the file system on the ASM dynamic volume device:

```
[grid]$ /sbin/mkfs -t acfs /dev/asm/acfsdgvol2-49
mkfs.acfs: version              = 11.2.0.2.0
mkfs.acfs: on-disk version      = 39.0
mkfs.acfs: volume               = /dev/asm/acfsdgvol2-49
mkfs.acfs: volume size          = 2147483648
mkfs.acfs: Format complete.
```

> **NOTE**
> *This command was run as the grid user because grid does have write access to the device through its asmadmin group. As the grid user, we must use the full path to **mkfs** because /sbin is not normally in the non-root user's $PATH.*

Step 3.   Mount the file system on all nodes of the cluster:

```
[root ~]# mount -t acfs /dev/asm/acfsdgvol2-49 /u02/app/oracle/diag/
```

Step 4.   Add the new file system to the ACFS mount registry:

```
[grid]$ /sbin/acfsutil registry -a -f -n racassur-ipfix01,racassur-
ipfix02,racassur-ipfix03 /dev/asm/acfsdgvol2-49 /u02/app/oracle/diag/

acfsutil registry: mount point /u02/app/oracle/diag successfully added
to Oracle Registry
```

> **NOTE**
> *The grid owner or root can run these commands.*
> *As shown, you should add all the nodes in one*
> *command. At this time, it appears that each*
> *command overwrites the registry record (though this*
> *could be fixed in later releases), so if you register*
> *one node at a time, only the last node will be*
> *registered. Finally, this can all be done on one node*
> *because the cluster registry is a clusterwide tool.*

Step 5. Check the registry entries using the **acfsutil registry** command. The following example does not use the –l flag, which can be either the mount point or the volume, as the output does not format neatly, as shown next. You should note that without the –l flag, all the registered file systems will be displayed.

```
[grid@racassur-ipfix01 bin]$ /sbin/acfsutil registry
Mount Object:
  Device: /dev/asm/acfsdgvol2-49
  Mount Point: /u02/app/oracle/diag
  Disk Group: ACFSDG
  Volume: ACFSDGVOL2
  Options: none
  Nodes: racassur-ipfix01,racassur-ipfix02,racassur-ipfix03
```

Step 6. Now remove the file system from the acfs registry, and clear the file system itself to re-create it using ASMCA, after unmounting on all nodes:

```
[grid]$ /sbin/acfsutil registry -d /dev/asm/acfsdgvol2-49
acfsutil registry: successfully removed ACFS volume /dev/asm/
acfsdgvol2-49 from Oracle Registry
[root]# umount /u02/app/oracle/diag
[grid@]$ /sbin/acfsutil rmfs /dev/asm/acfsdgvol2-49
```

> **NOTE**
> *The –d flag with **acfsutil** can be either the volume or*
> *the mount point, and the root user has to unmount*
> *the file system.*

Step 7. Start the ASMCA to re-create the same volume:

```
export DISPLAY=myvncserver:1
/u01/app/11.2.0/grid/bin/asmca
```

Step 8. When the Configuration Assistant screen appears, choose the ASM Cluster File Systems tab and click the Create button. You will see the following screen:

As we did earlier, select a previously created volume; this time, however, we select a general purpose file system and enter the precreated mount point. We also choose to register the mount point. Click OK and the assistant will run the **mkfs** command for you and add the file system to the ACFS mount registry. The file system will be mounted automatically on reboot or clusterware restart, and not as part of running the command.

Step 9. Mount the file system on all nodes:

```
[root]# mount -t acfs /dev/asm/acfsdgvol2-49 /u02/app/oracle/diag
```

Step 10. We are going to resize the file system, but first let's check how it looks using the **acfsutil info fs** command, which will show file system and volume information:

```
[grid@racassur-ipfix01 bin]$ /sbin/acfsutil info fs /u02/app/oracle/diag
/u02/app/oracle/diag
    ACFS Version: 11.2.0.2.0
    flags:        MountPoint,Available
```

```
    mount time:     Sun Sep 12 07:55:42 2010
    volumes:        1
    total size:     2147483648
    total free:     2033971200
    primary volume: /dev/asm/acfsdgvol2-49
        label:
        flags:                  Primary,Available,ADVM
        on-disk version:        39.0
        allocation unit:        4096
        major, minor:           252, 25090
        size:                   2147483648
        free:                   2033971200
        ADVM diskgroup          ACFSDG
        ADVM resize increment:  1073741824
        ADVM redundancy:        mirror
        ADVM stripe columns:    4
        ADVM stripe width:      131072
    number of snapshots:  0
    snapshot space usage: 0
```

Now let's resize the file system:

```
[grid]$ /sbin/acfsutil size +1G /u02/app/oracle/diag/
acfsutil size: new file system size: 3221225472 (3072MB)
```

When the resize is done, the system console and log will appear with this message:

```
[Oracle ADVM] Volume ACFSDG-ACFSDGVOL2 was resized, new size is 3072 MB.
```

Let's see how the file system and volume look now. We will show only the changed rows:

```
[grid]$ /sbin/acfsutil info fs /u02/app/oracle/diag
/u02/app/oracle/diag
    total size:     3221225472
    total free:     3105583104
    primary volume: /dev/asm/acfsdgvol2-49
        major, minor:           252, 25090
        size:                   3221225472
        free:                   3105583104
```

This shows us that the **acfsutil size** command will not only resize the ACFS but also the dynamic volume as required.

So now we have an ACFS that we can use to store almost anything, and it will be mounted at reboot. Our DBA Max will use his ACFS for RDBMS trace files.

ACFS Read-Only Snapshots

ACFS read-only snapshots, introduced with the first version of ACFS in 11.2.0.1, allow us to create a point-in-time copy of the file system that is always available when the file system is online. The method used to create the copy is called "copy on write" and occurs at the extent level.

When an extent is changed, the "before" copy is saved so that the changes can be recovered. When a recovery is required, any unchanged extents use the "before" copy on the file system, which makes this an extremely space-efficient function that can be used for general purpose and CRS-managed ACFSs.

Snapshots are managed using the **acfsutil snap** commands, but you should keep in mind that the new features in 11.2.0.2, such as ACFS encryption and ACFS security, cannot be applied to a file system that has a snapshot. Of course, you can delete snapshots if you want to use these features, but planning to use the features before you create snapshots will ensure that you do not need to do this. Let's go through a simple example of using snapshots with one of Max's files.

Max put a couple of ideas for his wife's anniversary gift in a text file on an ACFS he uses for tracing. He had been updating it and did not worry too much about losing it because he knew he could take snapshots of this file system. The original file looked like this:

```
[grid]$ cat /u02/app/oracle/diag/myanivlist
Date : 17 June
Years 11
Gift                   For                     Against
Diamonds -             She'll be happy         I am cheap
Washing Machine -      I'll get clean clothes  Only if she forgives me
```

He created a snapshot like so:

```
/sbin/acfsutil snap create snap01 /u02/app/oracle/diag/
```

The snapshot was immediately viewable with the same contents as the original file:

```
[grid]$ cat /u02/app/oracle/diag/.ACFS/snaps/snap01/myanivlist
Date : 17 June
Years 11
Gift                   For                     Against
Diamonds -             She'll be happy         I am cheap
Washing Machine -      I'll get clean clothes  Only if she forgives me
```

He later added a couple of new lines:

```
Go Out for food -     She will be happy      And expecting a present too..
Black Sabbath CD -    I like Ozzy            She is not so keen.
```

The newly edited file had the changes but the snapshot remained the same, so Max created a new snapshot to back up these changes:

```
/sbin/acfsutil snap create snap02 /u02/app/oracle/diag/
```

The file /u02/app/oracle/diag/.ACFS/snaps/snap02/myanivlist now has the latest changes, which is good, because Max had to delete the file one day when his wife, who also works for Trax, accessed the system. Luckily, she did not know about ACFS snapshots, so Max was in the clear despite two copies of the file still being on disk. He eventually bought the diamonds after he received a large bonus for implementing 11g Release 2 Oracle RAC and GI, so he removed all signs of the files:

```
[grid]$ /sbin/acfsutil snap delete snap01 /u02/app/oracle/diag/
acfsutil snap delete: Snapshot operation is complete.
[grid]$ /sbin/acfsutil snap delete snap02 /u02/app/oracle/diag/
acfsutil snap delete: Snapshot operation is complete.
```

This silly example shows that each snapshot provides a way to go back and view the file at that time. This is particularly useful if you need to take online backups of constantly changing file systems or if you need peace of mind that you can access an old copy of a file from a particular point in time. A snapshot works well, for example, for upgrading a database, because you can take a snapshot of the Oracle Home and create a restore point in the database that ensures you can get back to where you started before the upgrade.

ACFS Tagging

ACFS tagging was introduced in 11.2.0.2 for Linux. It allows you to group files together across directories or file systems—such as all files used by the HR department or all photos that include your daughters. It also allows you to group together all files in the file system you want to replicate, which means that you do not necessarily have to replicate an entire file system.

Tags can be up to 32 ASCII characters and can be created on files or directories. Tagging is accomplished by adding files and directories to or removing them from a tag set with the **acfsutil tag set/unset** command. If you tag a directory, only files created after that time will also inherit the tag—so you'd have to add the existing files manually.

Here's how you add files:

```
[root]# /sbin/acfsutil tag set mycriticalfiles
/u02/app/oracle/acfsdbhome1/emergency_procedures
```

Or you can add a whole directory's contents:

```
[root]# /sbin/acfsutil tag set -r myrdbmslogs /u02/app/oracle/diag/rdbms/
```

You can see the files in the tag set using the **acfsutil tag info** command:

```
[root]# /sbin/acfsutil tag info -t mycriticalfiles
/u02/app/oracle/acfsdbhome1/emergency_procedures
```

And you can remove them using **unset**:

```
/sbin/acfsutil tag unset -r myrdbmslogs /u02/app/oracle/diag/rdbms/
```

NOTE
*Tagging uses file extended attributes, and some operating system tools will clear those attributes when writing back a file, unless specific flags are used. For example, **tar** requires the **–xattrs** flag to keep attribute data, and **vi** requires the **bkc=yes** switch to ensure that the new file retains the tags and not the old copy. For **mv** and **cp**, you will need to be on Oracle Enterprise Linux 5 Update 4 and install coreutils-5.97-23.el5_4.1.src.rpm (32-bit) or coreutils-5.97-23.el5_4.2.x86_64.rpm (64-bit) or later to get the commands that preserve extended attributes. You should check the Oracle ASM Storage Administrator's Guide for the full set of requirements and test the tools before using them in production, because the tags can be lost.*

ACFS Replication

ACFS replication is a new feature in 11.2.0.2 on Linux; as its name suggests, it allows you to replicate files from one host to another. The terminology used is reminiscent of Oracle Data Guard, with a primary file system and a standby file system, with replication logs recording the changes. The replication logs are shipped across the network from the primary to the standby and the changes are applied.

When considering ACFS replication, your most important concern is probably file system space usage. Replication logs take up space in the file system being replicated; if you cannot complete a replication, you cannot complete a change on the file system, so running out of space in this setup can cause major problems. The standby must also not run out of space because that would stop the application of changes on the standby and cause replication logs to pile up on the primary, because they are deleted from both sites only when they have been applied.

You must also consider the network bandwidth to the standby, because slow transfer of logs will also mean that the standby will be out of date and logs will remain on the primary for longer than needed. Finally, the standby needs to be up to the job of applying the logs as fast as the primary generates them, so having a significantly lower powered standby machine is not a good idea.

Because the ability to determine the rate of change appears to be so important when sizing the file system, network connection, and standby, Oracle has provided a way to determine how to use the **acfsutil info fs** command. (Note that the 5 in the first line is the period in seconds we are reporting for each time we write the amount of change. The command will continue reporting statistics every 5 seconds until you break out of it.)

```
[grid]$ /sbin/acfsutil info fs -s 5 /u02/app/oracle/acfsdbhome1/
/u02/app/oracle/acfsdbhome1/
    amount of change since mount:        9851.31 MB
    average rate of change since mount: 154 KB/s

    amount of change: 0.50 MB    rate of change: 102 KB/s
    amount of change: 3.00 MB    rate of change: 612 KB/s
    amount of change: 1.00 MB    rate of change: 204 KB/s
```

We will not cover the calculations here to make sure you have enough resources to support replication. These can be found in the Oracle Automatic Storage Management Administrator's Guide.

Following are other considerations for ACFS replication:

- A server can be both a replication primary and standby system for different file systems.

- Each primary file system can have only one standby file system.

- You can replicate a file system only if it is mounted by eight or fewer nodes.

- Replication works on single-instance and clustered systems.

- ACFS tagging can be used to replicate only certain files within a file system, rather than the whole file system.

- File systems that are encrypted or under ACFS security control cannot be replicated.

- The standby file system must be running on a server that runs the same operating system and Oracle software distribution as the primary.

- The files on the standby are always available for reading, but they may change at any time.

MAA Workshop: *Set Up ACFS Replication*

Workshop Notes

In this workshop, we will quickly go through the general steps required to set up ACFS replication.

Step 1.   Create the replication admin user that will be used to connect between the primary and standby servers. This must be done in SQL*Plus on the ASM instance.

```
[grid@racassur-ipfix01 diag]$ $ORACLE_HOME/bin/sqlplus / as sysasm
create user acfs_repl_admin identified by maxpassword;
User created.
SQL> grant sysasm,sysdba to acfs_repl_admin;
```

Similarly on the standby site, issue the following:

```
SQL> create user acfs_repl_standby_admin identified by maxpassword;
SQL> grant sysasm,sysdba to acfs_repl_standby_admin;
```

Step 2.   Set up the Transparent Network Substrate (TNS) alias for accessing the services across the network. This must be done on all of the hosts that use either the primary or standby file system.

```
[grid]$ cat /u01/app/11.2.0/grid/network/admin/tnsnames.ora
ACFS_REPL_PRIMARY =
  (DESCRIPTION =
    (ADDRESS = (PROTOCOL = TCP)(HOST = racassur-ipfix01)(PORT = 1521))
    (ADDRESS = (PROTOCOL = TCP)(HOST = racassur-ipfix02)(PORT = 1521))
    (ADDRESS = (PROTOCOL = TCP)(HOST = racassur-ipfix03)(PORT = 1521))
    (CONNECT_DATA =
      (SERVICE_NAME = primary_service)
    )
  )
ACFS_REPL_STANDBY =
  (DESCRIPTION =
    (ADDRESS = (PROTOCOL = TCP)(HOST = racassur-ipfix06)(PORT = 1521))
    (LOAD_BALANCE = yes)
    (CONNECT_DATA =
      (SERVICE_NAME = standby_service)
    )
  )
```

NOTE
Do not use the scan name for the standby connection because the standby service will only be registered with a listener on one node and the scan could return the IP for any node.

Step 3. Create and mount, on only one node, the ACFS to be used on the standby site. See the preceding workshops for how to create the file system.

Step 4. Use **acfsutil** on the standby server to initialize the standby site:

```
[root]# /sbin/acfsutil repl init standby
-p acfs_repl_admin/maxpassword@acfs_repl_primary
-c standby_service /u02/app/oracle/acfsdbhome1_repl/
```

> **NOTE**
> *When this command runs, the service standby_*
> *service is registered only on the local node of the*
> *cluster. Also, the standby file system should be*
> *mounted only on the local node for initialization.*

Step 5. Use **acfsutil** on the primary server to initialize the primary site:

```
[root]# /sbin/acfsutil repl init primary
-s acfs_repl_standby_admin/maxpassword@acfs_repl_standby
-m /u02/app/oracle/acfsdbhome1_repl/ -c primary_service /u02/app/
oracle/acfsdbhome1
validating the remote connection
remote connection has been established
Registering with user specified service name-primary_service
waiting for the standby replication site to initialize
....
```

> **NOTE**
> *It is possible for the primary and standby to use the*
> *same service (–c). In addition, the –m flag is needed*
> *only if the mount point of the standby file system is*
> *different from that of the primary.*

Once the standby site has initialized, replication will occur for all files in the file system. We can use the **acfsutil repl info** command to check on the status of replication for our replicated mount points:

```
[root]# /sbin/acfsutil repl info -c /u02/app/oracle/acfsdbhome1
Site:                           Primary
Primary status:                 Initializing
    Primary:          0% complete
    Standby:          0% complete
Primary mount point:            /u02/app/oracle/acfsdbhome1
Primary Oracle Net service name: primary_service
```

```
Standby mount point:            /u02/app/oracle/acfsdbhome1_repl/
Standby Oracle Net service name: standby_service
Standby Oracle Net alias:       acfs_repl_standby_admin/****@acfs_
                                repl_standby
Replicated tags:
Log compression:                Off
Debug log level:                2
```

It is also possible to replicate only certain files by supplying a **TAGNAME** to the **acfsutil repl init primary** command.

As you can see, with ACFS replication even non-Oracle software can have a backup server that not only has an up-to-date copy of your database, but any files that are critical to your operations.

ACFS Security

Although ACFS by default utilizes the standard OS file system security, it is possible to provide a finer grained security using ACFS security, which was introduced in 11.2.0.2 for Linux. ACFS security is realm-based: a realm is a way to group files so that security rules or rule sets and authentication can be applied to it. To use ACFS security, you first need an OS user to serve as security administrator. After that user is registered, he or she can assign other security administrators to various realms as required. The security administrators can then manage the security rules for their realms.

Here's an example showing how this is done.

1. Let's first initialize security and create the first security administrator. The grid user is used here, but the user can be any existing user, and the password is not the OS user password, but is a new password you specify that will be used for all **acfsutil sec** operations. All security administrators must be part of the O/S group provided for the **–g** flag.

    ```
    [root]# /sbin/acfsutil sec init -u grid -g asmadmin
    Password for new ACFS Security administrator:
    Re-enter password for new ACFS Security administrator:
    acfsutil sec init: Security wallet created.
    ```

2. Now let's prepare the ACFS file system for security. We're asked for the realm management password that we set up in the previous step:

    ```
    [grid]$ /sbin/acfsutil sec prepare -m /u02/app/oracle/securefs/
    Realm management password:
    System realm (Backup) created.
    System realm (Logs) created.
    System realm (backup operator) created.
    ```

This creates the directory /u02/app/oracle/securefs/.Security, which holds information about the realm and rules as well as a log of operations. You can see the original preparation here and that root failed to look at the logs directory because that's a secure file:

```
[grid]$ cat /u02/app/oracle/securefs/.Security/realm/logs/
sec-racassur-ipfix01.log
09/13/10 10:56:18 UTC [uid: 500 gid: 500 Result: SUCCESS]
acfsutil sec prepare: ACFS 10627: Mount point '/u02/app/oracle/
securefs/' is now prepared for security operations.
09/13/10 10:59:26 UTC [uid: 0 gid: 0 Result: DENIED] Realm
authorization failed for OPEN on file 'logs'
```

3. Next, we actually create the security realm itself. Note the **–e off** flag, which simply states that we don't want to use encryption for this file system (since we haven't discussed encryption).

```
[grid]$ /sbin/acfsutil sec realm create secReal1 -m /u02/app/
oracle/securefs/ -e off -d "securefs security realm"
Realm management password:
```

Now we can create some rules that can be of the following types:

- **Application**   Allow access to the files by application.

- **Username**   Allow access for specific users.

- **Time**   Restrict the times of the day that the file system can be accessed.

- **Hostname**   Allow or deny access to a specific cluster node.

Rules are created against file systems and not realms. Let's allow Oracle to access the file system but disallow anyone on racassur-ipfix03 from accessing it:

```
[grid]$ /sbin/acfsutil sec rule create secRule1User
-m /u02/app/oracle/securefs/ -t username oracle -o ALLOW
[grid]$ /sbin/acfsutil sec rule create secRule2host
-m /u02/app/oracle/securefs/ -t hostname racassur-ipfix03 -o DENY
```

With a couple of rules created, we can create a couple of rule sets.

```
[grid]$ /sbin/acfsutil sec ruleset create secRuleSet1
-m /u02/app/oracle/securefs/ -o ALL_TRUE
[grid]$ /sbin/acfsutil sec ruleset create secRuleSet2
-m /u02/app/oracle/securefs/ -o ALL_TRUE
```

Notice **–o ALL_TRUE**, which is in fact the default value; we can also use **ANY_TRUE**, which means that only one of the rules would need to be *true* to allow access.

Now that rule sets are created, we can edit them to add the required rules. The first rule set will get both rules, and the second will just get the username rule:

```
[grid]$ /sbin/acfsutil sec ruleset edit secRuleSet1
-m /u02/app/oracle/securefs/ -a secRule1User,secRule2host -o ALL_TRUE
[grid]$ /sbin/acfsutil sec ruleset edit secRuleSet2
-m /u02/app/oracle/securefs/ -a secRule1User -o ALL_TRUE
```

Now we can add objects (files/directories) to the realm and rules or rule sets in one go, or we can do it separately. Here we will add a whole directory to the security realm, but we could also add single files if we omitted the **–r** flag.

```
[grid]/sbin/acfsutil sec realm add secReal1 -m /u02/app/oracle/securefs/
-f -r /u02/app/oracle/securefs/directory1
```

Before you can apply the ruleset to a realm, we need to have the grid user added to the security realm even though the grid user created it.

```
grid]$ /sbin/acfsutil sec realm add secReal1 -m /u02/app/oracle/securefs/
-u grid
```

Now let's apply a rule set to the realm for **ALL** operating system commands. The options, instead of **ALL**, could be a comma-separated list of any of the following: **APPENDFILE, CHGRP, CHMOD, CHOWN,CREATEFILE, DELETEFILE, EXTEND, IMMUTABLE, LINKFILE, MKDIR, MMAPREAD, MMAPWRITE, OPENFILE, OVERWRITE, READDIR, READ, RENAME, RMDIR, SYMLINK, TRUNCATE,** and **WRITE**.

```
[grid]$ /sbin/acfsutil sec realm add secReal1 -m /u02/app/oracle/securefs/
-l ALL:secRuleSet1
  [
```

The **acfsutil sec info** command is used to get and back up information on created security realms. Just one of the options is shown here to see the rule sets:

```
[grid]$ /sbin/acfsutil sec info -m /u02/app/oracle/securefs/ -s
Rule sets present on mount point '/u02/app/oracle/securefs/' as follows :
        secRuleSet1
        secRuleSet2
```

NOTE
The ASM Configuration Assistant can also be used to administer ACFS security.

By using ACFS security with many realms and rule sets, we can create fine-grained access to files on the ACFS that are configurable, and we can allow multiple administrators to manage different realms.

ACFS Encryption

Here, we'll quickly cover ACFS encryption, another new feature in 11.2.0.2 on Linux. ACFS encryption lets you encrypt stored data so that the file contents are never viewable as plain text and the encryption keys are also not accessible. Encryption cannot be applied to replicated file systems, but it can be used with secured file systems; however, that should be done through the security realm itself by the realm administrator instead of directly using **acfsutil encr**. To use encryption outside of a security realm at the most basic level, use the following steps:

1. Initialize encryption for the cluster, by running the following command as root on one node:

   ```
   [root]# /sbin/acfsutil encr init
   Creating SSO key store for encryption...
   acfsutil encr init: Encryption key store created.
   ```

2. Set up the encryption parameters for the file system.

   ```
   [root]# /sbin/acfsutil encr set -a AES -k 128 -m /u02/app/
   oracle/diag/
   FS-level encryption parameters have been set to:
   Algorithm (AES 128-bit), Key length (16 bytes)
   ```

3. Enable encryption on specific files or in the following example a whole directory using the **–r** flag with **acfsutil encr on**:

   ```
   [root]# /sbin/acfsutil encr on -m /u02/app/oracle/diag/
   -r /u02/app/oracle/diag/asm
   Using FS-level parameters: algorithm (AES), key length (16 bytes)
   Encrypting (/u02/app/oracle/diag/asm)... done.
   ```

   If we wanted to add encryption to our file system that is already secured, we would again need to initialize encryption on the cluster and set encryption on the file system. We'd then just need to add encryption to the realm itself and switch it on.

   ```
   [grid]$ /sbin/acfsutil sec realm add secReal1 -m /u02/app/
   oracle/securefs/
   -e on -a AES -k 128
   [root]# /sbin/acfsutil encr on -m /u02/app/oracle/securefs/
   ```

4. Then we use the **acfsutil encr info** command to view various pieces of information for the file system:

   ```
   [grid]$ /sbin/acfsutil encr info -m /u02/app/oracle/securefs/
   File system: /u02/app/oracle/securefs/
       Encryption status: ON
       Algorithm: AES 128-bits
       Key length: 16 bytes
   ```

NOTE
The ASM Configuration Assistant can also be used to administer ACFS encryption.

Summary

ASM has come a long way since Oracle Database 10g Release 1. Now you can store massive amounts of data, allowing ASM to spread the load to avoid hotspots. The most accessed data can be placed on the fastest parts of the disks, and you can ensure that data is safe with high-redundancy disk groups that are also managed seamlessly. If you have stretched clusters, ASM can be told to read your local copy first and even have a special disk group for the third site voting file copy.

All that ASM offered for database files is now available for files outside the database, as ACFS overlays standard ASM. Not only that, but other features have been added to tag, replicate, encrypt, secure, and snapshot those files. Oracle now provides all the tools you need to ensure maximum availability of your clustered database and/or file system implementations. Now it's time to let the database take over to see how it can ensure maximum availability of your data.

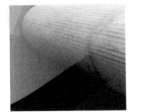

PART
II

Oracle Real Application Clusters (Oracle RAC)

CHAPTER
6

Oracle RAC
Setup/Configuration

n this chapter, we will drill down into the intricacies of installing, upgrading, and configuring 11.2 Oracle RAC. This includes the best practices for setting up the environment, such as configuring Oracle Homes, setting up the file system, and installing patches. We'll install Oracle RAC, and areas of interest or concern will be highlighted.

Oracle RAC/RDBMS Install Options

As discussed in Chapter 4, Oracle Database 11g Release 2 introduced a change in the relationship between Oracle Clusterware, Automatic Storage Management (ASM), and the RDBMS. In previous versions of Oracle Database, ASM used the same home as the RDBMS home or a separate home that was still considered an RDBMS home because it used the exact same RDBMS binaries. Oracle Clusterware and ASM are now installed into a single home directory, called the Grid Infrastructure (GI) home, which includes ASM, whether you intend to use it or not. Because we have already discussed the installation of the GI, including the clusterware and ASM, this chapter will focus on the installation and options for your Oracle RAC RDBMS home, which is now a completely separate home from ASM.

Shared Home vs. Private Drives for the RDBMS

We briefly touched on the concepts of shared homes in Chapter 4, but this was primarily in the context of the GI home. It was mentioned that shared homes for GI are not recommended and in fact will not be supported in the future. But how about the RDBMS home? Let's look a bit closer at the pros and cons of both options.

It is often tempting to think that having a single shared home is the simpler, and therefore better, solution. After all, especially with many nodes in an environment, installing, patching, and running backups can become complex when many copies of the same software are spread across multiple nodes. In addition, configuration and log files are distributed across all nodes, making it more difficult to view, monitor, and maintain them. Having everything in a single, shared home, where installs need to be done only once, with all of these files being centrally available, would seem to be the Nirvana of DBA-dom.

However, as a Maximum Availability Architecture (MAA) DBA, you should be aware of some of the downsides of this type of environment as well—for example, the option to perform a rolling upgrade of your Oracle RAC environment (see Chapter 7) or to apply patches in a rolling fashion are key elements in maximizing your availability, and key components of the Oracle Database grid. If you decide to set up your environment with a shared RDBMS home, it is more difficult to implement rolling upgrades or apply patches in a rolling fashion, since there is only a single copy of the software. In most cases, you must take down the entire software stack across *all* nodes to patch or upgrade. Another consideration in the same vein is that a shared Oracle home can be a single point of failure in other ways. Any damage to the binaries—whether from a file system corruption, hardware error, or human error of any type (deleting/overwriting of files)—will affect all nodes.

Oracle has recently introduced the concept of *hot* or *online patching*, which mitigates this argument for some patches; however, limitations to online patching prevent this from being used in all cases. With respect to rolling upgrades, if a standby database is available, rolling upgrades with a standby database can still be achieved with minimal downtime, even with a shared home. Nevertheless, a shared home still needs careful consideration before implementing your mission-critical environments.

Finally, it's generally a good idea to be in the mainstream. As of now, the predominant install variant in the user community is to have "homes on a private drive." If being part of the mainstream is important (which it should be for an MAA DBA), this is the option that gives you the most "company" in the world of the Oracle grid. Of course, over time, things will change and evolve, as always, but for the time being, we would advise going the route of private drives for the Oracle RDBMS home. The Oracle Universal Installer and the Oracle OPatch utility have both evolved to the point at which management of multiple private homes, even for a large number of nodes, is very manageable; the advantages of having separate homes on private drives outweighs the downside of the additional work necessary to manage these homes. The fact that Oracle Enterprise Manager (OEM) makes the control of many homes easy is another final point in favor of such a setup.

Owner of the DB Home

As discussed in Chapter 4, nearly all enterprises today have implemented role separation for their IT systems. In keeping with the discussion on role separation from that chapter, we recommend that you use separate accounts for the GI and RDBMS installations. As such, the examples in this chapter focusing on RDBMS installations are done as the *oracle* user account, assuming that the GI installation (in Chapter 4) was done as the *grid* user. Let's have a look at the typical OS groups created for an Oracle installation.

oinstall   oinstall is the OS group name typically used for the Oracle Inventory group. This group must be the primary group for Oracle software installation owners. Group members have access to the Oracle Inventory directory.

dba   dba is the OS group name typically used for the OSDBA group. It is required for Oracle database authentication.

asm   asm is the OS group name typically used for the OSASM group. It is required for ASM authentication. If not used, dba is the default OSASM group.

oper oper is the OS group name that is typically used for the OSOPER group. This group can be created if you want certain operating system users to have a limited set of database administrative privileges (SYSOPER).

asmdba asmdba is the OS group name that is typically used for the OSDBA group for ASM. Members of this group have read and write access to the files managed by ASM. The database software owner (*oracle*) must be a member of this group.

File System Choice for DB Files

Chapter 4 discussed the storage options for the Oracle Clusterware files—that is, the voting disk and Oracle Cluster Registry (OCR). This chapter covers the same points in the context of the RDBMS—that is, where should your database files be stored? Oracle provides several possible configurations for database file storage—the one available on all platforms is Automatic Storage Management (ASM) for the shared files, recommended for GI files and Oracle RAC. In addition, Oracle offers its own cluster file system (OCFS) for both the Linux and Windows platforms. Beyond the OCFS, other vendors also offer CFSs for certain platforms. Specific certification against the platform, Oracle version, and type of file system are required, so it is important to check the Oracle Certification Matrix to confirm which combinations are certified. Because we recommend the use of the full Oracle stack, we will not discuss these other options in detail, but you should be aware of other possibilities.

Yet another storage option is to use some type of certified network attached storage with a Network File System (NFS) mount option. This would mean that the file system used for storage would actually be an NFS file system. Again, this is not certified on all platforms, so check the Oracle Certification Matrix to confirm whether this is allowed for your platform. Assuming it is, you can then use the Oracle DirectNFS feature to manage access to these files.

Although these are all viable options for storing Oracle Database files, our preferred choice is to use Oracle ASM. As discussed in Chapter 5, ASM is built specifically for the Oracle RDBMS, and it provides the best choice for performance, manageability, and flexibility in an Oracle RAC environment. As such, the examples in this chapter will focus on using Oracle ASM as the storage mechanism for our files. Note that, as discussed in Chapter 5, ASM Cluster File System (ACFS) is not supported for any files that would normally reside in a standard ASM disk group. This includes data files, OCR or voting disks, archive logs, RMAN backup sets, and so on.

cluvfy

The cluvfy utility is helpful in identifying potential problems and pitfalls prior to embarking on the installation. It can be run in various stages, and we strongly recommend becoming familiar with cluvfy and incorporating it into your regular routine of maintenance and monitoring. (Grid control can help with this—see Chapter 13.)

At this point, if you are following along with our sequential process in the book, the GI home has been successfully installed and the environment is pristine and ready for the Oracle RAC installation. However, that may not always be the case. Your environment may have been inherited, or perhaps the GI installation occurred some time ago and changes have been made since then. Therefore, if you feel any uncertainty about the environment into which you are stepping, we would advise that you run the cluvfy utility again, prior to installation of the database, to help ensure that the installation will go smoothly and problem-free.

Following is the output from cluvfy to check readiness of the system prior to the database install. Remember that you execute this as the user who will be the database home owner (for example, *oracle*). The output should be reviewed for any failed checks, the causes should be fixed, and cluvfy should again be executed until the summary message "Pre-check for database installation was successful" is displayed. It is not recommended that you continue with the database creation before this is achieved.

```
[oracle@ratlnx01 bin]$ ./cluvfy stage -pre dbinst -n all

Performing pre-checks for database installation
Checking node reachability...
Node reachability check passed from node "ratlnx01"
Checking user equivalence...
User equivalence check passed for user "oracle"
Checking node connectivity...
Checking hosts config file...
Verification of the hosts config file successful
Node connectivity passed for subnet "10.143.90.0" with node(s)
ratlnx02,ratlnx01
TCP connectivity check passed for subnet "10.143.90.0"
Node connectivity passed for subnet "192.143.90.0" with node(s)
ratlnx02,ratlnx01
TCP connectivity check passed for subnet "192.143.90.0"
Node connectivity passed for subnet "172.143.90.0" with node(s)
ratlnx02,ratlnx01
TCP connectivity check passed for subnet "172.143.90.0"
Interfaces found on subnet "10.143.90.0" that are likely candidates for
VIP are:
ratlnx02 eth0:10.143.90.37 eth0:10.143.90.39 eth0:10.143.90.44
ratlnx01 eth0:10.143.90.36 eth0:10.143.90.38 eth0:10.143.90.45
eth0:10.143.90.46
Interfaces found on subnet "192.143.90.0" that are likely candidates for
VIP are:
ratlnx02 eth1:192.143.90.43
ratlnx01 eth1:192.143.90.42
Interfaces found on subnet "172.143.90.0" that are likely candidates for
VIP are:
```

```
ratlnx02 eth2:172.143.90.43
ratlnx01 eth2:172.143.90.42
WARNING:
Could not find a suitable set of interfaces for the private interconnect
Node connectivity check passed
Total memory check passed
Available memory check passed
Swap space check passed
Free disk space check passed for "ratlnx02:/oragrid"
Free disk space check passed for "ratlnx01:/oragrid"
Free disk space check passed for "ratlnx02:/tmp"
Free disk space check passed for "ratlnx01:/tmp"
User existence check passed for "oracle"
Group existence check passed for "oinstall"
Group existence check passed for "dba"
Membership check for user "oracle" in group "oinstall" [as Primary]
passed
Membership check for user "oracle" in group "dba" passed
Run level check passed
Hard limits check passed for "maximum open file descriptors"
Soft limits check passed for "maximum open file descriptors"
Hard limits check passed for "maximum user processes"
Soft limits check passed for "maximum user processes"
System architecture check passed
Kernel version check passed
Kernel parameter check passed for "semmsl"
Kernel parameter check passed for "semmns"
Kernel parameter check passed for "semopm"
Kernel parameter check passed for "semmni"
Kernel parameter check passed for "shmmax"
Kernel parameter check passed for "shmmni"
Kernel parameter check passed for "shmall"
Kernel parameter check passed for "file-max"
Kernel parameter check passed for "ip_local_port_range"
Kernel parameter check passed for "rmem_default"
Kernel parameter check passed for "rmem_max"
Kernel parameter check passed for "wmem_default"
Kernel parameter check passed for "wmem_max"
Kernel parameter check passed for "aio-max-nr"
Package existence check passed for "ocfs2-tools-1.2.7"
Package existence check passed for "make-3.81"
Package existence check passed for "binutils-2.17.50.0.6"
Package existence check passed for "gcc-4.1.2"
Package existence check passed for "libaio-0.3.106 (i386)"
Package existence check passed for "libaio-0.3.106 (x86_64)"
Package existence check passed for "glibc-2.5-24 (i686)"
Package existence check passed for "glibc-2.5-24 (x86_64)"
```

```
Package existence check passed for "compat-libstdc++-33-3.2.3 (i386)"
Package existence check passed for "compat-libstdc++-33-3.2.3 (x86_64)"
Package existence check passed for "elfutils-libelf-0.125 (x86_64)"
Package existence check passed for "elfutils-libelf-devel-0.125"
Package existence check passed for "glibc-common-2.5"
Package existence check passed for "glibc-devel-2.5 (i386)"
Package existence check passed for "glibc-devel-2.5 (x86_64)"
Package existence check passed for "glibc-headers-2.5"
Package existence check passed for "gcc-c++-4.1.2"
Package existence check passed for "libaio-devel-0.3.106 (i386)"
Package existence check passed for "libaio-devel-0.3.106 (x86_64)"
Package existence check passed for "libgcc-4.1.2 (i386)"
Package existence check passed for "libgcc-4.1.2 (x86_64)"
Package existence check passed for "libstdc++-4.1.2 (i386)"
Package existence check passed for "libstdc++-4.1.2 (x86_64)"
Package existence check passed for "libstdc++-devel-4.1.2 (x86_64)"
Package existence check passed for "sysstat-7.0.2"
Package existence check passed for "unixODBC-2.2.11 (i386)"
Package existence check passed for "unixODBC-2.2.11 (x86_64)"
Package existence check passed for "unixODBC-devel-2.2.11 (i386)"
Package existence check passed for "unixODBC-devel-2.2.11 (x86_64)"
Package existence check passed for "ksh-20060214"
Check for multiple users with UID value 0 passed
Current group ID check passed
Default user file creation mask check passed
Checking CRS integrity...
CRS integrity check passed
Checking Cluster manager integrity...
Checking CSS daemon...
Oracle Cluster Synchronization Services appear to be online.
Cluster manager integrity check passed
Checking node application existence...
Checking existence of VIP node application (required)
Check passed.
Checking existence of ONS node application (optional)
Check passed.
Checking existence of GSD node application (optional)
Check ignored.
Checking existence of EONS node application (optional)
Check passed.
Checking existence of NETWORK node application (optional)
Check passed.
Checking if Clusterware is installed on all nodes...
Check of Clusterware install passed
Checking if CTSS Resource is running on all nodes...
CTSS resource check passed
Querying CTSS for time offset on all nodes...
Query of CTSS for time offset passed
```

```
Check CTSS state started...
CTSS is in Active state. Proceeding with check of clock time offsets on
all nodes...
Check of clock time offsets passed
Oracle Cluster Time Synchronization Services check passed
Checking time zone consistency...
Time zone consistency check passed.

Pre-check for database installation was successful.
```

NOTE
The message "WARNING: Could not find a suitable set of interfaces for VIPs" can be ignored.

Installing Oracle RAC

Now that we have made our decisions about how our Oracle RAC should be designed, and we have prepared our hardware and installed the GI software. At this point, we can proceed with the next step and install the RDBMS software and the Oracle RAC database. To follow best practices, we'll use local homes for GI (see Chapter 4) and also for the RDBMS, we have used ASM to store all clusterware files, and we will do the same for database files. As mentioned earlier in this chapter, we will install the RDBMS homes with the *oracle* OS user account. Finally, we have verified that the underlying GI stack is properly configured by running the Oracle Cluster Verification Utility (CVU). If you've been careful during the preparation, the install itself will be a relaxed "type in a few parameters and click next" exercise.

MAA Workshop: *RDBMS Software Install*

Step 1. Because we will use different users for the GI home and the RDBMS home, we start the Oracle Universal Installer (OUI) for the RDBMS software installation as the OS user *oracle* that we created earlier.

```
#su - oracle
```

From the directory where we staged the RDBMS software, we start the OUI as follows:

```
./runInstaller
```

Step 2. In the first screen, add an e-mail address if you want to receive security updates from Oracle Support. Since we will install the database itself in a separate step, select the option Install Database Software Only.

NOTE
Beginning with version 11.2.0.2, the second screen of the Oracle Universal Installer allows you to download software updates. This feature allows the installer to download mandatory patches for itself as well as for the base product at installation time so that they do not need to be applied later.

Step 3. Select the option Install Database Software Only and click Next.

Step 4. In the next screen, OUI displays all nodes in the cluster and asks you to select the nodes where Oracle RAC should be installed. As done previously for the *grid* user, during the grid install, use the SSH Connectivity button to configure/ test the passwordless SSH connectivity between your nodes for the *oracle* user.

Step 5. Accept English as language and select to install the Enterprise Edition in the next two screens.

Step 6. At the Specify Installation Location screen, type in the locations for ORACLE_BASE and ORACLE_HOME. The ORACLE_HOME directory should be a subdirectory of the ORACLE_BASE directory, and the OUI will display a warning if this is not the case. Be aware that this differs from the GI installation.

Step 7. Specify the operating system (OS) groups for OSDBS select dba and OSOPER select oper.

Step 8. After you've provided this information, the OUI performs its prerequisite checks. As for the GI home installation, you can correct checks marked as "Fixable" by following the instructions when you click Fix & Check Again. Figures 6-1 and 6-2 show examples of how the fix for two OS kernel parameters can be performed by the OUI.

Step 9. After confirming the summary screen, OUI starts installing the RDBMS software. Shortly before completion, a window appears with instruction on how to run the root.sh script. Log into a terminal window as root user and run the root.sh script on the first node. When finished do the same for all other nodes in your cluster as well.

NOTE
root.sh should be run on one node at a time.

Step 10. At the Finish screen, you should see the message that the installation was successful. Click Close to finish the installation.

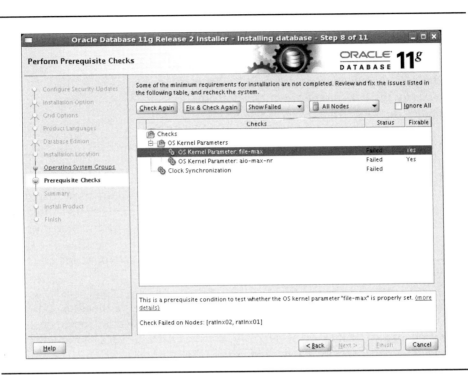

FIGURE 6-1. *Prerequisite Checks screen*

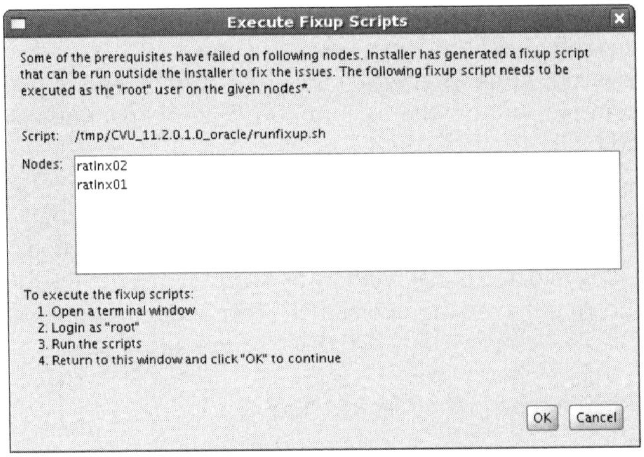

FIGURE 6-2. *Execute Fixup Scripts screen*

Patching the Environment

It is generally recommended that you apply the patches to the level you plan to patch after each installation step, before moving on to the next one. For example, you would patch the GI home before you start to install the RDBMS home, and you'd patch the RDBMS home before you start to create the database. In releases prior to 11*g* Release 2, this recommendation used to apply to patchsets as well as individual patches. So, for example, for an environment in which 11.1.0.7 was being installed, the recommendation would normally be to install the 11.1.0.6 BASE release, and then follow that up by applying the 11.1.0.7 PATCHSET. In 11*g* Release 1 and earlier versions, this required two separate steps. However, starting with 11.2.0.2 (which is the first patchset on top of 11.2.0.1), the patchsets are released as fully installable versions. For those customers who have Oracle Support and can access the patchsets, this greatly simplifies the initial installation for those who want to start out on the latest and greatest Oracle version, because it allows the MAA DBA to install the latest version, inclusive of the latest patchset, all in one step.

For additional patches beyond the patchsets, however, it is still advisable that you install those immediately after the base install. For example, the latest patchset updates (PSUs) should be installed to both the GI home and RDBMS home, prior to database creation, to ensure that the database is created with the latest set of fixes possible, and to minimize initial configuration steps. See Chapter 7 for more information on patches and patchsets.

ASM Disk Group Creation

With Oracle's grid infrastructure in 11*g* Release 2, it is recommended that you put the OCR and voting disks in Oracle ASM, using the same disk group you use for your database data. Using the same disk group for the Oracle Clusterware files (OCR and voting disks) simplifies (you need not create special devices to store those files) and centralizes the storage management (all Oracle related files are stored and managed in Oracle ASM), using the same characteristics for the data stored. Any disks/Logical Unit Numbers that you might want to use for other disk groups should be added into the existing disk group to allow for more flexibility in striping. Having said all that, in some circumstances, you may want to create a dedicated disk group for the Oracle Clusterware files, separate from the existing database data containing disk groups. This should not be required, but it can be configured.

Potential considerations that may affect your decisions on disk group layout include, but are not limited to, the following:

- A 1:1 relationship between disk groups and databases is preferred, and disk groups are generally not shared among databases.

- The backup and recovery for individual databases (more than one in the cluster) is based on a snapshot restore mechanism (EMC's BCV or Hitachi's Shadow copy are two examples). This approach is most likely used in conjunction with a 1:1 disk group to database relationship as mentioned.

- Certain and frequent system-specific maintenance tasks uncommonly require that specific database data containing disk groups be unmounted. This scenario can likely be avoided by using a different approach for those maintenance tasks.

- A higher protection level than the one provided for the "external redundancy disk groups," and therefore for the database data, is required for the Oracle Clusterware files.

- Your "Normal redundancy disk group" is designed for two failure groups only. An ASM disk group, which is supposed to hold voting files, requires three disks in separate failure groups.

- Different types/speeds of disks (that is, Solid State disks) are available. If you have, for example, a few Solid State disks, with much higher speeds than the rest of the storage, these disks should be placed in separate disk groups—perhaps for redo logs.

- A mix of multiple storage boxes with different technology are used in the cluster—such as Network Attached Storage (NAS) and Direct Attached Storage (DAS).

Whether you decide to store clusterware files and database files in the same disk group, you should maintain the ASM best practice that recommends that you create two disk groups for database files (for all databases)—one for data and the second for the Flash Recovery Area. (Chapter 11 discusses this in detail.)

To implement this, you must create at least one additional ASM disk group. Because ASM belongs to the GI home, we log in as the grid user and change into the GI home/bin folder.

1. To start the ASM Configuration Assistant (ASMCA), we execute the following:

   `./asmca`

2. In the next window, under disk groups, we will see the disk group we created during the GI install that stores the OCR and the voting disks. To create an additional disk group, we click Create.

3. In the new disk group, we type in a disk group name; here, it's ORAFLASH. Select the redundancy and tick the disks we want to use for the disk group and click OK to create the disk group.

4. We can perform the same steps for other disk groups we want to create. Now we are ready to create an Oracle RAC database.

Database Creation with DBCA

For Oracle veterans, using the Oracle Database Configuration Assistant (DBCA) to create a database was often considered an affront to their scripting and SQL skills. However, those days are long gone. DBCA significantly simplifies the creation of an Oracle RAC database by automatically setting the required initialization parameters, creating the required undo tablespaces, redo threads, and database views as well as creating the necessary GI resources to support the Oracle RAC database. With the automation of all of these Oracle RAC–specific configuration steps, in addition to all of the features and options available for creation of a database, DBCA has evolved into the de facto choice for creating databases. Even when scripting is necessary, you should use DBCA to generate those scripts instead of attempting to create a script on your own. Therefore, our examples will use the DBCA.

DBCA Functions

We use DBCA here to create an Oracle RAC database, but it offers many more functions. The DBCA can be used to create and delete databases, to add and delete instances, to set up network configuration for the database and its instances, to register a database in Oracle Enterprise Manager Grid Control, and to configure Database Control. It can be used to configure options for the database, such as Oracle Database Vault, and to start up the database and its instances. Prior to version 11.2, Cluster Managed Services, could be managed with the DBCA as well. From 11.2 on, this can be done via the Cluster Managed Services page in Oracle Enterprise Manager DB Control, accessible from the Cluster Database Availability page.

MAA Workshop: Oracle *RAC Database Creation*

Step 1. As the oracle user, start the Database Configuration Assistant (DBCA) from your RDBMS home bin directory:

```
#su - oracle
cd /u01/app/oracle/product/11.2.0/db_1/bin
./dbca
```

Step 2. The first window that pops up is the Welcome page for Oracle RAC, as shown in Figure 6-3. Here, we select the radio button to create an Oracle Real Application Clusters Database. The Oracle RAC Welcome page appears only if the Oracle home from which it is started was installed on a cluster. If you are on a cluster but DBCA does not display the Oracle RAC Welcome page, the DBCA was unable to detect whether the Oracle home is installed on a cluster. Start troubleshooting by

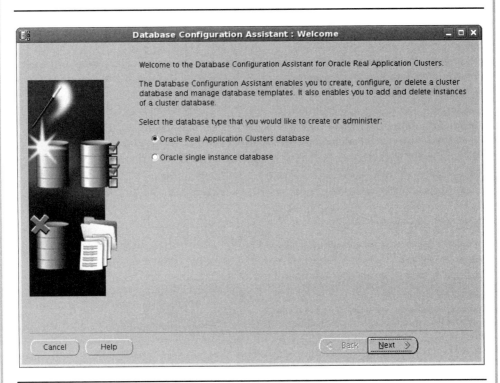

FIGURE 6-3. *Oracle RAC Welcome page*

checking that the OUI inventory is correctly located in the directory /etc/oraInst.loc, and that the oraInventory file is not corrupted. Run the **cluvfy** command with the **–post crsinst** switch and correct any failed checks:

```
[grid@ratlnx01 bin]$ ./cluvfy stage -post crsinst -n all
```

Step 3.   The next screen lists the functions that DBCA offers; if no database is present, only the options Create a Database and Manage Templates are available. For our task, we select Create a Database.

Step 4.   Now we have several options for specifying the purpose of the new database. The General Purpose or Transaction Processing or the Data Warehouse configuration type use preconfigured database templates that are optimized for each type of database. Custom Database does not use a template. We will use the General Purpose template for this example and confirm our selection by clicking Next.

Step 5.   We must now define certain database characteristics such as global database name and SID prefix. The Global database name can be up to 30 characters in length and must begin with an alphabetic character. The domain portion of the global database name can be no more than 128 characters and can contain only alphabetic and numeric characters, as well as the period (.) character. The SID prefix must begin with an alphabetic character. The maximum number of characters you can use for the SID prefix is 8 characters. Once the database name and SID have been specified, we select the cluster nodes where an instance should run; click Select All. In the radio buttons on top of the screen, we can specify the way the database will be managed. The available options are Policy-Managed and Admin-Managed. We'll select Admin-Managed.

Step 6.   In the next screens, we can decide whether we want to manage our database by grid control or database control, and we define the passwords for the SYS and SYSTEM accounts of the database.

Step 7.   Now the Database File Location screen appears. The list of values for Storage Type offers Automatic Storage Management (ASM) and Cluster File System. We want to store the database files using ASM. Under Storage Location, two options are available: Use Common Location For All Database Files and Use Oracle-Managed Files. We choose Use Oracle-Managed Files, because this feature simplifies tablespace creation, ensures data file location consistency, includes compliance with OFA rules, and reduces human error with data file management. We specify in the line for Database Area our disk group name, +ORADATA. We want to follow best practices and mirror our control files and redo log files, so we click Multiplex Redo Log and Control File Destination.

  In the window that appears, we type in the first line, **+ORADATA**, and in the second line we type **+ORAFLASH**. This way, we ensure that a mirror of each redo log and control file will reside in both disk groups.

Step 8.   In the Recovery Configuration screen, we define the Flash Recovery Area (Fast Recovery Area) location of +ORAFLASH and enable arching. The Database Content screen provides the option to include either sample schemas or to run custom scripts as part of database creation.

Step 9.   The Initialization Parameter screen, shown in Figure 6-4, appears, where we define how much memory our database instances should consume and specify the maximum number of OS user processes. We can specify the character sets the database should use and other options.

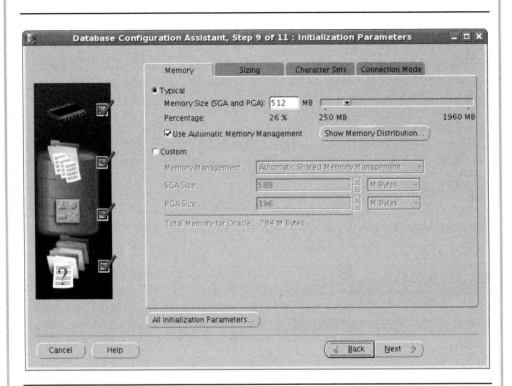

FIGURE 6-4. *Initialization Parameters screen*

In the Connection Mode tab, we can define whether our database should by default operate in dedicated or shared server mode. In the lower-left corner of the screen is the All Initialization Parameters button that opens a window with a list of the parameters that will be used for the new Oracle RAC database. Notice the buttons to display advanced parameters and to show a description of them.

Step 10.   After we confirmed the changes in the Initialization Parameters screen, the Database Storage screen appears, and because we selected to use a template that includes the data files, there is nothing for us to change. After confirming, the Create Options screen appears. Check the Create Database checkbox and click Finish; confirm the Summary screen to start the creation of the database. At the end of the creation, a window appears that informs us about the fact and lets us either change or unlock our passwords; or we can click Exit to finish the installation.

Oracle RAC–Specific Parameters

Even if DBCA is choosing what we consider to be the correct defaults, let's have a look at some cluster-related parameters and what is considered as best practice for setting them.

PRE_PAGE_SGA   Set **PRE_PAGE_SGA=false**. If set to true, it can significantly increase the time required to establish database connections. If clients might complain that connections to the database are too slow, consider setting this parameter to false, because doing so avoids mapping the whole SGA and process startup and thus saves connection time.

PARALLEL_MAX_SERVERS   Tune **PARALLEL_MAX_SERVERS** to your hardware. Start with $(2 \times (2\ threads) \times (CPU\_COUNT)) = 4 \times CPU\ count$ and repeat the test for higher values with test data.

FAST_START_PARALLEL_ROLLBACK   Consider setting the **FAST_START_PARALLEL_ ROLLBACK** parameter, which determines how many processes are used for transaction recovery that occurs after redo application. Optimizing transaction recovery is important to ensure an efficient workload after an unplanned failure. As long as the system is not CPU bound, setting this to a value of **HIGH** is a best practice. This causes Oracle to use four times the CPU count ($4 \times cpu\_count$) parallel processes for transaction recovery. The default for this parameter is **LOW**, or two times the CPU count ($2 \times cpu\_count$).

FAST_START_MTTR_TARGET   Set **FAST_START_MTTR_TARGET** to a non-zero value in seconds. (MTTR stands for Mean Time To Recovery.) Crash recovery will complete within this desired time frame. Use the Redo Logfile Size Advisor to determine the optimal, smallest online redo log file size based on the current **FAST_START_MTTR_ TARGET** setting and corresponding statistics. Note that the Redo Logfile Size Advisor is enabled only if **FAST_START_MTTR_TARGET** is set. **V$INSTANCE_RECOVERY** contains the size of the redo log file size (in megabytes) that is considered to be optimal based on the current **FAST_START_MTTR_TARGET** setting. It is recommended that you size all online redo log files to at least this value.

PARALLEL_EXECUTION_MESSAGE_SIZE   In pre-11.2 databases, increase **PARALLEL_ EXECUTION_MESSAGE_SIZE** from the default (normally 2048) to 8192. This can be set higher for data warehousing–based systems with a lot of data transferred through Parallel Query (in 11.2, the default is already16384).

CLUSTER_INTERCONNECTS (pre-11.2)   Parameter **CLUSTER_INTERCONNECTS** allows you to specify the network that is used for the IPC traffic for the cluster. Because the interconnect information is stored in the OCR, there is normally no need to set the parameter, and you should consider doing so only if you really need to. Having said that, it could be necessary in some cases.

One case is the use of IP network multipathing (IPMP) with Solaris. When using IPMP for the private interconnect, the **CLUSTER_INTERCONNECTS** parameter should be configured to ensure failover and load balancing. IPMP by itself can failover an address to another interface, but it cannot failover to another node. Oracle virtual IP (VIP) can failover to another interface on the same node or to another host in the cluster. So using **CLUSTER_INTERCONNECTS** will allow the VIP to function in concert with IPMP.

Another reason to set the parameter is to separate the interconnect traffic for databases on separate network cards. You need to be aware that in such a setup, when one of the several interfaces fails, clusterware will treat this as a complete failure and start instance eviction.

Starting from 11.2 onward, it is no longer required to set **CLUSTER_INTERCONNECTS**. The private interconnect information stored in the Oracle Cluster Registry (OCR) and the Grid Plug and Play (GPnP) profile will be used for the database layer as well.

The High Available IP (HAIP) feature (also known as Redundant Interconnect) is available on all platforms except Windows from 11.2.0.2 on. HAIP is used by the database for fault tolerance and load balancing. Your database alert log will indicate addresses used for cluster communication, including the HAIP. When IPMP or Linux bonding is used, outbound network traffic goes out on all active NIC's yet inbound traffic goes to only one active NIC. The use of HAIP is an elegant way to get around this problem.

Workload Management Considerations

One of the fundamental features of Oracle RAC is that it not only provides redundancy but can efficiently spread workload across several machines. To ensure minimal delays for the user requests, you should ensure that resources are available when requested or, to be precise, ensure that the user is connected to a node where resources are available. To address this, we make use of services and load balancing. Both methods are described in detail in Chapter 8.

Enabling Archiving

Remember that during the database creation with DBCA, we enabled archiving to ensure that the database will be configured with this option from the beginning. When you want to change the archiving mode, you can run the **ALTER DATABASE** SQL statements to change the archiving mode in Oracle RAC as long as the database is mounted by the local instance but not open in any instances. On the last open instance of the Oracle RAC, do the following to enable archiving:

```
[oracle@ratlnx01 bin]$ ./sqlplus /nolog
SQL*Plus: Release 11.2.0.1.0 Production on Fri Jul 2 13:00:51 2010
```

```
Copyright (c) 1982, 2009, Oracle.  All rights reserved.
SQL> connect / as sysdba
Connected.
SQL> shutdown immediate
Database closed.
Database dismounted.
ORACLE instance shut down.
SQL> startup mount
ORACLE instance started.
Total System Global Area  221294592 bytes
Fixed Size                  2212048 bytes
Variable Size             142610224 bytes
Database Buffers           71303168 bytes
Redo Buffers                5169152 bytes
Database mounted.
SQL> alter database archivelog;
Database altered.
SQL> alter database open;
Database altered.
```

To disable archiving, use the same sequence of steps but instead of **alter database archivelog**, use **alter database noarchivelog**. You do not need to modify parameter settings to run this statement.

Another option to change the archive log mode is to use the Recovery Settings page in the Maintenance tab of the Enterprise Manager Oracle RAC Database page. The view GV$ARCHIVE_PROCESSES can be used to query the status of the archiver processes for all database instances. The command archive log list can be used to determine from the SQL prompt if archiving is enabled:

```
SQL> archive log list
Database log mode              Archive Mode
Automatic archival             Enabled
Archive destination            USE_DB_RECOVERY_FILE_DEST
Oldest online log sequence     4
Next log sequence to archive   5
```

Extending Oracle RAC Databases to New Nodes

Chapter 4 discussed the steps required to add a node to your cluster from the perspective of the GI home. If you are adding a new node to your cluster, the first step is to get the underlying GI components to recognize that new hardware and incorporate it into your cluster. Once a node is added into your cluster, you may or may not decide to extend the database onto that node. Here, we will briefly discuss the steps to accomplish this.

Extending the Oracle RDBMS/Oracle RAC Home

Assuming you do not use a shared home for Oracle RAC, the software has to be transferred to the new node.

To get this done, go to the Oracle_home/oui/bin directory on one of the existing nodes and run the addNode.sh script in silent mode:

```
$ cd /u01/app/oracle/product/11.2.0/oui/bin
$ ./addode.sh -silent "CLUSTER_NEW_NODES={ratlnx03}"
```

When the script completes, run the root.sh script on the new node as the root user. The root.sh script resides in the Oracle home directory on the new node.

Add an Instance to a Policy-Managed Database

If your database is policy-managed and Oracle Managed Files (OMF) is enabled, you don't have much to do: simply increase the cardinality of the server pool for the database. The database instance and ASM instance on the new node are created and configured automatically when a node is added to the server pool. Use the **srvctl modify srvpool** command to increase the cardinality of the server pool. Note that OEM can be used as well to perform the task.

NOTE
If OMF is not enabled, you must manually add undo and redo logs.

Add an Instance to an Administrator-Managed Database

Remember that when a database is administrator managed, the database instance name is bound to the specific node where it can run. To add a new instance to the Oracle RAC cluster, we will use the Instance Management option of Database Configuration Assistant (DBCA). Start the DBCA from one of the existing nodes. The DBCA must be invoked from the $ORACLE_HOME/bin folder as user *oracle*.

1. $ ./dbca

2. Select the option Oracle Real Application Database in the first screen and Instance Management in the second screen.

3. You should see the option to Add An Instance and that's what you select. Ensure that the correct database is selected and provide a SYSDBA user and the appropriate password to continue. A list of the existing instances belonging to the database is displayed for information purposes.

4.   You'll see a default name for the new instance that can be changed to the instance name you prefer. Below the instance name, the available new node is displayed.

5.   After you confirm this, the default database storage options of the DBCA are displayed.

6.   Click Finish to see a summary for the instance to be created, and click the OK button to start the instance creation on the new node.

Deleting an Instance from the Oracle RAC Database

Any time something can be added, you need a way to remove it. Same is true for instances in an Oracle RAC database.

Delete an Instance from a Policy-Managed Database

To delete an instance from a policy-managed database, you decrease the cardinality of the server pool for the database. The database instance and ASM instance on the deallocated node are removed from the cluster, and the node is either reassigned to another server pool or placed in the free pool. The **srvctl modify srvpool** command can be used to decrease the cardinality of the server pool.

Delete an Instance from an Administrator-Managed Database

To delete an instance from an administrator-managed database, we again use the Instance Management option of the DBCA, similar to the steps we did for adding an instance. Note that the DBCA GUI has to be started on one node that remains in the cluster.

```
$ ./dbca
```

   Select the option Oracle Real Application Clusters Database and confirm, after selecting the Instance Management option in the next screen. From the available choices, select Delete An Instance and confirm. Provide logon credentials for the database and select the instance to be deleted. Read and confirm the information windows that appear, and the instance will be deleted by the DBCA.

Installing Earlier RDBMS Releases

In some cases, you'll need to run an earlier version of the Oracle RDBMS, even though you are running the 11g Release 2 of Grid Control. This may be the case because of certification requirements of third-party applications requiring an older release, because 11g Release 2 is not yet certified from an RBDMS perspective, or because internal testing requirements mandate that you use an older release for a specific amount of time. Because applications are interacting most heavily with the Oracle RDBMS, and not dealing directly with the underlying GI components, applications in most cases should not "care" what version of Oracle's grid infrastructure is being used, which allows the MAA DBA to take advantage of most of the new features of Oracle Database 11g Release 2 even when the database must remain on an older release. Oftentimes, the older RDBMS versions will already be in place, because the system is simply being upgraded. However, it is also often the case that new hardware has been procured for the new cluster environment, and the initial installation of the 11g Release 2 GI home needs to be followed up by an RDBMS installation of an older release (such as 10.2). Here, we will give a brief overview of the steps necessary to install a 10.2 RDBMS on 11.2 GI.

Using Older Oracle Database Versions with GI

You can use Oracle Database release 9.2, release 10.x, and release 11.1 with Oracle Clusterware release 11.2. We will explain the steps to install a 10.2 RDBMS on 11.2 GI, because this combination is probably the most requested. If you plan to install a 9.2 RDBMS, be aware that with GI 11.2, the Global Services daemon (GSD) is disabled by default. This daemon is required only for 9.2 databases, and you will have to enable it with these commands:

```
srvctl enable nodeapps -g
srvctl start nodeapps
```

The status check for the GSD resource should now return the following:

```
[root@ratlnx01 bin]# ./crsctl stat res ora.gsd
NAME=ora.gsd
TYPE=ora.gsd.type
TARGET=ONLINE           , ONLINE
STATE=ONLINE on ratlnx01, ONLINE on ratlnx02
```

Administer 11g Release 2 local and scan listeners using the **lsnrctl** command, and then set your **$ORACLE_HOME** environment variable to the path for the GI home (grid home). Do not attempt to use the **lsnrctl** commands from Oracle home locations for previous releases, because they cannot be used with the new release.

When Oracle Database version 10.x or 11x is installed on an 11g Release 2 cluster, keep in mind that the new cluster is configured for dynamic cluster configuration by default, which means that some or all IP addresses are provisionally assigned, and other cluster identification information is dynamic. This configuration is incompatible with older database releases, which require fixed addresses and configuration. Creating a persistent configuration for a node is called *pinning* a node. To check whether your nodes are pinned, execute the following:

```
[root@ratlnx01 bin]# ./olsnodes -t -n
ratlnx01        1       Unpinned
ratlnx02        2       Unpinned
```

To pin a node, use this:

```
[root@ratlnx01 bin]# ./crsctl pin css -n ratlnx01 ratlnx02
CRS-4664: Node ratlnx01 successfully pinned.
CRS-4664: Node ratlnx02 successfully pinned
```

Now the nodes are prepared for installing an older database version:

```
[root@ratlnx01 bin]# ./olsnodes -t -n
ratlnx01        1       Pinned
ratlnx02        2       Pinned
```

NOTE
When you execute the DBCA from an older release and the nodes are not pinned, the first DBCA screen will not display the option to install an Oracle Real Application Clusters Database.

If you have access to My Oracle Support, check before you begin for information regarding the setup you plan to use. My Oracle Support provides information on known issues with pre-11.2 Database in an 11*g* Release 2 GI environment.

Installing a Version 10.2 RDBMS on 11.2 GI

In the steps provided, a 10.2.0.1 Enterprise Edition RDBMS home is installed and patched to version 10.2.0.5 before the OUI is used to create a database.

1. Before you start with this, use the ASMCA either to confirm you have an ASM disk group available to store the database or to create such a disk group.

2. Stage the 10*g* Release 2 (10.2) database software and the 10.2.0.5 patch set we downloaded on the first node of the cluster, and make sure user *oracle* is the owner.

3. Create the directory to store the new 10.2 Oracle home, and do this on all nodes of the cluster:

```
# mkdir -p /u01/10.2/db
# chown -R grid:oinstall /u01/10.2/db
# chmod -R 775 /u01/10.2/db
```

4. Make sure user *oracle* has passwordless automatic SSH connectivity configured on all nodes. During the GI installation, this was done for the *grid* user not for the user *oracle*. The 10.2 OUI does not contain the option to configure this for you, as this option is new with version 11.2.

5. As the user *oracle,* start the **runInstaller** command from the directory where the Oracle Database 10*g* Release 2 (10.2) installation media is staged:

```
$ ./runInstaller
```

6. Select to install the Enterprise Edition and specify the location of the Oracle home we created earlier (in our example /u01/10.2/db).

7. In the next screen, the installer has detected the presence of Oracle Clusterware and uses this to populate this dialog box. As we want to install the 10.2 database on all nodes, we must ensure to select All Nodes here. The OUI will perform certain product-specific prerequisite checks. For our setup, one of the checks is supposed to be failing as the OUI expects Clusterware version 10.2. If other checks are failing, make sure you correct them before you continue.

8. Check the checkbox next to the Clusterware Is Not 10.2 message and the status will change to "User Verified," and you should be able to continue.

9. Confirm that no database needs to be upgraded and select to install the database software only (we will install the database at a later stage).

10. After you confirm the Summary screen, OUI starts to install the software. At the end a window will appear, asking you to run the root.sh script on all nodes. Make sure you run them sequentially on the nodes and not at the same time.

11. Because Patchset 10.2.0.5 has fixed most of the issues in a pre-11.2 Database, you patch the database home to this release. From the directory where the patch set is staged, as user *oracle,* start patching with this:

```
$ ./runInstaller
```

12. In the first screen, select the 10.2 Oracle home installed before (in our example, /u01/10.2/db).

13. The next screen will display all nodes, but you will not have the option to change anything here, because you can either patch all or none of the nodes. The OUI performs its checks and you are asked to confirm the Summary. OUI now starts patching the binaries and after root.sh was successfully run sequentially on all nodes, the patchset is applied.

Creating a 10.2 Database Using DBCA

1. To create the 10.2 Database, we use the DBCA, which must be invoked from the 10.2 Oracle home bin folder as user *oracle*:

```
$ cd /u01/10.2/db
$ ./dbca
```

2. The first screen should give you the options either to create an Oracle RAC database or a Single Instance database. If this screen is not displayed, your nodes might not be pinned. In this case, you have to cancel and correct this.

3. Choose Oracle Real Application Clusters Database, and in the next screen, select Create The Database On All Nodes and use the General Purpose template.

4. In the following screens, you'll provide information such as name and SID of the database, passwords to be used, and so on.

5. After you provide all this information, you are asked where the database should be stored. The options offered are cluster file system, ASM, or raw devices. Choose ASM and check the checkbox next to the disk group(s) we prepared before. Oracle Managed files is the preferred choice.

6. If you want to configure a Flash Recovery Area, enable archiving from the beginning, create services, or include a sample schema, make these selections as well.

7. Modify the default initialization parameters that size the SGA, character set, and so on.

8. Choose Create Database.

9. In the Summary screen, confirm the configuration and the database creation starts. When completed, you can click Password Management if you want to manage and/or unlock passwords.

10. After that, the database instances will be started on all nodes. To check the status of the database, you can use **crsctl** from the GI home or use **srvctl** from the 10.2 RDBMS home:

```
[root@ratlnx01 bin]# cd /u01/app/10.2/bin/
[root@ratlnx01 bin]# export ORACLE_HOME=/u01/app/10.2
[root@ratlnx01 bin]# ./srvctl status database -d orcl10
Instance orcl101 is running on node ratlnx01
Instance orcl102 is running on node ratlnx02
```

When you try to execute **srvctl** from the 11.2 home, you will see the following:

```
[root@ratlnx01 bin]# ./srvctl status database -d orcl10
PRCD-1027 : Failed to retrieve database orcl10
PRKP-1088 : Failed to retrieve configuration of cluster database orcl10
PRKR-1078 : Database orcl10 of version 10.2.0.0.0 cannot be
administered using current version of srvctl. Instead run srvctl
from /u01/app/10.2
```

Oracle RAC on Extended Distance Clusters

A special implementation of Oracle RAC lets you add an *extended distance cluster*, also called a stretched cluster, metro cluster, campus cluster, or geo cluster. With an extended distance cluster, components are deployed across two or more data center locations, allowing them to continue to function if one location fails. In normal operation, all nodes at all locations will be active. The distance for an extended Oracle RAC is determined by the type failure against which the Oracle RAC should be protected.

To make the Oracle RAC survive a fire in the server room, for example, it would be sufficient to have half of the nodes and the shared storage mirror in another server room, in another fire protection sector. To protect the Oracle RAC against an airplane crash or a terrorist attack, the distance between the Oracle RAC parts should be increased to at least a couple of miles. When making the decision regarding how far to stretch the cluster, remember that every mile adds latency for the network and the I/O operations, which can result in slow performance on a daily basis; this might not be a worthy tradeoff against the rare chance of losing the entire data center.

In most cases, Oracle Data Guard might be the better choice for protection. The new features of Oracle Data Guard integrated with Fast Start Fail Over (FSFO) will provide near seamless failover. In this section, we will look at the challenges of implementing an extended distance cluster.

Stretching a Cluster

In considering how far you can stretch a cluster, remember physics classes and recall how fast light can travel in a vacuum. For our calculation, we don't need the exact number (186,182 miles per second), because in optical fiber, the speed is slowed by approximately 30 percent and additional delays are introduced by electronic switches, for example. In addition, consider that any message requires a confirmation, so round-trip distances must be used for calculations.

We round up to 200 miles per millisecond (note we are now using milliseconds as opposed to seconds) and divide it by two because of the round trip. The result shows that a 100 mile distance of separation between nodes adds 1 millisecond delay. Being conservative, we add our 30 percent optical fiber delay, plus the additional delay for the switches and so on and end up using a value of 50 percent of that round trip delay; this results in a rule of thumb of 1 millisecond delay for every 50 miles of distance. So, for example, stretching a cluster over 1000 miles would result in 20 milliseconds additional latency of network and disk I/O. Normal disk access latency is around 10 milliseconds, so the extended design would triple the disk access latency, resulting in poor performance and other issues. Therefore, we recommend that an extended Distance Cluster architecture fits best when the two data centers are relatively close (equal to or less than 20 miles apart).

When selecting the data centers to host an extended Oracle RAC, only locations with existing direct cable connections with dedicated channels should be considered (which can be extremely costly).

Stretching Network Connections

Interconnect, Storage Area Network (SAN), and IP networking need to be kept on separate channels, each with required redundancy. Redundant connections must not share the same dark fiber (if used), switch, path, or even building entrances. Remember that cables can be cut.

Traditional networks can cope with a distance of approximately 6 miles before a repeater has to be installed. Because the use of repeaters introduces latency, network distances greater than 6 miles require dark fiber with Wavelength Division Multiplexing (WDM). Dark fiber is so named because it emits no light until a signal is added to it. WDM enables a single optical fiber to carry multiple signals simultaneously, thus increasing the capacity of a fiber. Each signal travels within its unique color band, which is modulated by the data. WDM distinguish between Dense Wavelength Division Multiplexing (DWDM) and Coarse Wavelength Division Multiplexing (CWDM) systems. CWDM systems have less than eight active wavelengths per fiber; DWDM systems provide more active wavelengths and can support more than 150 wavelengths, each carrying up to 10 Gbps.

The SAN and Interconnect connections need to be on dedicated point-to-point connections. For SAN networks, make sure you are using SAN buffer credits if the distance is more than 10km. The use of SAN buffer credits is a method of storage distance extension to limit the impact of distance at the I/O layer.

NOTE
Do not implement the Oracle RAC Interconnect over a WAN. This is the same as doing it over the public network, which is not supported.

Shared Storage

Although in the network considerations, distance is the only fact that distinguishes a "local" Oracle RAC from an "extended" Oracle RAC, when it comes to storage, other aspects must be considered. As the cluster will need to be able to survive a complete loss of one data center, the storage must be mirrored to both sides. The purpose of surviving a data center failure would be achieved only if the location hosting the storage survives. As this defeats the purpose of having an extended Oracle RAC, mirroring storage is essential for an extended cluster. The most common technologies for clusters are host-based mirroring, array-based mirroring, and ASM redundancy. ASM redundancy is the only supported storage mirroring for extended Oracle RAC in Oracle Database 11*g* Release 2.

Array-Based Mirroring
Array-based mirroring is a primary-secondary storage site solution. All I/O goes to one site and is mirrored to the other side. If a primary storage failure occurs, all nodes will crash and will have to be restarted after the secondary storage is made active. You must be aware as well that the instances from the secondary location will see slower I/O as it writes across the distance.

Host-Based Mirroring
From an availability viewpoint, host-based mirroring is preferred over array-based mirroring because it does not require a manual restart if one location fails. From a performance perspective, host-based mirroring requires CPU cycles from the host machines. Using host-based mirroring (software) for ASM disks can result in a major performance degradation and is not supported. Hardware mirroring of disks is not affected, so disk arrays that are not controlled by the host OS but by the array controller itself are supported.

ASM
As mentioned, ASM redundancy is the only supported option for the extended cluster shared storage mirroring from Oracle Database 11*g* Release 2 on. One failure group has to exist on each site. For a two-site setup, this means normal-redundancy disk groups have to be used. High-redundancy disk groups could keep the mirror on the same site and not in the failure group on the remote site. High-redundancy disk groups should be used only when the stretched cluster has three sites. With 11*g* Release 1, Oracle introduced two ASM improvements that are beneficial for extended cluster configurations: the preferred read feature and the fast disk resync.

ASM Preferred Read   Prior to 11*g* Release 1, ASM has always read the primary copy of a mirrored extent set. For stretched clusters, this resulted in possible reads from the remote site, even though a copy of the extent set existed on the local storage. To overcome this performance issue, Oracle introduced the **ASM_PREFERRED_READ_FAILURE_GROUP** initialization parameter, which allows you to specify a list of failure groups from which the local instances can read.

ASM Fast Mirror Resync   If the connection between the two sites is lost, one of the failure groups will be marked invalid. Restoring the redundancy of an entire ASM failure group is usually a time-consuming process. ASM fast mirror resync significantly reduces the time to resynchronize a failed disk in such situations. ASM fast resync keeps track of pending changes to extents on an offline disk during an outage. The extents are resynced when the disk is brought back online.

Voting Disks

The number and location of clusterware voting disks have a much bigger impact in an extended cluster than on a local cluster. You may be aware of the best practice needed to have an odd number of voting disks to ensure that a tie-breaking disk exists when the interconnect between nodes fails, but all voting disks reside on the same storage medium.

With the majority of extended clusters that reside on two sites, the odd number of voting disks introduces the question of where to place the tie-breaking voting disk. If one site hosts two, a primary-secondary setup is introduced. If the site with the majority of voting disks fails, the entire cluster will go down.

To address this issue and follow MAA best practices, a third alternative, independent site is recommended to be used for the stretch cluster. This site hosts the tie-breaking voting disk, which can reside on NFS. Beginning with Oracle Database 11g Release 2, along with the recommendation to store voting disks on ASM, Oracle introduced a failure group type called *quorum*. Disks in a quorum failure group do not contain user data and are not considered when determining redundancy requirements. During the clusterware installation, you are not offered the option of creating a quorum failure group. Thus, to create a disk group with a fail group on the second site and a quorum fail group on a third location, you must do the following:

```
SQL> CREATE DISKGROUP VOTE NORMAL REDUNDANCY
FAILGROUP fg1 DISK '<a disk in SAN1>'
FAILGROUP fg2 DISK '<a disk in SAN2>'
QUORUM FAILGROUP fg3 DISK '<disk or file on a third location>'
ATTRIBUTE 'compatible.asm' = '11.2.0.0';
```

NOTE
For more information on stretch clusters, consult the Oracle white paper, "Oracle Real Application Clusters on Extended Distance Clusters," by Erik Peterson, et al. In addition, refer to the paper "Extended Distance Oracle RAC," by Mai Cutler, Sandy Gruver, and Stefan Pommerenk. These papers served as a reference for the above section.

Summary

This chapter has provided you the information on configuring your Oracle RAC database in an Oracle grid infrastructure environment. Whether you are running an 11.2.0.x version of the database, or an older release, it should be apparent now how to get this environment up and running using the latest version of Oracle's grid infrastructure. We have discussed the pros and cons of shared versus private Oracle Homes, and discussed patching considerations for ongoing maintenance of these environments. Finally, we gave you tips on how to implement an extended distance cluster and pointed out that it is absolutely crucial that you use reliable hardware, a high performing network, and best practices. Before making a decision to implement an extended distance cluster, you need to understand the limitations and costs. Even more important is to understand that Oracle RAC and Oracle Data Guard are designed to protect against different kinds of failures. This means that when you're designing an MAA environment, Oracle Data Guard will most likely be a desired component of your MAA implementation, regardless of whether or not a stretch cluster is in place. Subsequent chapters will delve into more detail as to how and why Oracle Data Guard is a crucial component of your MAA environment.

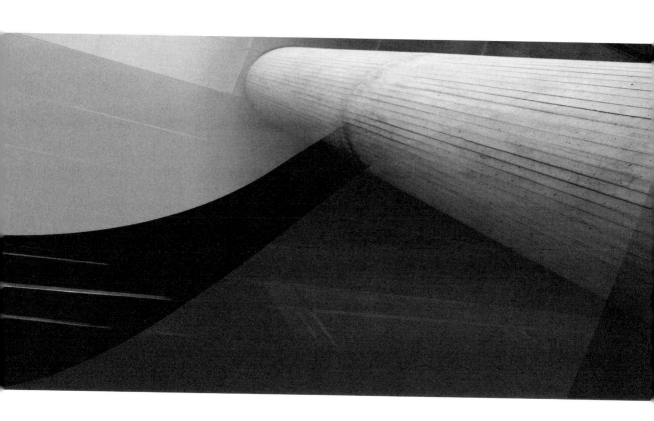

CHAPTER
7

Oracle RAC
Administration

his chapter focuses on administration of your database when it's running in an Oracle RAC environment. You will learn the differences between a single-instance database and an Oracle RAC database, how to tune effectively in an Oracle RAC environment, and how to patch an Oracle RAC database. In addition, the chapter covers details of using the SRVCTL utility to manage your Oracle RAC environment, and wraps up with a discussion of server policies and the managing of diagnostic data.

Oracle RAC vs. Single-Instance: Additional Processes

In an Oracle RAC environment, there are several additional background processes associated with each Oracle RAC instance, beyond what would normally be seen in a single-instance environment. These processes work together in a coordinated fashion to maintain the locks necessary for multiple instances to access resources simultaneously, and to ensure that these resources are made available to the instances where they are most needed, in a timely fashion.

A simple query such as the following will give you an idea of the background processes involved in an Oracle RAC environment:

```
SQL> set pages 50
SQL> select name, description from v$bgprocess where PADDR <> '00';
```

Comparing the list of processes between Oracle RAC and single-instance environments, you will see that there are several which are specific to an Oracle RAC instance. A brief description of these unique processes and how they interact in an Oracle RAC environment is provided next.

LCK: Lock Process

The *lock* process (LCK) manages requests that are *not* cache-fusion requests, such as row cache requests and library cache requests. Only a single LCK process is allowed for each instance. LCK maintains a list of lock elements and uses this list to validate locks during instance recovery.

LMD: Lock Manager Daemon Process

The *lock manager daemon* (LMD) process is also known as the global enqueue service daemon, because it manages global enqueue and global resource access. From within each instance, the LMD process manages incoming remote resource requests (that is, requests for locks that come from other instances in the cluster). It is also responsible for deadlock detection and monitoring for lock conversion timeouts.

LMON: Lock Monitor Process

The *lock monitor* (LMON) process is the global enqueue service monitor. It is responsible for the reconfiguration of lock resources when an instance joins the cluster or leaves the cluster and is also responsible for the dynamic lock remastering mentioned earlier. LMON will generate a trace file whenever a reconfiguration occurs (as opposed to remastering of a subset of locks). It is the responsibility of LMON to check for the death of instances clusterwide and to initiate reconfiguration as quickly as possible.

LMS: Lock Manager Server Process

The *lock manager server* (LMS, or global cache service process) process is in charge of shipping the blocks between instances for cache-fusion requests. In the event of a consistent-read request, the LMS process will first roll back the block, creating the consistent read (CR) image of the block, and will then ship that version of the block across the interconnect to the foreground process making the request at the remote instance. In addition, LMS must interact with the LMD process to retrieve lock requests placed by LMD. An instance may dynamically generate up to ten LMS processes; the number of LMS processes can be set with the parameter **GCS_SERVER_PROCESSES**, and the value is dependent on the number of CPUs. At startup time, **CPU_COUNT / 4** LMS processes are started, but at least two LMS processes are always started. From Oracle Database version 10.2 and on, only one LMS process is started if the server just has one CPU. If you are consolidating many small databases into a cluster, you may want to reduce the number of Global Cache Service (GCS) processes (LMSn) created by the Oracle RAC instance. To ensure the LMS processes get CPU time when needed, the LMS processes must run in a scheduling priority set to Real Time.

ACFS: ASM Cluster File System CSS Process

The *Automatic Storage Management (ASM) Cluster File System CSS* (ACFS) process delivers CSS membership changes to the ASM Cluster File System. These membership changes are required for the file system to maintain file system consistency within the cluster. This process is new with Oracle Database 11*g* Release 2.

ACMS: Atomic Control File to Memory Service Process

The *Atomic Control File to Memory Service* (ACMS) process works with a coordinating caller to ensure that an operation is executed on every instance in Oracle RAC despite failures. ACMS is the process in which a distributed operation is called. As a result, this process can exhibit a variety of behaviors. In general, ACMS is limited to small, nonblocking state changes for a limited set of cross-instance operations. This process is new with 11*g* Release 2.

GTXn: Global Transaction Process

Global Transaction (GTXn) processes help maintain the global information about (XA) global transactions throughout the cluster. Also, the processes help perform two-phase commit for global transactions anywhere in the cluster so that an Oracle RAC database behaves as a single system to the externally coordinated distributed transactions. This process is new with Oracle Database 11*g* Release 2.

LMHB: Global Cache/Enqueue Service Heartbeat Monitor

Another process new with 11*g* Release 2, *LM Heartbeat Monitor* (LMHB) monitors LMON, LMD, and LMSn processes to ensure that they are running normally without blocking or spinning.

PING: Interconnect Latency Measurement Process

Every few seconds, the *PING* process in one instance sends messages to each instance. The message is received by PING on the target instance. The time for the round trip is measured and collected. This is also a new process with 11*g* Release 2.

RMSn: Oracle RAC Management Process

The Oracle *RAC Management* (RMSn) process performs a variety of tasks, including creating resources related to Oracle RAC when new instances are added to a cluster.

RSMN: Remote Slave Monitor Process

The *Remote Slave Monitor* (RSMN) background process manages the creation of slave processes and the communication with their coordinators and peers. These background slave processes perform tasks on behalf of a coordinating process running in another cluster instance.

Oracle RAC vs. Single-Instance: The Basics

Aside from the additional background processes in an Oracle RAC environment, it is important to have an understanding of additional fundamental differences in an Oracle RAC environment versus a single instance environment. It is also key to have a grasp of the terminology. The next section discusses these fundamentals, and provides the background you need to have a deeper understanding of Oracle RAC functionality.

Cache Fusion: A Brief Intro

To help you understand what the Oracle RAC–specific background processes are doing, we'll take a moment to discuss the basics of how Oracle RAC works in terms of managing access to shared datafiles from multiple nodes. The centerpiece of

Oracle RAC technology, Cache Fusion, essentially enables the shipping of blocks between the SGAs of nodes in a cluster, via the interconnect. This avoids having to push the block down to disk, to be reread into the buffer cache of another instance.

When a block is read into the buffer cache of an instance in an Oracle RAC environment, a lock resource is assigned to that block (different from a row-level lock) to ensure that other instances are aware that the block is in use. Then, if another instance requests a copy of that block, which is already in the buffer cache of the first instance, that block can be shipped across the interconnect directly to the SGA of the other instance. If the block in memory has been changed, but that change has not been committed, a CR copy is shipped instead. This essentially means that, whenever possible, data blocks move between each instance's buffer cache without needing to be written to disk, with the key being to avoid any additional I/O being necessary to synchronize the buffer caches of multiple instances. This is why it is critical to have a very reliable, high-speed interconnect for your cluster—because the assumption is that the interconnect will always be faster than going to disk.

Dynamic Resource Mastering

Another feature in Oracle RAC is the concept of *dynamic resource remastering*. Each instance generally holds, or masters, a certain amount of cache resources. When an instance requests a cache resource, it must be obtained from the instance that is currently mastering this resource. This may or may not be the same instance that is requesting it. With dynamic remastering, if a certain instance is requesting a cache resource more often than any of the other instances, that cache resource will eventually be moved into the SGA of the requesting instance, making future requests more efficient. In database releases prior to 10g, remastering would take place only during reconfiguration, which happens automatically during normal operations such as instance startup or instance shutdown, or during abnormal events such as node evictions.

Reconfiguration

In the case of a node's death, the process of remastering that node's cache resources across the remaining instances is referred to as a *reconfiguration*. When a node or an instance dies or is taken offline, the locks (resources) that were previously mastered in that instance's SGA are distributed among the remaining instances. If an instance rejoins the cluster, a reconfiguration will also occur, and the new instance will end up mastering a portion of the locks previously held by the other instances in the cluster. This process, reconfiguration, is different from dynamic remastering.

You can view the allocation of resources between instances by querying the **gv$resource_limit** view. A reconfiguration can be seen in the alert log, prefaced with the line

```
Reconfiguration started (old inc 1, new inc 2)
```

and ending with the line

```
Reconfiguration complete
```

Cache Coherency in an Oracle RAC Environment

In addition to the normal performance metrics monitored in a single-instance environment, an Oracle RAC environment requires that some additional metrics be monitored. Primarily, we recommend that the MAA DBA focus on metrics related to messages across the interconnect, to gauge the amount of traffic across the interconnect and also the response time. This traffic essentially falls into two categories when it comes to your Oracle RAC database: *Global Cache Services* (GCS) and *Global Enqueue Services* (GES).

Global Cache Service

GCS relates to the concept of the global buffer cache, which is integral to the Cache Fusion concepts. As such, *global cache* is referring to database blocks. The GCS is responsible for maintaining cache coherency in this global buffer cache by ensuring that any time an instance attempts to modify a database block, a global lock resource is acquired, avoiding the possibility that another instance modifies the same block at the same time. The instance making the change will have the current version of the block (with both committed and uncommitted transactions) as well as a past image of the block. Should another instance request that block, it is the duty of the GCS to track who has the block, what version of the block they have, and what mode the block is held in. The LMS process is the key component of the GCS.

Global Enqueue Service

In addition to the maintenance and management of database blocks themselves, it is also incumbent in an Oracle RAC environment that certain other resources be coordinated between nodes. The GES is responsible primarily for maintaining coherency in the dictionary cache and the library cache.

The *dictionary cache* is essentially a cache of data dictionary information stored in the SGA of an instance for fast access. Since this dictionary information is stored in memory, changes on one node that result in dictionary changes (such as Data Definition Language [DDL] statements) must be immediately propagated to the dictionary cache on all nodes. The GES is responsible for handling this, and avoiding any discrepancies between instances.

By the same token, *library cache* locks are taken out on objects within the database for parsing of SQL statements that affect those objects. These locks must be maintained among instances, and the GES must ensure that deadlocks do not occur between multiple instances requesting access to the same objects. The LMON, LCK, and LMD processes work together to perform the functions of the GES.

GV$ Views

With all of this globalization discussed so far, it is only natural that we point out the addition of *global* views in an Oracle RAC environment. Global views are the same as the more commonly used V$ views, except that they will have a column added called INST_ID, which will map to the **instance_number** of each instance in the cluster. As such, in a three-node cluster, queries against a GV$ view will give you three times as many rows, because each instance will have its own set of data to display. Knowing this, you can query stats for a specific instance or all instances without needing to connect specifically to each node.

An example of some of the information you can gather is shown in the following query:

```
SQL> select * from gv$sysstat where name like '%gcs %';

INST_ID STATISTIC# NAME                              CLASS        VALUE
------- ---------- --------------------------- ---------- -----------
      1         38 gcs messages sent                   32          716
      2         38 gcs messages sent                   32        57325
```

This allows you to see, with one query, that instance number 1 has sent 716 gcs messages, whereas instance number 2 has sent 57325 messages, a disparity that may warrant further investigation.

Redo and Rollback with Oracle RAC

One of the keys of administration in an Oracle RAC environment is understanding how redo and rollback are managed. The key here is realizing that each individual instance requires its own independent set of redo logs, and secondly, its own undo tablespace. Generally speaking, redo and undo are handled on a per-instance basis. Therefore, if an Oracle RAC database comprises three instances, each instance must have two groups of redo logs, one set for each instance, for a minimum of six online redo log groups. Each instance can, of course, have more, but just as with a regular instance, two is the minimum. In the case of the undo tablespace, each instance also must have its own undo tablespace. These files still must reside on the shared drive.

Redo Logs and Instance Recovery

Instance recovery occurs when an instance goes down abruptly, either via a SHUTDOWN ABORT, a killing of a background process, or a crash of a node or the instance itself. After an ungraceful shutdown, it is necessary for the database to go through the process of rolling forward all information in the redo logs and rolling back any transactions that had not yet been committed. This process is known as *instance recovery* and is usually automatically performed by the SMON process.

In an Oracle RAC environment, the redo logs must be accessible from all instances for the purpose of performing instance recovery of a single instance or of multiple instances. Should instance recovery be required because a node goes down ungracefully (whatever the reason), one of the remaining instances must have access to the online redo logs belonging to the node that went down to perform the instance recovery. Thus, even though the instance is down, the data in the redo logs is accessible and can be rolled forward by a surviving instance, with any uncommitted transactions being rolled back. This happens immediately in an Oracle RAC environment, without the need to wait for the downed instance to come back online.

Here is an example of what you may see in the alert log of the instance performing instance recovery:

```
Sun Jun 13 12:32:54 2010
Instance recovery: looking for dead threads
Beginning instance recovery of 1 threads
Started redo scan
Sun Jun 13 12:33:10 2010
Completed redo scan
 read 1918 KB redo, 103 data blocks need recovery
Started redo application at
 Thread 1: logseq 11, block 2374
Recovery of Online Redo Log: Thread 1 Group 1 Seq 11 Reading mem 0
  Mem# 0: +DATA/orcl/onlinelog/group_1.262.721568027
  Mem# 1: +FLASH/orcl/onlinelog/group_1.258.721568047
Completed redo application of 0.44MB
Completed instance recovery at
 Thread 1: logseq 11, block 6211, scn 1538116
 95 data blocks read, 124 data blocks written, 1918 redo k-bytes read
```

The fact that instance recovery is done by a remaining node in the cluster means that when the crashed instance is restarted, no instance recovery is needed on that instance, because it will have already been done. If multiple instances go down, online instance recovery can still occur as long as at least one instance survives. If all instances go down, crash recovery is performed by the first instance to start up.

Redo Logs and Media Recovery

Media recovery differs from instance recovery in that it cannot be done automatically—it requires manual intervention, and it may also require the application of archived redo logs from all instances. If it is necessary to perform media recovery on some or all of the database files, you must do this from a single node/instance. If you are recovering the entire database, all other instances must be shut down, and then you can mount the database on the node from which you have chosen to do recovery. If you are recovering a single file (or set of files) that does not impact the entire database, all instances can be open, but the file(s) that needs to be recovered must be offline and will therefore be inaccessible. The node that performs the media recovery must have read access to all archived redo logs that have been generated from all nodes.

Redo Threads

As discussed, each instance is assigned a thread number, starting at 1, and the thread number for that instance should not change. The thread number is defined by the SPFILE parameter **<sid>.THREAD=*n***, where *n* is the thread number for that instance. Thus, when a redo log group is created, it is assigned to a given instance using the thread number, like so:

```
alter database add logfile thread 2 group 5
'/ocfs/oradata/grid/grid/redo02_05.log' size 100m;
```

This example is a database on an OCFS drive.

A query similar to the following can be used to view the online redo logs, their groups, and their threads. This example is on a cluster using ASM:

```
set linesize 120
col inst_id for 99
col group# for 99
col thread# for 99
col sequence# for 9999999
col status for a10
col member for a40
col bytes for 9999999999
select a.group#, a.thread#, a.sequence#, b.member
  2     from v$log a, v$logfile b where a.group#=b.group# order by 1,2,3;


GROUP# THREAD# SEQUENCE# MEMBER
------ ------- --------- ----------------------------------------
     1       1        14 +ASM_DISK/grid/onlinelog/group_1.265.3
     1       1        14 +ASM_DISK/grid/onlinelog/group_1.264.3
     2       1        15 +ASM_DISK/grid/onlinelog/group_2.263.3
     2       1        15 +ASM_DISK/grid/onlinelog/group_2.262.3
     3       2        11 +ASM_DISK/grid/onlinelog/group_3.258.3
     3       2        11 +ASM_DISK/grid/onlinelog/group_3.256.3
     4       2        12 +ASM_DISK/grid/onlinelog/group_4.257.3
     4       2        12 +ASM_DISK/grid/onlinelog/group_4.261.5
```

Parallelism in an Oracle RAC Environment

As you know, the focus of this book is primarily on maximizing the availability of your database, and Oracle RAC is an integral part of a Maximum Availability Architecture. However, Oracle RAC also has the dual benefit of scalability along with the role it plays in an MAA architecture. In Chapter 6, we discussed adding nodes; of course, inherent to this is the ability to spread out user sessions across nodes, adding and removing capacity as needed. But what about scaling within a single session?

The concept of splitting tasks into smaller parts and executing them in parallel can be implemented on one machine with multiple CPUs, for example, but Oracle RAC goes a step further and gives you the opportunity to extend this concept over several machines. Operations can run in parallel, using one, a subset, or all nodes of a cluster, depending on the workload, the characteristics, and the importance of the query. When a SQL statement is in the processes of being parsed, it gets optimized and parallelized. Once the optimization and parallelization have been completed, the original process becomes the query coordinator. Parallel execution servers (PX servers) are allocated from the pool of PX servers on one or more nodes and start working in parallel on the operation. After the statement has been processed completely, the PX servers return to the pool.

When Parallel Automatic Tuning is enabled, Oracle takes care of all relevant database settings for parallel execution. This is usually at least as efficient as manually derived parameters. However, you can adjust any of the settings, which gives you the flexibility to react to specific situations.

Types of Parallelism

Parallel query is the most common of parallel operations but is not the only type. For example, in data warehouse environments, where indexes often need to be rebuilt or large objects have to be created, these operations can be executed as *parallel DDL* for both partitioned and nonpartitioned objects. *Parallel Data Manipulation Language* (DML) operations (such as parallel insert, update, and delete) are mainly used to speed up DML operations against large database objects.

This covers the parallel SQL execution, but Oracle uses parallelism for other database operations as well. Parallel recovery and parallel load (SQL*Loader) are two examples of this. When a parallel operation is executed in a service that is allowed to be running only on a subset of the instances, the parallel query slaves will be generated only on the allowed instances. If, for example, a service runs on three out of five nodes, and you execute an operation in parallel, by default the PQ slaves are generated only on the instances where the services are running. This is important to mention, because it is a new feature in Oracle Database 11g Release 1. In 10g Release 2, for example, you could control PQ slaves across instances only via the parameter **PARALLEL_INSTANCE_GROUPS**. In Oracle Database 11g, the value of the **SERVICE_NAMES** parameter automatically becomes **INSTANCE_GROUPS** in which slaves can run. When a session is connected to a particular **service_name**, and an operation requires a parallel operation, the instance group with the same name as the service name is selected. It is still possible to use the **PARALLEL_INSTANCE_GROUP** parameter to override this setting. You may also want to consider tuning the **PARALLEL_EXECUTION_MESSAGE_SIZE** parameter (see the "Interconnect Performance" section later in this chapter) as increasing this parameter value can have a positive impact on the performance of parallelism.

NOTE
In conjunction with parallel execution, Oracle partitioning can be used to improve performance in large environments.

Monitoring the Environment

A key success factor for the MAA DBA is to monitor his or her Oracle RAC environment proactively. Although the MAA DBA may not have responsibility for the entire system (such as hardware or OS), it is incumbent upon him or her to ensure that all relevant aspects are monitored and under control at all times. When the MAA DBA starts to develop a concept for monitoring, he/she should carefully study the appropriate service level agreements (SLAs). Around the paragraphs in the SLA, you will define main areas for your monitoring strategy. One example may be the case where there is a certain required response time for the application. In the event of an operating system problem causing the response time on one node to suffer, the MAA DBA should develop a strategy for monitoring and reacting to this, even though the cause is external to the database.

Another example that almost always applies in an MAA environment is the definition of the uptime requirements, which can often be very challenging. A 99.999 percent availability for example means 5 minutes and 16 seconds allowed downtime—per *year*. The MAA DBA must employ monitoring techniques for all of the MAA components to ensure that these few minutes are not wasted for any unplanned downtime. Even in cases where a redundant component fails and the system continues to run, the MAA DBA must be notified of this immediately, because there has now become a risk of an outage in the event of a secondary failure. As such, diligent monitoring of the environment is crucial to maintaining high levels of availability.

When the main areas of the SLAs are defined, you drill down into each area and compose a list of components you have to monitor. Because every good MAA DBA has a certain degree of paranoia, you should monitor more rather than less. Some might object, saying that you should concentrate on monitoring only the usual suspects and that hypervigilant monitoring is too much. In such an approach, people define a monitoring subject but do not document why it is monitored and what to do when the monitoring threshold is reached. This creates the impression that many of the targets or thresholds being monitored can be ignored, which is of course a huge mistake. You should always consider that someone started to monitor a particular component for a good reason; it's worth your time to investigate why monitoring is being employed and document it for your colleagues and successors.

After you have defined monitoring needs, you can start looking for tools that help you to do the job most efficiently. Plenty of tools exist to help you monitor your enterprise database environment. Here we cover some of the tools provided by Oracle.

Database Control and Grid Control

Several areas throughout this book discuss Oracle Enterprise Manager (OEM), either in the form of the enterprise-wide Grid Control or in the form of the more targeted Database Control, and how it can help simplify certain management tasks. Chapter 13 is dedicated entirely to Oracle Grid Control, so here we'll offer just a quick introduction.

OEM has always set out to be an interface that can simplify the overwhelming duties of the DBA by consolidating all database management into a single suite of utilities that can be configured to monitor the entire enterprise. Let's have a quick look what OEM provides.

As you can see in Figure 7-1, the OEM welcome screen provides certain monitoring information for the machines configured in OEM Grid Control, such as CPU and memory utilization and the total I/O in seconds.

Drilling down into a specific server, alerts with certain severities are displayed, as shown in Figure 7-2.

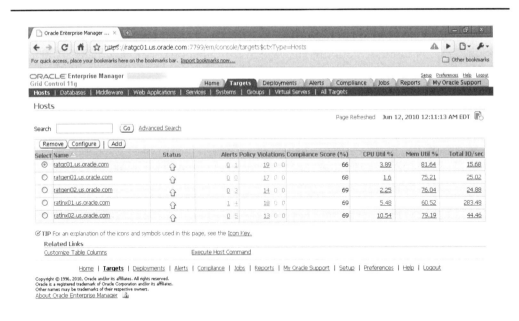

FIGURE 7-1. *Enterprise Manager hosts*

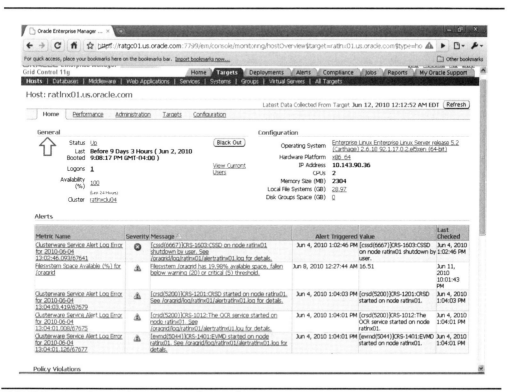

FIGURE 7-2.   *Enterprise Manager hosts alerts*

You can enable and customize thresholds for all possible events. Figure 7-3 shows the list of metrics that are bundled for specific areas such as database files, interconnect traffic, and more.

OS Watcher (OSW)

In addition to the monitoring capabilities of OEM, Oracle Support's Center of Expertise (COE) has developed a utility specifically for monitoring key operating system statistics useful for troubleshooting and debugging issues that can affect any environment. OS Watcher (OSW) is a collection of shell scripts intended to collect and archive operating system and network metrics. OSW collects basic OS information retrieved from standard commands such as **vmstat**, **iostat**, and **netstat**, and stores them in flat files. Since the data is stored in flat files, it is easily interpreted without requiring any special third-party tools or interfaces. If desired, OSW also includes a Java interface to display collected information in a graphical format. Because of its uniformity of data collection, ease of interpretation, and relatively short data collection intervals, OSW is widely used

ORACLE Enterprise Manager
Grid Control 11g

Setup Preferences Help Logout
My Oracle Support

Hosts | Databases | Middleware | Web Applications | Services | Systems | Groups | Virtual Servers | All Targets

Home **Targets** Deployments Alerts Compliance Jobs Reports

Database Instance: pitt_maadb2 >

All Metrics

Collected From Target Jun 12, 2010 12:13:20 AM EDT

Expand All | Collapse All

Metrics	Thresholds	Collection Schedule	Upload Interval	Last Upload
▼ pitt_maadb2				
▲ Archive Area	Some	Every 15 Minutes	Every Collection	-
▲ Data Failure	All	Every 5 Minutes	Every Collection	-
▲ Database Files	None	Disabled	Every Collection	-
▲ Database Limits	Some	Every 5 Minutes	Every Collection	Jun 11, 2010 8:11:57 PM EDT
▲ Database Services	None	Every 15 Minutes	Every Collection	Jun 11, 2010 8:02:57 PM EDT
▲ Database Vault Attempted Violations - Command Rules	None	Every 1 Hour	On Alert	-
▲ Database Vault Attempted Violations - Realms	None	Every 1 Hour	On Alert	-
▲ Database Vault Configuration Issues - Command Rules	All	Every 1 Hour	Every Collection	-
▲ Database Vault Configuration Issues - Realms	All	Every 1 Hour	Every Collection	-
▲ Database Vault Policy Changes	All	Every 1 Hour	Every Collection	-
▲ Dump Area	All	Every 15 Minutes	Every Collection	Jun 12, 2010 12:10:14 AM EDT
▲ Efficiency	None	Every 5 Minutes	Every Collection	Jun 11, 2010 8:11:57 PM EDT
▲ Global Cache Statistics	Not Applicable	Real-time Only	n/a	n/a
▲ Health Check	All	Every 15 Seconds	On Alert	Jun 11, 2010 7:51:53 PM EDT
▲ Incident	All	Every 5 Minutes	Every Collection	-
▲ Incident Status	All	Every 5 Minutes	Every Collection	Jun 12, 2010 12:13:20 AM EDT
▲ Interconnect	All	Every 12 Hours	Every Collection	Jun 11, 2010 10:31:32 PM EDT
▲ Interconnect Traffic	None	Every 5 Minutes	Every Collection	Jun 12, 2010 12:11:58 AM EDT
▲ Messages in the buffered queue	None	Every 30 Minutes	Every Collection	-
▲ Messages in the persistent queue	None	Every 30 Minutes	Every Collection	-
▲ Messages in the persistent queue per subscriber	Not Applicable	Every 30 Minutes	Every Collection	-
▲ Messages per queue per subscriber	None	Every 30 Minutes	Every Collection	-
▲ OCM Instrumenation	All	Every 24 Hours	Every Collection	Jun 11, 2010 10:35:31 PM EDT
▲ Operational Error	All	Every 5 Minutes	Every Collection	-

FIGURE 7-3. *Enterprise Manager All Metrics page*

by Oracle Support. Therefore, you may find that OSW data is requested by Oracle Support if you have to open a Service Request for various types of issues.

Cluster Health Monitor (CHM)

Cluster Health Monitor (CHM), sometimes called by its original name, IPD/OS, is another, more enhanced set of tools to collect OS performance data, though it is initially available only for Linux and Windows OSs. To store the automatic data collection captured by CHM for online and offline analysis, a Berkeley DB (an OS file based database from Oracle) is used.

As mentioned, OSW is useful because of its ability to make data collection uniform with relatively short collection intervals. CHM extends the OSW capabilities by ensuring that it is always scheduled and that data is collected in even more granular intervals (that is, 1 second). CHM uses not only OS commands but also calls ORACLE CRS APIs to collect data. In addition, CHM provides a client GUI to view current load and to replay information collected for a past period. Figure 7-4 shows an example of the GUI for CHM.

NOTE
CHM is installed by default with Grid Infrastructure (GI) 11.2.0.2 on the Solaris and Linux platforms. However, the version of CHM that is packaged with 11.2.0.2 does not currently support the GUI interface.

```
IPD Cluster Monitor V1.10 on win1, Logger V1.03.20090322, Cluster "MyCluster" (View 0), Refresh rate: 1 sec
Number of Nodes: 2
Top Resource Consumers On Each Node(Process(PID) Value):
NODENAME /   Process(PID) CPU       Process(PID) PRIV-MEM(KB)   Process(PID) WORKING-SET(KB)   Process(PID) #FDs   Process(PID) #THREADS
win1         java.exe(3212) 13.86   oracle.exe(1420) 429972     oracle.exe(1420) 229120        System(4) 14408     System(4) 60
win2         crsd.exe(1788) 10.10   oracle.exe(3964) 435672     oracle.exe(3964) 244952        System(4) 13585     System(4) 60
Cluster Stats:
NODENAME /  #CPUs  CPU     CPUQ  RAMFREE(KB)  MEMCACHE(KB)  SWAPFREE(KB)  IOR(KBps)  IOW(KBps)  #IOS(ps)  NETR(KBps)  NETW(KBps)  Procs  RTProcs  FDs    #Disks  #NICs
win1         1     94.92    26   76076        43012         1336          159        1632       181       243.16      171.11      52     3        28823  6       3
win2         1     72.46    19   151056       44855         1227          906        120        94        292.57      264.11      47     3        27136  6       3
Unresponsive Nodes:
NODENAME /  #CPUs  CPU     CPUQ  RAMFREE(KB)  MEMCACHE(KB)  SWAPFREE(KB)  IOR(KBps)  IOW(KBps)  #IOS(ps)  NETR(KBps)  NETW(KBps)  Procs  RTProcs  FDs    #Disks  #NICs
Alert 16 Red,  for NODENAME "win1", CPU = 99.31
   1: Time=06-16-10 11.38.34, CPU usage on node win1 (99.31%) is Very High (> 90%). 42 processes are waiting for only 1 CPUs.
Alert 17 Red,  for NODENAME "win1", CPU = 90.5
   1: Time=06-16-10 11.38.35, CPU usage on node win1 (90.50%) is Very High (> 90%). 29 processes are waiting for only 1 CPUs.
Alert 18 Red,  for NODENAME "win1", CPU = 90.5
   1: Time=06-16-10 11.38.35, CPU usage on node win1 (90.50%) is Very High (> 90%). 29 processes are waiting for only 1 CPUs.
Alert 19 Red,  for Process(PID) CPU "java.exe(3212) 96.5"
   1: Time=06-16-10 11.38.36, CPU usage (96.5%) of process java.exe pid 3212 is abnormally high (> 90%)
Alert 20 Red,  for NODENAME "win1", CPU = 100.0
   1: Time=06-16-10 11.38.36, CPU usage on node win1 (100.0%) is Very High (> 90%). 46 processes are waiting for only 1 CPUs.
Alert 21 Red,  for NODENAME "win1", CPU = 100.0
   1: Time=06-16-10 11.38.39, CPU usage on node win1 (100.0%) is Very High (> 90%). 65 processes are waiting for only 1 CPUs.
Alert 22 Red,  for NODENAME "win1", CPU = 100.0
   1: Time=06-16-10 11.38.40, CPU usage on node win1 (100.0%) is Very High (> 90%). 70 processes are waiting for only 1 CPUs.
Alert 23 Red,  for NODENAME "win1", CPU = 100.0
   1: Time=06-16-10 11.38.46, CPU usage on node win1 (100.0%) is Very High (> 90%). 50 processes are waiting for only 1 CPUs.
Alert 24 Red,  for NODENAME "win1", CPU = 100.0
   1: Time=06-16-10 11.38.50, CPU usage on node win1 (100.0%) is Very High (> 90%). 26 processes are waiting for only 1 CPUs.
Alert 25 Red,  for NODENAME "win1", CPU = 91.36
   1: Time=06-16-10 11.38.58, CPU usage on node win1 (91.36%) is Very High (> 90%). 37 processes are waiting for only 1 CPUs.
Alert 26 Red,  for NODENAME "win1", CPU = 90.58
   1: Time=06-16-10 11.39.00, CPU usage on node win1 (90.58%) is Very High (> 90%). 9 processes are waiting for only 1 CPUs.
Alert 27 Red,  for NODENAME "win1", CPU = 94.92
   1: Time=06-16-10 11.39.09, CPU usage on node win1 (94.92%) is Very High (> 90%). 26 processes are waiting for only 1 CPUs.
ipd>
```

FIGURE 7-4. *Cluster Health Monitor GUI*

ORION

When it comes to performance in an Oracle RAC, database I/O performance is of utmost importance. To ensure proper configuration so that performance will fall within expected levels, you should test the I/O subsystem before building the cluster. Oracle ORION (Oracle IO Numbers) is an ideal method for testing the I/O subsystem for servers that will be running an Oracle database. ORION can simulate database type workloads using the actual I/O stack that the Oracle Database uses without having to install any Oracle Database software. ORION measures the performance in terms of IOPS (I/O operations per second), MBps (megabytes per second), and I/O response time in milliseconds for different types of database workloads such as online transaction processing (OLTP), decision support systems (DSS), or mixed workloads.

Although it is beyond the scope of this chapter to provide details about how to set up and configure the Oracle ORION tool for testing, you can find all the information you need on the Oracle Technology Network (OTN). Type **Oracle ORION** into your favorite search engine to locate the ORION index page on OTN.

Tuning with AWR and ADDM

When we talk about high availability, we must consider more than just the question, "Is the database up?" More than just that simple question is at stake. What really matters is the users' perception. If the database is up, but its responsiveness is poor, uptime is affected from the end-user perspective.

Intelligent Infrastructure

Over the years, Oracle has made great strides in using the information that the database knows about its own inner workings, and turning that knowledge into an infrastructure that will allow the MAA DBA to take advantage of that information easily and automatically. This *Intelligent Infrastructure*, as termed by Oracle, begins with the Automatic Workload Repository (AWR). The AWR gathers information on activity in the database at regular intervals. Each run of the AWR is followed by an automatic run of the Automatic Database Diagnostic Monitor (ADDM), which interprets the information supplied by AWR and makes recommendations.

You can dig deeper into these recommendations by manually running one of a half-dozen advisors provided by Oracle. The combined tools in the Intelligent Infrastructure give the MAA DBA more immediate and instant access into the inner workings of the Oracle RDBMS than ever before.

MMON Background Process

The *Manageability Monitor* (MMON) background process is responsible for the automatic monitoring within the database. MMON monitors the ALERT_QUEUE, which is owned by SYS, once a minute for any new information/alerts. MMON can be used automatically either to take a corrective action or to send an alert via the ALERT_QUEUE. These alerts are then displayed on the database home page in OEM.

Automatic Workload Repository

The AWR is essentially a job-based, scheduled collection of statistics, gathered and stored in the Oracle database, containing information about the database itself. By default, this metadata repository is kept in an extra tablespace called SYSAUX. When creating a new database, the job of gathering statistics is automatically created as part of the database creation. By default, statistics collection will run every 60 minutes, gathering information from dynamic performance views (v$ Views) within the database on statistics such as I/O waits and other wait events, CPU used per session, sorts, I/O rates on various datafiles, and so on. For this to occur, the parameter **STATISTICS_LEVEL** must be set to **ALL** or **TYPICAL** (the default). At the end of a run, the repository is updated with current information for that period. Reports can then be generated, using begin and end values defined by the user, to measure activity during a given period of time.

Since AWR runs are scheduled by default when the database is created, you need do nothing special to enable this functionality. As mentioned, AWR runs at 60-minute intervals, collecting stats and storing that information. However, as you can imagine, this can lead to a rather large repository over time, so by default the data is purged after seven days. Should you want to change these defaults, either the frequency of the runs or how soon the repository is purged, you can do so easily using OEM. Should you want to disable AWR altogether, you can do that as well; however, we strongly recommend that you do *not* disable AWR. The overhead for AWR is minimal, and the gains achieved by allowing the statistic gathering can come in handy at the most unexpected times.

Viewing an AWR Report

The Workload Repository is populated every 60 minutes with statistics, and this happens automatically. Then what? What do you do with this information? You define times, outlined by AWR runs, in which to turn this information into a report. When creating an AWR report, you define the beginning and ending interval for the reports using snapshot IDs from the Workload Repository; your report will begin at one snapshot and end at a later snapshot.

An AWR report can be viewed in OEM from the Administration page. From there, select Workload Repository, and then click Snapshots. You can also change the interval for AWR snapshots here. As mentioned, you can determine the interval of the reports, with the beginning of the interval going back as far as the repository keeps the data. Reports can be viewed using a full report, or you can view the data with pertinent information summarized in the details view.

Creating Baselines for Comparing the Workload

Evaluating AWR reports is also made easier if you have a comparison point. You may suspect, as you evaluate sections of the AWR report, that something "doesn't look right"—for example, the Top SQL may show SQL statements with an excessive number of buffer gets. It would be valuable to be able to compare the report to a similar point in time in the past, when similar work was being done and performance was better. For example, perhaps the same SQL was run at points in the past, but the buffer gets for that same statement were much lower. This might indicate that an index has been dropped, or that the data distribution of the tables queried has somehow changed.

A *baseline* (also called a *preserved snapshot set*) is used as a comparison point of reference if and when performance suffers. The basic idea, for example, is that on a Monday morning, when poor MAA DBA Max is stumbling into work after a long weekend road trip to see his favorite football team, and all hell breaks loose with the database, Max can compare the current performance (or, say, the performance over the past hour) to the baseline that was set up for that timeframe. This will give him an immediate idea of what is different from last week and a head start on where to look for the solution to the problem.

Periods for Baseline Creation

As you can probably tell already, it is necessary to anticipate periods when you might expect to have performance problems. For this, you must understand the nuances of your particular business. For example, you may experience different peaks at different times of the day—for example, a busy period may occur between 8:30 A.M. and 1:00 P.M., and another peak from 2:30 P.M. to 4:30 P.M. Fortunately, you can create multiple baselines, each covering different points in time. Therefore, you may decide to create a different, separate baseline for each of those periods.

Automatic Database Diagnostic Monitor

After going through the information available in a Workload Repository Report, you might feel a bit daunted in trying to interpret it all. Further, you may ask yourself, "Do I need to read through these reports every 30 minutes? Once a day? Once a week?" The answer depends on the quality of your social life. In all seriousness, however, the good news is that you do not *have* to read these reports on a twice-hourly basis, because the ADDM will do that for you.

ADDM is constantly running in the background, monitoring information that is collected in the Workload Repository. ADDM uses this data, as well as data from the Active Session History (ASH), and automatically analyzes the information to provide proactive recommendations on tuning and performance issues. The Home screen in OEM has an Advice section, with links to ADDM findings, as well as an ADDM Analysis section where this information is displayed.

ADDM can be used in two separate modes—a proactive and a reactive mode. The *proactive* mode is defined by the automatic diagnosis already mentioned. In addition to these automatic ADDM checks, other ADDM tasks can be created to look for specific problems or to go back in time and look at a period when a problem was observed or reported. This is the *reactive* mode usage of ADDM.

Viewing the ADDM Reports

The ADDM is scheduled to run automatically at the end of each Workload Repository snapshot run, so each time a snapshot is gathered, ADDM runs automatically behind the scenes, gathering information on the last 30 minutes of activity. These reports can be viewed in OEM by querying the database directly via the **dbms_advisor.get_task_report** function against the **dba_advisor_tasks view**, or you can run the addmrpt.sql script from the rdbms_home/rdbms/admin folder: @addmrpt.sql.

For those not using OEM, you are able to view and generate reports (text and html) from the command line. Report generation is achieved by using awrrpt.sql, awrgrpt.sql (for Oracle RAC), or awrrpti.sql (instance level); these scripts are located in rdbms_home/rdbms/admin. Once the report is generated, it can then be viewed in either a web browser (if HTML was chosen) or your favorite text viewer.

What Drives ADDM?

ADDM uses a combination of sources for its findings and recommendations: wait events for individual sessions, the DB Time model to determine how much DB time is spent in database calls, with a focus on reducing the overall database time spent on operations; wait classes, which are a high-level grouping of the more fine-grained wait events; and operating system and database metrics. Using this information stored in the Workload Repository and the ASH lays the groundwork for ADDM to make the call to report a finding and a subsequent recommendation.

Wait Events and Active Session History

Wait events are essentially the lifeblood of diagnosing a performance problem. Oracle provides a view called **V$ACTIVE_SESSION_HISTORY**, which maintains data from active sessions, capturing the wait events and their wait times, the SQL_ID, and session information for the waiting session. This allows you to go back and view this detailed information as it existed in the past. ADDM can use this for proactive and reactive analysis purposes.

Monitoring Oracle RAC Metrics Using AWR

The reports generated from the AWR in an Oracle RAC environment will contain a section titled "Oracle RAC Statistics," where you can easily gather information on operations related to the global cache and global enqueues. You can take a quick look at the frequency of reads from the local cache, versus the remote cache, and how frequently you need to go to disk for a read; and you can view average get times for various operations. Generally, these average values should not be higher than 30 ms as the top range, but they are normally lower. For example, the average current block receive time may be as high as 30 ms, but the average CR block receive time should not be much higher than 15 ms. The sum of the global cache current block pin time (time to process a blocking asynchronous trap or BAST), plus send and receive time altogether account for the total average time to process a current block request, and this total should not exceed 30 ms.

NOTE
These numbers are ballpark figures and only given to provide an idea of minimum expected performance. Oftentimes, values less than 10 ms are expected and easily achieved.

Interconnect Performance

As explained, the interconnect in an Oracle RAC environment is the backbone of your cluster. A highly performing, reliable interconnect is a crucial ingredient in making Cache Fusion perform well. Remember that the assumption in most cases is that a read from another node's memory via the interconnect is much faster than a read from disk—except perhaps for Solid State Disks (SSDs). The interconnect is used to transfer data and messages among the instances. An Oracle RAC cluster requires a high-bandwidth solution with low latency wherever possible. If you find that the performance of the interconnect is subpar, your Oracle RAC cluster performance will also most likely be subpar. In the case of subpar performance in an Oracle RAC environment, the interconnect configuration, including both hardware and software, should be one of the first areas you investigate.

UDP Buffers

You want the fastest possible network to be used for the interconnect. To maximize your speed and efficiency on the interconnect, you should ensure that the User Datagram Protocol (UDP) buffers are set to the correct values. On Linux, you can check this via the following command:

```
sysctl net.core.rmem_max net.core.wmem_max net.core.rmem_default net
.core.wmem_default
net.core.rmem_max = 4194304
net.core.wmem_max = 1048576
net.core.rmem_default = 262144
net.core.wmem_default = 262144
```

Alternatively, you can read the associated values directly from the respective files in the directory /proc/sys/net/core. These values can be increased via the following SYSCTL commands:

```
sysctl -w net.core.rmem_max=4194304
sysctl -w net.core.wmem_max=1048576
sysctl -w net.core.rmem_default=262144
sysctl -w net.core.wmem_default=262144
```

The numbers in this example are the recommended values for Oracle RAC on Linux and are more than sufficient for the majority of configurations. Nevertheless, let's talk about some background of the UDP buffers. The values determined by **rmem_max** and **wmem_max** are on a "per-socket" basis. So if you set **rmem_max** to 4MB, and you have 400 processes running, each with a socket open for communications in the interconnect, then each of these 400 processes could potentially use 4MB, meaning that the total memory usage could be 1.6GB just for this UDP buffer space. However, this is only "potential" usage. So if **rmem_default** is set to 1MB and **rmem_max** is set to 4MB, you know for sure that at least 400MB will be allocated (1MB per socket). Anything more than that will be allocated only as needed, up to the max value. So the total memory usage depends on the **rmem_default**, **rmem_max**, the number of open sockets, and the variable piece of how much buffer space each process is actually using. This is an unknown—but it could depend on the network latency or other characteristics of how well the network is performing and how much network load there is altogether. To get the total number of Oracle-related open UDP sockets, you can execute this command:

```
netstat -anp -udp | grep ora | wc -l
```

NOTE
Our assumption here is that the UDP is being used for the interconnect. Although that will be true in the vast majority of cases, there are some exceptions. For example, on Windows, TCP is used for Cache Fusion traffic. When InfiniBand is in use (more details on InfiniBand are provided later in the section "Interconnect Hardware"), the Reliable Datagram Sockets (RDS) protocol may be used to enhance the speed of Cache Fusion traffic. However, any other proprietary interconnect protocols are strongly discouraged, so starting with Oracle Database 11g, your primary choices are UDP, TCP (Windows), or RDS (with InfiniBand).

Jumbo Frames

Another option to increase the performance of your interconnect is the use of *jumbo frames*. When you use Ethernet, a variable frame size of 46–1500 bytes is the transfer unit used between all Ethernet participants. The upper bound is 1500 MTU (Maximum Transmission Unit). Jumbo frames allows the Ethernet frame to exceed the MTU of 1500 bytes up to a maximum of 9000 bytes (on most platforms—though platforms will vary). In Oracle RAC, the setting of **DB_BLOCK_SIZE** multiplied by the **MULTI_BLOCK_READ_COUNT** determines the maximum size of a message for the global cache, and the **PARALLEL_EXECUTION_MESSAGE_SIZE** determines the maximum size of a message used in Parallel Query. These message sizes can range from 2K to 64K or more, and hence will get fragmented more so with a lower/ default MTU. Increasing the frame size (by enabling jumbo frames) can improve the performance of the interconnect by reducing the fragmentation when shipping large amounts of data across that wire. A note of caution is in order, however: Not all hardware supports jumbo frames. Therefore, due to differences in specific server and network hardware requirements, jumbo frames must be thoroughly tested before implementation in a production environment.

Interconnect Hardware

In addition to the tuning options, you have the opportunity to implement faster hardware such as InfiniBand or 10 Gigabit Ethernet (10 GigE). InfiniBand is available and supported with two options. Reliable Datagram Sockets (RDS) protocol is the preferred option, because it offers up to 30 times the bandwidth advantage and 30 times the latency reduction over Gigabit Ethernet. IP over InfiniBand (IPoIB) is the other option, which does not do as well as RDS, since it uses the standard UDP or TCP, but it does still provide much better bandwidth and much lower latency than Gigabit Ethernet.

Another option to increase the throughput of your interconnect is the implementation of 10 GigE technology, which represents the next level of Ethernet. Although it is becoming increasingly common, note that 10 GigE does require specific certification on a platform-by-platform basis, and as of the writing of this book, it was not yet certified on all platforms. Check with Oracle Support to resolve any certification questions that you may have on your platform.

Sequence Caches

The *sequence* is an object type that requires special attention in Oracle RAC. If you created your sequences with the default cache size of 20, or you decided not to cache, your performance may suffer. A general guideline regarding sequence cache size is that the higher the insert rate, the higher the sequence cache size should be configured. When sequences are not cached or the cache size is too small, contention may become an issue on the *SQ enqueue* in Oracle RAC environments and you may see messages in the alert log indicating that you are spending too much time waiting. The **row cache enqueue lock** essentially waits for the **DC_SEQUENCES** row cache. Review the sequences in your application and consult with the application developers to determine whether sequences can be cached. In most cases, if they can be cached at all, the cache value itself is open to adjustment, so sequences that are already cached at the default value of 20 can generally be increased without much concern. However, it is critical that you discuss this with the application designer, because improper handling of sequences can cause logical corruption and functionality issues when sequence cache modifications are implemented incorrectly. Note that sequences owned by internal Oracle schemas (such as SYS, SYSTEM, CTXSYS, DBSNMP, MDSYS, OLAPSYS, WMSYS, and XDB) should not be modified without direction from Oracle Support.

HugePages on Linux

When your cluster nodes are equipped with very large memory (that is, anything over 8GB, for example), the HugePages feature of the Linux OS is strongly recommended for better stability and performance. HugePages basically provides a method for having larger memory pages than the standard, greatly improving the efficiency of memory management in large systems. In most cases, the standard page size is only 4k, so on systems with a large amount of memory, the work needed to manage all of this memory in chunks of 4k can sometimes overwhelm the kernel, leading to hangs, sluggish response, and sometimes node evictions. On Linux x64 systems, enabling HugePages will increase the page size to 2MB from the default 4k, greatly enhancing the efficiency of the kernel. Similar benefits may be seen on other OSs as well, but because the examples in this book are focused on the Linux OS, we will limit our discussion to Linux in terms of specifics. If you are running on a different OS, you should investigate with your OS vendor the possibility of increasing the memory page size on your system.

HugePages are not swappable, so there is no page-in/page-out mechanism overhead. HugePages decrease a lot of overhead in memory management, providing a faster overall memory performance. Unfortunately, Automatic Memory Management (AMM) in your database and HugePages are not compatible, as you can have only one of the features enabled. This raises the question, then, of which feature to use.

As always, the best way is to test, but as a rule of thumb, we recommend for your ASM instances to configure AMM (by setting the **MEMORY_TARGET** init parameter, which automatically precludes HugePages from being used for the ASM instance) and for your RDBMS instances to make use of the HugePages feature.

Also note that this is an all-or-nothing proposition. So, let's assume that you have a 20GB system global area (SGA), but you allocated only 19.9GB for HugePages. In that case, the instance will not be able to use HugePages because there is not enough memory to allocate the entire SGA. My Oracle Support (MOS) provides a note with a script to calculate the optimal HugePages settings.

NOTE
Xen Linux kernels (Oracle VM is Xen) do not natively support HugePages, so you cannot use this configuration in Oracle VM environments such as the test environments and some other types described in this book.

Archiving and Backing Up

If you need to recover a datafile, or multiple datafiles, whether you are doing it with the database open or mounted from a single instance, you will need the archived redo logs from *all* threads of redo, and these will need to be made available in the archive destination of the instance doing the recovery. (This assumes, of course, that you are running in archivelog mode, as would any good MAA DBA.) How you accomplish this recovery depends greatly on the type of file system that you are using for your datafiles.

Recall that you have a few options for storing files on the shared disk—Automatic Storage Management (ASM), which is the preferred method; Oracle Cluster File System (OCFS) or some other cluster file system (depending on platform); and Network File System (NFS) (remember that, as discussed in Chapter 4, ASM Cluster File System is supported only for file types that cannot be stored in ASM). Although raw device support is still available for systems that have been upgraded from earlier releases, tools such as Database Configuration Assistant (DBCA) no longer support raw devices, and their use is strongly discouraged. We will discuss some of the file storage options, and how they affect the archival process, in the sections to follow. (In Chapter 10, these options are discussed more in conjunction with the use of Recovery Manager [RMAN] for backing up the database and archivelog.)

Archiving with NFS Mount Points for Your Archive Destination

One reason that raw device support has been deprecated in Oracle Database 11*g* Release 2 is the difficulty in managing files on raw devices. Recall that if your shared files are on raw devices, you must have a separate raw slice (with a link name) for *every* file. Therefore, in this situation, not only is it difficult to manage large numbers of files, but it is also not possible to have the archived logs created on raw slices themselves. Therefore, if you were using raw devices, the most common solution to archiving in the old days would have been to have the archive destination set to the private drive on each node. However, in the event that media recovery is necessary, it would then be required that all archived redo logs from all instances be copied to the archive destination from which recovery is being initiated.

To speed up the recovery process, and to simplify it greatly, this can be avoided by setting up NFS mounts on each node, similar to the following:

```
mount -t nfs rmsclnxclu2:/u01/app/oracle/oradata/test/archive /archive
```

Here we have mounted the archive destination from Node2 (rmsclnxclu2) to a directory called /archive on Node1 (rmsclnxclu1). Assuming that node rmsclnxclu1 has the same path for archiving, you can then have two archive destinations, as such:

```
LOG_ARCHIVE_DEST_1=location='/u01/app/oracle/oradata/test/archive/'
LOG_ARCHIVE_DEST_2=location='/archive/'
```

By doing this, Node1 is now archiving to two separate destinations—the first destination is its own local archive directory. The second destination, the /archive directory, is actually the NFS mounted archive destination used by Node2. If you reverse the process on Node2, issuing an NFS mount from Node2 back to the archive destination on Node1, what you will have is both instances archiving to their own local archive destination as well as the archive destination of the other node. What this means, in the event that media recovery is needed, is that no matter from which node you do the media recovery, you should have access to the archived logs from all threads. As you can see, this can get rather complicated if you have more than two nodes, but in a two-node cluster, this is a workable solution.

NOTE
If you make both archive destinations mandatory, you may cause a hang of the instance if the NFS mount point for LOG_ARCHIVE_DEST_2 is inaccessible. Therefore, we recommend that you make the second destination optional in this configuration, to lessen the impact if one of the nodes is down.

Direct NFS Client

Oracle Database 11g introduced the Direct NFS Client. This feature integrates the NFS client functionality directly into the Oracle software. This integration allows Oracle to optimize the I/O path between Oracle and the NFS server, which results in significantly improved performance. In addition, Direct NFS Client simplifies, and in many cases automates, the performance optimization of the NFS client configuration for database workloads.

Archiving in a Cluster File System Environment

If you are using OCFS or another supported third-party cluster file system for your datafiles, you can take advantage of this to simplify the archival process. You can accomplish the same thing by having a dedicated NFS server for handling the archive logs all in a single location. Simply specify the same directory on the OCFS/CFS/NFS drive as your **LOG_ARCHIVE_DEST** on each node. Each instance will then be writing archivelogs directly to the same partition. If you are using this option, we also strongly recommend that you specify a second archive destination, either on a private drive of each node or on a second shared mount point. This will protect you in the event of a catastrophic failure of the disk subsystem where your OCFS drive(s) are located.

CAUTION
If archiving to the same partition on OCFS, a directory lock is taken out when a new archived log file is generated. This directory lock will be held until the file is created, preventing another instance from being able to archive at the same time. This will manifest itself as a short delay on the second instance, until the directory lock is released. As such, it is advisable that you create separate partitions on the OCFS drive for each instance. This sacrifices convenience somewhat, because if a recovery is needed, you will need to move or copy files into the same partition. However, it avoids a possible performance hit during normal day-to-day operations.

Archiving in an ASM Environment

Finally, if you are using ASM as the storage medium for your datafiles, you can also use an ASM disk group as a location for your Flash Recovery Area. This will allow each instance to write out the archived logs to the location that is specified by the **DB_RECOVERY_FILE_DEST** for each instance, allowing you to store the archived logs in an area accessible by all nodes for recovery. RMAN can use this location to restore and recover whatever files are necessary, with access to archived logs from all instances. Note also that by default, the value for **LOG_ARCHIVE_DEST_10** is automatically set to be equal to the location for **DB_RECOVERY_FILE_DEST** and will be used if *no* other values are set for **LOG_ARCHIVE_DEST_n** parameters. You can explicitly set one of the **LOG_ARCHIVE_DESTINATION** parameters to use the Flash Recovery Area by setting it equal to the string **LOCATION=USE_DB_ RECOVERY_FILE_DEST**. Here's an example:

```
*.LOG_ARCHIVE_DEST_1='LOCATION=/u01/app/oracle/oradata/grid/archive/'
*.LOG_ARCHIVE_DEST_2='LOCATION=USE_DB_RECOVERY_FILE_DEST'
*.db_recovery_file_dest='+ASM_TEST'
*.db_recovery_file_dest_size=2147483648
```

This is discussed in more detail in Chapter 10. When archiving to an ASM disk group, Oracle will create a directory within the disk group for each day archived logs are generated. The directories containing the archived logs will stick around and cannot be deleted, even after they have been emptied (when the Flash Recovery Area and/or the archived logs are backed up via RMAN). Once a directory has been empty for seven days, it is deleted automatically when the controlfile is backed up using RMAN (either manually, or via a controlfile autobackup). ASM is clearly the preferred choice for not only archiving, but for datafiles in general.

NOTE
A Flash Recovery Area can also be used with OCFS.

Additional Notes on Archiving in an Oracle RAC Environment

During normal operations, it is highly likely that the rate of log switches will not be the same between all instances. Therefore, if one instance is having a large amount of redo and another instance is relatively idle, the gap between SCNs and logs may grow. To keep this gap from becoming too large, Oracle will periodically kick in and force a log switch on instances that are not seeing as much activity. In addition, redo threads that are closed but enabled are also subject to this redo log *kick*, meaning that if an instance is shut down for a long period of time but you do not disable the redo thread, you may find that another instance is still generating archive logs on its behalf, which will be needed in the event of a recovery. Therefore, it is important that you keep track of all archived redo logs generated by all instances. If a node is unavailable for an extended period of time, you may want to consider removing that node from the cluster, or at least removing the instance, to simplify the maintenance.

Patches and Patchsets

Product fixes for Oracle software are called *patches*. A patch can update the executable files, libraries, and object files in the software home directory. The patch application can also update configuration files and Oracle-supplied SQL schemas. The OPatch utility is used to apply patches. Opatch is supplied by Oracle or OEM. A group of patches form a *patchset*. When you apply a patchset, many different files and utilities are modified, and this results in a version change for your Oracle software—for example, from Oracle Database 11.1.0.6 to Oracle Database 11.1.0.7. A patchset is applied by the Oracle Universal Installer (OUI).

Rolling Patch Updates

During the discussion to use either a shared Oracle home or a local Oracle home, we mentioned the option of performing a rolling patch update. The concept for rolling patching is to shut only one node down, apply the patch to this node, and bring the node back up. The remaining node(s) will stay up. This is performed node after node, until all nodes in the cluster are patched. This is the most efficient way of applying an interim patch to Oracle RAC, as at least one instance is available during patching on a different node. Performing a rolling patch update means zero downtime for the cluster database, and the MAA DBA should use this method whenever possible. That said, you should be aware that although most patches can be applied in a rolling fashion, some patches cannot. In preparation for your update, you should check the README file for the patch, as this will tell you whether you can use the rolling patch method.

NOTE
Patchsets are not rolling from a database perspective—only from a clusterware perspective. However, patchset updates and one-off patches generally are rolling from a database perspective.

MAA Workshop: *Apply a Patch with the Rolling Patch Method*

Workshop Notes

This workshop will walk you through a rolling patch update, using the Oracle Enterprise Manager 11*g* Database Control. During the workshop, we will discuss at various stages what is being done via the OEM 11*g*.

Step 1. On the Database Home page, click Software and Support.

Step 2. On the Software and Support page, select Deployment Procedures. The Deployment Procedure Manager page appears.

Step 3. Select the option Patch Oracle RAC Database (Rolling Upgrade), and then click the Schedule Deployment button. The Select Patches page appears.

Step 4. Under the heading Oracle RAC Updates, click the Add Patches button. The Search and Select Patches page appears.

Step 5. Select the Search My Oracle Support option to check for patches online. Enter parameters to limit the Search performed, if desired, and then click Go.

Step 6. Check the box next to the patches you want to install, and then click Select. The Select Patches page appears again, with the selected patches displayed in the Oracle RAC Updates section.

Step 7. After you have selected all the patches you want to install, click Next. The Credentials and Schedule page appears.

Step 8. Choose to use the Preferred Credentials. In the Schedule section of the page, choose the option One Time (Immediately) to have the patch applied right away. Click **Next** and the Review page appears.

Step 9. Review the information on this page. Notice the warning telling you that you are not able to access DB Control during the patching operation. Check the Select The Check Box To Accept This Warning And Continue. After you have checked this box, you can click Finish and patching operation starts.

Online Patching (Hot Patching)

Oracle Database 11g introduced a new feature called *online patching* or *hot patching* for the RDBMS. Usually, a RDBMS patch contains object (.o) files and/or libraries (.a files). When a regular patch is applied, this requires that you shut down the RDBMS instance, relink the Oracle binary, and restart the instance. An online patch, however, can be applied to a running RDBMS instance. An online patch is a special kind of patch that contains only a single shared library. Applying the patch does not require that you shut down the instance or relink the Oracle binary. An online patch can be installed/uninstalled using OPatch (which uses oradebug commands to install/ uninstall the patch). Because of the current Oracle architecture, not all fixes and diagnostics can be bundled as an online patch.

The Out-of-Place Patchset Model

The concept of the *out-of-place patchset model* is to allow the installation of the patch (which is actually a whole new release) into a separate home while the database is still up. This means that downtime is greatly reduced, and it also enhances the ability to roll things back if needed, because the old home is left untouched. This has always been possible, but 11.2.0.2 makes it easier by not requiring two installations (that is, a base install plus a patchset are not necessary, because 11.2.0.2 is a full release).

Proactive Maintenance Strategy

A critical task of the MAA DBA is to stay in front of bugs and known issues. The MAA DBA has to avoid situations in which the business requirements will not allow a downtime when a patch has to be applied immediately because a bug seriously affects the system. Proactive/planned patching helps you to avoid having to install a patchset at an inconvenient time. This is often the case with reactive patching. You must be aware, that in each patchset many issues are fixed; thus, a proactive release and maintenance planning can avoid potential problems by keeping up with the various fixes delivered through patchsets.

Proactive application of patchsets, critical merge patches, and one-off fixes can avoid potential availability and integrity issues caused by encountering product defects in production environments. Although proactive patching provides significant benefits in terms of release stability and downtime avoidance, it does not guarantee a defect-free environment. Proactive patching will provide significant benefits when incorporated into a planned release and maintenance strategy.

Recommended Patches

My Oracle Support maintains a list with recommended patches in the My Oracle Support Note: 756671.1. Following are some of the advantages of recommended patches:

- Fix a set of critical issues commonly encountered in targeted environments and configurations.

- Stabilize production environments because the patches address known critical issues.

- Save time and cost by eliminating rediscovery of known issues.

- Patches are tested as a single combined unit, resulting in increased quality and eliminating the risk of combining patches that are only independently tested.

- It is easier to identify patches applicable for a targeted environment/ configuration.

Patchset Updates

To promote proactive patching strategies, patchset updates (PSUs) are released by Oracle on a quarterly basis. PSUs are proactive, cumulative patches that contain recommended bug fixes that are released on a regular and predictable schedule. PSUs are on the same quarterly schedule as the critical patch updates (CPUs), specifically the Tuesday closest to the 15th of January, April, July, and October. There is no need to apply the CPU and PSU for a specific quarter; the PSU contains the quarterly CPU.

NOTE
If you have applied a previous quarter's PSU and want to apply the latest quarter's CPU, the previously installed PSU will be rolled off (it will conflict). That said, once you adopt a PSU patching strategy you should not go back to applying CPU patches (remembering that CPUs are included in PSUs).

PSU patches are intended to be low-risk. This is accomplished by controlling content and thorough testing. By including the patch recommendations in one patch, Oracle is able to ensure that recommended fixes work well together. PSU patches include critical technical fixes that may affect a large number of customers and that are already proven in the field. They do not include changes that require recertification (for example, fixes that cause optimizer plan changes) or fixes that require configuration changes.

Needless to say, the MAA DBA should apply and test every new patch in a separated test environment before deploying them in a production system.

Managing the Oracle RAC Database with SRVCTL

Oracle provides certain command line utilities that allow you to query and change the status, or change the configuration of your cluster and Oracle RAC components. Chapter 3 discussed **crsctl**, **ocrcheck**, and **ocrconfig**. You also learned about the use of SRVCTL to manage the SCAN and the listeners. In this section, we will focus on examples of how to use SRVCTL correctly to manage your database and ASM. Managing services and node applications with SRVCTL is discussed in Chapter 8.

The Server Control Utility (SRVCTL)

The Server Control Utility (SRVCTL) is a command-line utility to administer your ASM instance, Oracle RAC instances, node applications, and database services. The key point to remember when using SRVCTL in your cluster is that SRVCTL retrieves and writes configuration data from and into the Oracle Cluster Registry (OCR). You should be aware that on your nodes exist two SRVCTL utilities—one at RDBMS home and another one in the Grid Infrastructure (GI) home—and that both are owned by different users. If you need to manage a database or instance, you should use RDBMS user and the SRVCTL from the RDBMS home. For GI-related tasks, use GI user and SRVCTL from GI home. Also note that from Oracle Database 11*g* Release 2 on, ASM is controlled by the GI user, but at 10*g* Release 2 and 11*g* Release 1, it needs to be controlled by the ASM/RDBMS user.

Manage ASM with SRVCTL

The SRVCTL from the Grid Infrastructure home can be used to manage ASM—but you cannot use the SRVCTL binary in the database home to manage ASM. Since Oracle Database 11*g* Release 2 ASM is part of the Oracle Clusterware stack, and when OCR and voting disks are stored on ASM, ASM starts when the Clusterware stack is started. The **srvctl disable asm** command does not prevent the ASM instance from starting. Oracle ASM, therefore, starts as needed by the Oracle Clusterware stack. The **srvctl disable asm** command prevents the ASM Oracle Clusterware proxy resource, and any resources that depends on it, from starting. So the command prevents Oracle Clusterware-managed objects, such as databases, disk groups, and file systems, that depend on Oracle ASM from starting. For example, the **srvctl start database | diskgroup | filesystem** command fails to start any of those objects on nodes where the ASM Oracle Clusterware proxy resource is disabled. The command also prevents the **srvctl start asm** command from starting Oracle ASM on remote nodes.

CAUTION
*To shut down ASM, CRS needs to be shut down with the **crsctl stop crs** command. Never kill the ASM instance!*

To get the configuration details of ASM, use the following command:

```
[grid@ratlnx01 bin]$ ./srvctl config asm
ASM home: /oragrid
ASM listener: LISTENER
```

The status switch gives you the status and names of ASM on each node by using the following syntax:

```
[grid@ratlnx01 bin]$ ./srvctl status asm -n ratlnx01
ASM is running on ratlnx01
[grid@ratlnx01 bin]$ ./srvctl status asm -n ratlnx02
ASM is running on ratlnx02
```

To get the information on what nodes a certain ASM disk group is running, execute the following command, where the **–g** switch specifies the disk group name, in our example **dbdata**:

```
[grid@ratlnx01 bin]$ ./srvctl status diskgroup -g dbdata
Disk Group dbdata is running on ratlnx01,ratlnx02
```

Managing Databases and Instances via SRVCTL

Similar to ASM, SRVCTL can be used to retrieve information regarding databases and instances registered in the Oracle Cluster Registry (OCR). The **srvctl config** command, for example, will show the names of any databases that are registered in the OCR:

```
[grid@ratlnx01 bin]$ ./srvctl config
maadb
```

You can use the database name to retrieve additional information, such as the instances and nodes associated with the database. For example, the following example shows a database with unique db_name of *maadb*. This command will give us information about the maadb database, as stored in the OCR:

```
[grid@ratlnx01 bin]$ ./srvctl config database -d maadb
Database unique name: maadb
Database name: maadb
Oracle home: /ora01/app/oracle/product/11.2.0/db_1
Oracle user: oracle
Spfile: +DBDATA/maadb/spfilemaadb.ora
Domain:
Start options: open
Stop options: immediate
```

```
Database role: PRIMARY
Management policy: AUTOMATIC
Server pools: maadb
Database instances: maadb1,maadb2
Disk Groups: DBDATA,DBFLASH
Services:
Database is administrator managed
```

This tells us that database has instances called *maadb1* and *maadb2*. We can get the status of these instances and the node names where they are running by using the **status** command:

```
[grid@ratlnx01 bin]$ ./srvctl status database -d maadb
Instance maadb1 is running on node ratlnx01
Instance maadb2 is running on node ratlnx02
```

A database can be added or removed from the configuration (OCR) using the **srvctl add database** or **srvctl remove database** commands as well. The remove operation may be necessary if a database has been deleted, but was not deleted through the Database Configuration Assistant (DBCA). This would leave information about the database in the OCR, which means that you would then be unable to re-create the database using the DBCA until that information has been removed. A command such as the following can then be used to remove the database from the OCR:

```
srvctl remove database -d maadb
```

A database can be manually added using the **add database** command. In our example with the grid database, and the grid1 and grid2 instance, we could re-create the basic configuration with a couple of simple commands such as these:

```
srvctl add database -d maadb -o /ora01/app/oracle/product/11.2.0/db_1
srvctl add instance -d maadb -i maadb1 -n ratlnx01
srvctl add instance -d maadb -i maadb2 -n ratlnx02
```

Here, **–d** signifies the unique database name, **–o** the ORACLE_HOME, **–i** the instance name, and **–n** the node name. These basic commands will define a database in the OCR as well as the instances and nodes associated with that database.

Disabling Objects via SRVCTL

Notice that the commands we have discussed so far are automatically run when the database is created using the DBCA. The information provided here is intended to help you understand the configuration operations undertaken by the DBCA and how they relate to CRS. Should you decide to create a database manually, you would need to run these commands manually to ensure that the database is properly registered with CRS via the OCR. However, it is strongly recommended that you use the DBCA to create the databases to avoid any issues with possible misconfiguration issues.

As mentioned at the beginning of this section, SRVCTL will come in handy for disabling the monitoring of these resources by CRS so that maintenance operations can be undertaken. Disabling an object with SRVCTL will prevent the cluster from attempting to restart it when it is brought down, thus allowing it to be repaired or allowing other maintenance operations. The Disabled status persists through reboots, avoiding automatic restarts of an instance or the database—an instance or database will remain as Disabled until a corresponding Enable command is run.

If you shut down the instance through SQL*Plus, CRS will leave it alone—but on a reboot, CRS will try to start the instance again, even though you do not want this until you are completely finished with your maintenance. To avoid this, you must first shut the instance down. You could do this via SQL*Plus, or you could use SRVCTL to stop the instance; after this, simply disable the instance with SRVCTL, as in the following example:

```
srvctl stop instance -d maadb -i maadb1 -o immediate
srvctl disable instance -d maadb -i maadb1
```

You can view the status of these targets from the OEM Grid Control screen by choosing the Targets tab and then All Targets. No special status indicates that the instance (maadb1) is disabled—the targets are simply noted as being Down or unavailable. Attempting to start the instances would be allowed—the disabled status simply indicates that CRS is not currently monitoring them. After the subsequent reboots, and confirmations that the maintenance or repair has been completed to your satisfaction on this node, the instance can be re-enabled again using SRVCTL in the reverse order from the preceding example:

```
srvctl enable instance -d maadb -i maadb1
srvctl start instance -d maadb -i maadb1 -o open
```

After a few moments, you should be able to refresh the screen in the Targets option of OEM Grid Control and see that the database is back online.

In addition to taking a single instance offline and disabling it, it is also possible to stop and disable the entire database using the **srvctl stop database** and **srvctl disable database** commands:

```
srvctl stop database -d maadb
srvctl disable database -d maadb
```

These commands will stop or disable *all* instances in the cluster. OEM 11g uses this command if you choose the Shutdown All option when you shut down the database from the Cluster Database screen.

NOTE
Although you may be able to cancel running SRVCTL commands by pressing CTRL-C, you may corrupt your configuration data by doing this. You are strongly advised not to attempt to terminate SRVCTL in this manner.

Management Through Policies

Chapter 3 explained the concept of *policy-managed databases*. To refresh your knowledge, remember that with an administrator-managed database (the traditional way), the DBA explicitly defines what instance runs on which node. With a policy-managed database, the resource requirements of the workload are defined, so you define how many instances you want your database to run on, and this cardinality can be increased or decreased if needed. Using a policy-managed database, you remove the hard-coding of a specific instance to a specific node. In this section, you'll learn about how you can manage the policies.

A server pool is defined by three attributes: the minimum number of servers on which it should run, the maximum number of servers, and the importance of that server pool. Suppose, for example, that you have two server pools, each with a minimum number of three servers defined. Usually six servers are available, but one server has gone down and only five servers remain up. In this case, the server pool with the lower importance has to run on two nodes only, and the server pool with the higher importance runs on three. You can define importance using a rating of 0 to 1000, where 0 is the lowest importance.

MAA Workshop: *Convert an Administrator-Managed Database into a Policy-Managed Database*

Workshop Notes

This workshop will walk you through the conversion of an administrator-managed database into a policy-managed database.

Step 1. Check the current configuration of all services and the database—so that if you make a mistake and need to recover, you will know what the configuration looked like when you began:

```
srvctl config database -d db_unique_name
srvctl config service -d db_unique_name
```

Step 2. Create a server pool for the policy-managed database (you must be a cluster administrator to do this), as follows:

```
srvctl add srvpool -g server_pool -l 0 -u n
```

In this command, **n** is the number of servers you want in the server pool.

Step 3. Modify the database to be in the new server pool, as follows:

```
srvctl modify database -d db_unique_name -g server_pool
```

Step 4. Check the status of the database to confirm that it is now policy managed, as follows:

```
srvctl status database -d db_unique_name
srvctl status service -d db_unique_name
```

> **NOTE**
> *Conversely, you cannot directly convert a policy-managed database to an administrator-managed database. Instead, you can remove the policy-managed configuration using the **srvctl remove database** and **srvctl remove service** commands, and then create a new administrator-managed database with the **srvctl add database** command.*

As you noticed, SRVCTL, in conjunction with the keyword **srvpool**, can be used to add a server pool. It can be used as well to modify, list the configuration of, or remove server pools. The following example changes the importance rank to 0, the minimum size to 2, and the maximum size to 4 for the server pool srvpool1 on the nodes mynode3 and mynode4:

```
$ srvctl modify srvpool -g srvpool1 -i 0 -l 2 -u 4 -n mynode3, mynode4
```

The next example removes the server pool:

```
$ srvctl remove srvpool -g srvpool1
```

If databases or services depend upon this server pool, remove them first so that this operation will succeed. If you successfully remove server_pool, the CRS daemon may assign its servers to other server pools, depending upon their minimum size, maximum size, and importance. The CRS daemon may also return these servers to the FREE server pool.

Managing Diagnostic Data

Beginning with Release 11*g*, Oracle Database introduced the advanced *fault diagnosability infrastructure* for collecting and managing diagnostic data. The infrastructure is designed to target critical errors such as those caused by code bugs, metadata corruption, and customer data corruption. When one of these critical errors occurs, it is assigned an incident number, and diagnostic data for the error is immediately captured and tagged with this number. The collected data is stored in the Automatic Diagnostic Repository (ADR), and from here it can be analyzed by the incident number.

Automatic Diagnostic Repository

The ADR is a special file-based repository that is automatically maintained by Oracle 11*g* to hold diagnostic information about critical error events. The diagnostic information includes trace files, dumps, and core files, plus new types of diagnostic data that enable customers and Oracle Support to identify and resolve problems more effectively.

ADRCI Command-Line Utility

The ADR Command Interpreter (ADRCI) is the command line utility that can be used to investigate incidents and to view health check reports. If you want to upload ADR data to Oracle Support, ADRCI can be used to package and upload first-failure diagnostic data. ADRCI also lets you view the names of the trace files in the ADR and view the alert log with XML tags stripped, with and without content filtering. To retrieve a list of incidents, do the following:

```
ADRCI> show incident
```

ADR Structure

The ADR root directory is known as the *ADR base*. Its location is set by the **DIAGNOSTIC_DEST** initialization parameter. Within ADR base, multiple ADR homes can exist, where each ADR home is the root directory for all diagnostic data. In an Oracle RAC environment with Oracle ASM, each database instance, Oracle ASM instance, and listener has an ADR home. The location of each ADR home is provided by the following path, which starts at the ADR base directory: diag/product_type/product_id/instance_id.

For example, for a database with a security identifier (SID) of *maadb1* and database unique name of *maadb*, the ADR home would be in the following location: ADR_base/diag/rdbms/maadb/maadb1/. Similarly, the ADR home path for the Oracle ASM instance +asm1 would be ADR_base/diag/asm/+asm/+asm1/.

Within each ADR home directory, you find the subdirectories, as listed next. These subdirectories contain the diagnostic data.

Alert	The XML-Formatted Alert Log
Cdump	Core files
Incident	Multiple subdirectories; each subdirectory is named for a particular incident and each contains dumps pertaining only to that incident
Trace	Background and server process trace files, SQL trace files, and the text-formatted alert log
(others)	Other subdirectories of ADR home, which store incident packages, health monitor reports, and other information

A query against the **V$DIAG_INFO** view lists all important ADR locations for the current Oracle Database instance:

```
SELECT * FROM V$DIAG_INFO;
INST_ID NAME VALUE
------- -------------------- -----------------------------------------
--------------------
1 Diag Enabled TRUE
1 ADR Base /u01/oracle
1 ADR Home /u01/oracle/diag/rdbms/maadb/maadb1
1 Diag Trace /u01/oracle/diag/rdbms/maadb/ maadb1/trace
1 Diag Alert /u01/oracle/diag/rdbms/maadb/ maadb1/alert
1 Diag Incident /u01/oracle/diag/rdbms/maadb/ maadb1/incident
1 Diag Cdump /u01/oracle/diag/rdbms/maadb/ maadb1/cdump
1 Health Monitor /u01/oracle/diag/rdbms/maadb/ maadb1/hm
1 Default Trace File /u01/oracle/diag/rdbms/maadb/ maadb1/trace/orcl_
ora_22769.trc
1 Active Problem Count 2
1 Active Incident Count 8
```

ADR in Oracle RAC

The ADR is stored outside of the database to be available for problem diagnosis when the database is down. This brings up the question of where to store the ADR. In an Oracle RAC environment, each node can have an ADR base on its own local storage, or the ADR base can be set to a location on shared storage. The following are two advantages of the shared storage approach:

- Diagnostic data from all instances can be displayed in a single report.

- You can use the Data Recovery Advisor to help diagnose and repair corrupted data blocks, corrupted or missing files, and other data failures. (For Oracle RAC, the Data Recovery Advisor requires shared storage.)

Nevertheless, you should keep in mind that you might need the ADR when certain functionality of your cluster is not available. If, for example, ASM or GI in general is not working and you configured ADR to be stored in ACFS, you would be left in the dark with no diagnostic data to use for troubleshooting. Thus, we recommend that you not use ACFS to store the ADR.

Reporting and Resolving a Problem

Problem resolution starts by accessing the Database Home page in OEM and reviewing critical error alerts. Select an alert for which you want to view details, and then go to the Problem Details page. Examine the problem details and view a list of all incidents that were recorded for the problem. Display findings from any health checks that were automatically run. Create a service request with My Oracle Support and record the service request number with the problem information. Package and upload the diagnostic data for the problem to Oracle Support. Then, set the status for the incidents to Closed.

Summary

Our goal in this chapter was to familiarize you with the nuances of administering a database in an Oracle RAC environment. Our hope is that you gained some sense of the tasks involved, and that ultimately you will realize that managing an Oracle RAC environment is not all that daunting. The chapters that follow will discuss additional database features (including Oracle Data Guard, RMAN, and Flashback) that will further your goal of becoming a Maximum Availability DBA; meanwhile, you should practice and master the skills and tasks discussed in this chapter.

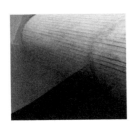

CHAPTER
8

Utility Computing:
Applications as Services

ou will hear the term "services" used often in Oracle Database 11*g* and in the realm of Maximum Availability. Although the concept of service is nothing new to the computing world, the concept of services in Oracle 11*g* needs to be explained in more detail. So, what exactly are services?

Services Concepts

Services are associated with an application's front end, which needs to connect to the database on the back end. Services enable the virtualization of an Oracle database server from the application using it. Instead of connecting to a physical host, the application connects to a service name.

In the grid computing world, customers (end users) do not care where the application is going when they run it. They do not think in terms of the database at the back end, behind it all. Customers think of computing in terms of services or applications at the front end—e-mail, calendaring applications, order entry, accounting, reporting, and so on. To the customer at the front end, it matters not where the power behind the scenes comes from. Just as a utility customer who plugs in an appliance does not care about the source of the electricity, an application user does not care where or how the data gets there. Utility customers do not think of appliances in terms of the power source; they think of appliances in terms of a hair dryer or a Nintendo—completely different things in the mind of the consumer, regardless of the fact that they both are plugged into the same grid. From the grid perspective, all that matters is that the electricity is there when it is needed.

Services as a Workload

By the same token, the application user cares not where the data comes from. All that matters is that when the application gets "plugged in" to the database, it gets what it requires—service, in the form of data.

In a general sense, services are essentially associated with an application that a customer may be using in the environment—connecting to, or plugging into, a database in a grid at the back end. In a more specific sense, however, services are defined as an abstract way to group logical workloads. Services should be representative of a workload generated by a group of consumers that have something in common—they are using the same functionality within the database, and they have the same needs with regard to availability and priority within the database. In addition, they generally use a similar amount of resources. You might also think of services in terms of a grouping of clients accessing the same or similar database objects, perhaps under the same Service Level Agreement (SLA).

Services as the Application's Interface to the Database

A simple way to think of a service is in terms of the application itself, rather than in terms of the database. The application connects to a service, which is defined within the database grid. A service gives the MAA DBA the ability to isolate workloads and manage them independently. This is more important than ever in an era of consolidation and centralized computing. More and more, applications are being consolidated to run against a single back-end database, which is part of a highly available, clustered environment. Services are a crucial part of this architecture, because they enable this isolation within the database and allow for individual prioritization and monitoring.

A service can be enabled or disabled based on the needs of the consumers of the service and the need to perform maintenance on all or a portion of the database. For example, by isolating services from each other, you can perform application-specific maintenance on a schema associated with the service, without affecting other services/applications. Simply disable the service for which the maintenance is scheduled, and then re-enable it once the maintenance is completed.

Aside from isolating different applications and workloads from one another, the service definition within the database grid determines on which nodes and/or instances the service (client application) can run. In the event of a failure, Oracle relocates services (client applications) based again on the service definition, which defines which nodes the service is allowed to run if the primary service has failed. All of this is irrelevant and transparent to the user/consumer of the service. The MAA DBA, on the other hand, has the power to determine where these services run, what is their priority, and how they are handled in the event of a failure.

Services from the Database Perspective

So, how is this managed on the back end? You know that a service is viewed by the user as a front-end application. But how does the MAA DBA make sense out of this? How is this controlled from the database perspective? There are several pieces to that puzzle. At the most basic level, services are defined at the database level via the parameter **SERVICE_NAMES = *comma delimited list of service_names***. With this parameter, the MAA DBA can define various connection types into the database, at the instance level, that are associated at the client end with various applications. For example, a given instance in a database cluster may have the following **SERVICE_NAMES** parameter defined:

```
SERVICE_NAMES=payroll, accounting, reporting, oltp
```

While another instance in the same database cluster may have a different value for **SERVICE_NAMES** defined:

```
SERVICE_NAMES=payroll, oltp
```

Thus, clients connecting via the payroll or OLTP service will be able to connect to either node, depending on its availability, while the accounting and reporting clients will be able to connect only to the first instance. This gives the MAA DBA the flexibility to segment different portions of the user population across different instances. In addition, we are prioritizing services by saying that the payroll and OLTP services are more critical and less tolerant of failure, so these services need to be able to run on either node in the cluster. Obviously, the more instances existing in the cluster, the more flexibility you will have.

Prioritizing Services for Availability

As you can see, one way of prioritizing services is to define which services get the most/best service by granting certain applications the ability to run on more than one node at any given time. For example, suppose you have a three-node cluster. Based on your business needs and the resources at your disposal, you may decide that the payroll and OLTP service can run on any of the three nodes, the accounting service can run on Node1 or Node2, and the reporting service can only run on Node3. When all three nodes are functioning correctly, all of these applications are running correctly and will have access to their defined node. However, in the event of a failure of one of the nodes, only the OLTP and payroll services are still guaranteed to have access to both remaining instances. The accounting service will have access to at least one remaining instance, but there is no guarantee that the reporting service would still have access.

By defining it this way, the MAA DBA is essentially saying that OLTP and payroll have higher priority than the other services. Should Node1, Node2, or Node3 go down, the OLTP and payroll services would still have access to the two remaining nodes, but we will not necessarily want *all* applications running against these remaining two nodes. Instead, we want only our highest priority applications running—that is, the applications that have the greatest requirements in our business environment for high availability. By giving the reporting service access only to one of the nodes, we are saying that the priority for that service is not as high. In the event of a failure of Node3, we do not want that service running on the other nodes, as the remaining two nodes are going to be more heavily loaded than they would be otherwise. If Node1 or Node2 fails, the reporting service could easily be disabled on Node3. This helps to ensure not only that these applications are running, but also that there is enough capacity to handle the load until such time as the failed node can be repaired or a new node brought back online.

Resource Manager and Services

In the preceding example, it is easy enough to see that, should a node fail, the OLTP and payroll services are guaranteed to have access to one of the remaining nodes. However, as we explained, there may be an undue load placed on those remaining nodes. Suppose that the surviving nodes are Node1 and Node3. These are nodes that we have also defined as being available for the reports and accounting services. Now, all of the services are still accessible, which is a good thing. However, all services are running on two nodes now instead of three. Ideally, this will have been planned out such that the nodes with the highest number of services assigned are also the nodes that are the most robust—that is, they have the greatest capacity, but this may not always be the case. Therefore, this could impact our most important services—namely, the payroll and OLTP services. As mentioned, we could easily disable the reporting service for a period of time, but that is a manual operation.

In this regard, Resource Manager can be used at the service level to define priorities for a given service. In prior releases, Resource Manager was used primarily at the session level, but since Oracle Database 10*g*, consumer groups can be defined for a given service so that services such as OLTP and payroll can be given a higher priority than services such as accounting and reporting. This can be done via Oracle Enterprise Manager (OEM) 11*g*, as we will discuss later in this chapter.

Resource Manager can intelligently manage resources such that when a machine is at full utilization of a given resource, certain groups/services are limited in how much of that resource they can use, based on the consumer group definition to which they are mapped. However, when the machine is not fully utilized, the database (knowing that there is excess capacity available) intelligently allows groups to consume more than their quota, because the capacity is there.

In our earlier example, assume that the reporting service was mapped to a consumer group that allots to it 10 percent of the total CPU. Thus, if the machine is 100 percent utilized, clients connecting to the reporting service will be allotted only 10 percent of the CPU, overall, while the remaining services are allowed to use 90 percent of the CPU. However, when the machine is *not* fully utilized (meaning the remaining services are not using their allotted 90 percent), the reporting service is allowed more than 10 percent of CPU, if needed, since the excess capacity is available. Therefore, at times when all three instances in our three-node cluster are running, the reporting service will most likely be able to run unfettered. However, if a node fails, leaving the remaining nodes running at higher loads than normal, the limits applied through Resource Manager will kick in automatically.

Services in Policy Managed Databases

A service for a policy-managed database is defined to a server pool where the database is running. You can define the service as either *uniform* (running on all instances in the server pool) or *singleton* (running on only one instance in the server pool). For singleton services, Oracle RAC chooses on which instance in the server pool the service is active. If that instance fails, the service fails over to another instance in the server pool. A service can run in only one server pool. The concept of policy-managed databases is explained in Chapter 3.

Distributing Work Among Oracle RAC Nodes for Performance

One of the fundamental features of Oracle RAC, in addition to providing redundancy, is the ability to spread workload efficiently across several machines. To achieve minimal delays for the user requests, you have to ensure that the user is connected to a node for which resources are available. Like the approach to avoid single points of failure, the load balancing approach is ideally performed on every level of your environment. Let's have a look at how load balancing is implemented across your Oracle RAC nodes.

Client-Side Load Balancing

Oracle has attempted to move more and more of the load-balancing configuration onto the server side, lessening the need to configure the client. With Oracle Database 11*g* Release 2 and the introduction of the Single Client Access Name (SCAN), this has been consequently improved. Prior to 11*g* Release 2 (you can still set up your clients that way), the client-side load balancing was implemented by providing a list of node addresses and setting the parameter **LOAD_BALANCE=yes** in the clients tnsnames.ora file:

```
grid_callcenter =
  (DESCRIPTION =
ADDRESS_LIST(
    (ADDRESS = (PROTOCOL = TCP)(HOST=ratlnx01-vip)(PORT = 1521))
    (ADDRESS = (PROTOCOL = TCP)(HOST=ratlnx02-vip)(PORT = 1521))
)
    (LOAD_BALANCE = yes)
    (CONNECT_DATA =
      (SERVER = DEDICATED)
      (SERVICE_NAME = grid_callcenter)
    )
  )
```

The client then randomly selects an address from the address list and connects to that node's listener. This is not actually real load balancing because it does not take any existing load of the instances into consideration. With 11*g* Release 2, when clients make use of the SCAN (with more than one IP address assigned to it), the client-side load balancing is moved to the Domain Name System (DNS) server. The client configuration contains only a single SCAN name, and this is resolved by the DNS to one of the assigned IP addresses and provided to the client. The client now connects to the SCAN listener running on that SCAN VIP.

Server-Side Load Balancing

When a SCAN listener receives a connection request, it will check which is the least loaded instance for the service provided in the connect request. The local listener on this node will then get the redirected connection request, provide its VIP address to the client, and create the connection to the database instance.

For each service, you can define the connection load-balancing goal that you want the listener to use. You can use a goal of either long or short for connection load balancing. These goals have the following characteristics:

- **Short**   Connections are distributed across instances based on the amount of time that the service is used. Use the short connection load-balancing goal for applications that have connections of brief duration.

- **Long**   Connections are distributed across instances based on the number of sessions in each instance, for each instance that supports the service. Use the long connection load-balancing goal for applications that have connections of long duration.

Load-Balancing Configuration

The server parameter files (SPFILE) parameter **REMOTE_LISTENER** ensures cross registration of the instances with listeners on other nodes. Oracle Database 11*g* Release 2 RAC instances register with SCAN listeners only as remote listeners. The **REMOTE_LISTENER** parameter must be set to **SCAN:PORT**. In 11*g* Release 2, the listener no longer requires tnsnames.ora file entries. Because the **REMOTE_LISTENER** is configured to reference the **SCAN:PORT**, there is no need for a tnsnames.ora entry.

Event Notification

One of the main requirements for an MAA system is to provide fast notification when the status of a critical component changes. The application user does not care that another instance could service his request, as he looks at a hanging screen caused by the application server waiting for a time-out from a failed instance. The application needs to be quickly notified if something happens to the database, the database server, or any other critical component. Such notification allows the application to execute programs that handle this event. If these programs are executed shortly after a cluster component failure or cluster reorganization occurs, costly connection time-outs or application time-outs can be avoided. In Oracle Clusterware, the Event Manager daemon (EVMd) is responsible for generating these events.

Notification Concepts

Notification is the first step in the process for application recovery, service recovery, offline diagnosis, and fault repair. Notification occurs in several forms.

In-band Notification   Using strong and weak dependencies in Cluster Ready Services (CRS) and special CRS events for check and fail actions, dependent resources receive an in-band notification to start and stop. These events occur as a result of starting or stopping interdependent resources, and as a result of dependent resources failing and restarting. These notifications are considered in-band because they are posted and processed synchronously as part of CRS managing the system. Dependent resources are, for example, listeners and database instances—the listeners depend on the virtual IPs (VIPs) and the database instances depend on Automatic Storage Management (ASM).

Out-of-band Notification   Using callouts, High Availability (HA) events, paging, e-mail, and so on, from the enterprise console, status changes, fault notifications, and fault escalation are forwarded to invoke repair and to interrupt applications to respond to the service change. These notifications are considered out-of-band because they are issued asynchronously through gateway processes out of CRS to listeners, enterprise consoles, and callouts.

Error and Event Logs   When a fault occurs in any layer, details of the error are reported to persistent event logs. This is the case for all error conditions, including those that are automatically recovered by the CRS system. For expediency, all event logs should have a consistent format and should be logged to a consistent location. Data collection is essential to ensure that a root cause for the condition can be found and found in minimal time. Once the condition is identified, a repair can be implemented.

Oracle Notification Service

The Oracle Notification Service (ONS) receives a subset of published clusterware events from the local EVMd. This is a publish-and-subscribe service to propagate messages within the Oracle RAC cluster and to clients or application-tier systems. ONS handles two types of events: Fast Application Notification (FAN) events and Load Balancing events. ONS is installed automatically as part of node applications (nodeapps) on each node of the cluster. The ONS daemons run locally, sending and receiving messages from other nodes' ONS daemons.

NOTE
Every node runs one ONS agent and one eONS agent within Cluster Ready Services daemon's (CRSD) oraagent process. The Enhanced ONS daemon (eONS) will be removed and its functionality included in EVM in 11.2.0.2.

Fast Application Notification

Oracle RAC uses FAN to notify processes about cluster configuration and service-level information. These events include status changes such as UP and DOWN for instances, services, and nodes. In addition, FAN publishes load balancing advisory events. When an instance failure occurs, a FAN event is published immediately and the application can react immediately. If the application is not written to handle FAN events, it would have to wait until the problem is detected, which usually means applications time out, resulting in frustrated users. FAN messages are propagated both internally, within the cluster, and externally, to client machines.

Fast Connection Failover The easiest way to make use of FAN is to use Oracle clients that support Fast Connection Failover (FCF). Examples of such clients are Java Database Connectivity (JDBC), Oracle Call Interface (OCI), and Oracle Data Provider for .NET (ODP.NET). When they are configured to use FCF, they automatically subscribe to FAN events and can quickly react to events from the database cluster. When an instance failure occurs, the client receives a down event and all connections to that instance using that service are terminated. Connections that are active at the time of failure are cleaned up and the application will immediately receive notification about the failure. Any uncommitted transaction will be rolled back through database recovery. The connection pool will create additional connections as it requires them. When the failed instance is restarted, it immediately receives an up event and the connection pool will create new connections to the instance. Assuming that connection load balancing is set up correctly, the new connections should go to the instance that was restarted.

NOTE
Do not configure Transparent Application Failover (TAF) with FCF for JDBC clients because TAF processing will interfere with FAN ONS processing. TAF can use FAN but cannot use it with FCF.

Load Balancing Advisory

We mentioned that applications can take advantage of the load balancing FAN events. The load balancing advisory provides information about the current service levels that the Oracle RAC database instances are providing. When such events are implemented, requests can be directed to the instance in the cluster that will provide the best performance based on the workload management directives that you have defined for that service.

The load balancing advisory is integrated with the Automatic Workload Repository (AWR) built into Oracle Database 11*g*. The AWR measures response time and CPU consumption for each service. The advice provided by the load balancing advisory takes into account the power of the server as well as the current workload of the service on the server. If you enable the load balancing advisory, you improve the throughput of applications, because workloads will not be directed to instances that are already overworked, slow, or not responding. The best way to take advantage of the load balancing advisory is to use an integrated Oracle client that has the Runtime Connection Load Balancing feature. As Oracle integrated clients have FAN integrated, they are always aware of the current Oracle RAC status.

To make use of the load balancing advisory, you must set up your service with a service-level goal. This enables the publication of FAN load balancing events. You can choose from two types of service-level goals:

- **Service Time**   Requests are directed to instances according to their response time. To make this decision, the load balancing advisory considers the elapsed time for work done by connections using the service, as well as available bandwidth to the service. Set this goal for workloads where the requests do not complete in a similar amount of time.

- **Throughput**   When the goal throughput is set, the efficiency of an instance is measured, rather than the response time. The load balancing advisory measures the percentage of the total response time that the CPU consumes for the service. Set this goal for workloads where each work request completes in a similar amount of time.

A service-level goal of *None* means that the load balancing for that service is disabled.

FAN Callouts

A *FAN callout* is a server-side executable file. The callout can be either a shell script or a precompiled executable written in any programming language. Oracle RAC will run the callout immediately when an HA event occurs. A FAN callout can, for example, send a text message automatically when an instance goes down or stop a server-side application when an instance goes down. FAN callouts can be used to address many issues, and Oracle Technology Network (OTN) provides FAN callout sample code you can reuse or customize for your needs.

The executable files for FAN callouts must be stored in the Grid_home/racg/usrco subdirectory. If this directory does not exist, you must create it with the same permissions and ownership as the Grid_home/racg/tmp subdirectory. All executables in Grid_home/racg/usrco are executed immediately, in an asynchronous fashion, when a FAN event is received. Copies of the FAN callout executable files must be stored on every node of the cluster.

Creating Services and Callouts

Now that you understand the concepts of services, events, and callouts, let's review some examples showing how to create services and callouts.

Creating Services

You can create services in two basic ways. The most common is using the GUI functionality from Oracle Enterprise Manager 11*g* Database Control/Enterprise Manager 11*g* Grid Control. (Note that the option to use the Database Configuration Assistant (DBCA) is no longer available in 11*g* Release 2.) The second way is to create services via the command line using the SRVCTL utility. In addition, the Net Configuration Assistant (NETCA) can be used to configure clients to connect to a service. However, by and large, we recommend that Oracle Enterprise Manager (OEM) 11*g* be used to create the services, because it will automate the process and do all of the necessary work for you. In addition, once the services are created, OEM 11*g* can be used to monitor and manage services—starting, stopping, and relocating services between nodes.

MAA Workshop: *Using OEM 11g Grid Control to Create Services*

Workshop Notes

This workshop will walk you through the creation and definition of services using the OEM 11*g* Grid Control. You'll see what is being done at various stages of the process using OEM 11*g*.

Step 1. Log into the OEM 11*g* Grid Control console using the SYSMAN account. By default, this will be located at http://<hostname_for_db_node>:7777/em.

Step 2. At the top of the screen, select Targets. When the Targets screen opens, select Databases. When the Databases page opens, click the Database for which you want to create the service. On the Cluster Database page, click Availability.

Step 3. On the Availability tab, click Cluster Managed Database Services in the Services section in the middle of the page, as shown here:

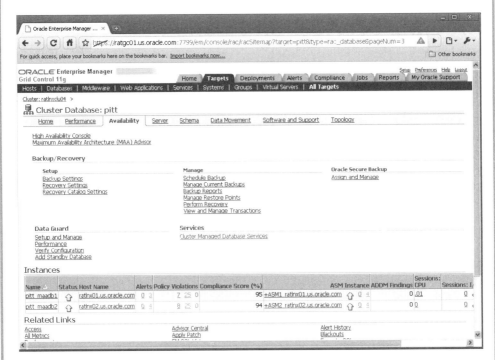

Step 4. Enter and confirm the credentials for the Oracle RAC database and the host operating system, and then click Continue.

Step 5. On the Cluster Managed Database Services page, click Create Service in the upper-right corner and wait for the Create Service page to appear.

Step 6. Enter the name of your service in the Service Name field—for example, grid_callcenter.

Step 7. Select Start Service After Creation to ensure that the service will be started after it is created. Select Update Local Naming Parameter (tnsnames.ora) File to ensure that Grid Control will add the new service to the local Oracle Net Services tnsnames.ora file, as shown here:

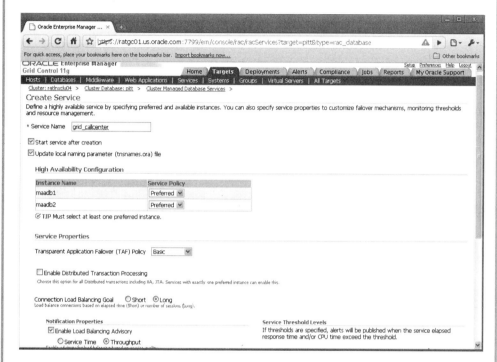

Step 8. Under Service Policy, define where this service can run. By default, the service can run on all nodes as Preferred, meaning that the application can connect to any given node, as long as it is running. Since the grid_callcenter application in our example is a critical application, we will leave it as is, with both nodes as preferred.

Step 9. Under TAF Policy, set the policy by selecting the Basic radio button. (Transparent Application Failover is discussed later in this chapter.) Be aware that if you do not want a service to run on an instance under any circumstances, you would set the Service Policy for that instance to Not Used.

Step 10. In the Service Properties section, select Long for Connection Load-Balancing Goal because we want to distribute the connection workload based on the overall number of connections. Selecting Short would be based on elapsed time instead.

Step 11. Select Enable Load Balancing Advisory under the Notification Properties subheading to enable the load balancing advisory for this service. Select a service-level goal of Throughput.

Step 12. Leave the Enable Fast Application Notification checked. This service would be used by an Oracle Call Interface (OCI) or ODP.NET application, and you want to enable FAN (discussed later in this chapter).

Step 13. In the Service Threshold Levels section, do not specify anything. Here you could optionally set service-level thresholds by entering a value in milliseconds for Warning and Critical thresholds for the Elapsed Time and CPU Time metrics.

Step 14. Use a Resource Plan to control the resources used by this service. As the grid_callcenter app in our example should get a default priority regarding resources, select the DEFAULT_CONSUMER_GROUP from the Consumer Group Mapping list in the Resource Management Properties section.

Step 15. Because this service will not be used by a specific Oracle Scheduler job class, do not specify the Job Scheduler Mapping.

Step 16. Click OK to create the service. The service will be listed in the Cluster Managed Database Services, as shown here:

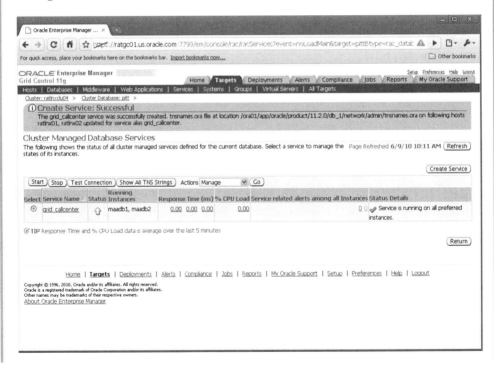

Step 17.   Now that the services are configured, you can see what has been done by connecting to the instances in SQL*Plus. From each instance, issue this command:

```
Show parameter service_names
```

You should see that the service_name of grid_callcenter is listed under each node. Note that the SPFILE is not actually updated with the new service_names value; however, you should be able to see an update in the alert log via an alter system command:

```
ALTER SYSTEM SET service_names='grid_callcenter' SCOPE=MEMORY
SID=' maadb1';
```

A similar command will be executed on each preferred instance on which the service will be run.

Step 18.   Open the tnsnames.ora file on each node (located in the $ORACLE_ HOME/network/admin directory). You should see a definition for the new service that looks similar to the following:

```
GRID_CALLCENTER =
  (DESCRIPTION =
    (ADDRESS = (PROTOCOL = TCP)(HOST = ratlnxclu02-scan.us.oracle.com)
(PORT = 1521))
    (LOAD_BALANCE = yes)
    (CONNECT_DATA =
      (SERVER = DEDICATED)
      (SERVICE_NAME = grid_callcenter)
      (FAILOVER_MODE =
        (TYPE = SELECT)
        (METHOD = BASIC)
        (RETRIES = 180)
        (DELAY = 5)
      )
    )
  )
```

Note that the hostname is actually defined as the SCAN.

Step 19.   Finally, test the connection using the new alias in the tnsnames.ora, and then run a quick query to verify the connection type:

```
SQL> connect scott/tiger@grid_callcenter
```

From another session with DBA privileges, you can check the connection type via a query such as the following:

```
SQL> select inst_id, username, failover_type, failover_method from
gv$session where username = 'SCOTT';
   INST_ID USERNAME    FAILOVER_TYPE   FAILOVER_METHOD
---------- ---------- --------------- -------------------------
        2 SCOTT       SELECT          BASIC
```

Viewing Services from Within the Database

After the services have been created, you can retrieve information about them in various ways. As noted, you can use the **show parameter** command to view the service names. Several additional views are also available in Oracle 11g to allow the DBA to view and monitor services and service activities from within the database. Some of the most useful of these views are the following:

- DBA_SERVICES

- V$SERVICES

- V$ACTIVE_SERVICES

- V$SERVICE_STATS

- V$SERV_MOD_ACT_STATS

Of course, all of the v$ views have their GV$ equivalents in an Oracle RAC environment. A query such as the following will allow you to view the services by instance (for Instance#1):

```
SQL> col inst_id for 99
SQL> col service_id for 99
SQL> col name for a15
SQL> col network_name for a15
SQL> select inst_id, service_id, name, network_name from gv$services
SQL> where inst_id = 1;


INST_ID SERVICE_ID NAME            NETWORK_NAME
------- ---------- --------------- ---------------
      1         10 grid_monthend   grid_monthend
      1         13 grid_payroll    grid_payroll
      1         12 grid_callcenter grid_callcenter
      1         11 grid_oltp       grid_oltp
      1          9 grid_reports    grid_reports
      1          8 grid_em         grid_em
      1          7 grid_erp        grid_erp
      1          5 grid           grid
      1          6 gridXDB         gridXDB
      1          1 SYS$BACKGROUND
      1          2 SYS$USERS
```

Modifying Services

Relocating a service can only be done to an instance that has been defined as Available for that service, when it was created via OEM. If you want to redefine a service so that it can run on additional nodes that were not part of the original service definition, you can do that through OEM. Go to the Cluster Managed Database Services page, as described in the MAA workshop, and select the service you want to modify. From the Actions list of values, select Edit Properties and click Go. Make the modifications and click OK, and the service will be reconfigured. At that point, the modified services will be available for relocation.

Using SRVCTL to Manage Services and Node Applications

In addition to using OEM 11g, you can manage services from the command line using the SRVCTL utility. OEM makes calls to SRVCTL behind the scenes to execute the operations involved in creating the database, stopping and starting instances, creating services, and so on. The SRVCTL utility can be used to take a database or an instance offline, add or remove services, modify services, and stop and start services, particularly built-in services that are not user-defined. This is of particular use when maintenance operations need to be performed, when CRS need not monitor or attempt to bring online certain services while maintenance work is being performed. When SRVCTL is used to add or remove services, databases, and instances, this information is written to the Oracle Cluster Registry (OCR).

Node Applications

Node applications on a cluster consist of components at the cluster layer that sit between the operating system and your Oracle RAC instances. Node applications, also known as nodeapps, comprise components such as the Virtual IP (VIP) address used by the node, the ONS daemon on the node, the Network resource (to monitor the public network), the eONS, and the Group Services daemon (GSD). The function of GSD is to service requests for Oracle 9i RAC management clients, so when no 9i databases are present, there is nothing for GSD to do. Therefore, in Oracle Database 11g Release 2, the GSD is set to offline by default. You might use SRVCTL in conjunction with the nodeapps option if you want to add any or all of these components to a node—for example, adding a VIP to a new node. When using SRVCTL to add a VIP to a node, you log on as root and then execute a command such as the following:

```
srvctl add vip -n ratlnx03 -A '138.1.144.129/255.255.255.0'
```

The **–A** creates a traditional VIP node application on the specified node. After the nodeapps have been added, you can start them via a **start** command:

```
srvctl start vip -n ratlnx03
```

Another area where you may need to use the nodeapps configuration is if you need to change the VIP for an existing node. To do this, you must first stop the nodeapps, and then modify them, using the following syntax:

```
srvctl stop nodeapps
srvctl modify nodeapps -n ratlnx03 -A '138.1.144.129/255.255.255.0'
```

The address specified by name or IP must match the subnet number of the default network. Again, these commands must be run as root. Of course, prior to attempting to add a VIP, it should be defined in the hosts, file.

Generally, the nodeapps are added when the **addnode** operation is run, when adding a new node. As a general rule, you should not need to add nodeapps to a node if it has been configured properly via the Oracle Universal Installer (OUI). The OUI should add the nodeapps at the time a new node is added to a cluster. (We illustrate the command here to help you get familiar with nodeapps and how they are created, or in the rare case, you may need to change the VIP.)

The SRVCTL utility can also be used to get the status of the nodeapps for your cluster:

```
srvctl status nodeapps
VIP ratlnx01-vip is enabled
VIP ratlnx01-vip is running on node: ratlnx01
VIP ratlnx02-vip is enabled
VIP ratlnx02-vip is running on node: ratlnx02
Network is enabled
Network is running on node: ratlnx01
Network is running on node: ratlnx02
GSD is disabled
GSD is not running on node: ratlnx01
GSD is not running on node: ratlnx02
ONS is enabled
ONS daemon is running on node: ratlnx01
ONS daemon is running on node: ratlnx02
eONS is enabled
eONS daemon is running on node: ratlnx01
eONS daemon is running on node: ratlnx02
```

This information is handy for checking the status of these services in a node, and also for confirming the configuration after installing or adding a node.

Managing Services via SRVCTL

Service creation, deletion, and management is also possible via the command line using the SRVCTL utility. The syntax is similar to what we have used so far, with some additional switches. As you have seen with OEM 11*g*, you can define services to run on a subset of nodes or on every node in the cluster, and you can also define certain nodes as being preferred nodes, or simply *available*. You have also seen through OEM that you can relocate services between nodes—and the same is also possible using SRVCTL.

Creating Services with SRVCTL

Services are created from the command line using the **add service** option. Several switches are used for defining the failover policy: **–P**, where the failover policy will be either **NONE**, **BASIC**, or **PRECONNECT**—the same options as seen in the OEM. For services created on administrator-managed databases only, use the **–r** switch for the list of preferred instances and the **–a** switch for the list of available instances. The following example will create a service within the maadb database called grid_ap, with a failover policy of **NONE**, and instance maadb2 being the preferred instance and maadb1 being available:

```
srvctl add service -d maadb -s grid_ap -r maadb2 -a maadb1 -P NONE
```

Note that this command alone does not start the service. After creating the service, you must follow it up with a **start service** command:

```
srvctl start service -d maadb -s grid_ap
```

At that point, you should see the alter system command in the alert log from maadb2, and the service will be available for connections. A key piece to note here, however, is that the entries do *not* get added to the tnsnames.ora, as they do when a service is created using the Database Configuration Assistant (DBCA). However, you can still connect using the Easy*Connection syntax. (Easy*Connection is explained later in this chapter in the "Easy Connect" section.) The syntax simply uses //<SCAN>/<service_name> as the connect string. So the following connections will now work, even though there is no entry in tnsnames.ora:

```
SQL> connect scott/tiger@//ratlnxclu02-scan.us.oracle.com/grid_ap
Connected.
```

Additional operations that can occur on services via SRVCTL include the disable and enable options, start and stop, modify, and relocate. As with OEM, the relocate operation will relocate the service only to an instance that has been defined initially as being available for that service. The command line operations also allow you to change the list of preferred or available instances for a service. For example, let's say that a third node is added to the cluster, with an instance of maadb3. Then the following command could be used to change our existing grid_ap service, as an available instance:

```
srvctl add service -d maadb -s grid_ap -u -a maadb3
```

The following command would then show us the status of that service:

```
srvctl config service -d maadb -s grid_ap
grid_ap PREF: maadb2 AVAIL: maadb3
```

A node can be upgraded from available to preferred using the modify syntax as follows:

```
srvctl modify service -d maadb -s grid_ap -i maadb3 -r
```

This command will upgrade instance maadb3 from an *available* instance to a *preferred* instance, so the **srvctl config** command should now show the following:

```
srvctl config service -d maadb -s grid_ap
grid_ap PREF: maadb2 maadb3 AVAIL:
```

So now, both maadb2 and maadb3 appear as preferred instances for this service. This change will not take full effect until the service is stopped and restarted.

Special Options for Policy-Managed Database Services

If your database is policy-managed, you have three switches to specify options only available for services in policy-managed databases:

- **g server_pool** to specify the name of the server pool.

- **c {UNIFORM | SINGLETON}** to specify the cardinality of the service, either **UNIFORM** (offered on all instances in the server pool) or **SINGLETON** (runs on only one instance at a time).

- **k network_number** to specify the optional network number from which SCAN VIPs are obtained. If not specified, the SCAN VIPs are obtained from the same default network from which the nodeapps VIP is obtained.

MAA Workshop: *Create a Simple FAN Callout*

Workshop Notes

This workshop will walk you through the creation of a simple FAN callout. The callout will print occurring FAN events with a timestamp to a file in the /tmp directory.

Step 1. Create files called callout.sh in the Grid_home/racg/usrco on each node.

Step 2. Populate the files with these code lines:

```
#! /bin/ksh
FAN_LOGFILE=/tmp/'hostname'_FAN.log
echo $* "reported="'date' >>$FAN_LOGFILE &
```

Step 3. Change the permissions on the files:

```
 chmod 775 callout.sh
```

Step 4. Use SRVCTL to start or stop an ASM or database instance:

```
srvctl stop instance -d maadb -i maadb1
srvctl start instance -d maadb -i maadb1
```

Step 5. Change into the /tmp directory of the node where you executed the command.

Step 6. Open the file called <node_name>FAN.log and you will see an entry for every FAN event that was published. The following is an example of an ASM stop and start:

```
cat /tmp/ratlnx01_FAN.log
INSTANCE VERSION=1.0 service=maadb database=maadb instance=maadb1
host=ratlnx01 status=down reason=USER timestamp=2010-06-07 04:43:17
reported=Mon Jun 7 04:43:19 EDT 2010
INSTANCE VERSION=1.0 service=maadb database=maadb instance=maadb1
host=ratlnx01 status=up reason=USER timestamp=2010-06-07 04:44:37
reported=Mon Jun 7 04:44:37 EDT 2010
```

You can see in the created file the payloads of the FAN events. The set of name-value pairs show you the name, type, and nature of the FAN event. If, for example, the service grid_callcenter is started and stopped, the following lines are reported in the file:

```
SERVICEMEMBER VERSION=1.0 service=grid_callcenter database=maadb
instance=maadb1 host=ratlnx01 status=down reason=USER timestamp=2010-
06-09 02:49:58 reported=Wed Jun 9 22:49:59 EDT 2010
SERVICEMEMBER VERSION=1.0 service=grid_callcenter database=maadb
instance=maadb1 host=ratlnx01 status=up reason=USER card=2
timestamp=2010-06-09 02:51:46 reported=Wed Jun 9 22:51:46 EDT 2010
```

Cluster Listener Configuration

The MAA DBA must understand the concept of listeners in the cluster, especially since 11g Release 2 introduced a new set of listeners, called SCAN listeners. When a SCAN name is used, the SCAN listener is first contacted. The SCAN listener knows about the placement of the VIPs and their associated local listeners and forwards the connect request to one of them. Like services which remove the hard linking between a node and an instance, the SCAN removes the hard linking between a client and a node. If you look at a client tnsnames.ora entry, you will not find a single hard link:

```
GRID_CALLCENTER =
   (DESCRIPTION =
     (ADDRESS = (PROTOCOL = TCP)(HOST = ratlnxclu02-scan.us.oracle.com)
(PORT = 1521))
     (CONNECT_DATA =
       (SERVER = DEDICATED)
       (SERVICE_NAME = grid_callcenter)
     )
   )
```

Grid Naming Service and Listeners

If you make use of the Grid Naming Service (GNS), manual listener configuration is not required. In a GNS configuration, one GNS daemon exists for the cluster. Service requests to the cluster domain managed by GNS are routed to the GNS virtual IP address, which routes these requests to the GNS daemon. The GNS daemon listens for registrations. When a SCAN VIP comes up, it registers its addresses with GNS. When GNS receives a request from a DNS for the SCAN, it sends back the registered addresses to the DNS.

SCAN Listeners

The SCAN listeners are configured during the installation of the Grid Infrastructure (GI). It is recommended that your network administrator creates a single name that resolves to three IP addresses using a round-robin algorithm. Note that this is recommended regardless of how many nodes are used in your cluster. During the installation, a SCAN VIP and a SCAN listener are created for each of the three IP addresses that the SCAN resolves. The SCAN listeners, along with their associated SCAN VIPs, will be distributed across the cluster. The clusterware will always try to put each pair of resources on a different node in the cluster. If a node hosting a SCAN VIP is failing, the SCAN VIP and its associated listener will failover to an available node in the cluster.

The following is an example listener.ora file that shows the three configured SCAN listeners:

```
LISTENER=(DESCRIPTION=(ADDRESS_LIST=(ADDRESS=(PROTOCOL=IPC)
(KEY=LISTENER))))              # line added by Agent
LISTENER_SCAN3=(DESCRIPTION=(ADDRESS_LIST=(ADDRESS=(PROTOCOL=IPC)
(KEY=LISTENER_SCAN3))))                   # line added by Agent
LISTENER_SCAN2=(DESCRIPTION=(ADDRESS_LIST=(ADDRESS=(PROTOCOL=IPC)
(KEY=LISTENER_SCAN2))))                   # line added by Agent
LISTENER_SCAN1=(DESCRIPTION=(ADDRESS_LIST=(ADDRESS=(PROTOCOL=IPC)
(KEY=LISTENER_SCAN1))))                   # line added by Agent
ENABLE_GLOBAL_DYNAMIC_ENDPOINT_LISTENER_SCAN1=ON        # line added by Agent
ENABLE_GLOBAL_DYNAMIC_ENDPOINT_LISTENER_SCAN2=ON        # line added by Agent
ENABLE_GLOBAL_DYNAMIC_ENDPOINT_LISTENER_SCAN3=ON        # line added by Agent
ENABLE_GLOBAL_DYNAMIC_ENDPOINT_LISTENER=ON              # line added by Agent
```

This configuration file does not provide much information, but you can use the SRVCTL commands to get information such as where the SCAN listener is running, what port is used, and so on. To determine on which node the SCAN listeners are running, use the **srvctl status scan_listener** command:

```
srvctl status scan_listener
SCAN Listener LISTENER_SCAN1 is enabled
SCAN listener LISTENER_SCAN1 is running on node ratlnx01
SCAN Listener LISTENER_SCAN2 is enabled
SCAN listener LISTENER_SCAN2 is running on node ratlnx02
SCAN Listener LISTENER_SCAN3 is enabled
SCAN listener LISTENER_SCAN3 is running on node ratlnx02
```

As the cluster in our example has only two nodes, two SCAN listeners (LISTENER_SCAN2 and LISTENER_SCAN3) have to run on one node (ratlnx02). If this node has to go down, all three will reside on the remaining node.

To configure your clients or troubleshoot a problem, you might have to find out what port the SCAN listeners are using. The **srvctl config scan_listener** command provides that information for you:

```
srvctl config scan_listener
SCAN Listener LISTENER_SCAN1 exists. Port: TCP:1521
SCAN Listener LISTENER_SCAN2 exists. Port: TCP:1521
SCAN Listener LISTENER_SCAN3 exists. Port: TCP:1521
```

At the client, you specify the SCAN name. To find out what SCAN name is in use and what SCAN VIPs are associated with it, execute **srvctl config scan**:

```
srvctl config scan
SCAN name: ratlnxclu02-scan.us.oracle.com, Network:
1/10.143.90.0/255.255.255.0/eth0
SCAN VIP name: scan1, IP: /ratlnxclu02-scan.us.oracle.com/10.143.90.44
SCAN VIP name: scan2, IP: /ratlnxclu02-scan.us.oracle.com/10.143.90.45
SCAN VIP name: scan3, IP: /ratlnxclu02-scan.us.oracle.com/10.143.90.46
```

Local Listeners

As described, the SCAN listener passes the connection request over to the local listener that finally establishes the connection to the instance. The database instance(s) local_listener parameter is automatically set on instance startup by the oraagent in accordance to node local listener definition in the OCR. It is recommended that you leave the parameter unset so that the database agent can maintain it automatically. If you set **LOCAL_LISTENER** manually, the agent will not automatically update this value. If you do not set **LOCAL_LISTENER**, the database agent automatically keeps the database associated with the grid home's node listener updated, even as the ports or IP of that listener are changed.

The endpoints_listener.ora contains the configuration of the local listener. This is listening on the VIP (not the SCAN VIP):

```
LISTENER_RATLNX01=(DESCRIPTION=(ADDRESS_LIST=(ADDRESS=(PROTOCOL=TCP)
(HOST=ratlnx01-vip)(PORT=1521))(ADDRESS=(PROTOCOL=TCP)(HOST=10.143.90.36)
(PORT=1521)(IP=FIRST))))            # line added by Agent
```

As you probably have guessed already, SRVCTL can also be used to get the status of the listener:

```
srvctl config listener
Name: LISTENER
Network: 1, Owner: grid
Home: <CRS home>
End points: TCP:1521
```

and

```
srvctl status listener
Listener LISTENER is enabled
Listener LISTENER is running on node(s): ratlnx01,ratlnx02
```

Listener Registration and PMON Discovery

When a local listener starts after the Oracle instance was started, you might find that the instance is not registered with the listener, even though the listener is listed for service registration. This can be explained by the fact that the Oracle Database Process Monitor (PMON) discovery routine, by default, occurs only every 60 seconds. To avoid a delay for users to be able to connect, use the following SQL command:

```
SQL> ALTER SYSTEM REGISTER;
```

This statement forces the PMON process to register the service immediately. You should consider creating a script that runs this statement immediately after starting the listener. The statement has no effect when the listener is up and the instance is already registered, or when the listener is down.

Why a Virtual IP? TCP Timeouts

Why must we use a VIP address in an Oracle RAC environment? The simple answer to this question is TCP timeouts. Let's discuss this a bit more.

TCP timeouts, believe it or not, play a huge part in the perceived availability of applications. When a node in an Oracle RAC environment goes down, or in any MAA environment with multiple addresses to attempt, there may be no way for the client to know this. If a client is connecting using a TNS alias or a service that allows connection to multiple nodes, the client may unknowingly try its first connection attempt to the node that is down. This in and of itself is not a problem, as multiple addresses should be in the list, so that when the client fails to get a response from the first address in the list, the next address will be tried, until the connection succeeds. The problem lies with the time that it takes to go to the next address in the list.

How long does the client wait to determine that the host it is trying to reach is not accessible? The time can range anywhere from a few seconds, to a few minutes, and in some environments this is simply unacceptable. If a node goes down for several hours, days, or weeks, the database may still be humming along just fine, with x number of nodes still accessing the database. However, some clients may always be trapped into making the initial connection attempt to the down node, and will therefore be stuck in front of a (seeming) interminable hourglass while the connection is timing out, before being rerouted to the next address in the list.

Reigning in TCP Timeouts at the OS

Unfortunately, this time is something that is generally outside of the control of Oracle. In addition, it varies from client to client, and operating system to operating system. It is controlled by the operating system timeout values, on the client side, so making modifications to all clients can be cumbersome, since there may be many clients and many variations to configuration changes need to be made. In addition, changing the timeout values may also result in adverse consequences on other applications that the clients are running, if other applications rely on a higher TCP timeout value, for whatever reason.

To make matters worse, the behavior may not be consistent. If client-side load-balancing is enabled, it is possible that some connections will succeed immediately on their first attempt, because they just happened to connect randomly to a node that is available. At other times, however, the connection time increases, because the client randomly and unwittingly picks the down node for its first connection attempt. The result of this is confusion and frustration at the client side, even though from the database's perspective everything is functioning as it should.

Giving the MAA DBA Control over TCP Timeouts

Enter the VIP address. By using a VIP address, Oracle eliminates the problem with TCP timeouts on the initial connection, without the need to make any changes to a single client machine. This is done by enforcing client connections first to come in on the VIP address for all connections. When all nodes are functioning properly, each VIP is running on its assigned node, and connections are directed to the appropriate listener and service. When the unthinkable happens, and a node fails (gasp!), CRS will kick in, and the VIP for that node will actually be brought online on one of the remaining nodes of the cluster, where it can respond to a ping and also to connection attempts. Note that this VIP will *not* be accepting connections to the database at this time. However, since the IP address is available, it will be able to respond to a connection attempt immediately.

The response given to the client will generally be in the form of an ORA-12541, advising that no listener is available. This is because the node where the VIP now resides has its own listener, but it is listening on its own VIP, not the VIP of any other nodes. The client, receiving the message that there is no listener, will then immediately retry, using the next IP in the ADDRESS_LIST, rather than waiting up to 2 minutes for the timeout we would normally expect. Thus, a connect-time failover has still occurred, but the connection attempt succeeds within a second or even faster. Even though a client uses the SCAN, the local listener is still listening on the VIP.

Why a SCAN Virtual IP?

Having answered the question of why we need VIPs, your next logical question might be, "Why a SCAN VIP?" and subsequently, "Why does Oracle recommend three of them?" The SCAN VIP works a bit differently from the "normal" VIP. We will call the "normal" VIP a *local VIP* for the moment, as these VIPs are associated to the local listener. We know that if a node fails, the VIP fails over to another node. So far, the SCAN VIP and local VIP act the same. The difference comes into the game as the failed over local VIP replies to a ping, but its local listener does not listen, for SQL*Net connections because it cannot failover. The SCAN listeners in comparison can run on any node of the cluster. So the SCAN VIP not only has the task of avoiding a wait for the TCP timeout, but it must also ensure that the SCAN LISTENER associated with the SCAN VIP can be started on every available node in the cluster, if needed.

Why does Oracle recommend that you set up the SCAN name with three IP addresses, thus having three SCAN VIPs and three SCAN listeners? The answer is related to the subject of this book: Maximum Availability. You can configure your cluster with only one SCAN VIP/listener, but this would make a responsible MAA DBA very nervous. An MAA DBA could not sleep at night, concerned that her SCAN listener would fail. Redundancy is the answer to the question, but it's not the whole story, because the question of Why not two? or Why not one SCAN per node? can still be asked. Having two would cover the redundancy requirement, but having three ensures that the connect load of the SCAN listener would not get exhausted, would reduce the CPU cost per node, and would require the least amount of decision on the part of the cluster. Having three is plenty.

NOTE
The benefit of using SCAN is that the network configuration files on the client computer do not need to be modified when nodes are added to or removed from the cluster.

Connect-Time Failover

Connect-time failover is a technique used to set up your tnsnames.ora, and it has been made redundant by the use of SCAN. Clients can still be set up this way, however, so it's worth discussing. Connect-time failover is defined as a failed initial connection attempt, which must be retried against a different address. Consider the following entry in a client's TNSNAMES.ORA:

```
grid_callcenter =
  (DESCRIPTION =
    (ADDRESS = (PROTOCOL = TCP)(HOST=ratlnx01-vip)(PORT = 1521))
    (ADDRESS = (PROTOCOL = TCP)(HOST=ratlnx02-vip)(PORT = 1521))
    (CONNECT_DATA =
      (SERVICE_NAME = grid_callcenter)
    )
  )
```

Here, the alias grid_callcenter is called when a client attempts to connect. The first address in the list will be tried initially—in this case, ratlnx01-vip. Should the initial connection attempt to ratlnx01-vip be unsuccessful, the next address in the list will be tried. This is known as a *connect-time failover*. You can add as many entries to the list as you have available nodes to accept connections. Note also that the entries in the list do not have to be Oracle RAC nodes. Connect-time failover can also be implemented in an Oracle Streams or Advanced Replication environment, or one of the entries in the list may be a standby database—physical or logical—as long as an available service is defined and running on that node.

The other criteria, of course, is that the addresses in the list will all allow the client to get to the data that is needed by the application. With an Oracle RAC environment, we know that the data is always the same, as it is the same database. In the case of Streams, Advanced Replication, and physical or logical standby, whether or not the data is accessible depends on how these options are configured.

Transparent Application Failover

The TAF feature allows application users to reconnect to surviving database instances if an existing connection fails. When such a failure happens, all uncommitted transactions will be rolled back and an identical connection will be established. The uncommitted transactions have to be resubmitted after reconnection. The TAF reconnect occurs automatically from within the OCI library. To use all features of TAF, the application code may have to be modified. When your application is query-only, TAF can be used without any code changes. In general, TAF works well for reporting.

Server-Side vs. Client-Side TAF

TAF can be implemented either client-side or server-side. Service attributes are used server-side to hold the TAF configuration; client-side the TNS connect string must be changed to enable TAF. Settings configured server-side supersede their client-side counterparts if both methods are used. Server-side configuration of TAF is the preferred method.

You can configure TAF in two different failover modes. In the first mode, Select Failover, SELECT statements that are in progress during the failure are resumed over the new connection. In the second mode, Session Failover, lost connections and sessions are re-created.

- **Select** Selects will resume on the new connection

- **Session** When a connection is lost, a new connection is created automatically

When TAF is set up client-side, it can be configured to establish from the beginning a second connection to another (backup) instance. This eliminates the reconnection penalty but requires that the backup instance support all connections from all nodes set up this way.

- **Basic** Establishes connections only when failover occurs

- **Preconnect** Pre-establishes connections to the backup server

Implementing TAF

Depending on the parameters discussed, you can implement TAF in several ways. Oracle recommends the following three methods.

TAF with Connect-Time Failover and Client Load Balancing

If you implement this option, Oracle Net connects via the SCAN to one of the VIPs of your nodes. If the instance fails after the connection, the TAF application fails over to the other node's listener, reserving any SELECT statements in progress.

```
grid_callcenter=
(DESCRIPTION=
(LOAD_BALANCE=on)
(FAILOVER=on)
(ADDRESS=
(PROTOCOL=tcp)
(HOST=ratgen-scan.us.oracle.com)(PORT=1521)
)
(ADDRESS=
(PROTOCOL=tcp)
(HOST=ratlnxclu02-scan.us.oracle.com)(PORT=1521)
)
(CONNECT_DATA=
(SERVICE_NAME=grid_callcenter)
(FAILOVER_MODE=
(TYPE=select)
(METHOD=basic)
)
)
)
```

TAF Retrying a Connection

TAF will retry connecting automatically if the first connection attempt fails if you set the **RETRIES** and **DELAY** parameters. In the following example, Oracle Net tries to reconnect to the listener. If the failover connection fails, Oracle Net waits 15 seconds before trying to reconnect again. Oracle Net attempts to reconnect up to 20 times.

```
grid_callcenter=
(DESCRIPTION=
(ADDRESS=
(PROTOCOL=tcp)
(HOST=ratgen-scan.us.oracle.com)(PORT=1521)
)
(CONNECT_DATA=
(SERVICE_NAME=grid_callcenter)
(FAILOVER_MODE=
(TYPE=select)
(METHOD=basic)
(RETRIES=20)
(DELAY=15)
)
)
)
```

TAF Pre-establishing a Connection

For this option, you must explicitly specify the initial and the backup. In the following example, clients that use net service name sales1.us.example.com to connect to the listener on sales1-server are also preconnected to sales2-server. If sales1-server fails after the connection, Oracle Net fails over to sales2-server, preserving any SELECT statements in progress. Similarly, Oracle Net preconnects to sales1-server for those clients that use sales2.us.example.com to connect to the listener on sales2-server.

```
grid_callcenter1=
(DESCRIPTION=
(ADDRESS=
(PROTOCOL=tcp)
(HOST=ratgen-scan.us.oracle.com)(PORT=1521)
)
(CONNECT_DATA=
(SERVICE_NAME=grid_callcenter)
(INSTANCE_NAME=maadb1)
(FAILOVER_MODE=
(BACKUP=ratlnxclu02-scan.us.oracle.com)
(TYPE=select)
(METHOD=preconnect)
)
)
)
grid_callcenter2=
(DESCRIPTION=
(ADDRESS=
(PROTOCOL=tcp)
(HOST=ratlnxclu02-scan.us.oracle.com)(PORT=1521)
)
(CONNECT_DATA=
(SERVICE_NAME=grid_callcenter)
(INSTANCE_NAME=maadb2)
(FAILOVER_MODE=
(BACKUP=ratgen-scan.us.oracle.com)
(TYPE=select)
(METHOD=preconnect)
)
)
)
```

MAA Workshop: *Configure and Test TAF*

Workshop Notes

In this workshop, you'll perform a simple test to get a feeling of how TAF works. To demonstrate this, you'll use the grid_callcenter service that we created in the MAA workshop "Using OEM 11g Grid Control to Create Services." Here, you will test the failover of an in-flight query when the instance in which the query started goes down.

Step 1. Verify the tnsnames.ora entry for the grid_callcenter alias. This should look similar to this:

```
GRID_CALLCENTER =
  (DESCRIPTION =
    (ADDRESS = (PROTOCOL = TCP)(HOST = ratlnxclu02-scan.us.oracle.com)
(PORT = 1521))
    (LOAD_BALANCE = yes)
    (CONNECT_DATA =
      (SERVER = DEDICATED)
      (SERVICE_NAME = grid_callcenter)
      (FAILOVER_MODE =
        (TYPE = SELECT)
        (METHOD = BASIC)
        (RETRIES = 180)
        (DELAY = 5)
      )
    )
  )
```

Step 2. Connect to the grid service:

```
sqlplus scott/tiger@grid_callcenter
```

Step 3. Confirm which node you are connected to, and the failover method, with the following query:

```
SQL> select inst_id, username, failover_type, failover_method, failed_over
  2  from gv$session where username = 'SCOTT';
   INST_ID USERNA FAILOVER_TYPE FAILOVER_METHOD FAILED_OVER
---------- ------ ------------- --------------- -----------
         2 SCOTT  SELECT        BASIC           NO
```

From this you can see that user SCOTT connected to instance #2, the **FAILOVER_TYPE** is selected, and the session has not yet failed over.

Step 4. Create or populate a table with a large amount of data—enough so that a long-running query can be performed (long enough that we can shut down Instance 2 in the middle). In this case, you have granted select on DBA_OBJECTS to SCOTT, and you create a table called *TEST_TAF* as select * from SYS.DBA_OBJECTS:

```
Create table TEST_TAF as select * from SYS.DBA_OBJECTS;
```

Step 5. Connect as SYSDBA to Instance 2, and prepare to issue a **SHUTDOWN ABORT**, but do not press ENTER yet.

Step 6. Toggle back over to user SCOTT's session on the client. Execute a query against the TEST_TAF table from within SCOTT's session:

```
select * from test_taf where object_name like 'D%';
```

Step 7. As soon as the query begins, switch to your SYSDBA connection to Instance 2 and execute the **SHUTDOWN ABORT** command.

Step 8. After a brief pause, your query from within the client session (as user SCOTT) should continue on. On Instance 1, open up another SYSDBA connection and run the same query as before to get the session information for SCOTT:

```
SQL> select inst_id, username, failover_type, failover_method, failed_
over  from gv$session where username = 'SCOTT';
   INST_ID USERNA FAILOVER_TYPE FAILOVER_METHOD FAILED_OVER
---------- ------ ------------- --------------- -----------
         1 SCOTT  SELECT        BASIC           YES
```

Note that the session now resides on INST_ID 1, and the FAILED_OVER column says YES.

> **NOTE**
> *The **DELAY** parameter in the configuration shown tells you to wait 5 seconds after the failure is first noted, and then attempt to reconnect. **RETRIES** tells you to retry this 180 times, with a 5-second delay each time. The length of the pause you see in step 8 will depend on how far the query had gotten and will also depend on these parameters. If neither parameter is set, your session may error out rather than failing over as expected.*

Easy Connect

In some situations, you may want to connect to a database without having to create an entry in the TNSNAMES.ORA. This could be because it is only a test or a one-time connection. This is possible using Oracle Easy*Connection: the client may connect by simply specifying the connect string in the form **//<scan:port>/<service_name>**. This type of connection is available with only Oracle Database 10g and later clients.

A connection using the Easy*Connection syntax will connect you to any available node on which the service is running, similar to using a TNSNAMES.ORA entry. Note that it is not necessary to specify the port if you are using port 1521. For example, the following client connection to the grid_callcenter service can be made with and without specifying the port, as the scan listener is running on the default port 1521:

```
sqlplus /nolog
SQL*Plus: Release 11.2.0.1.0 Production on Wed Jun 9 04:37:20 2010
Copyright (c) 1982, 2009, Oracle.  All rights reserved.
SQL> connect system/oracle123@//ratlnxclu02-scan.us.oracle.com:1521/
grid_callcenter
Connected.
```

or

```
sqlplus /nolog
SQL*Plus: Release 11.2.0.1.0 Production on Wed Jun 9 04:52:18 2010
Copyright (c) 1982, 2009, Oracle.  All rights reserved.
SQL> connect system/oracle123@//ratlnxclu02-scan.us.oracle.com/ grid_
callcenter
Connected.
```

When using the Easy*Connection syntax, ensure that you specify the SCAN, because the SCAN provides load-balancing and failover of client connections to the database.

Oracle RAC/Standby/Replication Environments

Oracle Data Guard (see Chapter 9) is one of the core components in a Maximum Available Architecture. With Oracle Data Guard, you implement one or more standby databases for your Oracle RAC database, which can be either Oracle RAC or a single instance. We discussed in this chapter how you can take advantage of TAF within your Oracle RAC database, as this is the primary environment suited for use of TAF. With Oracle RAC, you can always be assured that when failing over to another node, you are still accessing the same data as before—because it is the same database. However, TAF can also be used in other environments, such as physical or logical standby environments.

Determining the suitability depends on how these environments are used. For example, with a standby database, users can experience a transparent failover, when the database is switched over to the standby. This depends, however, on how quickly the switchover occurs and also on the settings for **RETRIES** and **DELAY**. With logical standby, clients can failover as well, without necessarily having to perform a switchover, because in this case, the target databases for failover is open. However, successful select failover would depend on the availability of the data at the target sites, as the propagation of data to a logical standby does not necessarily have to be synchronous.

The DB_ROLE_CHANGE System Event

As you will see in Chapter 9, the Oracle Data Guard database failover process is straightforward. But especially in complete site failover, life is not that easy, and more steps are involved to failover an entire application. Certain components need to be either reconfigured or restarted to make the application work again as expected.

To address this, you can use the **DB_ROLE_CHANGE** system event. This event (event inside the database) fires every time the role of the database is changed. When a physical or logical standby is converted to a primary or a primary is converted to a physical or logical standby, the **DB_ROLE_CHANGE** system event is fired. This event then can be caught by a trigger that fires after the role change event happens. The trigger is coded to call the **DBMS_SCHEDULER** and the scheduler executes an external script. This script can contain all kind of actions you need to perform to make your application failover, such as starting the application servers.

The following is an example of how the trigger could look. Once the trigger is created, as a result of a role change, the script /u01/scripts/role_change_actions.sh would be executed. The script should be placed on all nodes.

```
SQL> CREATE OR REPLACE TRIGGER role_change_actions AFTER DB_ROLE_CHANGE
ON DATABASE
  BEGIN
   dbms_scheduler.create_job(
   job_name=>'role_change_actions',
   job_type=>'executable',
   job_action=>'/u01/scripts/role_change_actions.sh',
   enabled=>TRUE
   );
  END;
```

Setting Up the Client

The connect string of the client should contain the SCAN of the primary and the standby cluster because this avoids any reconfiguration during a failover. The connect string should use a service name as well:

```
TEST =
  (DESCRIPTION =
    (ADDRESS_LIST =
      (ADDRESS = (PROTOCOL = TCP)(HOST = ratgen-scan.us.oracle.com)(PORT = 1521))
      (ADDRESS = (PROTOCOL = TCP)(HOST = ratlnxclu02-scan.us.oracle.com)(PORT =
1521))
```

```
 (LOAD_BALANCE = yes)
 )
 (CONNECT_DATA =
  (SERVICE_NAME = TEST)
 )
)
```

The service, however, should be running only on the primary side. If the service is running on the standby side as well, client connections would attempt to connect to the standby side; therefore, the service name should not be listed under **SERVICE_ NAMES** in the SPFILE. To automate the starting of the service when the role of the database is primary, you can deploy a database startup trigger:

```
SQL> CREATE OR REPLACE TRIGGER start_service_test AFTER STARTUP ON DATABASE
 DECLARE
 role VARCHAR(30);
 BEGIN
 SELECT DATABASE_ROLE INTO role FROM V$DATABASE;
  IF role = 'PRIMARY' THEN
   DBMS_SERVICE.START_SERVICE('TEST');
   END IF;
 END;
```

This trigger would not cover the situation that would occur when a logical database is converted into a primary database, because this action does not require a restart of the standby database. Subsequently, the startup database trigger will not fire. In this case, a second trigger (the first one is still needed) dependent on the **DB_ROLE_ CHANGE** can catch that situation:

```
SQL> CREATE OR REPLACE TRIGGER start_service_test_role_change AFTER
 DB_ROLE_CHANGE ON DATABASE
 DECLARE
 role VARCHAR(30);
 BEGIN
 SELECT DATABASE_ROLE INTO role FROM V$DATABASE;
  IF role = 'PRIMARY' THEN
   DBMS_SERVICE.START_SERVICE('TEST');
   END IF;
 END;
```

NOTE
When using the Oracle Data Guard Broker in an 11g Release 2 Data Guard environment, a new feature called Role-Based Services allows database services to start on a designated database when that database is in a specific role. This avoids much of the complexity described above but does require the use of the Oracle Data Guard Broker to manage the role of the database within the clusterware. More details on this feature are in Chapter 12.

FAN and Oracle Data Guard

When an Oracle Data Guard failover is performed using the Oracle Data Guard Broker (see Chapter 12), the FAN OCI event is automatically created and published to the application. The Java Database Connectivity (JDBC) application makes use of FAN Oracle Notification Service (ONS), but FAN ONS is designed to work only within a cluster; thus, FAN events cannot send FAN events to another cluster. Having said that, this is exactly what is needed in the event of a failover to the standby cluster. To resolve this, an external ONS publisher must be configured. This external publisher will create events that tell the application that the primary database is down and where it can find the new primary database.

Integration with OEM

As you saw in the workshop "Using OEM 11g Grid Control to Create Services," the service features are tightly integrated into OEM 11g. Although you might be one of those DBAs who avoid using GUIs, you should be aware that OEM does a great job when it comes to creating and managing services for your cluster. Don't get us wrong—you still need a deep understanding of what services can do for you and what features

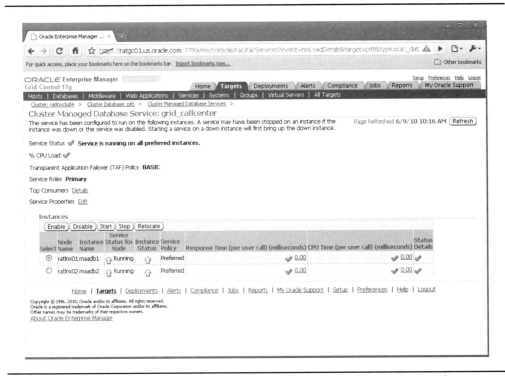

FIGURE 8-1. *Cluster Managed Database Service Screen in OEM Grid Control*

you can use to set them up, but using OEM means that you don't need to remember every command line syntax exactly when you need it. It performs necessary checks in the background that you might have forgotten about. It shows you all available options for a particular setting, helping you rethink whether you are performing the most optimal configuration.

In the workshops, you saw how to use the Database Control version of OEM. The Grid Control version will be discussed in detail in Chapter 13, and it will hopefully make you curious enough to give it a try. For now, remember that OEM can make your cluster, database, and service management tasks much easier. Figure 8-1 shows you the Cluster Managed Database Service screen in Grid Control with the options to enable, disable, start, stop, and relocate the services.

To stop the grid_callcenter service, simply click the Stop button and confirm in the next screen that you really want to do this. The Clustered Managed Database Services screen now shows that the service is down on one more preferred instances. If you click the service, you'll see on what instances the service is running and stopped, as shown in Figure 8-2.

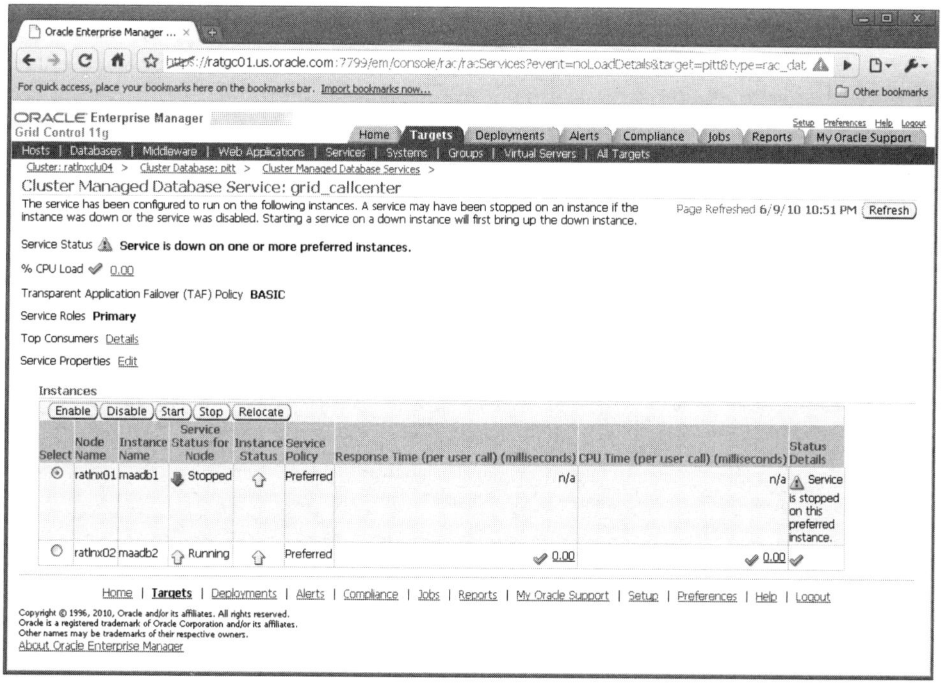

FIGURE 8-2.   *Service stopped on one preferred instance*

Summary

This chapter discussed the importance of addressing Maximum Availability from an application, and more specifically, an end-user perspective. To ensure Maximum Availability, your application must be prepared to handle failures and seamlessly transition users to an available node, as well as effectively balance the work across the available instances in an Oracle RAC. Furthermore, the ability to failover between clusters (aka clusters using Oracle Data Guard or other replication mechanisms) provides a complete application failover solution to match the complete database solution provided by Oracle's MAA.

Although every application is different, this chapter's intent was to lay the foundation to ensure that applications can fully utilize that back-end infrastructure, while also ensuring that the MAA DBA is familiar with new concepts, such as SCAN VIPS, to attain smooth yet simple client connectivity to critical data. In the next chapter, you'll learn how to harden that back-end database grid using Oracle Data Guard.

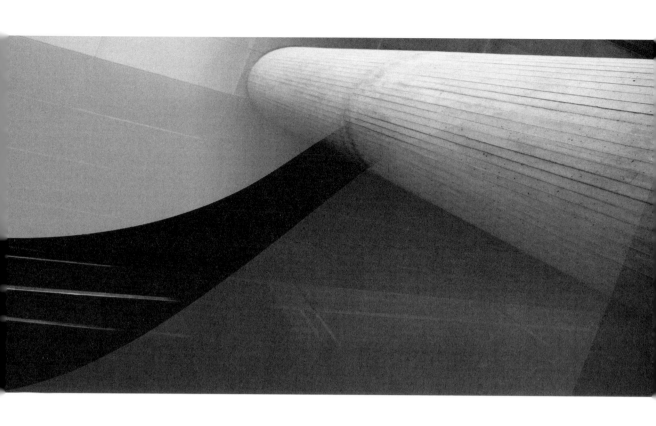

PART III

Disaster Planning

CHAPTER
9

Oracle Data Guard

o far you have learned how a proper Oracle RAC implementation can make a highly available database system that is able to scale out to meet the performance demands of LunarTrax's thriving business. At this point, Oracle RAC node and database instance failures are virtually transparent to the end-user community. Max is ecstatic with his increase in productivity. Life is good; it's time to sit back in his chair, put his feet up on the desk, and take in the well-deserved praise for his work of art. His success has been duly noted; Max is the envy of others within the company and expects a hefty salary increase this year!

Then it happens….
It's a quiet Saturday night, and Max gets "the call" that the data center that houses his Oracle RAC cluster has burned to the ground. LunarTrax's business has come to a grinding halt. How long will it take Max to acquire new hardware and get it configured? How long will it take him to install all the software and restore the database? Days? Weeks? Max wonders whether the company is still shipping the tapes off site. He wonders how much data he is going to lose. Max knows he can probably have the database up and running within 48 hours, with data loss of about six days. But with this fire, LunarTrax has lost hundreds of thousands of dollars, with more to come over the next 48 hours. At this point, Max thinks, the 48 hours of work required to get the database back to an operational state is probably better spent updating his resume.

Obviously, Oracle RAC *cannot* save you from corruptive disasters, but you can relax a bit, because there is an Oracle solution. Oracle Data Guard has been designed from the ground up to provide an efficient disaster recovery solution that will save your database from a fiery death, massive tsunami, or crippling earthquake.

When properly implemented, Oracle Data Guard can even protect against a disk corruption within the storage subsystem. Oracle Data Guard provides the ability to failover the database in the event of such disasters, enabling end users to access the database in minutes instead of days or weeks. Oracle Data Guard can be configured to guarantee zero data loss, minimize maintenance downtime through role transitions, and reduce workloads on the primary database by offloading reporting and backup operations. In this chapter, you will learn how to take advantage of Oracle Data Guard's robust features and how to build a configuration that will provide data safety and security while making efficient use of the additional resources.

Making the Right Choice

Oracle Data Guard is a key component within Oracle MAA that provides an efficient disaster recovery solution. It enables the creation, maintenance, and monitoring of transactional consistent copies of the production database at an alternate location. The production database in an Oracle Data Guard configuration is commonly referred to as the *primary database,* while the transactional consistent copies are referred to as *standby databases*. With Oracle 11g Release 2, a single Oracle Data Guard configuration can contain up to 30 standby databases in 3 standby database configurations: physical, snapshot, and logical. All three types of standby databases can be Oracle RAC or single-instance, regardless of the configuration of the primary database. The overall layout of your Oracle Data Guard configuration is dependent on what business requirements must be satisfied by the configuration.

NOTE
Beginning with 11g, you can implement a cross-platform Linux-to-Windows (and vice versa) Oracle Data Guard configuration. More information on cross-platform Oracle Data Guard configurations can be found in MOS Note: 413484.1.

Physical Standby Databases

A physical standby database is synchronized with the primary database by using media recovery to apply redo that was generated on the primary database. The use of media recovery ensures that a physical standby database is a block-for-block identical copy of the primary database. For this fact, a physical standby database is the preferred choice for disaster recovery. In the event of a failure, you can rest assured that your data will be intact and consistent with data that existed on the primary.

A physical standby database in Oracle Database 11*g* Release 2 provides the following key benefits:

■ Offers fast and efficient failover to a block-for-block copy of the primary database.

■ Applies no restrictions on data types.

■ Lets you perform role reversal of the primary and standby databases (switchover) for planned maintenance.

■ Lets you offload backups from the primary database.

■ Allows for minimal downtime upgrades and/or patching with the use of the Transient Logical Standby Database feature.

■ Allows use of the Oracle Active Data Guard option, which lets you open the physical standby database in read-only to perform reporting while redo data is being applied. In addition to the Physical Standby database being open for read write operations Oracle Active Data Guard also provides the following features/benefits:

　■ If block corruption occurs on the primary database (resulting in a ORA-1578), automatic block recovery will be performed in an Oracle Active Data Guard configuration without the end user realizing that corruption was even encountered.

- Allows for the use of block change tracking on the standby database to facilitate fast incremental backups (not possible without Oracle Active Data Guard).

- Integrates the Oracle Active Data Guard option with the support of up to 30 standby databases, allowing for the creation of reader farms. A *reader farm* is a set of physical standby databases running the Oracle Active Data Guard option from a single primary database. These Oracle Active Data Guard–enabled physical standby databases are used to support and/or offload read-only workloads from the primary database.

Snapshot Standby Databases

Oracle Database 11*g* Release 1 introduced a new type of standby database called a *snapshot standby*, a physical standby that has been temporarily opened in read-write mode. Flashback Database technology is used to facilitate this functionality. When a physical standby is converted into a snapshot standby, an implicit guaranteed restore point is created for the standby database. After a physical standby has been converted to a snapshot standby, the database still receives all of the redo data, but instead of immediately applying the redo, it is archived into the archivelogs at the standby site. When the snapshot standby is converted back to a physical standby, all changes made while the database was in read-write mode will be discarded and the archived redo data will then be applied from the restore point forward, making the physical standby database transactionally consistent with the primary database. Switchover and/or failover operations are *not* permitted on a snapshot standby until the database is converted back to a physical standby.

Snapshot Standby databases are often used in the following situations:

- For troubleshooting application-related issues that are dependent on production data sets

- With application load testing tools, such as Real Application Testing, to ensure proper application functionality and performance prior to application upgrades take place on the production system

Logical Standby Databases

A logical standby database is kept in sync with the primary by transforming redo data received from the primary into logical SQL statements and then executing those SQL statements against the standby database. Because we are applying SQL statements instead of performing media recovery, it is possible for the logical standby to contain the same logical information but at the same time have a different physical structure. A logical standby is open for user access while applying changes, making it an ideal solution for a reporting database while maintaining its disaster recovery attributes.

Following are a few of the primary benefits for a logical standby:

■ Allow near zero downtime for database upgrades

■ Ability to offload reporting from the primary database

■ Ability to create additional objects to better support reporting operations

Your choice of the type of standby database to implement is a decision that will be heavily influenced by the same business requirements that justified the need for the standby database in the first place. Given the scenario of our database dying in a fiery death, Max wants to ensure this amount of downtime and data loss will never occur again. The requirements laid forth by the business is to ensure that the database is available for user access (Recovery Time Objective, or RTO) within minutes of such a disaster, and that the database is in the exact same structure that it was in prior to the fire. Given the fact that a physical standby database is a block-for-block copy of the primary database, the decision to implement a physical standby database is easy.

Now assume that Max has been dealing with complaints from the sales team that the application performance is resulting in a significant lack of productivity. The primary reason for the application slow-downs is the fact that the bean-counters in accounting are constantly running resource-intensive reports in the middle of the day to meet their own deadlines. Max is tired of these complaints and wants to see some return on investment (ROI) from the hardware and software that was purchased to facilitate the standby database. With Oracle Database 11*g* Release 2, three options can make the bean-counters and the sales team happy: logical standby, snapshot standby, or a physical standby using the Oracle Active Data Guard option.

Obviously, with all of these options, the decision is a bit complex. We know that a snapshot standby will not be "up-to-date" when it is opened in read-write mode, so increasing our RTO beyond the acceptable limitation narrows us now down to two options: logical standby or a physical standby using the Oracle Active Data Guard option. We do know that with a logical standby database, we can create additional database objects to enhance the reporting functionality, but these changes will make the structure of the database slightly different, thus invalidating the business requirement of our disaster recovery solution being identical in structure. By using the business objectives laid out by management, we used our powers of deduction to make our choice of using a physical standby with the Oracle Active Data Guard option. Oracle Active Data Guard will provide the ultimate HA solution by allowing real-time reporting while still maintaining a transactionally consistent block-for-block copy of our primary database.

In the real world, a single standby database of any specific type may not meet the needs of your business. As mentioned, Oracle Database 11*g* Release 2 supports up to 30 standby databases of any type in a given Oracle Data Guard configuration type, providing the ability to use all of the above standby types from a single primary server and allowing for the implementation of a solution tailored to meet the high availability and scalability needs of just about any application.

Creating a Physical Standby

Now that you understand the types of standby databases available as well as the potential uses for each, let's create a physical standby database. Why start with the creation of a physical standby? Well, the concepts and procedures used in the creation of a physical standby database will carry over to the creation of the other types of Standby databases not to mention the fact that a physical standby database is the most common of the available types of standby databases.

Our first Oracle Data Guard MAA workshop covers the steps required to create the physical standby: create a backup of the primary, transfer the backup files to the standby site, and mount the standby database. The details for each step along the way are provided to allow for proper decisions to be made during implementation with the goal of preventing headaches after implementation.

MAA Workshop: *Creating an Oracle RAC Physical Standby Database*

Workshop Notes

The following table shows the names that will be used when building our Oracle Data Guard physical standby configuration:

Host	Database Role	DB Name	DB SIDs	DB Unique Name
ratlnx01, ratlnx02	Primary	maadb	maadb1, maadb2	pitt
ratgen01, ratgen02	Physical standby	maadb	maadb1, maadb2	cosp

Properly configuring the database environment prior to creating the standby will ensure easier maintenance and will pave the road to later role transitions and use of the Oracle Data Guard Broker (covered in Chapter 12). While some steps are not mandatory, we will explain the benefits to illustrate how those choices can result in a more robust disaster recovery solution. Also, because several steps involve restarting the primary database, you should attempt to consolidate those steps to reduce the number of database restarts.

To simplify the configuration, we have divided this MAA workshop into three parts: network configuration, primary database configuration, and standby database configuration. These pieces of this MAA workshop are separated by Workshop Notes that describe each section. Let's get started.

To support log transport services and RMAN active database duplication (we will talk more about this later) for standby instantiation, we must update the Oracle network configuration for the primary database and the standby database on both the primary and standby hosts. Perform the following steps to configure the Oracle network for Oracle Data Guard.

Step 1. To instantiate the standby database, we will be using RMAN. To support the RMAN standby instantiation, we must create a static listener entry for the standby database on the node used for instantiation. We could choose to create the static entries only on the primary and standby cluster nodes used for instantiation, but we want to ensure that we are able to reinstantiate from any primary node to any standby node when a role reversal or failover has occurred. To ensure that we are able to reinstate after a role transition or failover from any node in the Oracle Data Guard configuration, we must create a static listener entry for each of the primary and standby database instances on their respective node.

Add the following to the $GI_HOME/network/admin/listener.ora file on all the nodes that the primary database will be running on, replacing <sid> and <oracle_home> with the appropriate SID and ORACLE_HOME for that particular node:

```
SID_LIST_LISTENER =
  (SID_LIST =
    (SID_DESC =
      (GLOBAL_DBNAME = pitt)
      (ORACLE_HOME = <oracle_home>)
      (SID_NAME = <sid>)
    )
  )
```

Add the following to the $GI_HOME/network/admin/listener.ora file on all the nodes that the standby database will be running on, replacing <sid> and <oracle_home> with the appropriate SID and ORACLE_HOME for that particular node:

```
SID_LIST_LISTENER =
  (SID_LIST =
    (SID_DESC =
      (GLOBAL_DBNAME = cosp)
      (ORACLE_HOME = <oracle_home>)
      (SID_NAME = <sid>)
    )
  )
```

After making these configuration changes to the listeners, reload the listeners (on all nodes) to pick up the configuration changes as the Grid Infrastructure (GI) software owner:

```
# lsnrctl reload
```

Step 2. With 11*g* Release 2, the log transport services fully support access via the Single Client Access Name (SCAN) address; therefore, we will need to create Transparent Network Substrate (TNS) aliases to support log shipment and communication between the primary and standby databases using the SCAN. Add the following tnsnames.ora entries to the $ORACLE_HOME/network/admin/tnsnames.ora file on all nodes on the primary and standby systems:

```
pitt =
  (DESCRIPTION =
    (ADDRESS = (PROTOCOL = TCP)
      (HOST = ratlnxclu02-scan.us.oracle.com)(PORT = 1521)
    (CONNECT_DATA =
      (SERVER = DEDICATED)
      (SERVICE_NAME = pitt)
    )
  )
cosp =
  (DESCRIPTION =
    (ADDRESS = (PROTOCOL = TCP)
      (HOST = ratgen-scan.us.oracle.com)(PORT = 1521)
    (CONNECT_DATA =
      (SERVER = DEDICATED)
      (SERVICE_NAME = cosp)
    )
  )
```

Step 3. In addition to these tnsnames.ora entries, we will also need to create entries to support the RMAN instantiation of the standby database. If you want, you can create entries for only the database instances that will be used for instantiation, but it is recommended that entries are created on all primary and standby nodes to ensure instantiation is possible on any system in the configuration. These entries must use the node VIP and not the SCAN VIP, because these TNS aliases will be used to connect to the database using the static listener entries created in the preceding step. Add the following to the tnsnames.ora on all nodes in the Oracle Data Guard configuration replacing <node_vip> and <sid> with their appropriate values:

```
pitt_<server_name> =
  (DESCRIPTION =
    (ADDRESS = (PROTOCOL = TCP)(HOST = <node_vip>)(PORT = 1521))
    (CONNECT_DATA =
      (SERVER = DEDICATED)
      (SERVICE_NAME = pitt)
      (INSTANCE_NAME = <sid>)
    )
  )
```

```
cosp_ratgen01 =
  (DESCRIPTION =
     (ADDRESS = (PROTOCOL = TCP)(HOST = <node_vip>)(PORT = 1521))
     (CONNECT_DATA =
       (SERVER = DEDICATED)
       (SERVICE_NAME = cosp)
       (INSTANCE_NAME = <sid>)
     )
  )
```

Workshop Notes

We will now cover the steps necessary to prepare the primary database to support our physical standby database.

Step 1. As you probably know by now, Oracle Data Guard is dependent on redo data to synchronize the standby database with the primary; therefore, we must ensure that the database is in archivelog mode.

   If the primary database is not in archivelog mode, enable archivelog mode as follows:

```
# srvctl stop database -d maadb
SQL> startup mount;
SQL> alter database archivelog;
SQL> alter database open;
# srvctl start database -d maadb
```

   As for Oracle Database 10g, the **log_archive_start** parameter has been deprecated and is no longer necessary. Automatic archiving is enabled by default when the database is placed into archivelog mode.

Step 2. Nologging operations performed on the primary database can result in missing data on the standby database. To ensure that all transactions generate the required redo data to maintain the standby database, it is highly recommended that force logging be implemented on the standby database. Execute the following within SQL*Plus as the sys user to enable force logging:

```
SQL> alter database force logging;
```

Step 3. Oracle Data Guard uses Oracle Net for log transport services; therefore, authentication is required for the log transport services. With Oracle 11g Release 2, authentication can be achieved by using Secure Sockets Layer (SSL) or by using the traditional remote login password file. SSL authentication requires that Oracle Internet Directory be implemented, which is beyond the scope of this book, so we will be using the traditional method of remote login password file authentication. This password file must reside in the $ORACLE_HOME/dbs directory on UNIX systems or the $ORACLE_HOME\database directory on Windows systems, with the format of orapw<sid>.ora. It must be identical on both the primary and standby databases (more on this later). If the primary database does not yet have a password file, create one on all cluster nodes running the primary database by using the **orapwd** command line utility as follows:

```
# orapwd file=$ORACLE_HOME/dbs/orapw<oracle_sid> password=oracle123
```

Once the password file has been successfully created on the necessary cluster nodes, you must set the following parameter in the SPFILE and restart the database.

```
SQL> alter system set remote_login_passwordfile=exclusive scope=spfile
sid='*';
```

Step 4.   Standby redo logs are required on the standby database for maximum protection and maximum availability protection modes. Standby redo logs are a highly recommended best practice when in maximum performance mode because they will allow real-time apply to be used on the standby database. Real-time apply was introduced in 10*g* to provide a higher level of transactional consistency by allowing for redo data to be applied from the standby redo log as that log is being written by the Remote File Server (RFS) process, as opposed to the traditional method of waiting for a full archivelog to be cut prior to applying the redo data in that log. The result of real-time apply is decreased data loss during failover and better performance of switchover and failover operations, making real-time apply a best practice for your Oracle Data Guard environment.

The creation of standby redo logs on the primary database is also a highly recommended best practice that allows for seamless role transitions (switchover) and reinstatement of failed databases (more about this later in the chapter in the section "Reinstating a Database After a Failover"). By creating standby redo logs on the primary database at this stage, we are ensuring that they exist on both the primary and yet-to-be-created standby databases.

When creating standby redo logs, you must create them to be the same size as the online redo logs, and best practice is to create one additional standby redo log group per thread beyond what exists for the online redo logs. This extra redo log per thread acts as a buffer to allow for more efficient handling of redo data during high transactional periods. Standby redo logs should not be multiplexed to avoid unnecessary I/O overhead during log transport.

Perform the following to create the standby redo logs within Automatic Storage Management (ASM):

```
SQL> alter database add standby logfile thread 1
group 10 '+DBDATA' size 500M,
...
group 13 '+DBDATA' size 500M;
```

```
alter database add standby logfile thread 2
group 14 '+DBDATA' size 500M,
...
group 17 '+DBDATA' size 500M;
```

Step 5.   When configuring initialization parameters on the primary database, we need to consider future role transitions. We must configure the parameters to control log transport services and log apply services so that the database will seamlessly operate in either role with no parameter modification. While the database is mounted on a primary control file, the standby parameters are not read and are not put into effect, so they will not affect the operation of the database while in the primary role. Configure the primary database with the following initialization parameters (SPFILE) by logging into the database as sysdba and running the following:

```
SQL> alter system set db_unique_name='pitt' scope=spfile sid='*';
SQL> alter system set log_archive_config = 'DG_CONFIG=(pitt,cosp)'
scope=both sid='*';
SQL> alter system set standby_file_management=AUTO scope=both sid='*';
SQL> alter system set db_file_name_convert='pitt','cosp','cosp','pitt',
'maadb','cosp','cosp','maadb' scope=spfile sid='*';
SQL> alter system set log_file_name_convert='pitt','cosp','cosp',
'pitt','maadb','cosp','cosp','maadb' scope=spfile sid='*';
SQL> alter system set log_archive_dest_2='SERVICE=cosp VALID_
FOR=(ONLINE_LOGFILES,PRIMARY_ROLE) DB_UNIQUE_NAME=cosp' scope=spfile
sid='*';
SQL> alter system set log_archive_dest_state_2=defer scope=spfile;
SQL> alter system set fal_server='pitt' scope=spfile sid='*';
```

Notice the setting of **db_unique_name**; although recommended on the primary database (for ease of identification), it is not required, but this parameter *must* be set on *all* standby databases to ensure unique identification of that database. Next, if you are familiar with pre-11*g* Oracle Data Guard configurations, you are probably thinking that we missed the setting of the **FAL_CLIENT** parameter. Well, in 11*g* Release 2 this parameter has been deprecated and is no longer necessary. Third, in this example we did specify the **db_file_name_convert** and **log_file_name_convert** parameters. If you are using Oracle Managed Files (OMF), these parameters are not necessary, because you will not be explicitly specifying locations/filenames for datafile and/or redo log creation. We specified these parameters for demonstration purposes only; if you are *not* using OMF, these parameters are indeed required.

   After making these changes to the database SPFILE, we must restart the database to allow the parameter changes to take effect. We will do this using the Server Control Utility (SRVCTL):

```
# srvctl stop database -d maadb
# srvctl start database -d maadb
```

Step 6. Assuming the **db_unique_name** was modified in the parameter changes for step 5, we now need to update the Clusterware database resources to reflect this change. This could be avoided by specifying the appropriate **db_unique_name** when creating the database or by setting the **db_unique_name** to the database name, but for educational purposes we will make the modification. The only way to make this change is to completely remove and re-create the Clusterware database resource.

First, let's print out the current configuration of the database resource:

```
# srvctl config database -d maadb
```

Now that we have the current configuration, we can remove and re-create the database resource:

```
# srvctl stop database -d maadb
# srvctl add database -d pitt -n maadb -a "DBDATA,DBFLASH" -r PRIMARY
-o /ora01/app/oracle/product/11.2.0/db_1 -p +DBDATA/maadb/spfilemaadb.ora
# srvctl add instance -d pitt -i maadb1 -n ratlnx01
# srvctl add instance -d pitt -i maadb2 -n ratlnx02
# srvctl start database -d pitt
```

> **TIP**
> *Use **srvctl –h** to list the available syntax options.*

Workshop Notes

Now that our primary database has been prepared and our Oracle network has been configured to support the standby database, we can create the standby database. With 11g Release 1 and 11g Release 2, two RMAN methods can be used to perform the instantiation of the standby database: *backup-based duplication* and *active database duplication*.

Backup-based duplication is the traditional method that involves creating a database and archivelog backup, copying the backup to the standby system, preparing the standby database, and using the RMAN **duplicate** function to instantiate the standby. This method is often used when a backup of the database already exists.

RMAN active database duplication was introduced in 11g Release 1 to simplify the standby database creation (and duplication) process by copying the active datafiles from the primary database directly to the standby (or auxiliary) site. As you can see, this method has eliminated three of the most time-consuming tasks performed using the traditional method of standby database creation. We will discuss RMAN in detail in Chapter 10; for now, we will be using the active database duplication process for standby creation.

Step 1. We will be specifying the SPFILE clause in the RMAN **duplicate** command to allow RMAN to duplicate and appropriately modify the SPFILE as part of the database duplication process. This makes the creation of our parameter file simple, because we need to specify a single parameter, **db_name**; to keep things simple, we will set this parameter to the **db_unique_name** of the standby database. This setting is not permanent, however: it is necessary only to allow us to **startup nomount** the standby database instance to provide a target for duplication. This parameter value will be corrected when RMAN creates the standby database SPFILE. This text-based parameter file should reside in the $ORACLE_HOME/dbs directory on UNIX systems or the $ORACLE_HOME\database directory on Windows systems, having the format init<sid>.ora. The parameter file can be created as follows:

```
# echo db_name=cosp > $ORACLE_HOME/dbs/initmaadb1.ora
```

Step 2. Because RMAN active database duplication uses Oracle .NET, we must create a password file on each of the standby systems. Oracle 11g uses strong password authentication by default, so we must copy (not re-create) the password file from the primary systems to the standby systems. This password file must reside in the $ORACLE_HOME/dbs directory on UNIX systems or the $ORACLE_HOME\ database directory on Windows systems, having the format orapw<sid>.ora.

> **NOTE**
> *Using **orapwd** to create the password file on the standby systems will likely result in an ORA-16191 error when connecting to the standby database.*

If you are using the Windows OS, a Windows service must be created for the standby database instance(s) on the standby host. To create the service, perform the following command:

```
oradim -NEW -SID maadb1 -INTPWD oracle123 -STARTMODE manual
```

> **NOTE**
> *The password file can also be copied by the RMAN duplication procedure, assuming the **password file** option is used.*

Step 3. Oracle 11g has **audit_trail** set to **DB** by default and the **audit_file_dest** parameter is set to **$ORACLE_BASE/admin/<db_name>/adump**. Therefore, to allow our standby database to start up, we must create the admin directory structure for the standby database prior to startup. On all standby nodes, create the following directories:

- $ORACLE_BASE/admin/cosp/
- $ORACLE_BASE/admin/cosp/adump

Step 4. When using RMAN duplicate functionality, the standby database must be started in nomount state. To start the database, set the **ORACLE_SID** appropriately and issue a **startup nomount** within SQL*Plus:

```
# export ORACLE_SID=maadb1 (windows will use the set command)
# sqlplus / as sysdba
SQL> startup nomount
```

Step 5. Finally, it is the moment we have been waiting for. It is time to instantiate our standby database using RMAN active database duplication. When using RMAN database duplication, the primary system is always referred to as the *target* database and the duplicate is referred to as the *auxiliary* database.

We will use the following RMAN duplicate parameters to create our standby:

- **FOR STANDBY**   This tells RMAN that the duplication is for a standby database allowing RMAN to create the standby controlfile and not rename the database.

- **DORECOVER**   Allows RMAN to perform a point-in-time recovery of the standby database.

- **SPFILE**   Directs RMAN to copy the SPFILE from the target system with the modifications listed below the SPFILE directive.

- **NOFILENAMECHECK**   Allows the reuse of the target datafile names for the duplicate database.

Since RMAN active database duplication requires the use of Oracle Net, the duplication can be initiated on either the primary system or the standby system. Issue the following to instantiate the standby database:

```
# rman
rman> connect target sys/oracle123@pitt_ratlnx01
rman> connect auxiliary sys/oracle123@cosp_ratgen01
rman> DUPLICATE TARGET DATABASE
  FOR STANDBY
  FROM ACTIVE DATABASE
  DORECOVER
  SPFILE
    PARAMETER_VALUE_CONVERT "pitt","cosp","maadb","cosp"
    SET DB_UNIQUE_NAME="cosp"
    SET LOG_ARCHIVE_DEST_2="service=pitt
     VALID_FOR=(online_logfile,primary_role) DB_UNIQUE_NAME=pitt"
    SET FAL_SERVER="cosp"
    SET FAL_CLIENT="pitt"
    SET REMOTE_LISTENER="ratgen-scan.us.oracle.com:1521"
  NOFILENAMECHECK;
```

Step 6. RMAN duplicate will create the SPFILE in the $ORACLE_HOME/dbs directory as part of the duplication process. Because we are creating an Oracle RAC standby, we must move this SPFILE to a shared location to allow it to be accessed by all standby database instances. In our case, this is ASM.

```
SQL> create pfile='$ORACLE_HOME/dbs/inittmp.ora' from spfile;
SQL> create spfile='+DBDATA/spfilemaadb.ora' from pfile='$ORACLE_HOME/
dbs/inittmp.ora'
SQL> shutdown immediate;
```

Now we perform the following to make use of the SPFILE stored in ASM on all standby cluster nodes, replacing <sid> with the appropriate value:

```
# echo spfile='+DBDATA/spfilemaadb.ora' > $ORACLE_HOME/dbs/init<sid>.ora
# rm $ORACLE_HOME/dbs/spfilemaadb1.ora --will only exist on node 1
```

> **NOTE**
> *If you have changed the SID(s) for your standby database (not demonstrated here), the modification of the SID will not be modified by the Active Database Duplication process. You must manually modify the instance-specific parameters as appropriate for your environment.*

Step 7. Now we'll restart our standby database in mount state and place it in managed recovery mode. If you are familiar with 9*i* and earlier standby databases, you will notice that the **startup mount** command does not contain the **standby database** clause. Where did it go? Well, starting with Oracle 10*g*, the control file is read during startup, and if the control file is a standby control file, the database is automatically mounted as a standby database.

```
SQL> startup mount
```

The "Managing a Physical Standby Database" section later in the chapter covers the details of the enablement of managed recovery for our standby database. For now, we are going to keep things simple by using the following:

```
SQL> alter database recover managed standby database disconnect;
```

Step 8. Now that we have created our standby database, we need to tell the Oracle Clusterware on the standby cluster that it has a new database resource to monitor.

To do so, we use SRVCTL, making sure that we specify the database to start up in mount state, as follows:

```
# srvctl add database -d cosp -n maadb -a "DBDATA,DBFLASH" -r physical_
standby -s mount -o /ora01/app/oracle/product/11.2.0/db_1 -p +DBDATA/
spfilemaadb.ora
# srvctl add instance -d cosp -i maadb1 -n ratgen01
# srvctl add instance -d cosp -i maadb2 -n ratgen02
# srvctl start database -d cosp
```

Step 9.   Remember in step 5 that we deferred **LOG_ARCHIVE_DEST_2** on the primary database until we had the standby mounted. Now it is time to enable that destination and begin shipping redo data the standby. On the primary database, enter the following command:

```
SQL> alter system set log_archive_dest_state_2=enable scope=both sid='*';
```

Now we'll perform a log switch on the primary and verify that the transmission of that log was successful:

```
SQL> alter system switch logfile;
SQL> select status,error from v$archive_dest where dest_id=2;
```

If the transmission was successful, the status of the destination should be valid. If the status is invalid, investigate the error listed in the error column to correct any issues.

Creating a Snapshot Standby

As mentioned in the overview of the three different types of standby databases, a snapshot standby is essentially an extension of a physical standby that allows the database to be opened in read-write mode for periods of time before being reverted back to a physical standby. Since we have just created a physical standby database, this is a logical time to try out the conversion of that standby into a snapshot standby. Before breaking out into our second Oracle Data Guard MAA workshop, let's start off with a use-case scenario.

Galaxy Travel is a customer of LunarTrax that places weekly automated travel reservations. Week after week, Galaxy calls to complain that travelers are being confirmed on the incorrect flights. Clearly, the automated system has a problem, but the developers have not been able to uncover the issue in their test systems. The developers suspect that it is an application induced data issue, but it is simply not feasible to replicate the 10 terabyte database on the development or QA systems.

Max is weary of hearing excuses. It's time for the DBAs to take action and show what the database can do by converting the 11g physical standby database to a snapshot database. We still have the level of protection provided by log transport, and we can get this issue solved once and for all by opening our standby database for developers to perform their magic…so how do we do that?

In this MAA workshop, we will convert our physical standby database into a snapshot standby and then reverse the procedure converting the snapshot standby back into a physical standby.

MAA Workshop: *Converting an Oracle RAC Physical Standby to a Snapshot Standby*

Workshop Notes

We will use the physical standby database created in the preceding workshop. If you have destroyed this standby or you simply skipped over that section, go back and create the physical standby database per the workshop instructions.

Step 1. Because we will be opening this standby database, we first need to complete any active recovery that is in progress and tell the database to halt standby recovery operations:

```
SQL> alter database recover managed standby database cancel;
```

Step 2. When a physical standby database has been converted to a snapshot standby, it will still receive redo data from the primary database via log transport services as well as generating its own redo data. Therefore, it is important that prior to converting the physical standby to a snapshot standby, the Flash Recovery Area must be sized to handle the backlog of redo data as well as the flashback logs (before image block copies; more on this in Chapter 11) required for a snapshot standby database.

Step 3. To perform the conversion, we must first shut down all but one instance of our standby database. After all but one instance is shut down, we can perform the conversion and open all instances in read-write mode:

```
# srvctl stop instance -i maadb2 -d cosp
SQL> alter database convert to snapshot standby;
SQL> alter database open;
# srvctl start instance -i maadb2 -d cosp -o open
```

Step 4. At this point, the snapshot standby is a fully updateable database. The fact that it is a snapshot standby is completely transparent to the end user. We DBAs need to realize that we *cannot* switchover or failover to this standby database until it is converted back into a physical standby.

Step 5. Once we have finished using our snapshot standby, we must convert it back into a physical standby. Converting a snapshot standby back to a physical standby will utilize Flashback Database to flash the standby back to the point in time prior to the conversion. The procedure, once again, must be performed when only a single instance of our cluster database is running:

```
# srvctl stop database -d cosp
SQL> startup mount;
SQL> alter database convert to physical standby;
SQL> shutdown abort;
SQL> startup mount;
SQL> alter database recover managed standby database disconnect;
# srvctl start database -d cosp
```

The amount of time it will take for the conversion to complete depends on the amount of redo data that was generated while the database was a snapshot standby (for information on estimation of flashback logging, see Chapter 11). If the redo volume was high, be patient, it will complete. Once the conversion back to a physical standby has completed, we restart the standby database to enable managed recovery.

Creating a Logical Standby

Let's start with a short discussion on the supported objects of a logical standby. The use of unsupported objects in the primary database is often the determining factor regarding whether or not we should implement this type of a standby database. After we understand more about the unsupported objects, we will move into the actual creation of a logical standby database. The high-level steps first create a physical standby database and then convert it into a logical standby. If you are wondering, no, that is not a typo; the first step in the process is indeed to create a physical standby database. Even though the steps are quite simple, we break each step down into parts that will be discussed in detail to help you understand the process.

Logical Standby Unsupported Objects

The first step in creating a logical standby is to examine the applications on the primary and make sure that logical standby has support for all of the data types and tables. Determining support for your application database objects on the primary database before you create a logical standby database is an important step. Changes made on the primary database to any objects that are not supported will not be propagated to the logical standby. When the log apply services on the logical standby encounters any unsupported objects, it will silently exclude all changes made to those objects with no warning provided to the user.

Determining Unsupported Objects

Fortunately, Oracle makes it easy to determine exactly which objects are supported and which are not. To obtain a list of unsupported tables, issue the following query on the primary database:

```
SQL> select distinct owner,table_name from dba_logstdby_unsupported
order by owner,table_name;
```

Tables that are returned from this query are unsupported for one of several reasons: either it's an unsupported data type or it belongs to a default Oracle schema that is not maintained. In most cases, the tables are unsupported due to data type restrictions. To see exactly which column/data type is unsupported, we can modify the previous query to include column information:

```
SQL> select column_name,data_type from dba_logstdby_unsupported
where table_name = 'foo';
```

In Oracle Database 11*g* Release 2, the following data types are *not* natively supported with a logical standby:

- BFILE

- VARRAYS

- ROWID

- Nested tables

- UROWID

- XML type stored as object relational

- User-defined types

- Binary XML

- Multimedia data types (such as spatial, image, Oracle text)

Uniquely Identifying Rows on the Primary

When you update a row on the primary database, a redo record is created that can uniquely identify the exact row that was changed. In the absence of a primary key or unique key index, Oracle will use the ROWID to locate the row. While this is a fast and efficient method for uniquely locating rows on the primary, it does not work in the case of a logical standby. A logical standby can have a drastically different physical layout, which makes the use of ROWID impossible. Without getting into a deep discussion of the architecture of SQL Apply (covered later in the section

"Managing a Logical Standby Database"), this can cause performance issues. To resolve the issue, Oracle recommends that you add a primary key or unique key index to as many of your application tables as possible. Doing so will allow SQL Apply to apply updates efficiently to those tables on the logical standby.

To identify tables on the primary that do not have a primary key or do not have a unique index, run the following query:

```
SQL> select owner, table_name,bad_column from dba_logstdby_not_unique
where table_name not in
(select table_name from dba_logstdby_unsupported)and bad_column = 'Y';
```

Note that tables returned in this query can still be supported by SQL Apply as long as the row is able to be uniquely identified. To allow this functionality, Oracle uses supplemental logging to add information into the redo stream that will enable the rows to be uniquely identified. However, performance might be impacted. If your application ensures uniqueness, you should consider adding a RELY constraint onto that table on the primary database along with an index of the unique columns on the logical standby. The RELY constraint will tell Oracle to assume that the specified columns uniquely identify the row on the primary database, while the index on the standby will prevent full table scans by SQL Apply when applying the transactions.

MAA Workshop: *Creating an Oracle RAC Logical Standby Database*

Workshop Notes

Now that you have confirmed that a logical standby is able to support your application or you've made accommodations within your application to allow the use of a logical standby, you can perform the actual task of creating a logical standby database. For this workshop, we will again be using same database naming conventions used for the "Creating an Oracle RAC Physical Standby Database" workshop. If you have forgotten, **pitt** was the **db_unique_name** for the primary database and **cosp** was the **db_unique_name** for the standby database.

Step 1. The first step of creating a logical standby database is to create a physical standby. To create the physical standby, go back to the MAA workshop "Creating an Oracle RAC Physical Standby Database" and follow those steps through completion.

Step 2. A logical standby database makes use of LogMiner behind the scenes to mine the redo data necessary to generate SQL apply transactions. Prior to creating the LogMiner dictionary, we must stop the managed recovery on the standby database to ensure that we do not apply redo beyond the redo that contains the LogMiner dictionary:

```
SQL> alter database recover managed standby database cancel;
```

Step 3.   If you are using your logical standby database for disaster recovery, minimal downtime patching, or any other scenario that would require a role transition, it is recommended that you implement the parameters to support this transition prior to performing it. This will minimize the number of tasks required to be executed when performing the role transitions, thus minimizing the time required to perform the transition.

```
SQL> alter system set LOG_ARCHIVE_DEST_1='LOCATION=USE_DB_RECOVERY_FILE_
DEST' VALID_FOR=(ALL_LOGFILES,ALL_ROLES) DB_UNIQUE_NAME=PITT' scope=both
sid='*';SQL> alter system set LOG_ARCHIVE_DEST_STATE_1=ENABLE scope=both
sid='*';
```

Here we used **LOG_ARCHIVE_DEST_1** for **ALL ROLES**. Alternatively, we could have specified a separate location for **ONLINE_LOGFILES** and **STANDBY_LOGFILES**, but this is not necessary (and we will not cover this in the subsequent steps).

Step 4.   As mentioned, a logical standby uses LogMiner to mine the online redo data to generate the transactions that are executed by the SQL Apply process. This requires that we build a LogMiner dictionary in the redo data. To perform this task, we will use the **dbms_logstdby.build** procedure.

In addition to building the LogMiner dictionary, the procedure will also enable supplemental logging on the primary key and unique index columns. This supplemental logging will ensure that the table rows are able to be uniquely identified by the SQL Apply process.

```
SQL> exec dbms_logstdby.build;
```

Be patient; the **dbms_logstdby.build** will wait for all active transactions to complete, and the more busy the database, the longer this will take.

Step 5.   Assuming that we have created an Oracle RAC physical standby, the first step in the process is to shut down all database instances, set the **cluster_database** parameter to **false**, and mount a single instance in exclusive mode:

```
# srvctl stop database -d cosp
SQL> startup nomount;
SQL> alter system set cluster_database=false scope=spfile sid='*';
SQL> shutdown abort;
SQL> startup mount exclusive;
```

Step 6. At this point, all of the information necessary to convert our physical standby to a logical standby is in the redo data from the primary database. To begin the conversion, we must recover the database to a logical standby:

```
SQL> alter database recover to logical standby cosplg;
```

This command will result in the database being recovered up to the point at which the LogMiner dictionary is found. Again, be patient, as the time it takes to complete is dependent on how much redo data was generated after the cancellation of the managed recovery process of the physical standby.

You have probably noticed that the preceding command specified a new database name of *cosplg* for our standby database. This will change the database name from *maadb* to *cosplg* in the controlfile, make the modification to the SPFILE for our logical standby database, and create a new unique DBID for the database. If you are familiar with the logical standby creation procedures prior to Oracle 11g, you'll realize that this greatly simplifies the process.

Step 7. We can now take the database out of the exclusive mount and reset the **cluster_database** parameter to **true**. Even though we are setting the parameter to **true**, we are mounting only a single database instance.

```
SQL> alter system set cluster_database=true scope=spfile sid='*';
SQL> shutdown;
SQL> startup mount;
```

Step 8. Now we configure the local archive destination parameters to support this role transition and logical standby functionality. Again, keep in mind that **LOG_ARCHIVE_DEST_2** should have already been configured as part of the build process for the physical standby to support log transport services when the database is in the primary role. No modifications should be necessary for the **LOG_ARCHIVE_DEST_2** parameter. Also, we are not specifying a separate location for standby log files (note the **ALL_LOGFILES** setting), so no changes should be necessary in this step.

```
SQL> alter system set LOG_ARCHIVE_DEST_1='LOCATION=USE_DB_RECOVERY_FILE_
DEST VALID_FOR=(ALL_LOGFILES,ALL_ROLES) DB_UNIQUE_NAME=COSP' scope=both
sid='*';
SQL> alter system set LOG_ARCHIVE_DEST_STATE_1=ENABLE scope=both sid='*';
```

Step 9. At last! We are ready to open our newly created logical standby database, but those anxious management team members must wait: we are not quite ready to support those TPS reports. We still need to enable managed recovery and provide the Oracle RAC performance they expect, but we are moments away:

```
SQL> alter database open resetlogs;
```

Step 10.   A database link that points to the primary will be necessary for role transitions and for the use of the **DBMS_LOGSTDBY.INSTANATIATE_TABLE** procedure:

```
SQL> create database link pitt connect to <user> identified by
<password> using 'PITT';
```

Step 11.   To allow the clusterware to monitor and manage our logical standby database properly, we must update the database resource configuration that was added when creating the physical standby.

```
# srvctl modify database -d cosp -n cosplg -r logical_standby -s open
# srvctl start database -d cosp
```

Step 12.   Finally, the last step in the process is to enable SQL Apply to allow the logical standby to remain in sync with the transactions performed on the primary database:

```
SQL> alter database start logical standby apply immediate;
```

The management team can now run those reports.

Log Transport Services

By now, you have probably noticed the mention of *log transport services* in the previous Oracle Data Guard MAA workshops. Log transport services are at the heart of Oracle Data Guard. The basis of Oracle Data Guard is the fact that we are effectively able to ship changes generated on the primary database to a secondary site. Once those changes exist on the secondary site, we are protected from the dreaded disaster. But log transport services does more than simply ship redo from one site to another site. It also lets us determine the level of data protection for our database. Log transport services configuration can be performed to balance data protection and availability against any performance impact. We will examine how to configure log transport services and discuss items that should be considered when designing your disaster recovery solution.

Defining Log Transport Services Destinations

We define where and how log transport services will transmit redo using the **log_archive_dest_n** initialization parameter. Using this parameter in Oracle 11*g*, we can define up to 30 destinations, each of which can send redo to distinct destinations. When defining the destination for redo data, we use the **LOCATION** attribute to store the redo locally on disk and the **SERVICE** attribute to enable shipment to a remote location via Oracle Net.

The following example will ship redo via Oracle Net to the specified netservice name using the default attributes:

```
SQL> alter system set LOG_ARCHIVE_DEST_2='SERVICE=cosp' scope=both sid='*';
```

Once the parameter is set, log transport services will redo data to the specified Oracle netservice name. If we want to disable the shipment of redo data to this destination, we would simply modify the **log_archive_dest_state_*n*** parameter from **enabled** to **defer** as follows:

```
SQL> alter system set LOG_ARCHIVE_DEST_STATE_2=defer scope=both sid='*';
```

Although the parameter in even its simplest form is very effective, numerous attributes allow fine-grained control over how and when data is sent. Because covering all attributes is not practical for this chapter, we will describe some of the more frequently used attributes.

NOTE
*If you are familiar with log transport attributes available prior to Oracle 11g, you will notice that we are not covering the **ARC** or **LGWR** attributes. These attributes were deprecated in favor of always using the more efficient LNS process to perform redo shipment.*

ASYNC (Default) and SYNC Attributes

When the default mode of **ASYNC** is used, the log network server (LNS) process does not wait for each network I/O to complete before proceeding to minimize the overhead of Oracle Data Guard on the primary database. To ensure minimal overhead of Oracle Data Guard when operating in **ASYNC** mode, LNS will always attempt to read redo from the log buffer to avoid disk I/O; should the log buffer have been flushed, LNS will then read from online redo and subsequently archived redo. Obviously, in this case it is more efficient for LNS to read from the log buffer (instead of performing physical I/O), so we should ensure that LNS is reading from the log buffer as often as possible. To check how often LNS is reading from the log buffer, we can query **x$logbuf_readhist**.

The **SYNC** attribute specifies that network I/O is to be performed synchronously for the destination, which means that once the I/O is initiated, the archiving process waits for the I/O to complete before continuing. That being said, a transaction is not committed on the primary database until the redo data necessary to recover that transaction is received by all destinations in which the **SYNC** attribute has been specified. With Oracle Database 11g Release 2, the local write and remote write(s) will occur at the same time to minimize the performance impact of **SYNC** on the primary database. The **SYNC** attribute is not available with **log_archive_dest_11** through **log_archive_dest_31**.

AFFIRM Attribute

The **AFFIRM** attribute is valid only when using **ASYNC** log transport in 11g Release 2 (defaulted when using **SYNC**). When configured, this setting ensures that all disk I/O at the standby site are performed synchronously and that they have completed successfully prior to returning control to the user on the primary.

NET_TIMEOUT Attribute

During normal Oracle Data Guard operations, the LNS process establishes an Oracle Net service connection to the standby. If for some reason the network between the primary and standby hosts is lost, the network connection will go through normal TCP processing before determining that the connection no longer exists. Depending on the log transport configuration, this can negatively impact processing on the primary database. Oracle developed the **NET_TIMEOUT** attribute so that the user could specify the amount of time in seconds for Oracle Net services to respond to a **LGWR** request. The **NET_TIMEOUT** attribute has a default value of 30 seconds and is applicable only when the **SYNC** attribute has been specified. Oracle recommends that this value not be set lower than 10 seconds to avoid false disconnects.

REOPEN Attribute

If an archive destination receives an error, the destination will close and will not be retried until the period of time (in seconds) as specified by the **REOPEN** attribute. Once **REOPEN** has expired, the destination is once again valid and will be attempted at the next log switch. This attribute has a default value of 300 seconds.

MAX_FAILURE Attribute

The **MAX_FAILURE** attribute defines the number of times we will reopen a destination that has been closed due to a failure.

COMPRESSION Attribute

Log transport compression is a feature within the Advanced Compression database option that allows for compression of redo data prior to transporting that redo data to the specified destination (not only in Fetch Archive Log [FAL] as in previous releases). With 11g Release 2, compression is available for use when shipping redo in both **ASYNC** and **SYNC** modes. This is definitely a feature worthy of consideration if you have enough CPU capacity to perform the compression but are tight on network bandwidth between the primary and standby databases. That being said, if you do have sufficient bandwidth between the primary and standby databases, it is recommended that you not incur the overhead of compression, because the increased need for CPU resources may result in unnecessary latency in redo transport and/or apply.

VALID_FOR Attribute

Both the primary and standby initialization parameters should be configured to support either the primary or standby role so that role reversals via switchover are seamless. To prevent the DBA from having to enable or defer archive destination depending on when that destination should be used, Oracle developed the **VALID_FOR** attribute. The **VALID_FOR** attribute is used to specify exactly when an archive destination is to be used and what types of redo logs are to be archived.

The **VALID_FOR** attribute comprises two keywords: archival source and database role. The archival source keywords are as follows:

- **ONLINE_LOGFILE**   Archive online redo logs only for this destination.

- **STANDBY_LOGFILE**   Archive standby redo logs only for this destination.

- **ALL_LOGFILES**   Archive both online and standby redo logs for this destination.

The database role keywords are as follows:

- **PRIMARY_ROLE**   Archive to this destination only when in the primary role.

- **STANDBY_ROLE**   Archive to this destination only when in the standby role.

- **ALL_ROLES**   Archive to this destination when in either primary or standby role.

Let's consider the following example from a physical standby to see how the **VALID_FOR** attribute works. First, the PITT database:

```
LOG_ARCHIVE_DEST_1='LOCATION=USE_DB_RECOVERY_FILE_DEST'
     VALID_FOR=(ALL_LOGFILES,ALL_ROLES) DB_UNIQUE_NAME=PITT' scope=both
sid='*'
LOG_ARCHIVE_DEST_2='SERVICE=cosp
   VALID_FOR=(ONLINE_LOGFILES,PRIMARY_ROLE)
   DB_UNIQUE_NAME=COSP' scope=both sid='*';
```

Then the COSP database:

```
LOG_ARCHIVE_DEST_1='LOCATION=USE_DB_RECOVERY_FILE_DEST'
     VALID_FOR=(ALL_LOGFILES,ALL_ROLES) DB_UNIQUE_NAME=COSP' scope=both
sid='*'
LOG_ARCHIVE_DEST_2='service=pitt
     VALID_FOR=( ONLINE_LOGFILES,PRIMARY_ROLE)
     DB_UNIQUE_NAME=PITT' scope=both sid='*';
```

In this example, when the PITT database is in the primary role, we will archive the online redo logs only to destination 1, because the standby redo logs are not active in the primary role. We will also archive the online redo logs to destination 2 while we are in the primary role. In the COSP database, we will archive the standby redo logs to destination 1 because the online redo logs are not active in the standby role. We will not archive to destination number 2 because the COSP database is not in the primary role. When a role reversal occurs, no change to the parameters is necessary to achieve the desired effect. The **VALID_FOR** attribute makes enabling or deferring destinations during role reversals unnecessary.

Log Transport Services Security

In today's IT environment, security and availability cannot be separated. To ensure availability, we must be able to guarantee that the data comes from an authorized agent and that the data is intact and unmodified. In 11*g*, Oracle Data Guard is a disaster recovery solution that includes authentication and data integrity checks out of the box. It optionally offers the ability to provide encryption via the industry standard Secure Socket Layer (SSL).

Oracle Data Guard provides for authenticated network sessions between the primary and the standby for transferring redo by default by using password files and optionally using SSL when Oracle Internet Directory (OID) is used for authentication. Because OID is well beyond the scope of this book, we will focus on the default password file authentication method.

Password file authentication is achieved by comparing the SYS password from the password file on both the primary and standby database to verify that they are the same. This means that your primary database and all standby databases within an Oracle Data Guard configuration must use a copy of the password file from the primary database. If the SYS user is not acceptable for log transport authentication within your environment, Oracle 11*g* provides the flexibility for a user other than SYS to perform log transport services. The log transport user can be modified by specifying the **REDO_TRANSPORT_USER** parameter and adding that user to the password file.

Standby Redo Logs

You have learned how to configure the log transport services on the primary to assure that the redo data is getting transmitted to the standby according to your configuration. What we haven't discussed is what is happening on the standby where the redo is being received. This section discusses the process flow that occurs on the standby once the primary's redo data has arrived.

With Oracle 11*g*, by default, LNS is used on the primary to initiate a connection with the standby; the standby listener responds by spawning a process called the *remote file server (RFS)*. The RFS process will create a network connection with the primary and will sit waiting for data to arrive. Once data begins arriving from the primary, the RFS process will place it either into standby redo logs or into archive redo logs. You can think of standby redo logs as exact twins to online redo logs, except the former are active only when a database is in the standby role. Basically, standby redo logs are just a separate pool of redo logs. The RFS process will pick the first available standby redo log and begin placing changes into that log. When a log switch occurs on the primary, we switch standby redo logs and the RFS process will go to the next available standby redo log. The standby redo log that was being written prior to the log switch will be archived by the standby database. Oracle highly recommends that you use standby redo logs. If you plan on setting one of the higher level protection modes or using Real-Time Apply (we will discuss this later in the section "Starting and Stopping Managed Recovery"), the use of standby redo logs is mandatory.

When creating standby redo logs, it is recommended that you adhere to the following guidelines:

- Standby redo logs should be created with one more log group per thread than the number of online redo log groups on the primary database.

- The standby redo logs must be exactly the same size as the online redo logs.

- You should create standby redo logs on both the primary and standby to facilitate seamless role changes.

- In an Oracle RAC environment, all standby redo logs should be on a shared disk and should be thread-specific.

Protection Modes

The last step in the Oracle Data Guard decision-making process is perhaps the most importation decision that will be made when designing your disaster recovery solution. It all comes down to a single question: How much data are you willing to lose (that is, what is your Recovery Point Objective, or RPO)? Naturally, everyone answers that they can risk none. As we all know from everyday life, there is no such thing as a free lunch. Oracle Data Guard can provide zero data loss, but the resources involved in this configuration often drive the cost-to-benefit ratio beyond budgets set forth for disaster recovery. Thankfully, Oracle Data Guard provides three levels of protection that allow the solution to meet the needs of the business and capabilities of the underlying infrastructure.

Maximum Protection

Holding true to its name, this protection mode guarantees zero data loss in the event of a primary database failure. To facilitate this guaranteed zero data loss level of protection, the redo data needed to recover each transaction must be written both to the local redo log and to a standby redo log on at least one standby database before the transaction commits on the primary database. To ensure this transaction consistency, the primary database will shut down if a fault occurs when writing the redo stream to at least one of the standby destinations.

The following requirements must be met to enable a Maximum Protection Oracle Data Guard configuration:

- The primary database must use the **SYNC** attribute to stream redo to the standby database (**AFFIRM** is defaulted for all **SYNC** transports in 11*g* Release 2).

- The standby database must have standby redo logs configured.

- A minimum of one standby database must be available.

- A snapshot standby cannot be the only standby database in a Maximum Protection configuration.

The use of **SYNC** for streaming of redo data defines that commit complete will not be returned to the user until the transaction has successfully been written to the standby redo logs on the standby host. To put it simply, a user will not be able to continue entering transactions until the primary database receives confirmation of the write having been completed on the standby. Although with 11*g* Release 2, the local and remote redo will be written at the same time, the speed of the network between the primary and standby database have a direct relationship on the speed in which commits can be performed on the primary database. That being said, you would not want to implement a standby in Maximum Protection mode on a high-latency or unreliable network. To help mitigate the risk of network latency or a slow/unresponsive standby in Maximum Protection mode, it is a recommended best practice to have a minimum of two standby databases available, one of which should be on a low-latency high-speed network.

Maximum Availability

The second highest level of protection for a standby database is Maximum Availability. Maximum Availability operates in the same manner as Maximum Protection: we do not return commit complete to the user until we have guaranteed the redo has been completely written to the local and standby redo logs of at least one standby database. The difference is in the fact that if for some reason the standby database becomes unavailable and we are unable to write to the standby redo log, the primary database does not shut down. In this case, the primary database will temporarily drop its protection mode to Maximum Performance and continue allowing transactions. Upon service restoration of the standby database, gap resolution will automatically begin to resolve any archivelog gaps between the primary and standby. Once gap resolution is complete, the primary database will automatically switch back to Maximum Availability at the time of the next log switch. This configuration allows for near zero or zero data loss in the event of a primary database failure.

The following requirements must be met to enable a Maximum Availability Oracle Data Guard configuration:

■ The primary database must use the **SYNC** attributes to stream redo to the standby database.

■ The standby database must have standby redo logs configured.

■ A minimum of one standby database must be available.

You can see by the requirement to use the **SYNC** attributes to supply redo to the standby destination that Maximum Availability will also be impacted by a slow network. Although a slow network will impact the time to return commits to the primary, an error condition will cause the protection mode to drop to Maximum Performance temporarily, thereby avoiding impact on the primary. Keep in mind that with 11g Release 2, we will be performing the local and remote writes of redo data in parallel so the commit latency will be reduced in 11g Release 2, but, obviously, the commit latency will still be driven by the network latency of the network used for Oracle Data Guard. That being said, to run efficiently in a Maximum Availability configuration, a low-latency network between the primary and standby database(s) is very important.

Maximum Performance

Maximum Performance is the default protection level for the Oracle database. It offers the highest level of database protection (minimal to zero data loss) without affecting the availability or performance of the primary database. User transactions on the primary database are allowed to commit immediately as soon as the transaction is written to the local redo logs.

With Maximum Performance, no specific rules or requirements are enforced. The primary ships redo data in **ASYNC** mode, thus minimizing any performance impact on the primary database. The standby does not have to have standby redo logs although their use is recommended. The primary database is allowed to open even if the standby is not available, unlike Maximum Availability and Maximum Protection.

MAA Workshop: *Changing the Protection Mode*

Workshop Notes

When you first create your standby database, its protection mode is set to Maximum Performance by default. Once you have decided which protection mode is best for your business needs and objectives, you will need to change the default mode. Changing the mode involves setting the archivelog destination to meet the requirements of the desired protection mode, and then placing the database into the correct mode. In this MAA workshop, we will modify the protection mode of our physical standby database default from Maximum Performance to Maximum Availability.

Step 1. To set our protection mode to Maximum Availability, we must first configure the remote destination for our standby to use the **SYNC** method for log transport.

```
SQL> alter system set log_archive_dest_2='SERVICE=cosp SYNC
    VALID_FOR=(ONLINE_LOGFILES,PRIMARY_ROLE)
    DB_UNIQUE_NAME=COSP' scope=both sid='*';
```

Step 2. We are now ready to set our protection mode for the standby database to Maximum Availability. With Oracle Database 11*g*, you can modify the protection mode from Maximum Performance to Maximum Availability without restarting the primary database as long as you have specified the **log_archive_config** parameter (as we did in the MAA workshop "Creating an Oracle RAC Physical Standby Database"). Changing the protection mode to Maximum Protection will require a database restart if the protection level is not at Maximum Availability and if the standby database is not synchronized.

```
SQL> alter database set standby database to maximize availability;
```

Step 3. We can now validate that the protection mode has been increased from Maximum Performance to Maximum Availability by running the following query:

```
SQL> select protection_mode from v$database;
```

Handling Network Disconnects

The speed and latency of the network used for log transport can have a considerable impact on how Oracle Data Guard operates. An equally important topic to understand is how network disconnects impact Oracle Data Guard. Let's consider what happens during a simple network disconnect between a primary and standby database.

When the network connection between two hosts is disconnected or when one host within a TCP session is no longer available, the session is known as a *dead connection*. A dead connection indicates that there is no physical connection, but to the processes on each system, the connection still appears to exist. When the LGWR and RFS process are involved in a dead connection, LNS will discover the dead connection when attempting to send a new message to the RFS process. At this point, LNS will wait on the TCP layer to timeout on the network session between the primary and standby before establishing that network connectivity has indeed been lost.

The TCP timeout, as defined by TCP kernel parameter settings, is key to how long LNS will remain in a wait state before abandoning the network connection.

On some platforms, the default for TCP timeout can be as high as two hours. To avoid this lengthy TCP timeout from severely impacting Oracle Data Guard, the **MAX_FAILURE**, **REOPEN**, and **NET_TIMEOUT** attributes were developed.

On the standby, the RFS process is always synchronously waiting for new information to arrive from the LNS process on the primary. The RFS process that is doing the network read operation is blocked until more data arrives or until the operating system's network software determines that the connection is dead.

Once the RFS process receives notification of the dead network connection, it will terminate itself. However, until the RFS process terminates itself, it will retain lock information on the archivelog or the standby redo log on the standby database, whose redo information was being received from the primary database. Any attempt to perform a failover using the **RECOVER MANAGED STANDBY DATABASE FINISH** command will fail while the RFS process maintains a lock on the standby redo log or archivelog. The **RECOVER** command will fail with the following errors:

```
ORA-00283: recovery session canceled due to errors
ORA-00261: log 4 of thread 1 is being archived or modified
ORA-00312: online log 4 thread 1:'+DBDATA/cosp/onlinelog/
group_10.259.718137303'
```

At this point, we must wait for either the network stack on the OS to clean up the dead connection or kill the RFS process before the failover attempt will succeed. The preferred method to decrease the time for the OS network software to clean up the dead connection is the use of Oracle's Dead Connection Detection (DCD) feature.

With Oracle's DCD feature, Oracle Net periodically sends a network probe to verify that a client-server connection is still active. This ensures that connections are not left open indefinitely due to an abnormal client termination. If the probe finds a dead connection or a connection that is no longer in use, it returns an error that causes the RFS process to exit. Though DCD will minimize the detection time of a network disconnect, we are still dependent on the OS network stack for timeouts and retries, so a delay will occur before termination of the RFS process.

Once the network problem is resolved, and the primary database processes are again able to establish network connections to the standby database, a new RFS process will automatically be spawned on the standby database for each new network connection. These new RFS processes will resume the reception of redo data from the primary database.

Gap Detection and Resolution

We now know that once network communication is reestablished between the primary and standby database, the shipment of redo data will automatically resume, but what happens to all the redo data that was generated during the disconnect?

Let's assume that we had a network disconnect at redo sequence 50, and communication was not reestablished until redo sequence 55. In this situation, we have a gap of four archived redo logs. This situation is appropriately named "gap" or "archive gap." Oracle Data Guard provides two methods for gap resolution, *automatic* and *Fetch Archive Log (FAL)*. Automatic gap resolution holds true to its name by occurring automatically without any configuration. FAL, on the other hand, must be configured via primary and standby initialization parameters.

Automatic Gap Resolution

Automatic gap resolution is implemented during log transport processing. As the LNS process begins to send redo to the standby, the sequence number of the log being archived is compared to the last sequence received by the RFS process on the standby. If the RFS process detects that the archivelog being received is greater than the last sequence received plus one, then the RFS will piggyback a request to the primary to send the missing archivelogs. Since the standby destination requesting the gap resolution is already defined by the **LOG_ARCHIVE_DEST_*n*** parameter on the primary, the ARC process on the primary sends the logs to the standby and notifies the LGWR that the gaps have been resolved.

In addition, the ARC process on the primary database polls all standby databases every minute to see if there is a gap in the sequence of archived redo logs. If a gap is detected, the ARC process sends the missing archived redo log files to the standby databases that reported the gap. Once the gap is resolved, the LGWR process is notified that the site is in sync.

FAL Gap Resolution

As the RFS process on the standby receives an archived log, it updates the standby controlfile with the name and location of the file. Once the Media Recovery Process (MRP) sees the update to the controlfile, it attempts to recover that file. If the MRP finds that the archived log is missing or is corrupt, FAL is called to resolve the gap or obtain a new copy. Since MRP has no direct communications link with the primary, it must use the **FAL_SERVER** parameter and the **LOG_ARCHIVE_DEST_*n*** parameter for the **DB_UNIQUE_NAME** client to resolve the gap. Note that **FAL_CLIENT** is no longer required in 11.2 because the client is actually pulled from the **LOG_ARCHIVE_DEST_*n*** parameter (as previously mentioned). The **FAL_SERVER** parameter is defined as follows:

> An Oracle Net service name that exists in the standby tnsnames.ora file defines connectivity to the primary database listener. The **FAL_SERVER** parameter can contain a comma delimited list of locations that should be attempted during gap resolution.

After MRP had determined that a gap needs to be resolved, it uses the value from **FAL_SERVER** to call the primary database. Once communication with the primary has been established, the **DB_UNIQUE_NAME** value of the **LOG_ARCHIVE_DEST_***n* parameter is used to ship the missing redo data from the primary database to the requesting standby database. If the first destination listed in **FAL_SERVER** is unable to resolve the gap, the next destination is attempted until either the gap is resolved or all **FAL_SERVER** destinations have been tried.

Managing a Physical Standby Database

Up to this point, our discussion has been focused on how to configure Oracle Data Guard properly in a physical standby, logical standby, and snapshot standby configuration. We have provided the pros and cons of each and discussed the three protection modes available with Oracle Data Guard. By now you have enough information to implement Oracle Data Guard in a configuration tailored to your business needs.

This section will discuss the management of day-to-day operations of your Oracle Data Guard environment. These operations include starting the standby database, enabling managed recovery, opening the standby in read-only, as well as general maintenance tasks. This section ends with an MAA workshop demonstrating the much anticipated 11g Oracle Data Guard new feature, Oracle Active Data Guard.

Starting a Physical Standby

If you are a veteran of Oracle Data Guard, you probably remember the startup of a physical standby database is a two-step process requiring us DBAs to tell Oracle to mount the database on a standby controlfile. To refresh your memory, the commands are similar to the following:

```
SQL> startup nomount;
SQL> alter database mount standby database;
```

Good news. Starting with Oracle 10g, the startup task has been condensed into a single step:

```
SQL> startup mount;
```

Notice that there are no references to a standby database anywhere in this statement; it is a simple **startup mount** command. During startup, Oracle will read the controlfile when mounting the database to make the determination to mount the database as a standby database or as a primary database.

In an Oracle RAC environment, our physical standby database will be registered with the clusterware. When creating the clusterware resource for the standby database, we need to use SRVCTL to perform this registration, as follows:

```
# srvctl add database -d <db_unique_name> -n <db_name > -a <diskgroups>
-r physical_standby -s mount -o <oracle_home> -p <spfile>
# srvctl add instance -d cosp -i <sid> -n <node>
```

In this **srvctl add database** command, we specified the **–r** option to tell the clusterware that the database is a physical standby database and the **–s** option to set the start mode to mount. Once the standby database has been properly registered with the clusterware, we can start the database as we would start any other Oracle RAC database:

```
# srvctl start database -d <db_unique_name>
```

Starting and Stopping Managed Recovery

Once the standby database has been started, it will begin receiving redo data from the primary database. This redo data will stack up in the form of archivelogs until we instruct the standby database to begin applying the redo data to the standby database. For a physical standby, the redo application is performed via the MRP. The following SQL statement will start the MRP as a foreground process:

```
SQL> alter database recovery managed standby database;
```

This command will appear to hang because MRP is part of the session that it was started in. If we cancel out of this session, the MRP will also exit. As you can imagine, this is really not a desirable functionality for day-to-day operations, but it's handy in troubleshooting or maintenance operations.

For day-to-day operations, we want the MRP to run as a background process, thus allowing us to close our session of the database and allowing MRP to continue applying redo data to the standby database. Here's an example:

```
SQL> alter database recover managed standby database disconnect;
```

When the MRP is started with the two preceding commands, changes are applied to the standby database when either a complete archivelog is received from the primary or when one of the standby redo logs is completely archived. It's important to note that changes are applied only at an archivelog boundary.

If your physical standby has standby redo logs configured, it is possible to have the MRP begin applying changes as soon as they arrive to the standby instead of waiting for a log switch boundary and for the standby redo log to be archived. This functionality was introduced in 10*g* and is called *Real-Time Apply*. Real-Time Apply can shorten the role transition time by minimizing the redo that needs to be applied to the standby database during the role transition. To start Real-Time Apply, you initiate MRP by issuing the following command:

```
SQL> alter database recover managed standby database using current
logfile disconnect;
```

In some cases, you may want to have the standby database lag behind the primary database. This is often useful during application upgrades, bulk load operations, or other situations that may modify database data in an undesirable way. To achieve this time lag, we will start MRP with a delay interval expressed in minutes. The redo data is still shipped immediately from the primary database, but the MRP will not apply the changes until the specified time interval has passed.

Let's assume LunarTrax's development team is deploying a new version of the application with major database changes. It is going to take the QA team two hours to validate the database changes. If the QA test fails, the back-out plan is to switch over to the standby database. To facilitate this, we are going to start the MRP with a delay of 120 minutes:

```
SQL> alter database recover managed standby database delay 120 disconnect;
```

NOTE
It is generally recommended that Flashback Database be enabled and used to handle these types of situations. Flashback Database puts more control in the hands of the DBA, because an exact point in time can be specified for flashback, which provides assurance that the entire set of transactions is rolled back. See Chapter 11 for more information on Flashback Database.

The QA team has finished early and now wants the standby database immediately synchronized with the primary. We can make this happen by issuing the following:

```
SQL> alter database recover managed standby database nodelay;
```

Stopping the MRP is even simpler than starting the process. We could simply perform a normal shutdown on the database, or we could cancel managed recovery, leaving the standby database up and running. To cancel managed recovery, issue the following:

```
SQL> alter database recover managed standby database cancel;
```

At this point, you are probably wondering about Oracle RAC. From a MRP perspective, Oracle RAC is no different than single instance. The same commands are used to enable managed recovery, and the MRP will run on a single instance in the cluster even if there are multiple available (running) instances for your standby database. In Chapter 12, we will talk about enhancing MAA with the Oracle Data Guard Broker. To give you a quick preview, the Oracle Data Guard Broker provides the ability for the MRP to failover to a surviving instance in the event of a failure of an instance running the MRP.

Accommodating Physical Changes on the Primary

It is important that you make sure that any physical database changes performed on the primary, such as adding datafiles or tablespaces, are also performed on the standby.

Nobody wants to perform a failover during a disaster and realize that the new tablespace added last week didn't make it across to the standby. It's also important that many of these changes on the standby be performed without user intervention, to reduce undue work on the DBA. To accommodate these needs, the standby parameter **standby_file_management** was created. When this parameter is set to **AUTO**, actions from the following types of commands will automatically be performed on the standby:

- Create a tablespace.

- Alter tablespace commands that add datafiles.

- Alter tablespace commands that change the status of a tablespace.

- Alter database commands that enable or disable threads.

- Drop tablespace commands that have the including contents and datafiles clause (you must physically remove the file on the standby if the including contents and datafiles clause was not specified).

The following primary database changes will require user intervention regardless of the **standby_file_management** parameter setting:

- **Dropping a tablespace without the including contents and datafiles clause**   The datafile must manually be removed from the OS unless OMF is used.

- **Using a transportable tablespace on the primary database**   The datafiles must manually be copied to the standby database prior to plugging in the tablespace.

- **Renaming datafiles**   If the file is to be renamed on the standby database as well, the equivalent command must be run on the standby database.

- **Adding or dropping redo logs**   It is not required (though recommended) that redo logs are in sync with the primary. However, the standby redo log size should match that of the primary redo logs, and one additional group per thread should exist on the standby. Therefore, it is recommended that you review the standby redo log configuration after modifications of the primary redo logs to determine whether modifications are necessary.

- **Modifying password file**   The password file should be recopied from the primary system to the standby system (all nodes) when any change is made to the password file.

■ **Modifying Transparent Data Encryption (TDE) master encryption key**   The encryption wallet must be replaced on the standby database if a TDE master key is reset on the primary database.

■ **Changing database initialization parameter**   Database initialization parameters should be kept in sync whenever possible to ensure expected performance and functionality in the event of a role transition.

Monitoring a Physical Standby

You will often want to verify that the physical standby's MRP is able to keep up with the rate at which redo is being sent from the primary or that it has not aborted with some type of error. This section examines several techniques that will allow you to see the status of the Oracle Data Guard configuration.

Let's start by taking a look at the overall Oracle Data Guard protection mode and current protection level. To do so, we query v$database on the primary and/or standby, as follows:

```
SQL> select protection_mode, protection_level, database_role role, from
v$database;
PROTECTION_MODE      PROTECTION_LEVEL      ROLE
-------------------- -------------------- ----------------
MAXIMUM AVAILABILITY MAXIMUM AVAILABILITY PHYSICAL STANDBY
```

Now that we know what protection mode we are running, let's check to see whether we are using Real-Time Apply:

```
SQL> select dest_id, recovery_mode from v$archive_dest_status
where recovery_mode <> 'IDLE';
DEST_ID    RECOVERY_MODE
---------- ----------------------
2          MANAGED REAL TIME APPLY
```

This query can be run on either the primary or the standby database; if it's run on the primary database, the **dest_id** will be the ID defined for log transport services.

From the information we have just queried, we now know that we are in Maximum Availability mode using Real-Time Apply. With this information, we expect that our standby database is in sync with our primary database with minimal or no lag. Let's check by running the following query on the standby database:

```
SQL> select name, value, time_computed from v$dataguard_stats;
NAME                    VALUE             TIME_COMPUTED
----------------------- ----------------- --------------------
transport lag           +00 00:00:00      05/10/2010 21:40:08
apply lag               +00 00:00:00      05/10/2010 21:40:08
apply finish time       +00 00:00:00.000  05/10/2010 21:40:08
estimated startup time  31                05/10/2010 21:40:08
```

NOTE
*An additional column in the **v$dataguard_stats***
*view, **unit**, defines the unit for the calculated value.*
This column was omitted from this example to
ensure the readability of the output.

We can see that we have a transport and apply lag of 0 seconds, there is no pending redo to apply, and the estimated time to open our standby database is currently 31 seconds. Obviously, there is no load on the primary database; but even if there were, we would expect extremely low lag times since we are using Real-Time Apply and are running in Maximum Availability mode.

In the old days, we would have been querying **v$archived_log**, **v$log_history**, and **v$log**, and then we'd perform various calculations to determine our lag. The **v$dataguard_stats** view greatly simplifies this by performing these calculations for you. It's not that querying v$ views for the archive and online logs is something you should forget about, but you should always keep them in your back pocket for troubleshooting.

With Oracle 11g, several v$ views are available, and various queries on these views can be constructed to help you understand exactly what is happening within the Oracle Data Guard configuration. Here is a listing of v$ (and gv$) views that should be considered when monitoring a physical standby Oracle Data Guard configuration:

- **v$managed_standby** Displays information for the database processes related to the physical standby such as LGWR, RFS, LNS, ARCH, MRP, and so on.

- **v$archived_log** When queried on the standby database, displays the logs that have been received by that standby database.

- **v$log_history** Displays details on the archival history.

- **v$dataguard_status** Shows messages generated by Oracle Data Guard that are written to the alert log or trace files of that particular database (primary or standby).

- **v$recovery_progress** Displays statistics related to the recovery of the standby database.

- **v$standby_event_histogram** Shows a histogram of the apply lag for a physical standby database.

Read-Only Physical Standby Including Oracle Active Data Guard

Not only can a physical standby protect your primary from disasters, but it can also relieve some of the users' workload by allowing users to perform reporting. With Oracle 11g, this functionality is facilitated in two ways: by opening the standby in traditional read-only mode and by using Oracle Active Data Guard. While both Oracle Active Data Guard and traditional read-only mode both allow reporting applications or user queries that do not perform any type of updates to be performed on the standby database, the two options are distinctly different. Oracle Active Data Guard will allow the standby database to continue applying redo, thus keeping the standby database synchronized with the primary. This functionality does come at an extra licensing cost, but the alternative comes at a cost in the form of consequences.

Read-Only Considerations

Before you decide to open the standby in traditional read-only mode for use in reporting, you should be aware that redo changes generated from the primary are not being applied while open in this mode. For this reason, reporting applications run against the standby will see only data that has been applied just prior to opening in read-only. Although the redo from the primary is not being applied while open, the changes are still being received and stored until such time as managed recovery is once again started. While the standby is out of sync from the primary, you should be aware that switchover and failover times will be greater, because the standby must first apply all outstanding redo from the primary.

To avoid this negative impact on failover times and potential data loss while allowing queries on up-to-date data, check into acquiring a license for the Oracle Active Data Guard option. Oracle Active Data Guard, also called real-time query, enables the standby database to be opened in read-only mode while still allowing MRP to continue to perform its task of applying redo to the standby database. With Oracle Active Data Guard enabled, role transitions are efficiently performed due to the standby database being kept in sync with the primary database.

MAA Workshop: *Opening a Standby in Read-Only Mode Including Oracle Active Data Guard*

Workshop Notes

In this MAA workshop, we'll open a standby in read-only mode; then we'll take this one step further by enabling real-time query (Oracle Active Data Guard) on the standby database. Should you not have an Oracle Active Data Guard license or if you are not enabling it, some of the steps in this workshop will not apply. The steps specific to Oracle Active Data Guard are indicated in the description of each step.

Step 1. Oracle Active Data Guard was introduced with Oracle Database 11g Release 1; therefore, to enable it, we must first ensure that the database **COMPATIBLE** initialization parameter is set to a minimum of 11.1.0.0. This setting is necessary only if Oracle Active Data Guard will be enabled on the read-only standby database.

Step 2. To open the standby database in read-only mode, we must first cancel the active managed recovery:

```
SQL> alter database recover managed standby database cancel;
```

To open the standby database in read-only mode, we issue the following SQL statement:

```
SQL> alter database open;
```

Note that we purposely left off the **readonly** attribute from the command. If you remember the discussion about starting the standby database and Oracle's ability to read the control file to determine whether it is a standby controlfile, the same holds true here. Oracle is fully aware that we are mounted on a standby controlfile, so when the database is opened, it will automatically be placed in read-only mode. The same will be true if we completely shut down the database and issue a **startup** command.

Step 3. When we are open in read-only mode, no updates to the database can occur. So how do we handle user queries that need sorting space? First, the queries will make use of memory sorting using **sort_area_size**. If the required sort space exceeds that space, then we must go to disk. By making use of tempfiles in locally managed temporary tablespaces, we can provide disk-based sorting space to the users without directly updating the dictionary. Issue the following SQL statement to add the tempfile(s):

```
SQL> alter tablespace temp add tempfile size 10M;
```

If you are unsure of your temporary tablespace name or if your standby database already has tempfiles, you can consult the alert log of the instance that was opened in read-only.

If you are not implementing real-time query, this is the last step in the process of making the standby database available for read-only access. Assuming real-time query is not being used, you can now restart remaining Oracle RAC database in read-only mode via SRVCTL if you choose:

```
# srvctl stop instance -i maadb2 -d cosp
# srvctl start instance i maadb2 -d cosp -o open
```

To close the database and re-enable managed recovery, move ahead to step 6.

Step 4. To enable real-time query, we simply need to restart the managed recovery process with the database opened in read-only mode:

```
SQL> alter database recover managed standby database using current
logfile disconnect;
```

You can now restart remaining Oracle RAC databases in read-only mode via SRVCTL if you choose:

```
# srvctl stop instance -i maadb2 -d cosp
# srvctl start instance i maadb2 -d cosp -o open
```

If we query **open_mode** from gv$database, we can see that the open mode is now READ-ONLY WITH APPLY for all database instances. If you plan on using Oracle Active Data Guard as a permanent solution within your environment (as recommended), you will want to modify the clusterware resource for the database to ensure the database has a start mode of opened (instead of mounted):

```
# srvctl modify database -d cosp -n maadb -s open
```

Workshop Notes

Now that Oracle Active Data Guard is active on our physical standby database, let's talk about some of the features that are available with this option before we return to the workshop.

Automatic Block Recovery avoids the dreaded ORA-1578 block corruption errors that an end user would typically see when a block corruption is encountered. How does it do that? Upon detection of a block corruption on the primary database that would normally result in an ORA-1578 error, the corrupt block is shipped from the standby database, and the corrupt block on the primary database is replaced with the standby copy of the block. The user who ran the query to "discover" the block corruption will notice a slight pause in his/her query while the block is replaced, but no error is ever thrown. No human intervention is required. Now *that* is high availability! Even if you are not taking advantage of the real-time query features that Oracle Active Data Guard provides, this feature alone can make the additional licensing costs worth the cost.

If you are using Oracle Active Data Guard to offload those high resource consuming read-only types of operations, you can scale out your read-only workload by creating several real-time query standby databases (up to 30 in 11g) to meet those ever-growing demands of your application. Configurations involving multiple real-time query standby databases are commonly referred to as *reader farms*. Client connectivity to read-only versus read-write can be managed by the use of role-based database services (more on this in Chapter 12) to allow for seamless integration into the application. Read-mostly workloads can also be accommodated by a real-time query standby database with the use of database links and synonyms. Obviously, as you grow dependent on real-time query, you will indeed need to tune the standby database and/or workload, which is made possible with in-memory Active Session History (ASH) and Standby Statspack (MOS Note# 454848.1). As these are fairly advanced topics that are beyond the scope of this chapter, you can find more information by reading the Oracle MAA Whitepaper "Oracle Active Data Guard Oracle Data Guard 11*g* Release 1" (also applies to 11*g* Release 2).

Step 5.   We will now configure the **STANDBY_MAX_DATA_DELAY** session parameter to specify the lag tolerance for queries issued against the standby database. This parameter is session-specific and is completely optional unless your business demands that data queried from the standby database be up-to-date within a defined threshold. Let's assume that Max considers any data that is greater than 30 seconds old to be stale. To accommodate this requirement, Max sets the **STANDBY_MAX_DATA_DELAY** parameter to 30 seconds when he logs into SQL*Plus:

```
SQL> alter session set standby_max_data_delay=30;
```

If the apply lag is greater than the specified threshold, when a query is executed, the query will fail with an ORA-3172 error. You are probably thinking, My CEO will never log into SQL*Plus directly, so how do I enforce this policy for application users? Common methods of overcoming this include adding the **alter session** statement to the application code or creating a logon trigger. Obviously, if you plan to use this feature, you will want to review the lag time of the standby database to ensure that redo apply is able to accommodate the desired setting—a good starting point would be the **v$standby_event_histogram** view.

Another approach is to synchronize the standby database prior to running a query:

```
SQL> alter session sync with primary;
```

This statement will not return user control until all redo data has been applied to the standby database. As with the **STANDBY_MAX_DATA_DELAY** parameter, this **alter session** command can be inserted into the application code or implemented via a logon trigger.

To allow the execution of the sync with primary or setting of **STANDBY_MAX_DATA_DELAY** parameter to 0, the standby database *must* be using the **SYNC** attribute for log transport, be running at the Maximum Availability or Maximum Protection level, and Real-Time Apply must be enabled.

> **NOTE**
> *For information on how to monitor the log transport and redo apply performance of the real-time query standby database, see the section "Monitoring a Physical Standby" earlier in this chapter.*

Step 6. To disable read-only access to our standby database, we must first disable any active managed recovery. This would be applicable only if you have enabled real-time query and want to disable this feature.

```
SQL> alter database recover managed standby database cancel;
```

Now shut down and restart all database instances in mount state. Assuming the database definition in the Oracle Cluster Registry (OCR) still has the mount option specified, we can easily perform this task via SRVCTL as follows:

```
# srvctl stop database -d cosp
# srvctl start database -d cosp
```

Re-enable managed recovery on the desired database instance:

```
SQL> alter database recover managed standby database using current
logfile disconnect;
```

We are now back to our typical physical standby database configuration—easy as that!

Managing a Logical Standby Database

Although the log transport or the method of delivering changes to a physical and logical standby are the same, changes are applied in a very different way. Logical standbys read redo data from either archivelogs or standby redo logs and convert that redo data into SQL statements. These SQL statements are then applied to the database tables while the database is open in read-write. Understanding the processes involved can greatly help you manage the configuration.

First, let's look at the processes involved in SQL Apply. The SQL Apply engine comprises six processes that, as a whole, read the redo, transform the redo, construct transactions, and apply the transaction to the database tables. These processes are spawned from a pool of parallel query slaves.

The following is a list of the processes along with a description of their purpose:

- **Reader process**   Reads redo as it arrives from the primary database.

- **Preparer process**   Converts the redo into Logical Change Records (LCRs) as well as identifying dependencies between the LCRs.

- **Builder process**   Takes individual LCRs and builds complete transactions.

- **Analyzer process**   Takes the transactions completed by the Builder process and computes dependencies between them.

- **Coordinator process**   Monitors the dependencies between transactions, and correctly schedules the application of those transactions with the apply slaves.

- **Apply processes**   Accept transactions from the Coordinator process and physically apply the changes to the database tables.

Starting and Stopping SQL Apply

The first step in starting logical apply is to bring the database to an open state. Once the standby database is open, you can start logical apply by issuing the following statement:

```
SQL> alter database start logical standby apply;
```

This statement will spawn all six processes involved in SQL Apply and will read redo from archived redo logs as they are registered with the logical standby. To start SQL Apply and have it immediately apply changes as they arrive (real-time apply) from the primary, issue the following statement:

```
SQL> alter database start logical standby apply immediate;
```

Before shutting down the standby database or before changing attributes to the SQL Apply engine, you should stop SQL Apply. The following statement stops the apply engine:

```
SQL> alter database stop logical standby apply;
```

Much like MRP from our physical standby, SQL Apply will run only on one database instance at any given time. That being said, Oracle RAC is really no different from single instance. The same commands are used to enable and disable SQL Apply in an Oracle RAC environment that are used in single instance. High availability of the SQL Apply process is enabled with the use of the Oracle Data Guard Broker, which is covered in Chapter 12.

Monitoring SQL Apply Progress

After you start SQL Apply, you will likely want to check the processes to see what actions they are performing by querying the v$logstdby view. This view displays one row for each process that is part of the apply engine and describes what that process is doing as well as what System Change Number (SCN) that process has worked on. The following query returns each process name, the highest SCN that it has worked on, as well as its current status:

```
select type, high_scn, status from v$logstdby;
```

When querying the v$logstdby view, pay special attention to the **HIGH_SCN** column. This is an indicator that progress is being made—as long as it is changing each time you query the v$logstdby view.

The **DBA_LOGSTDBY_PROGRESS** view describes the progress of SQL Apply operations on the logical standby databases. Here's an example:

```
SELECT APPLIED_SCN, APPLIED_TIME, READ_SCN, READ_TIME,
NEWEST_SCN, NEWEST_TIME
FROM DBA_LOGSTDBY_PROGRESS;
```

The **APPLIED_SCN** indicates that any transactions below that SCN have been committed and applied. The **NEWEST_SCN** column is the highest SCN that the standby has received from the primary database. When the value of **NEWEST_SCN** and **APPLIED_SCN** are the same, all available changes have been applied. If the **APPLIED_SCN** value is lower than the **NEWEST_SCN** value and is increasing, then SQL Apply is currently applying changes. The **READ_SCN** column reports the SCN at which the SQL Apply engine will start, should it be restarted.

The following views are of interest when monitoring a logical standby database:

- **v$dataguard_stats** Provides information of the current status as well as statistics related to SQL Apply

- **v$logstdby_process** Displays the current state of each of the SQL Apply processes

- **v$logstdby_state** Provides a summary view of the state of SQL Apply

- **dba_logstdby_log** Displays information about archived logs that have been processed or are being processed by SQL Apply

- **dba_logstdby_events** Contains records of recent SQL Apply events such as abnormal termination; these events are also present in the database instance alert log for the instance running SQL Apply

Deletion of Standby Archived Logs

With Oracle 11g, we can store archivelogs shipped from the primary database as Flash Recovery Area files. This means that once the redo data from a particular log has been applied, that log will be automatically purged after the flashback retention period has expired. This retention period is controlled by the **DB_FLASHBACK_RETENTION_TARGET** initialization parameter, which carries a default value of 1440 minutes, or 1 day. To enable this functionality, we would specify **LOCATION=USE_DB_RECOVERY_FILE_DEST** for the log archive destination used for our standby redo logs.

To get more control over the retention, we can store the archived standby redo logs outside the Flash Recovery Area (**LOCATION=<diskgroup>**) and set the SQL Apply parameter **LOG_AUTO_DEL_RETENTION_TARGET** to the desired value (in minutes) using the **dbms_logstdby.apply_set** procedure:

```
SQL> exec dbms_logstdby.apply_set('LOG_AUTO_DEL_RETENTION_TARGET',10);
```

To disable the automatic deletion of consumed archived standby redo logs, again do not use the Flash Recovery Area for storage (**LOCATION=<diskgroup>**) and execute the following:

```
SQL> exec dbms_logstdby.apply_set('LOG_AUTO_DELETE', 'FALSE');
```

NOTE
If the Flash Recovery Area is used as the target for storage of archived standby redo logs, you will not be able to manage the log files manually using the preceding commands.

Protecting the Logical Standby from User Modifications

At this point, you should be asking this question: If the logical standby is open and users can connect, what is stopping the users from trashing the tables being maintained by the logical standby? Upon conversion from a physical standby to a logical standby, by default, only the SYS user is able to make Data Manipulation Language (DML) or Data Definition Language (DDL) modifications to the logical standby database. This behavior is controlled with the **alter database guard** statement, which comes in three flavors to control user access:

- **ALL**   Prevents all users other than SYS from performing DML and DDL on the logical standby.

- **STANDBY**   All non-SYS users can create new objects on the logical standby. Only the SYS user is able to perform DML and DDL to tables and/or sequences maintained by SQL Apply.

- **NONE**   The database guard is disabled and all updates are allowed.

Should we want to allow users of our logical standby database to create their own tables but not be able to modify the tables maintained by SQL Apply, we would set database guard to standby, as follows:

```
SQL> alter database guard standby;
```

Users with the logstdby_administrator privilege are allowed to modify the database guard either at the database level or at the session level. For what should be obvious reasons, changing the guard at the database level can be dangerous and is not recommended. If only temporary corrections need to be made, it is better that you temporarily disable the guard for the session only. To do this, issue the following statement:

```
SQL> alter session disable guard;
```

Once you're done with the modifications, re-enable the guard for your session:

```
SQL> alter session enable guard;
```

Recovering from Errors

Whenever the SQL Apply engine encounters an error while applying a SQL statement, the engine will stop and give the DBA the opportunity to correct the statement and restart SQL Apply. The error and the statement that stops the engine is logged in a view called DBA_LOGSTDBY_EVENTS. Before we start discussing how to skip transactions, let's first cover some of the dangers.

As a DBA, your number one concern is to keep the data on the logical standby in sync with data that exists on the primary. If the SQL Apply engine receives an error during a DDL transaction, it is safe to issue a compensating transaction manually and then skip the failed transaction. However, if a DML transaction receives an error, you should proceed very cautiously. For instance, suppose that transaction X consists of 500 inserts and 27 updates. If one of the inserts receives an error during apply and you then skip that single insert, you have logically corrupted the entire transaction. In general, how you recover from DDL transaction errors versus DML transactions errors can be very different.

Recovering from a DDL Transaction

One common type of DDL transaction that can fail involves physical modification such as **create tablespace** commands. It is important to note that the **db_file_name_convert** and **log_file_name_convert** parameters do not function on a logical standby. If the directory structure between the primary and standby are the same or if you are using ASM with Oracle Managed Files (as we are), DDL transactions that create files will succeed without error. However, if the directory structure between the primary and standby are different, the DDL transaction will fail, because the create file will fail. The following procedure can be used to correct the failed DDL statement:

1. Determine the failed SQL Statement:

```
SQL> select event_time, commit_scn, event, status
from dba_logstdby_events
order by event_time;
```

2. Re-issue the failed statement with the appropriate corrections. For example, the failing statement was

```
create tablespace mytbs datafile '+DBDATA/pitt/datafile/
mydbfile.dbf' size 5M
```

To correct this issue, we would execute the following:

```
SQL> create tablespace mytbs datafile '+DBDATA/cosp/datafile/
mydbf.dbf' size 5m:
```

3. Restart the SQL Apply process. We must instruct the process to skip the failed DML transaction; otherwise, the SQL Apply process will fail upon restart with an ORA-01543 error. (Note that this is one of the few cases that we actually need to skip the failed transaction.)

```
SQL> alter database start logical standby apply immediate skip
failed transaction;
```

Recovering from a Failed DML Transaction

In general, a failed DML statement indicates that the table associated with the DML is not correctly in sync with the table on the primary. The table could have gotten out of sync by a user modifying the table on the logical standby or defining skips on that object. The most simplistic remedy for failed DML transactions is to reinstantiate the table so that it is once again in sync with the primary. You can use the following procedure to accomplish the table reinstantiation:

1. Stop the logical standby apply:

```
SQL> alter database stop logical standby apply;
```

2. Use the **DBMS_LOGSTDBY.INSTANTIATE_TABLE** procedure to resynchronize the table with the primary. The values passed to this procedure are schema name, table name, and database link name to the primary database.

```
SQL> exec dbms_logstdby.instantiate_
table('MTSMITH','MTS1','pitt_dblink');
```

3. Restart the logical standby apply:

```
SQL> alter database start logical standby apply immediate;
```

Changing the Default Behavior of the SQL Apply Engine

No matter how well intentioned, default values will not cover all possible situations. Depending on the transaction profile of your primary database, you might find it necessary to fine tune the default values for several components of the SQL

Apply engine. The different parameters are all modified by using the **DBMS_ LOGSTDBY.APPLY_SET** procedure, which takes as the first value the parameter that is being changed and the second value set to the new value. In releases prior to 11*g* Release 2, you were required to stop SQL Apply prior to making any changes, but with 11*g* Release 2 this restriction has been lifted for the majority of the parameters. A full listing of all the available parameters along with their descriptions is available in the "Oracle Database PL/SQL Packages and Types Reference 11*g* Release 2 (11.2)" manual.

Performing a Role Transition Using Switchover

Let's start by defining a *role transition* so that we are all on the same page. A database can operate in one of two modes in an Oracle Data Guard configuration: primary or standby. When we change the role of either a primary or standby, we call this a *role transition*. We can use two methods to change the roles: switchover and failover. Which one you use is a very important decision. Choosing the wrong one can result in extra work on the part of the DBA to get the configuration back in sync, although a lot of that work has been eliminated with the advent of Flashback Database.

A *switchover* allows a primary and standby to reverse roles without any data loss and without any need to re-create the previous primary. In contrast, a *failover* implies potential data loss and can result in the need for the old primary to be re-created. Switchovers are normally performed for planned maintenance. For example, if the primary host needed to replace a faulty CPU that required downtime, we could perform a switchover and have users automatically redirected to the new primary. The impact to the user base could be greatly reduced, thus increasing our availability.

A switchover can be performed using either a physical or logical standby. However, you should be aware of some issues. If you have a configuration with a primary database, a physical standby, and a logical standby, and you perform a switchover to the logical standby, your physical standby will no longer be a part of the configuration and must be re-created. In the same scenario, if you perform a switchover to the physical standby, the logical standby remains in the configuration and does not need to be re-created. For this reason, a physical standby is a better option for a switchover candidate than a logical standby when multiple standby types exist in the configuration.

The secret to performing a switchover successfully is proper planning and testing. The following is a list of items that you should consider prior to performing a switchover:

- First and most important, verify that initialization parameters for both the primary and the standby support both roles. Pay special attention to the **VALID_FOR** attributes to the **LOG_ARCHIVE_DEST_*n*** parameter, as this will play greatly into the switchover.

■ Verify that the primary and standby host each have TNS aliases that point to one another and that those aliases function correctly. Also verify that those functioning aliases are used in the **LOG_ARCHIVE_DEST_n** parameters.

■ For a fast and efficient switchover, disconnect all user connections. If that is not feasible, restrict the user activity as much as possible. It is possible to failover user connection if they have connected via an OCI application and the proper transparent application failover setup has been performed.

■ Verify that both the primary and standby temporary tablespaces are populated with tempfiles.

■ Have the standby, either physical or logical, applying changes from the primary. Verify that the application of redo is current with the primary. Using the Real-Time Apply method will speed up the switchover.

MAA Workshop: *Switchover to a Physical Standby*

Workshop Notes

After a review of the switchover recommendations, we are ready to perform the switchover. We highly recommend that you test switchover in your test environment prior to attempting it on your production system. This testing will root out any small configuration errors and will make the production event smooth and painless.

Step 1. When performing a switchover in an Oracle RAC environment, we must shut down all instances except the one that will be used to execute the switchover commands:

```
# srvctl stop instance -d pitt -i maadb2
```

Step 2. Before beginning the switchover, we need to validate that the primary database is able to be switched over. To validate that switchover is possible, we will look at the **switchover_status** of the v$database view on the primary database:

```
SQL> select switchover_status from v$database;
```

If this query returns a value of TO STANDBY, then everything is good. If the query returns SESSIONS ACTIVE, then we should issue the switchover command with the **session shutdown** clause. If neither of these two values are returned, some type of configuration issue is likely making switchover impossible.

Step 3. Assuming that the switchover status from step 2 has returned a value of TO STANDBY, we can convert our primary database to a physical standby by running the following:

```
SQL> alter database commit to switchover to physical standby;
```

If the switchover status is reporting SESSIONS ACTIVE, we must use the **session shutdown** clause:

```
SQL> alter database commit to switchover to physical standby with
session shutdown;
```

Step 4. To complete the conversion of the primary database to a physical standby, we must shut down and mount the former primary database:

```
SQL> shutdown immediate;
SQL> startup mount;
```

Time to celebrate; we now have two physical standby databases.

Step 5. As with the primary, when performing a switchover in an Oracle RAC environment, we must shut down all instances of the standby except the instance that will be used to execute the switchover commands:

```
# srvctl stop instance -d cosp -i maadb2
```

Step 6. When we converted the primary to a standby, we generated a marker in the redo stream and sent that marker to the standby. That marker states that no more redo has been generated. As soon as the standby receives and recovers that marker, it is eligible to become a primary database. Query the **switchover_status** column of V$DATABASE on the standby to ensure that the marker has been recovered and that it is ready for the switchover to primary:

```
SQL> select switchover_status from v$database;
```

If **switchover_status** returns TO PRIMARY, then the redo marker has been received and we can proceed with the switchover to primary command. If the status is SESSIONS ACTIVE, then we should either disconnect active sessions or issue the switchover command with the **session shutdown** clause. If the status states NOT ALLOWED, then the marker has not been received and recovered by the standby and switchover cannot proceed.

Step 7. Assuming that the switchover status from step 6 has returned a value of TO PRIMARY, we can convert our physical standby to a primary database by running the following:

```
SQL> alter database commit to switchover to primary;
```

If the **switchover_status** is reporting SESSIONS ACTIVE, we must use the **session shutdown** clause:

```
SQL> alter database commit to switchover to primary with session shutdown;
```

Step 8. To allow the clusterware to monitor and manage our new primary and physical standby databases properly, we must update the database resource configuration. After we have modified the configuration, we can open the remaining database instances in their respective modes.

On the new primary, execute the following:

```
# srvctl modify database -d cosp -n maadb -r primary -s open
# srvctl start database -d cosp
```

On the new standby, execute the following:

```
# srvctl modify database -d pitt -n maadb -r physical_standby -s mount
# srvctl start database -d pitt
```

Step 9. Finally, it's time to start managed recovery of our new physical standby database:

```
SQL> alter database recover managed standby database using current
logfile disconnect;
```

At this point, the switchover process is complete. If you have configured the **VALID_FOR** attribute to the **LOG_ARCHIVE_DEST_*n*** parameter, then your new primary is already configured to send redo to the new standby. If you performed the switchover to perform maintenance on the primary host, you can shut down the new standby and perform the required maintenance. Before shutting down the standby, you should consider the protection mode you are in on your new primary and make sure that it is satisfied.

Performing a Role Transition Using Failover

Hopefully, you are reading this section at your leisure and not when a disaster has occurred. Ideally, everything mentioned in this section should be a part of your disaster recovery plan and should have been tested to the Nth degree. A failover implies that the primary database is unavailable and that, depending on our protection mode, the possibility of data loss exists. In a failover, being prepared means more than anything else in the world.

Your decision to failover, in most cases, depending on your company structure, will be made along with management. The role of the DBA is to provide the best option—one that incurs the least amount of interruption of service and data loss. For instance, if the primary database fails, it might be faster to restart the primary database and perform crash recovery than it would be to perform a failover to a disaster site. If the primary is unable to be restarted and multiple standbys exist, the DBA will have to decide which one is the best option. In a configuration that contains both a physical and logical standby, we should always consider the physical standby as the best option, because a logical standby can contain a subset of primary database's data. The DBA must also consider which standby is transactional closest to the primary database, thus taking the least amount of time to failover.

Chapter 12 discusses a feature available with the Oracle Data Guard Broker called *Fast-Start Failover*. Fast-Start Failover allows the Oracle Data Guard Broker to automatically perform the failover from a primary database to a designated standby database when a specific (user-definable) condition is met. This feature eliminates the need for DBA involvement as part of the failover process. We will save the nitty-gritty details of Fast-Start Failover for Chapter 12; next, we'll cover the failover procedures the "old-fashioned" way to ensure that you fully understand the process.

Failover First Steps

Prior to performing the actual failover commands that convert the standby into a primary, we need to take some steps to ensure that we have as much data as possible from the primary. We also need to prepare the standby to assume the role of a primary, to smooth the transition. The following factors should be addressed:

- First and foremost, attempt to get all unapplied data off of the primary host and onto the standby host. This could include any archivelogs that did not get transferred.

- Ensure that any temporary tablespaces on the standby are populated with tempfiles.

- If the standby will become an Oracle RAC primary, make sure that all but one instance are down.

- Remove any delay setting for recovery of redo from the primary.

- Change the protection mode of the standby database to Maximum Performance.

MAA Workshop: *Failover to a Physical Standby*

Workshop Notes

Prior to beginning this workshop, you should enable Flashback Database on the primary. We will talk more about the role of Flashback Database after a database failover in the "Reinstating a Database After a Failover" section. For now, enable Flashback Database on the primary, as follows:

```
SQL> alter database flashback on;
```

Step 1. If possible, we need to mount the primary database. Version 11*g* Release 2 offers zero data loss failovers regardless of the protection mode by providing the ability to flush redo to a designated standby. Assuming that we can get the database to mount on any one of the primary cluster nodes, we issue the following:

```
SQL> alter system flush redo to 'COSP';
```

Note that the time necessary for this statement to complete depends on the amount of redo that needs to be sent to the standby, so be patient. If you are in a serious time crunch, you can cancel out of the execution of the statement and move on to the next step, but remember that *data loss may occur*.

Step 2. This step is necessary only if step 1 wasn't completed for one reason or another. To identify any redo gaps that may exist, run the following query on the standby database:

```
SQL> select thread#, low_sequence#, high_sequence# from v$archive_gap;
```

If this query returns any rows, manually copy the archivelogs for the thread and sequence numbers identified by the query from the primary to the standby database. Once the archivelogs have been copied to the standby, you must register the logs to allow them to be identified by MRP:

```
SQL> alter database register physical logfile '/tmp/archive_1_250.arc';
```

If it is not possible to copy the logs manually, continue to the next step, but note that *data from the time of the gap forward will be lost*.

Step 3 After we have recovered as much redo as possible on our physical standby, we must cancel out of media recovery as follows:

```
SQL> alter database recover managed standby database cancel;
```

Step 4. Perform terminal recovery by using the **finish** clause with the **recover managed standby database** command:

```
SQL> alter database recover managed standby database finish;
```

If the command fails, do not worry—we can still perform the failover, but data loss will likely occur. For this reason, errors returned by this command should be resolved before you continue.

Step 5. Query the **switchover_status** column of V$DATABASE on the standby to ensure that it is ready to assume the primary role:

```
SQL> select switchover_status from v$database;
```

Step 6. Assuming that the switchover status from step 5 has returned a value of TO PRIMARY, we can convert our physical standby to a primary database by running the following:

```
SQL> alter database commit to switchover to primary;
```

If the switchover status reports SESSIONS ACTIVE, we must use the **session shutdown** clause:

```
SQL> alter database commit to switchover to primary with session shutdown;
```

If the switchover status reports any other state, the terminal recovery likely returned an error. If all efforts to correct the error have been exhausted, we must complete the failover as follows:

```
SQL> alter database activate physical standby database;
```

Step 7. At this point, all the instances for our Oracle RAC database should be at mount state and ready to be opened. Normally with Oracle RAC, we would use SRVCTL to start and stop the database, but SRVCTL is not able to take a database from the mount state to open, so we must manually open all database instances individually via SQL*Plus to avoid shutdown. It is recommended to allow the first database instance to open before moving on to the other instances.

```
SQL> alter database open;
```

Step 8. To allow the clusterware to monitor and manage our new primary database properly, we must update the database resource configuration. Once we have modified the configuration, we can then open the new primary database:

```
# srvctl modify database -d pitt -n maadb -r primary -s open
```

We have just completed a failover to a physical standby database.

Reinstating a Database After a Failover

Prior to Oracle 10g, when a failover was performed, the old primary database could no longer be a member of the Oracle Data Guard configuration and had to be re-created (reinstated) from a backup of the new primary. Although this procedure is still entirely valid and necessary in physical corruption situations, it is an extremely expensive operation because it involves a lot of time and often numerous resources. By using Flashback Database, we can "rewind" the old primary database to the point just before the failure occurred and convert that database into a standby. In configurations having multiple standby databases, a failover can result in the new primary database being behind the other standby databases in the configuration, thus requiring that those standby databases be reinstated. For this reason, it is highly recommended that Flashback Database be enabled on all databases in a given Oracle Data Guard configuration.

MAA Workshop: *Reinstating a Failed Primary as a Standby After Failover*

Workshop Notes

Hopefully, you read the workshop notes in the "Failover to a Physical Standby" workshop. If so, you enabled Flashback Database on what was your primary database and are ready to perform the tasks in this workshop.

Step 1. On the new primary, run the following query to determine at what SCN it became the new primary:

```
SQL> select to_char(standby_became_primary_scn) from v$database;
```

Step 2. To flashback the old primary database, we must first bring the database to mount state on a single instance:

```
SQL> startup mount;
```

Once the old primary database has been mounted, flashback the database to the SCN returned from the query in step 1:

```
SQL> flashback database to scn <scn from step 1>;
```

Step 3. Now that we have returned the old primary database to the point in time just before the failure, we must convert it to a physical standby:

```
SQL> alter database convert to physical standby;
```

Step 4. After converting the old primary into a physical standby, the database will be in nomount state; therefore, we must restart the database in mount state:

```
SQL> shutdown immediate;
SQL> startup mount;
```

Step 5. To allow the clusterware to monitor and manage our new physical standby database properly, we update the database resource configuration and mount the remaining instances:

```
# srvctl modify database -d pitt -n maadb -r physical_standby -s mount
# srvctl start database -d pitt
```

Step 6. Complete the process by enabling managed recovery of our new physical standby database:

```
SQL> alter database recover managed standby database using current
logfile disconnect;
```

If for some reason we flashed back to a SCN prior to that of the failure, we may need to restart MRP, because it will halt on all redo records that were generated as a result of the role transition.

We just saved ourselves countless hours of work by completely avoiding the need to rebuild the standby database.

Summary

Oracle Data Guard is a key component within Oracle MAA that enables the creation, maintenance, and monitoring of transactional consistent copies of the production database at an alternate location, thus protecting our valuable data from disasters such as fire or earthquake. If a disaster occurs, a properly implemented Oracle Data Guard solution will provide end users access to the database with zero (or minimal) data loss in a matter of minutes instead of days or weeks.

With the Oracle Active Data Guard option, block-consistent physical standby databases can be used to improve scalability of the database by offloading read-only workloads. In addition, with this option, we can avoid those scary ORA-1578 errors. Should you need additional objects (indexes, summary tables, and so on) to support your reporting operations, a logical standby will allow this functionality while maintaining a transactional consistent copy of your database.

Need to troubleshoot a problem using production data? Oracle Data Guard can accommodate this as well with the use of a snapshot standby. The bottom line is that Oracle Data Guard will indeed enhance your MAA environment, not only by protecting your valuable data but by also providing the ability to improve scalability with the use of the real-time query and/or logical standby databases.

Chapter 12 discusses enhancing your MAA environment with the use of the Oracle Data Guard Broker, which not only simplifies the typical Oracle Data Guard monitoring, maintenance, switchover, and failover activities, but also allows for automatic failover of a failed primary database and redo apply failover for Oracle RAC standby databases.

CHAPTER
10

Backup and Recovery for
MAA Environments

o far, we've focused on creating a highly available database using Oracle Real Application Clusters (Oracle RAC), Oracle Data Guard, and internal database features. These technologies are all critical components of Oracle Maximum Availability Architecture (MAA) that are typically researched, proofed, and rolled out by DBAs with specific high availability requirements.

This chapter will take a different track. Every DBA performs backups (at least they should), and most seasoned DBAs have spent time perfecting their backup scripts to be efficient while still protecting the critical data within the database from media failures, corruption, user errors, and other problems. Traditionally, the use of these backups is a last resort or a fall back when the database has already gone down and is unavailable, and the DBA has no other choice but to restore and wait. For this reason, database backups are not commonly considered part of a high availability or MAA design. The very nature of backups is to accept that, occasionally, the database will go down. A common argument when discussing backups with a successfully integrated Oracle RAC and Oracle Data Guard solution in place is that backups are an antiquated notion of the past.

We are here to change that perception.

The Importance of Media Backups

An analysis of backup and recovery service requests that are opened with Oracle Support Services revealed an interesting point: When backups existed for recovery, a full restore of the entire database was initiated 40 percent of the time. In other words, when a hardware failure or a data corruption occurred, the DBA initiated a restore of every datafile in the database. Certainly, in some cases, a full restore of the database may be required due to the nature of the problem. But a survey of the reported issues showed that, in most cases, recovery of a single datafile, subset of datafiles or set of data blocks (yes, data blocks) would have sufficed to resolve the issue, saving hours of lost time with the entire database down. Why restore the entire database? Well, typically, this is a trained reaction by the DBA who has been conditioned to believe that there is only one method to recover the database, and that is to recover the entire database. Quite often, these database restores are scripted to restore the entire database, and the DBA is simply dot-slashing a shell script that was built back in the days of Oracle 7. (To be honest, I have a few sets of my own scripts from back in the old days.)

A defense of this technique is very simple. No "gray area" surrounds restore and recover decisions. A clear roadmap exists to completion of the recovery, after which the database will be up and running. But if that were really the case, if it were that simple, *why do DBAs keep calling Oracle Support for help?*

First, we must accept the fact that recovery situations are sticky, sweaty, nervous times for the DBA. Business is at a standstill, and dollars are being lost by the minute. When caught in this situation, a DBA will often go with what he or she understands best—a vanilla, full database restore looks very appealing, regardless of downtime exceptions. So what is to be done?

First, we must realize that media backups are a required component of any MAA implementation. Oracle RAC provides scalability, performance, and protection against node failure, but Oracle RAC nodes still share the same datafiles, so the possibility of datafile corruption still impacts all nodes in the cluster. Oracle Data Guard guarantees our system against site failure and complete disaster scenarios, but Oracle Data Guard failover is expensive, and we generally try to avoid it at all costs.

Do we failover when a single datafile goes belly up or when a single database block has become corrupt? The correct answer here is absolutely not. Why burden ourselves and our coworkers by having to repoint application servers, reconfigure database jobs (such as backups), reconfigure system monitoring, and so on, not to mention the fact that we probably have to take a full outage for the majority of these tasks to occur. This is the exact niche where a proper database backup and recovery strategy fits, like that last missing piece of the puzzle. For that piece to fit properly, we must first instill in our minds that a full database restore and recovery must be avoided at *all* costs!

For MAA environments requiring those famous "5 9s," a full database restore from backup is the kiss of death. Better to use Oracle Data Guard to failover to the standby system, and then reinstate the primary, than to waste valuable time with a full database restore and recovery. But having a sound backup strategy means having access to files for restoration of individual datafiles or even single data blocks. Given a specific recovery scenario, the best approach may be a datafile or block-level recovery instead of an Oracle Data Guard failover. Given the recoverability enhancements in 11*g*, restoration of database availability can be achieved faster than ever before, which leads us to Oracle Recovery Manager.

Oracle Recovery Manager (RMAN) is a requirement for any true MAA implementation. RMAN is no longer the painful little utility best eschewed by seasoned DBAs empowered with tried-and-true shell scripts. RMAN now comes equipped with the kind of functionality that makes it a critical component in an overall MAA implementation. No other backup utility packs the features that RMAN has to offer. RMAN has been developed specifically to assist in MAA environments, so it not only integrates with Oracle RAC, Oracle Data Guard, and Flashback, but it complements the entire MAA stack, making all components greater than their sum. Did I mention it is free?

This chapter is dedicated to getting the most from an RMAN backup strategy, and not just for recovery, but for assisting with load balancing, maintaining uptime, minimizing downtime, as well as chipping in with Oracle RAC and Oracle Data Guard maintenance.

RMAN: A Primer

It is worth spending a moment to come to terms with the underlying architecture of an RMAN backup, and how it is different from an OS copy. To do so, it is best to know exactly what RMAN is: It is a client utility, like export or SQL*Loader. RMAN comes installed with the database utilities suite within every Oracle database. As such, it can be installed at a client system that has no database and can be used to connect remotely to any number of databases. This is becoming less common, but it is worth pointing out: RMAN makes a SQL*Net connection to the Oracle Database that needs to be backed up.

Typically, the connection from RMAN to the database is a local connection, because RMAN is running from the same environment as the database: same ORACLE_HOME, same ORACLE_SID. But sometimes you need to set up a Transparent Network Substrate (TNS) alias to the database in the tnsnames.ora file, in which case RMAN does not require the same environment as the database—it will connect via the listener, same as a remote SQL*Plus connection, for instance. Note that SQL*Net RMAN connections must use a dedicated server connection (opposed to a shared server connection), so for those who are using shared server, you must create a tnsnames.ora entry specifying **SERVER=DEDICATED** for use by RMAN.

Before jumping into details on RMAN, let's get some vocabulary out of the way:

- **Target database**   In RMAN, the database for which you are currently attempting to perform backup and recovery operations is the target database.

- **RMAN executable**   The RMAN executable is the client utility itself, made up of both the RMAN executable and the recover.bsq (the library file).

- **Recovery catalog**   The recovery catalog is a set of tables, indexes, and packages that are installed into a user schema of an Oracle database. These tables store information about RMAN backups that occur for all the target databases in your enterprise.

- **Catalog database**   The catalog database is the database you choose to house the recovery catalog schema.

- **Auxiliary database**   When you use RMAN to create a clone of your target database, you will make a connection to the clone as the auxiliary database.

This list provides a good roadmap of the components in play during any RMAN operation (say, a backup). From the RMAN prompt, you make a connection to the target:

```
# rman target /
```

If you use a recovery catalog, you make the connection to the catalog as well; typically, the catalog connection is going to be using a TNS alias. This is because you cannot make two local connections to two different databases, and you should never put the recovery catalog in the target database.

```
# rman target / catalog username/password@rmancatalog
```

If you are performing a cloning operation, you would also make a connection to the auxiliary database:

```
# rman target / catalog username/password@rmancatalog auxiliary sys/
oracle123@cosp
```

Alternatively, you invoke RMAN and use the **connect** command to perform any of the previous connections individually:

```
# rman
rman> connect target /
rman> connect catalog username/password@rmancatalog
rman> connect auxiliary sys/oracle123@cosp
```

The RMAN utility is nothing more, really, than a command syntax interpreter. It takes as input simple commands to backup or restore, and turns them into remote procedural calls that are passed to PL/SQL packages at the target database. These packages, dbms_backup_restore and dbms_rcvman, are found in the sys schema and have complementary duties. dbms_rcvman accesses the controlfile to build file lists and dictates work flow in the backup job. This backup job is then passed to dbms_backup_restore for actual file access for backups or restore. That is all you need to know about that, for now.

RMAN and the Controlfile

RMAN has unprecedented access to information about the target database, and this access provides the unprecedented features that make RMAN backups so compelling. First and foremost, RMAN makes a server process connection to the target database as a sysdba user; therefore, it has access to the best source of all important information in the database: the controlfile. RMAN checks the controlfile for information about the datafiles and compiles backup lists based on the number and size of the files. The controlfile also guides RMAN with operations concerning archivelogs: RMAN automatically adjusts for existing archivelogs and backs up only those that are complete. RMAN can also delete all archivelogs in all destinations (except those that are listed as a service in the database, such as archivelogs created at a standby system).

In addition to accessing the controlfile for information about what to back up and what to restore, when RMAN performs a backup or delete (deletion of backups or archivelogs) operation, it records the data about the backup or deletion itself in the controlfile. This data includes information about what files have been backed up, when the backup was taken, as well as checkpoint information and the names of the backup pieces (the output files created by a backup).

RMAN and the Data Block

After gathering the required data from the controlfile, RMAN performs a backup by initializing one or more channel processes. These channel processes access the datafiles and stream the Oracle data blocks from the files into memory buffers within the Oracle Program Global Area (PGA) of the target database. Once a buffer is filled, the channel process does a memory-to-memory write of each data block from the input buffer to an output buffer. Once the output buffer fills, the entire buffer is written to the backup location.

The following illustration shows the RMAN architecture, including controlfile access.

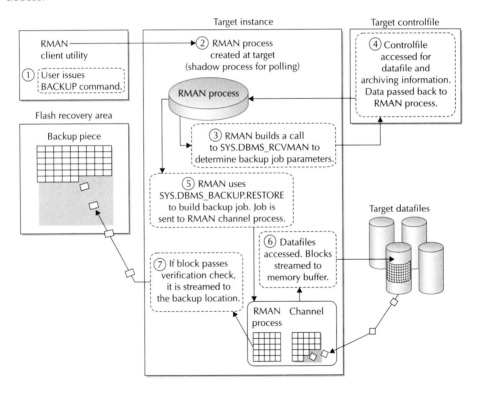

The fact that RMAN has knowledge of and full access to the Oracle data block pretty much sums up why RMAN is so valuable. Nearly everything good that comes from RMAN is due to the fact that data blocks are pulled through the Oracle memory window and then streamed to the backup location. When the memory write occurs from input buffer to output buffer, RMAN checks the block for corruption. If corruption is found, the corrupt block is logged and the backup is aborted to ensure that no corrupt blocks exist in the backup. At the same time, RMAN checks to see if the block is even worth streaming to the backup. If the block has never been initialized, the block is skipped so that it does not take up space in the backup. Also at this time, if an incremental backup is being taken, RMAN will check the block header for an incremental system change number (SCN) and determine whether the block should be backed up during an incremental backup (more on this later).

With so much good stuff to say about RMAN, there's simply no room in this chapter to cover all the territory. RMAN uses the controlfile to guide a back up or recovery, and records its own data in it. RMAN backs up the database at the data block level, streaming them through a memory buffer to perform checks. Now let's concentrate on what RMAN can do for the MAA DBA.

RMAN Command-Line Usage

As a stand-alone client utility, RMAN's command-line syntax is exceptional in the ease-of-use category. Want proof? You can go to any Oracle database, version 9.0.1 or higher, and run the following:

```
# rman target /
rman> backup database;
```

Simple as that, RMAN will back up your database, assuming you are running 10g or higher and have specified a location of the backup will be that specified for the **db_ recovery_file_dest** (Fast Recovery Area—more on this later) initialization parameter. Granted, in this raw form without any additional arguments or parameters specified, the backup is not likely to meet the requirements of your MAA backup and recovery strategy, but you will still have a usable backup after typing four words and a slash.

Likewise, if you still don't believe that a full database restore and recovery must be avoided at *all* costs, you can do the same thing to restore your database (if your database is mounted off a current controlfile):

```
# rman target /
rman> restore database;
```

This command will read the current controlfile to determine which files need to be restored and which backup is best used to do the restoring and perform the restoration. The simplicity saves you from knowing where the backups are, when they were last taken, or what the schematic layout of the datafiles might be at the time of restore.

Many good sources of RMAN command-line syntax are available, and we don't have the space to go into the details here. Check out Oracle Press's own *Oracle RMAN 11g Backup and Recovery* (McGraw-Hill, 2010) or the *Oracle Backup and Recovery Reference 11g Release 2* within the Oracle documentation.

Preparing an RMAN Backup Strategy

RMAN performs invaluable services to achieve high availability, even if you are not using Oracle RAC or Oracle Data Guard and are merely looking for simple, straightforward solutions for your stand-alone database running on a modest server. RMAN provides perhaps the single most powerful out-of-the-box backup experience on the market, but to fully unlock its potential, you need to spend a few moments configuring RMAN to meet your backup and recovery needs.

The Flash Recovery Area

The Flash Recovery Area (FRA) is not a requirement for using RMAN, but it should be. If you are just now coming out of the 9i or even pre-9i days, the FRA was introduced as a new feature in 10g. In Oracle Database 11g Release 2, the Flash Recovery Area was renamed Fast Recovery Area, just to keep us DBAs on our toes!

The functionality of "the area" has not changed, however. It is a specific location on disk that you set up to house all the Oracle recovery files. These include any files that might be required for a media recovery operation: full datafile backups, incremental backups, datafile copies, backup controlfiles, archivelogs, and flashback logs (see Chapter 11). The FRA also functions as a repository for mirrored copies of online redo log files, the block change tracking file, a current controlfile, and an Oracle Data Guard Broker configuration file (see Chapter 12). Although the name has changed in the documentation, many of the database utilities still use the *Flash Recovery Area* name; therefore, within this chapter (and book for that matter), we will stick with the more familiar name of Flash Recovery Area, or FRA for short.

The concept behind the FRA is to simplify the management of your backup and recovery duties by consolidating the requisite files into a single location that Oracle and RMAN can then micromanage, while the DBA moves on to other important MAA duties. This simplification is based on some underlying principles of a solid backup strategy that focuses on availability:

- At least one backup of important datafiles, if not the entire database, should be kept on disks that are locally accessible to the database.

- Backups past a certain age should be moved to tape based on storage pressure on local disks.

- Long-term backup management should be almost completely automatic, based on business rules.

The FRA that you set up can be either a directory on a normal disk volume or an Automatic Storage Management (ASM) disk group (see Chapter 5 on ASM setup and usage). You specify the size of the FRA as an initialization parameter. When determining how large to make your FRA, you should consider the types and number of files that you will be putting there and whether or not compression of backups will be used. This, of course, gets to the heart of your backup and recovery strategy, which we have not yet discussed. Let's just say, for now, that what you need is space for two complete copies of your database, a few days' worth of archivelogs, and then add 20 percent on top of that.

The FRA is defined by two initialization parameters: **db_recovery_file_dest** and **db_recovery_file_dest_size**. The first determines the location, and the second, as denoted by its name, the size. These can be set in your init.ora file, if you still use one (you shouldn't be), or in the SPFILE via an **alter system set** command.

With a FRA configured, you are not required to set any other **log_archive_dest_*n*** parameter for archivelogs; by default, with FRA configured, Oracle will default the archivelog destination to the FRA. It should also be noted that with an FRA in use, you cannot use **log_archive_dest** or **log_archive_duplex_dest**. In fact, these parameters have been deprecated for 11*g* Enterprise Edition (but are still applicable if you are running Standard Edition).

FRA functionality comes on the tail of two other Oracle technologies: Oracle Managed Files (OMF), the means by which initialization parameters determine the size, name, and function of database files; and ASM, the technology that allows Oracle to manage disk volumes for easy DBA management of disk space. You can use the FRA without using OMF and ASM, but they work well together to provide a complete management solution to disk space management for all files related to Oracle. For the MAA DBA, using these three technologies in tandem provides the best of all worlds: availability, manageability, and top-notch performance.

MAA Workshop: *Configure the Flash Recovery Area*

Workshop Notes

The FRA is determined by initialization parameters. In this workshop, we will add a recovery area to a running, operational database for the purpose of RMAN database backups. Although you may have performed this task in previous chapters, this section is a bit different, because it demonstrates the sizing calculations for the FRA. These sizing calculations are to be used as an estimate; actual space usage will be dependent on your backup strategy (compressed, incremental, and so on) and the actual space used in the database datafiles.

Step 1. Determine the size you need for your recovery area. For this example, we are setting up a strategy to account for 24 hours of archivelogs and two full backups of the database.

```
SQL> select sum(bytes)/1024/1024 MB from v$datafile;
       MB
----------
    2762.5
```

Now determine the total size of archivelogs over the last 24 hours:

```
SQL> select sum(blocks*block_size)/1024/1024 MB from v$archived_log
where completion_time > sysdate-1;
       MB
----------
158.212402
```

We then multiply our database size by two, and then take the sum of the datafile and archivelog values and multiple them by 1.2 to get a 20 percent increase from this size to cover file header blocks and other files that may exist in this space:

$$((2762.5 \times 2) + 158.212402) \times 1.2 = 6819.8548824MB$$

For simplicity purposes, we can round up this value to the nearest GB, making our size requirement for the **db_recovery_file_dest_size** parameter 7000MB.

Step 2. Determine the location for the recovery area. For this workshop, we are using our ASM disk group +DBFLASH, which is designated solely for this purpose. Before continuing, we ensure that sufficient space exists in the disk group. To refresh your memory, we can use a simple ASMCMD command to review the disk group sizing:

```
# asmcmd lsdg
```

> **NOTE**
> *Don't forget to set your Oracle Home and ASM SID*
> *properly before running ASMCMD.*

Step 3. Now set the **db_recovery_file_dest** and **db_recovery_file_dest size** values. The values set for these parameters *must* be the same on all Oracle RAC database instances for a particular database. You will notice that in our example, we are using OMF; thus, we are required to specify only the disk group to be used for the destination:

```
SQL> ALTER SYSTEM SET DB_RECOVERY_FILE_DEST='+DBFLASH' SCOPE=BOTH SID='*';
SQL> ALTER SYSTEM SET DB_RECOVERY_FILE_DEST_SIZE=7000M SCOPE=BOTH SID='*';
```

Final Notes on the FRA

Following are a few closing remarks on the FRA, before we move on with our RMAN configuration.

Automatic Maintenance   Transient files (archivelogs, flashback logs, backups, and so on) are managed by the Oracle Database based on retention policies. When these files are no longer needed for recovery of the database based on the retention policies you define, they become candidates for deletion. Should space pressure exist in the FRA, they will automatically be deleted by Oracle to alleviate the pressure. When this "cleanup" occurs, a message will be posted in the database alert log. Static files (online log files, current controlfiles, and so on) are *never* candidates for deletion. Nervous? Don't be! The database does indeed know what it needs for recoverability.

OMF Usage   With OMF, it's not recommended that you set your **db_recovery_file_ dest** to the same location as the **db_file_create_dest** or **db_file_create_online_log_ dest_1** parameters. This is for performance as well as data-protection purposes. Oracle will actually throw a warning if you set these to the same value.

Sharing the FRA Across Multiple Databases   The same FRA can be used by multiple databases. This can provide significant advantages in terms of manageability. It can also prove handy when it comes time to clone production for test purposes. The requirement here is that all the databases using a given FRA must have a unique **db_ name** or utilize the **db_unique_name** parameter.

RMAN Configuration Parameters

Now we have set up the location for our backups. Next, we have to configure the RMAN parameters of the backup itself. In the old days of RMAN in version 8.1.7 or lower, every single backup job you ran from RMAN had to be configured at the time of job execution in a **run{}** block. This resulted in lengthy backup scripts that were often complex in nature—not to mention having to remember all this syntax in a recovery situation when you're under extreme pressure!

Ahh, the good old days..... Or were they? Rest assured that, if you come from 8*i* and you have a pile of RMAN scripts you still want to use, these scripts will still run successfully in 11*g*. However, starting with 9*i*, Oracle acknowledged that certain parameters of a backup are the same across every backup job and should be stored persistently for use on every backup. The ability to set values for RMAN execution that can be used by all subsequent jobs are referred to as *persistent configuration parameters*. These parameters are set at the RMAN command prompt using the

configure command. To list the current configuration parameters, execute the **show all** command within RMAN:

```
RMAN> show all;
RMAN configuration parameters for database with db_unique_name PITT are:
CONFIGURE RETENTION POLICY TO REDUNDANCY 1; # default
CONFIGURE BACKUP OPTIMIZATION OFF; # default
CONFIGURE DEFAULT DEVICE TYPE TO DISK; # default
CONFIGURE CONTROLFILE AUTOBACKUP OFF; # default
CONFIGURE CONTROLFILE AUTOBACKUP FORMAT FOR DEVICE TYPE DISK TO '%F'; # default
CONFIGURE DEVICE TYPE DISK PARALLELISM 1 BACKUP TYPE TO BACKUPSET; # default
CONFIGURE DATAFILE BACKUP COPIES FOR DEVICE TYPE DISK TO 1; # default
CONFIGURE ARCHIVELOG BACKUP COPIES FOR DEVICE TYPE DISK TO 1; # default
CONFIGURE MAXSETSIZE TO UNLIMITED; # default
CONFIGURE ENCRYPTION FOR DATABASE OFF; # default
CONFIGURE ENCRYPTION ALGORITHM 'AES128'; # default
CONFIGURE COMPRESSION ALGORITHM 'BASIC' AS OF RELEASE 'DEFAULT' OPTIMIZE FOR
LOAD TRUE ; # default
CONFIGURE ARCHIVELOG DELETION POLICY TO NONE; # default
CONFIGURE SNAPSHOT CONTROLFILE NAME TO
'/ora01/app/oracle/product/11.2.0/db_1/dbs/snapcf_maadb1.f'; # default
```

With persistent configuration parameters, you can set up job control information that will exist for all backups of the database. For example, if you always back up to tape and would like to configure four channels to do so, you could set the following parameters:

```
RMAN> configure default device type to 'sbt_tape';
RMAN> configure channel device type 'sbt_tape' parms = "env=(nb_ora_
server=linx02)";
RMAN> configure channel device type 'sbt_tape' maxpiecesize = 8G;
RMAN> configure device type 'sbt_tape' parallelism 4;
```

After doing so, the backup can be executed day after day as follows:

```
RMAN> backup database format = 'FULL_DB_%U';
```

You are probably asking why we didn't persistently configure the backup format. Well, the format we are using implies a full database backup, and there may come a time when we want to use this configuration to take an incremental backup to tape. We can get around this by using *backup tags* (text strings used to identify backups). *Backup tags* can be user defined by specifying the **tag** keyword followed by a text string as part of the backup command or a system generated name if the **tag** keyword is not specified in the backup command. If you wanted to set a *backup tag* named "FULL_DB" for the previously shown example, you would do so as follows:

```
RMAN> backup database tag FULL_DB format = 'FULL_DB_%U';
```

We will work more with backup tags in the upcoming MAA workshops.

By now, you have executed the **show all** command and are wondering, "What the heck am I suppose to do with all these parameters?" Numerous options can be configured and books are dedicated to RMAN, all of which describe these configurations in detail. That said, throughout the remainder of this chapter, we will cover various RMAN backup scenarios for MAA environments, many of which involve the setting of persistent configuration parameters for the type of backup we will be performing. As we set various persistent configuration parameters, we will describe the meaning and impact of these settings to your backup and recovery plan.

MAA Workshop: *Setting Persistent Configuration Parameters*

Workshop Notes

This workshop will set up the parameters for a backup strategy that maximizes the functionality of RMAN. The actual backup commands, restore/recover commands, and additional persistent configuration parameters can be found in the subsequent workshops this chapter. The persistent configuration parameters outlined in this workshop will be common to every subsequent MAA workshop in this chapter.

Step 1. Establish the default device as disk, and then configure the disk channels to a parallel degree of 2. This will allow us to back up two datafiles at the same time, allowing for decreased backup times.

```
RMAN> configure default device type to disk;
RMAN> configure device type disk parallelism 2;
```

Step 2. We don't want RMAN to waste time backing up files that we have already backed up, so we must tell RMAN to skip the backup of a file when that identical file has already been backed up. RMAN uses the following criteria to determine whether an identical backup of a given file already exists:

- **Datafile** The DBID, checkpoint SCN, creation SCN, and the reset logs SCN must match that of the backup. For this to happen, the datafile would be either offline normal, read-only, or closed.

- **Archivelog** The DBID, thread, sequence, reset logs SCN, and time must all match.

- **Backup set** The DBID, backup set record ID, and stamp must match. And we can backup a backup set (which you'll soon see).

  ```
  RMAN> configure backup optimization on;
  ```

Step 3. Now we must protect ourselves against the loss of all controlfiles by turning on the controlfile autobackup. We will discuss this in more depth in the "Caring for Your Controlfile" section, but for now let's just turn it on:

```
RMAN> configure controlfile autobackup on;
```

Step 4. Although these configuration parameters are called persistent, they are easily able to be reset to their default values by using the **CLEAR** keyword. For example, let's say we want to reset backup optimization to its default value. We would do so as follows:

```
RMAN> configure backup optimization clear;
```

This is just an example, and after testing this parameter, you should set it as we did in step 2.

Caring for Your Controlfile

The persistent configuration parameters can be applied to every backup of the target database because they are stored in the target database controlfile. You can always view the parameters by looking at v$rman_configuration (this view is not populated with default configuration parameters).

RMAN adds an increased amount of reliance on the presence of a controlfile for its continual operation: the controlfile is the lookup table for what to backup and restore, the lookup table for where the RMAN backups reside and when they were taken, and the home of our backup job controls. This reliance on the controlfile make it a critical component for database recoverability.

It's important that you have an accessible backup of the controlfile that includes data from your most recent backup. In other words, the controlfile needs to be backed up after the successful completion of your database and archivelog backup. By default, RMAN takes a backup of the controlfile whenever it notes that the system datafile is being backed up. The problem with this controlfile backup, however, is that it is initiated at the same time as the datafile backup, so by its very nature it does not contain information about the backup in which it is contained.

The preferred approach to ensure complete controlfile backups is to allow RMAN to back up the controlfile automatically. To allow this to happen, we must set the persistent configuration parameter **controlfile autobackup** to **on** (see MAA workshop "Setting Persistent Configuration Parameters" earlier in the chapter). After we set this parameter to **on**, it will automatically take a controlfile backup to the FRA or a specified location (on disk or tape) after every backup operation, and any structural change to the database (datafile additions, datafile extends, and so on). Note that the default value for this parameter is **off**.

This backup comes at a very small cost—the controlfile is typically only a few megabytes in size. This controlfile autobackup has a few features that are extremely desirable to use in a MAA environment. First, this controlfile autobackup will always contain the RMAN backup metadata that is most recent. Second, the autobackup control file will be written in a format that is immediately recognizable by RMAN; RMAN will be able to find the autobackup controlfile, even when all it knows about the database it is trying to restore is the DBID. Third, without a recovery catalog, the controlfile autobackup lets you avoid having to contact Oracle Support in the event of the loss of all controlfiles. Yes, without this feature and without a recovery catalog, you can still restore the database after the loss of all controlfiles, but the procedure is extremely complex and as mentioned does require the assistance of Oracle Support.

When turned on, the default location for the controlfile autobackup is the FRA. In the absence of an FRA, the location for disk backups is the $ORACLE_HOME/dbs directory. If you configure the default device type to tape, this backup goes to tape. If you back up to disk, lack an FRA, and want to set the controlfile autobackup to a smarter location than the DBS directory, it is done like so:

```
RMAN> configure controlfile autobackup format='/u02/backup/cf_%F';
```

The only requirement is that the format contain the **%F** format so that the backup is recognizable to RMAN during a restore operation. As you move through the MAA workshops in this chapter involving database backups, you will see that we always turn on controlfile autobackup.

The Snapshot Controlfile

When reviewing the RMAN configuration parameters, you may have noticed the presence of a snapshot controlfile. What is this? Well, let's start with what it is *not*. It is *not* a replacement to the controlfile autobackup. RMAN needs a read-consistent view of the controlfile for the backup operation, but by its nature, the controlfile is extremely volatile. Instead of putting a lock on the controlfile and causing all kinds of database enqueue problems, RMAN makes a copy of the controlfile called the snapshot controlfile and uses it instead of the actual controlfile. The snapshot is refreshed at the beginning of every backup. You can relocate the snapshot if it makes sense in your environment, but for the most part it does no harm to leave it in the $ORACLE_HOME/dbs directory. If you are in an Oracle RAC environment, you could place the snapshot controlfile on some type of shared storage, as discussed later in this chapter.

The Recovery Catalog

As previously stated, RMAN, by default, stores all information required for backup and recovery of the database, information about the database backup, as well as configuration settings in the controlfile of the target database. Although the controlfile is always the primary data store for RMAN, a separate copy of this data can be stored in schema within a separate Oracle database. This schema, called the recovery catalog, provides a centralized repository (for multiple databases) for RMAN backup metadata. In addition to providing this centralized repository for RMAN metadata, the recovery catalog provides the following benefits:

- **Increased backup retention** The length of time that backup records are maintained in the controlfile is governed by the **CONTROLFILE_ RECORD_KEEP_TIME** initialization parameter. The longer they keep time, the larger the controlfile (large controlfiles exposed several issues in pre-11g databases). The use of a recovery catalog will allow longer backup retention without the overhead of increasing the **CONTROLFILE_ RECORD_KEEP_TIME** value.

- **Ease of recovery** In the event of the loss of all controlfiles, recovery is simplified because of the controlfile backup information being stored in the recovery catalog. Although with a recovery catalog it is possible to recover without the controlfile autobackup, it is still recommended that the controlfile autobackup be set to **on**.

- **Added features** Some RMAN features such as backup of a physical standby database (more on this later in the section "Block Media Recovery") and storage of backup scripts are available only when using a recovery catalog.

When you are implementing a recovery catalog database, it is recommended that a dedicated database be used. There is no need for multiple recovery catalog databases because a single recovery catalog can be used for all databases within your environment. A recovery catalog should never be created in the database whose metadata is being stored by the same recovery catalog—after all, that would be pointless since the information is already in the controlfile of that database! Tight on space? No worries, because the RMAN recovery catalog database will consume little space. A good estimation is about 15MB (per year) for every database in which it serves, along with about 90MB of additional space consumed in the SYSTEM tablespace.

MAA Workshop: *Implementing a Recovery Catalog*

Workshop Notes

In this workshop, we will create a recovery catalog using an existing 11*g* Release 2 database called *rmancat*. Once the recovery catalog has been created, we will then register a target database (in our case, the pitt database from Chapter 9) with the recovery catalog.

Step 1. Create a tablespace of the appropriate size to house the recovery catalog schema. We are using OMF in our example, so you will notice that there is no explicit filename definition in our syntax.

```
SQL>  create tablespace rmancat datafile size 100M;
```

Step 2. Create a user to own the recovery catalog schema. We will use rman for simplicity, but you can use any username that complies with Oracle standards.

```
SQL> create user rman identified by rman
temporary tablespace temp
default tablespace rmancat
quota unlimited on rmancat;
```

Step 3. Grant the RECOVERY_CATALOG_OWNER role to the user that will own recovery catalog (rman in our case):

```
SQL> grant recovery_catalog_owner to rman;
```

Step 4. Using the RMAN command-line interface, log into the recovery catalog database as the soon-to-be recovery catalog owner and create the recovery catalog schema:

```
# rman catalog rman/rman@rmancat
RMAN> CREATE CATALOG;
```

Step 5. Register a target database with the recovery catalog. We will perform this registration from the host (or one of the hosts in an Oracle RAC environment) running the target database instance, so we will need to be able to connect to the recovery catalog database from this host. We could edit TNSNAMES, but for the sake of this example we will use EZCONNECT. If you are unfamiliar with EZCONNECT, the format is //<hostname>:<listener_port>/<service_name>.

```
# rman target / catalog rman/rman@//ratgc01:1521/gcrep
RMAN> register database;
```

Backups for the MAA Database

Finally, let's get into what this chapter is really all about: backups for the MAA database. Our database backup strategy must put heavy emphasis on availability of the database. Backing up for availability requires that you envision your recovery requirements prior to establishing the backup strategy. It means looking at the different types of failures for which your media recovery strategy must account, and then preparing in advance for as fast a recovery as possible.

The High Availability Backup Strategy

The MAA backup strategy is based on the following high-level principles:

- A complete restore of the database must be avoided at all costs.

- Datafile recovery should take minutes, not hours.

- User errors should be dealt with using Flashback technology, and not media recovery.

- Backup operations should have minimal performance impact on normal database operations.

- Backup maintenance should be automated to fit business rules.

When you consider these principles when designing a backup strategy, they lead toward a specific configuration for your backups in the MAA environment.

Whole Datafile Backups

It might seem obvious, but the centerpiece of your backups must be, of course, backups of the Oracle datafiles. You can ignore your temporary tablespace tempfiles; RMAN does not consider them when backing up, and neither should you. They are built from scratch every time you open the database anyway. Every other file needs a complete, whole backup.

RMAN Backup Sets   RMAN's specialty, leading up to version Oracle Database 10g, was taking a backup using a format called the backup set. The backup set was an RMAN-specific output file that was a multiplexed catchall for all the datafiles of the database, streamed into a single backup piece (think of a backup set as a logical unit, like a tablespace; think of a backup piece as a physical unit, like the datafile). This is an extremely efficient method for getting a backup taken that minimizes the load by eliminating unused blocks. This is the *only* way RMAN can back up to tape.

The only problem with backup sets is that you have to stream the blocks from the backup set through the Oracle memory area, through input/output buffers, and then back to the datafile locations—then rebuild any empty blocks from scratch. So the restore takes a little time. No big deal if you are restoring from tape; the tape restore is the bottleneck, anyway.

RMAN Compressed Backup Sets   Now that you have an understanding of what an RMAN backup set is, you should know that RMAN can create these backup sets in a compressed format. This can and will provide great benefit if you are tight on space. The ability to create compressed backup sets is not really new—it was introduced in 10g. However, with 11g this functionality has been enhanced, allowing for three additional backup compression algorithms:

- **HIGH**   This algorithm allows for the highest level of compression at the cost of increased CPU utilization and increased backup times. This is a good choice for those backing up over a slow network or those who are extremely tight on space.

- **MEDIUM**   This option provides a nice balance between CPU utilization and speed. For this reason, this is the recommended level for most environments.

- **LOW**   If CPU resources are limited within your environment and you would like to take advantage of compression, this is the option for you.

At this point, you are probably wondering what the actual size and resource consumption difference is between all of these compression levels. And the answer is...drum roll, please...well, it depends. The actual level of compression and resource consumption of each of these algorithms is highly dependent on the structure of your database and the type of data within. For this reason, we suggest you test each of these compression levels to determine which one best suits your needs.

As with many of the Oracle advanced features, the ability of running these various compression levels does come at a cost, because you must be licensed for the Advanced Compression Option (ACO) to use them. If you are not licensed for ACO, you can still take advantage of the BASIC compression that was available in previous releases free of charge.

MAA Workshop: *Compressed Backup Sets*

Workshop Notes

This workshop covers the implementation of a compressed backup set backup strategy. With this backup strategy, we will take a full database backup on a daily basis using the ACO compression option of MEDIUM. The destination of this backup will be our FRA. These backups will be maintained for seven days. This workshop assumes that the persistent configuration parameters in the MAA workshop "Setting Persistent Configuration Parameters" have already been set.

Step 1. To implement this backup strategy, we must first configure our persistent configuration parameters to allow for all to use the same configuration. That being said, this step needs to be executed only once.

The first persistent configuration parameter tells Oracle how long a backup is retained. We will configure the retention policy to a recovery window of seven days. (The later section "Backup Housekeeping" offers details on how to do this.) For now, we set the parameter as follows:

```
RMAN> configure retention policy to recovery window of 7 days;
```

In the next command, we are using a compression level of MEDIUM. The **AS OF RELEASE** clause is used to ensure that compression algorithms are maintained across releases; we are specifying **DEFAULT**, which in our case will be 11.2. Finally, the optimize for load clause is used to specify whether precompression block processing will be used. When optimize for load is set to true (the default), no precompression block processing is performed. When set to false, Oracle will perform block defragmentation to improve compression ratios. Obviously, a setting of false results in increased CPU utilization and increased backup times, and for this reason we are using the default value of true. The full persistent configuration parameter setting is as follows:

```
RMAN> configure compression algorithm 'MEDIUM' as of release 'DEFAULT'
optimize for load true;
```

Last but not least, we need to configure our backup type to a compressed backup set. As part of this persistent configuration parameter, we will also be telling RMAN to perform two operations at once by defining parallelism to 2:

```
RMAN> configure device type disk parallelism 2 backup type to
compressed backupset;
```

Step 2. Now to back up the database to a compressed backup set, we execute the next command. In this syntax, we will be using the **plus archivelog** keyword to allow the archivelogs to be backed up in compressed format along with the database.

This will free up space in our FRA by allowing the archivelogs to be candidates for deletion after they are backed up.

```
RMAN> backup database plus archivelog tag compfull_plus_arc;
```

A four-word command on a daily basis would achieve our backup and recovery goals as defined in the workshop notes provided earlier.

Step 3. Previously, we went through a rough estimation of the FRA sizing in the MAA workshop "Configure the Flash Recovery Area." While this sizing was sufficient for two full uncompressed database backups, plus 24 hours of archivelogs, in this workshop we need space for eight full compressed database backups plus seven days of compressed archivelogs and 24 hours of uncompressed archivelogs. As mentioned, the level of compression will vary from database to database, while also being dependent on the compression algorithm in use. For this reason, it is highly recommended that we review the space utilization after our first compressed backup and fine-tune our FRA sizing. To determine the size of the compressed backup set created in the previous step, we execute the following query from SQL*Plus:

```
SQL> select sum(bytes)/1024/1024 MB from v$backup_files where bs_tag
like 'comp_%';
               MB
--------------------
        497.570801
```

Now, going back to the MAA workshop "Configure the Flash Recovery Area," we know that we average about 158MB of redo per day, so let's do some math. First multiply our database size by 8, and then take the sum of the compressed backup set and archivelog values and multiply by 1.2 to get a 20 percent buffer for database growth and/or increased activity:

$$(497.570801 \times 8) + 158.212402) \times 1.2 = 4966.534572MB$$

As you can see, we are getting fairly good compression from the MEDIUM compression algorithm, resulting in an overall space requirement of 4967MB for our FRA. This is well under our initial estimation of 7000MB. We will take comfort over space pressure any day, so we will leave our recovery area sizing as is.

RMAN Datafile Copies to Disk Starting with Oracle 10g, RMAN can take copies of the Oracle datafiles (opposed to backup sets). It still uses the memory buffers during the backup to take advantage of corruption checking, but empty blocks are not eliminated—and the end result is a complete, block-for-block copy of the datafile. Datafile copies can be taken only to disk; it doesn't make sense to do it to tape because backup sets are far more efficient.

The benefit of datafile copies is that, given a restore operation, the copy can quickly be switched to by the Oracle database, instead of physically restoring the file to the datafile location. The restore goes from minutes (or hours) to mere seconds. Once we have told the database to use the datafile copy, we immediately apply archivelogs to recover the datafile to the current point in time. Now that is a desirable feature for availability!

The problem, of course, is that you need the disk space to house a complete copy of the datafiles in your database. Of course, this is becoming less and less of a problem as Storage Area Networks (SANs) become commonplace and disk prices continue to drop. But given a multi-terabyte database, using disk-based copies might prove impossible.

It is recommended that in Oracle Database 10g and above, you take advantage of disk-based copies whenever possible. Using local datafile copies is the best way to decrease the mean time to recovery (MTTR), thus increasing the overall availability of our MAA environment. Creating them using RMAN means you have all the benefits: corruption checking, backup file management, block media recovery, and so forth. If you don't have space for copies of all your files, prioritize your files based on those that would be most affected by an extended outage, and get copies of those files. Send the rest directly to tape or alternate media.

Incremental Backups

Once you have decided to use datafile copies or backup sets for your backup strategy, you can consider using incremental backups. RMAN lets you take a backup of only those data blocks that have changed since the last full backup, or the last incremental. That means backup times are decreased, and for those of you who are tight on disk space, backup sets are generally much smaller in size. Using incremental backups during datafile recovery is typically more efficient than using archivelogs, so you usually improve your MTTR as well.

If you have the disk space to do so, taking full database backups every night is definitely preferred over taking a full backup once a week, and then taking daily incrementals. The first step of any recovery will be to restore the last full datafile backup, and then begin the process of replacing blocks from each subsequent incremental backup. So if you have a recent full backup, recovery will be faster. Incremental strategies are for storage-minded DBAs who feel significant pressure to keep backups small due to the size of the database.

RMAN divides incremental backups into two levels: 0 and 1 (if you used incremental backups in RMAN9i and lower, levels 2–4 have been removed because they really never added much functionality). A level 0 incremental backup is actually a full backup of every block in the database; a level 0 is the prerequisite for any incremental strategy. Specifying a level 0 incremental, versus taking a plain old backup, means that RMAN records the incremental SCN (the marker by which all blocks will be judged for inclusion within an incremental backup). The incremental SCN is not recorded when level 0 is not specified when the backup is taken.

After you take your level 0 backup, you are free to take as many level 1 backups as you require. Incremental level 1 backups come in two flavors: cumulative, which will back up all modified blocks since the level 0 was taken; and differential (the default), which will back up only those blocks that have changed since the last level 1. During a level 1 backup, RMAN determines whether a block has been modified since the level 0 (for cumulative) or level 1 (for differential) backup. If so, the block makes the pass from the input buffer to the output buffer and ends up in the backup piece. When complete, the level 1 backup is a pile of blocks that, by itself, is a significant subset of the actual datafile it represents (depending on your database volatility, of course).

Incrementally Updated Backups   With Oracle Database 10g, Oracle introduced the ability to leverage incremental backups for fast recovery via incrementally updated backups. In a nutshell, RMAN now allows you to apply an incremental backup to a copy of the datafiles on an ongoing basis so that the copy is always kept as recent as the last incremental backup. Upon switching to a datafile copy, you would need to apply only archivelogs since the last incremental backup, and you'd be back in business. This reduced recovery window makes this backup strategy our preference for the MAA DBA.

Obviously, the reduction in downtime in recovery situations is a huge advantage, but incrementally updated backups offer other enormous advantages: you can mimic taking a new, full copy of the datafiles every night without the overhead of such an operation. You also extend the lifespan of your full datafile copy, because you can theoretically apply incremental backups to the copy forever without taking a new full copy of the file.

If you are planning on using a recovery window or a redundancy greater than 1 for backup retention, you must take this into account when merging the incremental backup with the full backup; otherwise Oracle, by default, will not honor retention policies greater than a redundancy of 1. We will show this in the next MAA workshop "Using Incrementally Updated Backups."

The requirements are minimal for incrementally updated backups:

- You need to tag your full level 0 backup so that it can be specified for the incremental apply.

- You can apply an incremental only to a copy, and not a backup set.

- The incremental backup must be taken with the keywords **for recover of copy**.

MAA Workshop: *Using Incrementally Updated Backups*

Workshop Notes

This workshop assumes that the persistent configuration parameters in the MAA workshop "Setting Persistent Configuration Parameters" have already been set. We will be maintaining a single copy of the database that will utilize FRA for the backup location.

Step 1. As with the implementation of any RMAN backup strategy, we must first configure our persistent configuration parameters to allow for all to use the same configuration.

We will start off by telling Oracle to maintain one complete backup of the database. To do so, we will configure the retention policy to redundancy 1. (More in "Backup Housekeeping.")

```
RMAN> configure retention policy to redundancy 1;
```

Now configure RMAN to back up as a copy instead of the default backup set, and as with the preceding MAA workshop, we will use a degree of parallelism of 2.

```
RMAN> configure device type disk parallelism 2 backup type to copy;
```

Step 2. Take the full, level 0 backup. Be sure to tag it, because this is how we will refer to it during the application of the incremental backup. Be sure there is enough space in the recovery area to house full copies of all your datafiles.

```
RMAN> backup incremental level 0 tag 'inc_4_apply' database;
```

Step 3. Take the level 1 incremental backup. If this is production, you should schedule your level 1 to meet your business needs—every night is a common approach. If you are merely testing incremental application at this time, be sure to run some Data Manipulation Language (DML) changes against your database after making the level 0 backup, and before running the level 1. Switch the log files a few times as well, to put some distance between the two backups.

```
RMAN> backup incremental level 1 for recover of copy
tag 'inc_4_apply' database;
```

Step 4. Apply the incremental backup to the datafile copies of your database:

```
RMAN> recover copy of database with tag 'inc_4_apply';
```

After applying the first incremental level 1, you can script the incremental backup and the incremental application to the backup copy so that you apply the latest incremental backup immediately after taking it.

If you are maintaining a recovery window of, let's say, seven days for your retention policy (we will discuss retention policies shortly), defined in your persistent RMAN configuration:

```
RMAN> CONFIGURE RETENTION POLICY TO RECOVERY WINDOW OF 7 DAYS
```

This poses an issue when we run the **recover copy of database** command for it, since it will merge the latest incremental with the latest datafile copies, leaving us with an up-to-date copy of our database. So if we wanted to restore and recover to seven days prior, we would be unable to do so. Two solutions are available for this issue.

First, we can include the **UNTIL TIME** clause of the **recover** command, as follows:

```
RMAN> recover copy of database with tag 'inc_4_apply'
until time 'sysdate -7';
```

This will allow for recoverability of the database to any point within the last seven days. Without this **UNTIL TIME** clause, the **recover copy** command will merge the latest incremental with the level 0, resulting in recoverability of the database from the latest incremental forward.

The second approach is to back up our database copy after the recover copy has completed. This provides the best of both worlds. We can use the incremental strategy described previously on a daily basis (without the **UNTIL TIME** clause), leaving a full up-to-date copy of our database in the FRA, and take that full copy to an alternate location (tape or disk) on a daily basis. We will discuss backups of the FRA in more detail shortly, but for now, here's the syntax required to back up our database copy from the FRA to an alternate disk location (new in 11g):

```
RMAN> backup recovery area to destination '/nas/fra_backups' tag
'fra_backup';
```

To back up our database copy to a configured System Backup to Tape (SBT) device (more on SBT later in the section "The SBT Interface"):

```
RMAN> backup device type sbt tag "fra_backup" recovery area;
```

In addition to backing up the database copy, this will also back up every recovery file in the FRA, including the archivelogs.

Using Block Change Tracking for Better Incremental Performance   If you do decide to use incremental backups in your recovery strategy, you should consider implementing a performance feature called *block change tracking*. When enabled, this feature will allow RMAN to keep track of all blocks that have been modified since the last backup. When the incremental level 1 backup is taken, RMAN looks at the block change tracking file to determine which blocks to back up.

Prior to the introduction of this feature in 10*g*, the only way that RMAN could determine which data blocks to include in a level 1 incremental backup was to read every block in the database into an input buffer in memory and check it. This led to a common misconception about incremental backups in RMAN: that they would go significantly faster than full backups. This simply didn't hold up to scrutiny, as RMAN still had to read every block in the database to determine its eligibility—so it was reading as many blocks as the full backup.

With block change tracking, the additional I/O overhead is eliminated almost entirely, as RMAN will read only those blocks required for backup. Now, there is a little bit of robbing Peter to pay Paul, in the sense that block change tracking does incur a slight performance hit for the database to maintain the change tracking files, but if you plan on using incremental backups, chances are you can spare the CPU cycles for the increased backup performance and backup I/O decrease.

To enable block change tracking, you simply execute the following from SQL*Plus:

```
SQL> ALTER DATABASE ENABLE BLOCK CHANGE TRACKING;
```

As briefly mentioned, the block change tracking information is maintained in a binary file. By default, this file will be created using OMF; however, you can manually specify a location if you choose. If you are in an Oracle RAC environment, keep in mind that this location *must* be shared across all cluster nodes. Here's the syntax:

```
SQL> alter database enable block change tracking using file '/dir/blck_
change_file';
```

Execute the following to turn off block change tracking:

```
SQL> alter database disable block change tracking;
```

NOTE
After you turn block change tracking on, it does not have any information about block changes until the next level 0 backup is taken.

Backing Up the Flash Recovery Area

With all backups being taken to the FRA and archivelogs being generated to this same location, we have the peace of mind of a quick and simplistic recovery. However, these backups and archivelogs will pile up over time, and as we all know, disk space is not infinite. RMAN provides built-in functionality that allows the FRA to be essentially a staging area for taking these recovery files to alternate media so that we can easily maintain historical backups to meet business requirements. The syntax involves three words and the rest is magic:

```
RMAN> backup recovery area;
```

There's actually a lot of internal logic behind this command, which automatically backs up all recovery files in the recovery area: full backups, copies, incrementals, controlfile autobackups, and archivelogs. Block change tracking files, current controlfiles, and online redo logs are not backed up (these are not recovery files).

In releases prior to Oracle Database 11g Release 2, this command could back up only to channel type SBT (tape), so it would fail if you did not have tape channels configured. With 11g Release 2, Oracle recognized that backing up to media other than tape is becoming more popular. For this reason, the **TO DESTINATION** clause was added to the **backup recovery area** command. If you are backing up the FRA to tape, we will be demonstrating this later in this chapter. For now, we are going to use the destination clause:

```
RMAN> backup recovery area to destination '/my_backup_location';
```

Alternatively, if you want the same magical functionality but you do not use a FRA, you can use this:

```
RMAN> backup recovery files to destination '/my_backup_location';
```

This has the same effect: full backups, copies, incrementals, controlfile autobackups, and archivelogs are backed up.

Backup Housekeeping

As you probably know, backups are not often used, and yes, this is a good thing. However, as we surpass our recovery requirements, backups can leave quite a long trail of useless files consuming precious space in our FRA and will result in quite the large media library. These outdated backups not only clog storage media, but they leave a lengthy trail of metadata in our controlfile or recovery catalog, making reports more and more useless with every passing day. For these reasons, we must consider housekeeping chores as a key part of any serious MAA backup strategy.

Determine, Configure, and Use Your Retention Policy

The key to our MAA backup housekeeping lies in a RMAN configuration parameter called the *retention policy*, which refers to the rules by which you dictate which backups are obsolete, and therefore eligible for deletion. RMAN distinguishes between two mutually exclusive types of retention policies: redundancy and recovery windows.

Redundancy policies determine whether a backup is obsolete based on the number of times the file has been previously backed up. So if you set your policy to "redundancy 1" and then back up the database, you have met your retention policy. The next time you have successfully completed a backup of your database, all previous backups are marked obsolete, making them candidates for deletion. Setting "redundancy 2" would mean that you keep the last two backups, and all backups prior to that are obsolete.

The *recovery window* refers to a time frame in which all backups will be kept, regardless of how many backups are taken. The recovery window is anchored to sysdate, and therefore is a constantly sliding window of time. So if you set your policy to "recovery window of 7 days," all backups older than seven days would be marked obsolete, making them candidates for deletion. As time rolls forward, new backups are taken and older backups become obsolete.

You cannot have both retention policies, so choose one that best fits your backup practices and business needs. There is a time and a place for both types, and it always boils down to how you view your backup strategy: Is it something that needs redundancy to account for possible problems with the most recent backup, or do you view a backup strategy as defining how far back in time you can recover?

After you determine what policy you need, configuration is easy: use the **configure** command from the RMAN prompt to set it in the target database controlfile (this was shown in previous MAA workshops). By default, the retention policy is set to redundancy 1, but this can easily be changed as follows:

```
RMAN> CONFIGURE RETENTION POLICY TO RECOVERY WINDOW OF 7 DAYS;
```

After you have configured your desired retention policy, you'll find it simple to use. You can list obsolete backups and copies using the **report** command, and then when you are ready, use the **delete obsolete** command to remove all obsolete backups. Note that RMAN will always ask you to confirm the deletion of files.

```
RMAN> report obsolete;
RMAN> delete obsolete;
RMAN retention policy will be applied to the command
RMAN retention policy is set to recovery window of 7 days
allocated channel: ORA_DISK_1
channel ORA_DISK_1: SID=34 instance=maadb1 device type=DISK
allocated channel: ORA_DISK_2
channel ORA_DISK_2: SID=164 instance=maadb1 device type=DISK
Deleting the following obsolete backups and copies:
Type                  Key    Completion Time    Filename/Handle
--------------------  -----  -----------------  --------------------
Backup Set            32     26-JUL-10
  Backup Piece        35     26-JUL-10          +DBFLASH/pitt/
backupset/2010_07_26/nnndf0_tag20100726t200258_0.337.72540018
Archive Log           3693   26-JUL-10                +DBFLASH/pitt/
archivelog/2010_07_26/thread_1_seq_924.358.725400259
Do you really want to delete the above objects (enter YES or NO)?
```

You can automate the **delete obsolete** command so that a job can perform the action at regular intervals (just after a successful backup is logical) and save you the effort. To do so, include the **noprompt** keyword to override the deletion prompt:

```
RMAN> delete noprompt obsolete;
```

Retention Policies and the FRA

As mentioned, the FRA is self-cleaning (kind of like an oven without all the buttons and the horrid smell of burning food). What this means is that as files build up in the FRA and storage pressure begins to appear, the FRA will age-out old files that have passed the boundaries of the retention policy you have implemented. Consider, for example, a retention policy of redundancy 1. You take a full database backup on Monday, and on Tuesday, you take a second full database backup. On Wednesday, you take a third full database backup. However, three full backups won't fit in the FRA. So Oracle checks the policy, sees that it requires only one backup, and it deletes the backup taken on Monday—and the Wednesday backup completes.

NOTE
Even with redundancy set to 1, you must have enough space in your FRA for two whole database backups. This is because RMAN will not delete the only backup of the database before it completely writes the new one, because the possibility exists for a backup failure—and then you'll have no backups. So before the Monday backup is truly obsolete, the Tuesday backup has to exist in its entirety, meaning two backups exist.

If the FRA fills up with files, but no files qualify for deletion based on your retention policy, you will see an error, and the backup that is currently underway will fail:

```
RMAN-03009: failure of backup command on ORA_DISK_1 channel at
07/19/2010 19:23:38
ORA-19504: failed to create file "+DBFLASH"
ORA-17502: ksfdcre:4 Failed to create file +DBFLASH
ORA-15041: diskgroup "DBFLASH" space exhausted
```

A full FRA can be a far more serious problem than just backup failures. If you set up your FRA as a mandatory site for archivelog creation, the archive (ARCH) process can potentially hang your database waiting to archive a redo log to a full location. By all estimations, it behooves the MAA DBA to keep the FRA open for business. Fortunately for us MAA DBAs, Oracle has provided the v$recovery_area_usage view to give us some insight into our FRA usage:

```
SQL> select * from v$recovery_area_usage;
```

Retention Policies and FRA Backups

Our preferred MAA backup strategy is to keep an up-to-date copy of our database in the FRA for quick simplistic recovery, but we also want to maintain a retention policy that requires more than a single backup of the database be available for restore. The way to accomplish this, of course, is to back up the FRA. As discussed earlier, with Oracle Database 11g Release 2, you now have the ability to back up the FRA to an alternate disk location or tape, thus proving you have more flexibility to achieve your backup and recovery goals.

The retention policy that you configure applies to all backups, whether they be on disk or tape. However, if you use the FRA as a staging area that is frequently moved to tape, you will never be required to clean up the FRA. When you back up the recovery area, you free up the transient files in the FRA to be aged out when space pressure occurs, so the errors noted previously don't impair future backups or archivelog operations. That being said, you must ensure that you run your maintenance commands to ensure that you are cleaning up your FRA backup location (whether it be on tape or disk).

We did just this (with the exception of maintenance) in our script from the MAA workshop "Using Incrementally Updated Backups," and now we'll modify it to include a FRA backup and a backup maintenance command to delete obsolete backups from the location of the FRA backups (this is using a retention policy set to a recovery window of seven days):

```
RMAN> backup incremental level 1 for recover of copy
tag 'inc_4_apply' database;
RMAN> recover copy of database with tag 'inc_4_apply';
RMAN> backup recovery area to destination '/nas/fra_backups';
RMAN> delete obsolete;
```

Archivelog Deletion Policy

With RMAN, archivelogs are deleted using the backup archivelog **delete input** and **delete archivelog** commands. When run with the default archivelog deletion policy of none, these commands will delete archivelogs that are not needed for any required standby destination and any archivelogs not required for a flashback database operation (restore point or flashback retention policy). If you are using a FRA for archival, you may opt out of performing any manual archivelog deletions, allowing Oracle to delete archivelogs that are no longer needed for recovery when there is space pressure in the FRA.

Although both manual and automatic deletion methods are fine for most environments, we can customize the archivelog deletion policy to ensure that the desired archivelogs are available for one reason or another (business rules, applied on standby, and so on). To facilitate this, we can explicitly define an archivelog deletion policy using RMAN persistent configuration parameters—for example, if we wanted to tell RMAN not to delete archivelogs that have never been backed up to disk, we can perform the following (for tape we would modify the device type to **sbt**):

```
RMAN> configure archivelog deletion policy to backed up 1 times to
device type disk;
```

If you are using Oracle Data Guard, you will likely want to configure your archivelog deletion policy to be applied on standby or shipped to standby. For example, to make sure that archivelogs that have not been applied to **all** standby databases are not deleted, we would set the archivelog deletion policy like so:

```
RMAN> configure archivelog deletion policy to applied on all standby;
```

Similarly, if we wanted to tell RMAN to allow deletion of archivelogs only after the log data has been shipped to **all** standby databases, we would set the deletion policy to this:

```
RMAN> configure archivelog deletion policy to shipped to all standby;
```

In the two preceding commands, we used the **all** keyword. Omitting the **all** keyword in the commands will allow the deletion of archivelogs that were shipped and/or applied to mandatory destinations. Non-mandatory destinations are not included in the policy and therefore are candidates for deletion whether or not they were shipped and/or applied.

Performing Recovery

Here's one of our favorite sayings: Every DBA has a backup strategy. Few of them, however, have a recovery strategy. Our advice here is not to be the cliché. Make sure you understand your recovery options and test them once in a while to keep your recovery skills sharp.

Back when I was a day-to-day DBA, we had a common practice at the company that I worked at of regularly corrupting one of our DBA-only test databases (block corruption, delete datafiles, and so on). It started off as a joke to annoy other DBAs on the team, but it quickly became a useful exercise in keeping our recovery skills sharp. Basically, to use the database, you were forced to recover it first.

Maintaining availability through the failure event requires that you have the knowledge and trust in your backups to take immediate action that is not a knee-jerk reaction that leads to further downtime due to the recovery itself. The key, as always, is not to initiate a full restore of the database in a blind panic.

Database Recovery: Restore and Recover

Recovering from some sort of failure (database corruption, hardware loss, and so forth) typically involves two distinct steps for an Oracle database: restore and recovery. Datafile *restore* refers to the act of getting a copy of the lost or broken file back (or data block with RMAN) in place from the backup. *Recovery* refers to the process of applying archived redo log changes to the restored file.

As you know, the goal is to avoid a full database restore at all costs. When you encounter an error, it is critical that you come to terms with the full extent of the problem and be mindful of overreacting. Think first to restore a single datafile back for recovery. You can always bring the file or group of files manifesting the problem first and recover them, and then investigate for other possible problem files.

This approach is assisted in a huge way by incrementally updated datafile copies that live in the FRA. Because the files exist on disk and are independent of each other (that is, not multiplexed into a single backup piece), you can perform restore and recovery one piece at a time without slowing down the overall performance.

Stream through a day's worth of archivelogs two or three times and you will soon realize that a piecemeal approach does have its downside. So trying to diagnose the entire problem prior to recovery is extremely useful.

If you are taking backup set–type backups directly to tape, restoring a single datafile from the backup set is going to be extremely expensive. RMAN must restore the entire backup piece from tape before it can extract just the blocks for the single datafile. So multiplexing multiple files into the same backup set can be very costly at the time of recovery. Better, then, to set **filesperset** to 1, which will slow down the backup but provide the most flexibility during restore.

Full Database Recovery

Although extremely rare with a proper backup and recovery strategy, we must face the fact that sometimes it's absolutely required to perform a full recovery of a database. In those cases, the code is simple and straightforward. Note that the following code for restoring the database assumes that you have the current controlfile and the target database is mounted. If there is no controlfile, you should read the upcoming section, "Recovery from Complete Loss (Loss of all Controlfiles)."

```
rman> restore database;
rman> recover database;
```

If you need to specify a point in time in the past to which to recover, use this:

```
rman> run {set until time = '27-JUL-10 12:00:00';
restore database;
recover database; }
```

Datafile or Tablespace Recovery

The most common form of recovery should be datafile recovery. To perform datafile recovery, you must offline the datafile prior to restoration. You can do this from the SQL prompt or from within RMAN (as shown). These recovery commands assume the database is still open and running.

```
RMAN> sql 'alter database datafile 8 offline';
```

Once the file is offline, from the RMAN prompt, issue **restore** and **recover** commands. To save yourself typing, you can refer to the files by their file numbers instead of their names.

```
RMAN> connect target /
RMAN> run {
 restore datafile 8;
 recover datafile 8;
 sql 'alter database datafile 8 online';}
```

The same basic structure is used for tablespaces:

```
rman> run { sql 'alter tablespace users offline';
restore tablespace users;
recover tablespace users;
sql 'alter tablespace users online'; }
```

Recovery from Complete Loss (Loss of all Controlfiles)

If the controlfile has been lost along with the rest of the database, we hope you took our advice and configured RMAN for controlfile autobackup. If you did not take our advice and do not have a recovery catalog database to identify the backup set that contains the backup of the controlfile, you will be forced into contacting Oracle Support to assist you with your recovery. That said, if you have not done so already, take our advice and turn on the controlfile autobackup feature!

MAA Workshop: *Recovering from a Complete Loss*

Workshop Notes

This workshop guides you through the restoration and recovery of an Oracle database that has been completely lost. This example shows how to recover using RMAN when there is no RMAN catalog and all controlfiles have been lost; we'll use the controlfile autobackup feature.

Step 1.   Determine the database ID (DBID) of the lost database; this is required for RMAN to identify the appropriate controlfile autobackup. That said, you should take note of your DBID and keep it handy for these situations. If your database is already corrupt and you have lost all the controlfiles, don't worry, because you can still find your DBID in the following locations:

- In the recovery catalog database.

- Within the controlfile autobackup filename (unless you are using OMF to store the file in the FRA). The DBID will be the first numerical value of the **%F** format—for example, **c-<dbid is here>-xxx-xxx**.

- Within the RMAN log files from backups (assuming you log your backups). The DBID will be displayed just after connecting to the target database.

Step 2. Using RMAN, **startup nomount** a default instance for your database and set the DBID you identified in step 1:

```
RMAN> startup nomount
RMAN> set dbid 12345678934
```

Step 3. Restore your SPFILE from the autobackup and restart the database instance in nomount state to pick up the restored SPFILE:

```
RMAN> restore spfile from autobackup;
RMAN> startup force nomount;
```

RMAN will automatically locate the latest autobackup if it is stored in one of the default locations (FRA or $OH/dbs) having the default format. If you have specified a non-default autobackup location, you must use a run block to specify the autobackup location as follows:

```
RMAN> run {
set controlfile autobackup format for device type disk to '/nas/c_%F';
restore spfile from autobackup;
startup force nomount; }
```

Step 4. Restore the controlfile from the autobackup and then mount the database:

```
RMAN> restore controlfile from autobackup;
RMAN> alter database mount;
```

As with the SPFILE, if you have specified a non-default autobackup location, you must use a run block to specify the autobackup location as follows:

```
RMAN> run {
set controlfile autobackup format for device type disk to '/nas/c_%F';
restore controlfile from autobackup;
alter database mount; }
```

Step 5. Restore and recover the database files:

```
RMAN> restore database;
RMAN> recover database;
```

Step 6. Once the database has been recovered, open the database using the **resetlogs** option:

```
RMAN> alter database open resetlogs;
```

If this were an Oracle RAC database, we would now open the remaining database instances and be back in business. Technically, we could have created a run block with all of the commands from steps 2–6, but for demonstration purposes, we have shown this recovery one command at a time.

Recovery Using the Incrementally Updated Datafile Copy

No extra step is required to use the incrementally updated datafile copies for restore operations. They will be used automatically, because their incremental update time will show them to be the most recent copies of the files. Cool, huh?

Block Media Recovery

Now we get to the feature with RMAN that is absolutely too cool for words: *block media recovery (BMR)*. BMR refers to RMAN's ability to restore from backup a single data block and then perform media recovery on that single block. This is huge, people. ORA-1578? No problem. Plug in the file number and block number from the 1578 error, and RMAN will search, in order, the physical standby, flashback logs, and then within database backups. Once RMAN identifies a copy of this block, it will restore the block, and then scroll through the archivelogs to see if any of the redo needs be applied to the block. Here's the kicker: The file that has the corrupt block remains available through the recovery process. Wait, it gets better: The segment that contains the corrupt block is available during the recovery process. This means that you can continue to use the table that has a corrupt block, as long as you don't try to select from the bad block.

Usage is simple. Take your average ORA-1578 error:

```
ORA-1578: ORACLE data block corrupted (file # 7, block # 1234)
```

Note the file number and block number, and plug them into the RMAN command:

```
RMAN> recover datafile 7 block 1234;
```

You can specify multiple blocks:

```
RMAN> recover datafile 7 block 1234
   datafile 10 block 3265;
```

When numerous corrupt blocks are visible in v$database_block_corruption, you can tell RMAN to recover all of those blocks:

```
RMAN> recover corruption list;
```

If you are familiar with block recovery in pre-11g, you may be thinking we have the incorrect syntax for BMR. Not true—Oracle has deprecated the blockrecover syntax to allow for the recovery command to fall in line with other types of RMAN media recovery.

Now that we have explained BMR with RMAN, let's take this one step further by totally eliminating the ORA-1578 error in the first place. If you already read Chapter 9, this will be nothing new to you because it was covered there, but this is such an awesome feature we have decided it was appropriate for two chapters! How do we do this? First, we need a physical standby database running with the Oracle Active Data Guard option. Upon detection of a block corruption on the primary database that would normally result in an ORA-1578 error, the corrupt block is shipped from the standby database and the corrupt block on the primary database is replaced with the standby copy of the block. The user who ran the query to "discover" the block corruption will see a slight pause in his/her query while the block is replaced, but no error is ever thrown. No human intervention is required. Now *that* is high availability!

Database Recovery: Data Recovery Advisor

You know how to perform recovery the hard way. If you are running Oracle RAC, the hard way (which really isn't so hard) is the only way at this point, because the Data Recovery Advisor does not support Oracle RAC databases just yet. Please do keep reading, though, because this feature is truly interesting and at some point will support Oracle RAC.

NOTE
If you are running in an Oracle RAC environment, the Data Recovery Advisor can be used if you shut down all database instances and start in single instance mode (cluster_database=false).

As discussed, the general steps in performing recovery are to assess the situation, determine what recovery steps need to be performed based on your assessment, perform the recovery, and then cross your fingers and hope that you have taken the proper corrective actions to minimize the outage window and data loss (if any). With careful assessment of the situation and proper planning, you will be able to uncross those fingers and ensure success, but this is a stressful situation for even the most experienced DBA. These situations become even more stressful when management looks over your shoulder while you are performing a task that you don't often practice (though it should be, but we are being realistic here). Needless to say, human error in these situations is likely.

And this is why the Data Recovery Advisor was introduced with Oracle Database 11g Release 1—to assist in diagnosing and repairing data corruption and/or data loss issues. Oracle will now diagnose corruption issues within single instance databases and advise DBAs on how to take corrective action on the corruption issues. Taking this one step further, the MAA DBA can implement the recommendations generated by the Data Recovery Advisor with a few strokes on the keyboard. The driving source of any recovery is detection of the corruption, and for corruption detection, Oracle uses a new framework introduced in 11*g* Release 1 called the *Health Monitor*.

Health Monitor

The Health Monitor can be invoked in either a reactive method, which means that corruption has resulted in a database error, or in a proactive method, which allows for detection of corruption prior to users experiencing errors related to the corruption. Regardless of how the Health Monitor is invoked, it will always log its findings to the Automatic Diagnostic Repository (ADR). The Health Monitor currently has the ability to execute the following five Health Checks (which are also viewable by querying the v$hm_check view):

- **DB Structure Integrity Check**   Detects and reports corrupt, inconsistent, or missing datafiles.

- **Data Block Integrity Check**   Detects and reports on database block corruptions; also populates the v$database_block_corruption view.

- **Redo Integrity Check**   Detects and reports redo and archivelog corruptions including inaccessible redo logs.

- **Undo Segment Integrity Check**   Detects logical undo corruptions and invokes System Monitor (SMON) and Process Monitor (PMON) to recover the corrupt transaction. Should the transaction be unrecoverable, the corruption is logged in v$corrupt_xid_list view.

- **Transaction Integrity Check**   Performs the Undo Segment Integrity Check on a specific transaction.

- **Dictionary Integrity Check**   Detects and reports on corruption within the dictionary objects in the following areas: data dictionary entries, object relationships (parent-child), and row-level constraints.

In its default reactive form, Health Monitor will automatically run the appropriate Health Check for the error that was encountered. For example, if the database encounters an ORA-1110 error, the DB Structure Integrity Check would automatically be invoked. To invoke this check proactively, we use the **DBMS_HM.RUN_CHECK** procedure as follows:

```
SQL> BEGIN
  DBMS_HM.RUN_CHECK (
    check_name   => 'DB Structure Integrity Check',
    run_name     => 'proactive_struct_chk');
END;
/
```

As with the majority of internal PL/SQL procedures and/or packages, the **DBMS_HM.RUN_CHECK** procedure comes with various variables for each check. Depending on the check, some of these variables may be required. To determine the available and/or required variables for each of the Health Checks, execute the following:

```
SQL> select chk.name check_name, parm.name parameter, parm.default_value,
parm.description
from v$hm_check chk, v$hm_check_param parm
where parm.check_id = chk.id and chk.internal_check = 'N'
order by chk.name;
```

For those GUI fans out there, the Health Monitor can also be invoked through Enterprise Manager (Grid Control or Database Control, whatever your flavor may be), and regardless of the interface being used, the features and functionality are the same. To access the Health Monitor Checks from EM, navigate to the Advisor Central page for your target database and click the Checkers link.

Once a Health Check has been run, whether it be proactive or reactive, the results are able to be viewed through Automatic Diagnostic Repository Command Interface (ADRCI), SQL*Plus via DBMS_HM, or EM. The following example shows a corrupt block in file number 6 block 150:

```
SQL> select * from lunar.customers
*
ERROR at line 1:
ORA-01578: ORACLE data block corrupted (file # 6, block # 150)
ORA-01110: datafile 6: '+DBDATA/pitt/datafile/lunar_data.261.726002631'
```

As a result of this error, Health Monitor reactively spawns a Data Block Integrity Check. We will later use this corruption to demonstrate the powers of the Data Recovery Advisor, but first let's take a look at the Health Check results through the most commonly used interface, SQL*Plus. Although HTML, XML, and text reports are available through SQL*Plus, we are keeping things simple here by demonstrating only the text output.

To allow us to view the correct Health Check run, we should first query the reactive Health Checks that were the result of an incident within the past hour from the v$hm_run view:

```
SQL> select run_id, name, check_name, src_incident from v$hm_run
where run_mode='REACTIVE'
and start_time > SYSDATE-(60/1440)
and src_incident <> 0;

    RUN_ID NAME           CHECK_NAME                     SRC_INCIDENT
---------- -------------- ------------------------------ ------------
        21 HM_RUN_21      Data Block Integrity Check              241
```

Now that we have identified the Health Check spawned by our ORA-1578 error, we can generate a report of the Health Check findings to see the findings and recommendations:

```
SQL> set long 100000
SQL> set longchunksize 1000
SQL> set pagesize 1000
SQL> set linesize 512
SQL> select dbms_hm.get_run_report('hm_run_21') from dual;
```

NOTE
*You must be in a non-Oracle RAC database for this to work properly. If you have only Oracle RAC databases, you can shut down all instances and set **cluster_database=FALSE** to test this feature.*

This execution of **dbms_hm.get_run_report** will produce a report similar to the following:

```
Basic Run Information
 Run Name                        : HM_RUN_21
 Run Id                          : 21
 Check Name                      : Data Block Integrity Check
 Mode                            : REACTIVE
 Status                          : COMPLETED
 Start Time                      : 2010-08-02 23:09:26.835942 -04:00
 End Time                        : 2010-08-02 23:09:28.044229 -04:00
 Error Encountered               : 0
 Source Incident Id              : 241
 Number of Incidents Created     : 0

Input Paramters for the Run
 BLC_DF_NUM=6
 BLC_BL_NUM=150

Run Findings And Recommendations
 Finding
 Finding Name  : One or more corrupted blocks
 Finding ID    : 22
 Type          : FAILURE
 Status        : OPEN
 Priority      : HIGH
 Message       : Datafile 6: '+DBDATA/pitt/datafile/lunar_data.261.726002631'
                 contains one or more corrupt blocks
 Message       : Some objects in tablespace LUNAR_DATA might be unavailable
 Finding
 Finding Name  : Media Block Corruption
 Finding ID    : 25
 Type          : FAILURE
 Status        : OPEN
 Priority      : HIGH
 Message       : Block 150 in datafile 6:
                 '+DBDATA/pitt/datafile/lunar_data.261.726002631' is media
                 corrupt
 Message       : Object CUSTOMERS owned by LUNAR might be unavailable
```

The same procedures described previously can be used to view any of the available Health Checks, whether they be proactive or reactive. The full report view shown in the illustration is helpful, but you could query the v$hm_finding and v$hm_recommendation views to pull select pieces of information from ADR.

Data Recovery Advisor

The Data Recovery Advisor has two interfaces: RMAN and EM. Regardless of the interface being used, the features and functionality are the same. Since our focus in this chapter is backup and recovery with RMAN and we know that RMAN will exist on all Oracle 11g Release 2 systems (EM may not be installed or configured), we will focus on the RMAN CLI into the Data Recovery Advisor. GUI fans can access the Data Recovery Advisor by clicking the Perform Recovery link (in Grid Control or Database Control) under the Availability tab for your database. Just to reiterate, this feature is available only with single instance databases within 11.2.0.1—but again, keep reading, because this is interesting.

With the Data Recovery Advisor, it is all about failures. That said, four basic RMAN commands are used to interface with the Data Recovery Advisor: **LIST FAILURE**, **ADVISE FAILURE**, **CHANGE FAILURE**, and **REPAIR FAILURE**. Have you noticed that all of the commands contain *FAILURE*? Like I said, it's all about failures! Rather than straining your eyes with more text, let's just break out into an MAA workshop to demonstrate the ease of use and power of the Data Recovery Advisor.

MAA Workshop: *Using the Data Recovery Advisor*

Workshop Notes

Within this workshop, we will use the RMAN interface to the Data Recovery Advisor to list, advise, and repair a corrupt data block within the LunarTrax Data tablespace. This workshop assumes the use of a single instance database (Oracle RAC is not supported by the Data Recovery Advisor) and assumes that data block corruption exists and has been detected by Health Monitor (proactive or reactive). Alternatively, if you want, you can detect the corruption with **RMAN VALIDATE**; the end result will be the same.

Step 1. Within RMAN, execute the **LIST FAILURE** command to report the detected failures:

```
RMAN> list failure all;
List of Database Failures
=========================
Failure ID Priority Status    Time Detected  Summary
---------- -------- --------- -------------- -------
22         HIGH     OPEN      02-AUG-10      Datafile 6: '+DBDATA/pitt/
datafile/lunar_data.261.726002631' contains one or more corrupt blocks
```

Failures have three priorities: low, high, and critical. As you can see, this data block corruption has been prioritized as high and has a status of open. This status will remain open until the corruption is repaired, at which time it will be marked as closed. Should you have performed a manual block recovery, the status will still remain open until the **list failure** command is run, at which time it will reassess the failure, marking it closed. The **ALL** keyword at the end of the command will list all failures; omitting the **ALL** keyword will report only low priority failures if no other failures exist.

Step 2. Although not typically necessary unless you experience numerous failures, you do have the ability to reprioritize failures to low or high (changing to critical is not possible) using the **CHANGE FAILURE** command:

```
RMAN> change failure 22 priority low;
```

If you wanted to change all failures to high, you would execute the following:

```
RMAN> change failure all priority high;
```

Step 3. Now that we understand our failure and know we can prioritize the failure as we please, let's check to see what the Data Recovery Advisor recommends for corrective action by using the **ADVISE FAILURE** command:

```
RMAN> advise failure 22;
. . .
Mandatory Manual Actions
========================
no manual actions available
Optional Manual Actions
========================
no manual actions available
Automated Repair Options
========================
Option Repair Description
------ -------------------
1      Perform block media recovery of block 150 in file 6
  Strategy: The repair includes complete media recovery with no data loss
  Repair script:
/ora01/app/oracle/diag/rdbms/pitt/maadb1/hm/reco_3186838308.hm
```

If we omitted the Failure ID, failure advisory would be generated only for high and critical failures. Similarly, if we specified the **ALL** keyword, advisory would be given for all failures.

Step 4. Now let's ask the Data Recovery Advisor exactly what it will do to repair the failure(s):

```
RMAN> repair failure preview;
Strategy: The repair includes complete media recovery with no data loss
Repair script:
/ora01/app/oracle/diag/rdbms/pitt/maadb1/hm/reco_2361325379.hm
contents of repair script:
   # block media recovery
   recover datafile 6 block 150;
```

Step 5. Finally, repair the failure using the **repair failure** command as follows:

```
RMAN> repair failure;
...
executing repair script
Starting recover at 03-AUG-10
using channel ORA_DISK_1
using channel ORA_DISK_2
channel ORA_DISK_1: restoring block(s) from datafile copy +DBFLASH/
pitt/datafile/lunar_data.371.726004363
...
media recovery complete, elapsed time: 00:00:17
Finished recover at 03-AUG-10
repair failure complete
```

As you can see, we repaired this failure in a matter of seconds with minimal brain power and much lower levels of stress!

Media Management Considerations

RMAN is a fully functional backup utility that provides unparalleled functionality, particularly in a high-availability environment. However, one thing RMAN cannot do by itself is back up directly to tape. To back up directly to tape, RMAN must pass the stream of data blocks to a media management layer (MML), which can redirect the data flow to a media management server that controls your tape devices.

The SBT Interface

The MML is provided by a third-party vendor (unless you are using Oracle Secure Backup—see "Oracle Secure Backup and the OSB Cloud Module" a bit later) and is written specifically to receive data from an RMAN backup session and redirect it to tape. Common media management products include Symantec NetBackup, EMC NetWorker, HP OpenView Omniback, and Tivoli Data Protection. These vendors provide an Oracle integration file called the SBT library, which gets loaded by

RMAN into the Oracle memory stack when a tape channel is allocated for backup. RMAN can locate the library file provided by the media management vendor in two ways: the file can be symbolically linked in the $ORACLE_HOME/lib directory, or you can call the **sbt_library** as a parameter in the channel allocation command.

Prior to version 9*i*, Oracle looked to load the SBT library by initializing the file $ORACLE_HOME/libobk.so (or libobk.a or libobk.sl, depending on the operating system). This file is merely a symbolic link file that is re-created to point to the actual SBT library file provided by the vendor. By default, this pointed to a dummy SBT library file provided by Oracle, libdsbtsh8.so. This file allowed you to allocate a tape channel and then back up to disk so that tape channels could be tested and debugged. To use the default SBT interface, you had to set the environment variable **BACKUP_DIR** to a disk location.

If you are looking for the default libobk.so file, you won't find it, because it's no longer included with the installation (hasn't been since 8*i*). This file will exist only in the $ORACLE_HOME/lib directory if it is created by your media management provider (therefore, not default). Instead, you now specify the SBT library file as a value in the PARMS specification of your tape channel allocation. This is the approach recommended by Oracle, because it is more specific and requires less work in the Oracle software stack.

```
RMAN> configure channel device type sbt parms='SBT_LIBRARY=/fullpath/
libraryfilename';
```

Believe it or not, many media management vendors still use the libobk.so symbolic link. Refer to your vendor documentation to find out.

If you want to test a tape channel usage using the Oracle-provided default SBT interface, you can specify it at the PARMS line, as noted earlier, and then you provide an additional **ENV** variable for the place on disk to which you would like to write the tape backup:

```
RMAN> configure channel device type sbt parms 'SBT_LIBRARY=oracle
.disksbt, ENV=(BACKUP_DIR=/nas/fake_tape_backups)';
```

NOTE
It's not a good idea to take your production-level backups using the disk SBT file (it is not supported). This gives you all the drawbacks of backing up to tape and none of the benefits of backing up to disk. It is merely a troubleshooting or proofing exercise.

Once you have configured your SBT device, you can then back up the FRA to tape (remember our preferred MAA backup strategy) as follows:

```
RMAN> backup device type sbt tag "fra_backup" recovery area;
```

How do we restore the FRA from tape? When we back up the FRA, we are essentially backing up our backups. That said, it really doesn't make sense to restore a backup of a backup to restore our database. As you can imagine, that would be far too time-consuming. For this reason, FRA backups can be used directly to restore the respective database just like any other backup to tape would be used.

Backing Up Directly to Tape

We've covered the use of the FRA as a staging area for backups: first the backups go to disk, and then, after a predetermined amount of time elapses, we move the backups to alternate media such as tape. However, in your environment, backups might need to go directly to tape.

Configuration for backing up directly to tape is pretty straightforward. Change your default device to SBT. Configure your SBT channels to contain the proper PARMS values to match your media management setup. Determine your level of parallelization and multiplexing. Then simply schedule your backups.

```
RMAN> configure default device type to sbt;
RMAN> configure channel device type sbt parms = 'SBT_LIBRARY=/fileloc/
libobk.so, EN=(NB_ORA_SERV=ratlnx01,NB_ORA_CLASS= oracle)';
RMAN> configure device type sbt parallelism 4;
RMAN> configure channel device type sbt filesperset=4;
```

Determining Parallelization and Multiplexing

Parallelization refers to the number of tape channels you allocate simultaneously for an RMAN backup (same as we discussed for disk backups). Multiple channels run simultaneously to speed up the backup process. However, seriously bad side effects can occur during restore if your allocated channels during backup outnumber the tape devices that will house the backup pieces. If you allocate two channels and you have only one tape device, the two backup sets will be interspersed together on the same tape. On restore, unless you are restoring the entire database, you will have to read through a lot more tape to get access to all the writes that are required for the restore.

The same problem applies to multiplexing. If you do not limit the number of files that go into each backup set (**filesperset** greater than 1), you will have to wait longer for a single file restore. During the restore, RMAN will have to read the entire backup set into a memory buffer at the target database to determine which blocks are needed for the one file being restored. So the more files you multiplex, the longer you will have to wait and the more network bandwidth is used during the restore of a single datafile or single data block.

In the best possible scenario, you can write to dozens of tape devices simultaneously during a backup so that you can set a higher level of parallelization during backup where only one backup set is being written to any one tape at a time. Then you set **filesperset=1** at the time of backup so that every backup set contains only one file. If this is not possible in your environment, try coming to terms with some middle ground for your multiplexing solution. One channel per tape device is pretty much set in stone, so what you are determining is a cost-to-return ratio between how long you can run your backup, and how long it will take to restore a file during recovery.

Oracle Secure Backup and the OSB Cloud Module

With all this talk about tape backups, you may be thinking, "But I don't have a media manager in my environment." No problem, Oracle Secure Backup (OSB) will provide this functionality for you. OSB is a complete tape backup solution designed for Linux, Windows, and Unix file systems as well as database files through its tight integration with RMAN.

No access tape device? Well, no problem there either. With Oracle Database 11*g* Release 2 you can utilize the OSB Cloud Module allowing for the integration of RMAN with the Internet-based Amazon Simple Storage Service (S3) to facilitate your tape backup and offsite backup storage needs. Since these technologies are beyond the Grid Infrastructure and database scope, they are indeed beyond the scope of this book; however, you should be aware that these services are available. More information on OSB and the OSB Cloud Module can be found on the Oracle Technology Network.

RMAN and Oracle Data Guard

The relationship between RMAN and Oracle Data Guard is based on the technology that underpins the Oracle Data Guard product: the standby database. As you learned in Chapter 9, the standby database stands at the center of the DG environment: a complete duplicate copy of the production database is mirrored to a similar hardware configuration (this, of course, refers to a physical standby database). As demonstrated in Chapter 9, RMAN can easily facilitate the database duplication portion of the standby build process. In this chapter, we'll describe this functionality in a bit more detail.

Using RMAN to Build the Standby Database

A common use of Oracle backups in any environment is to move them to a new location and then open the backup copy of the database as a clone copy of the database for test and development purposes. It's a good way to get some value out of backups, other than merely as a "just in case" fallback. With RMAN, the ability to clone a database has been built into the CLI as the **duplicate** command, and it's quite simple:

```
RMAN> duplicate target database to <clone_db_name>;
```

We can also facilitate the creation of a standby database using RMAN backups:

```
RMAN> duplicate target database for standby;
```

Of course, that is the icing on the cake: A certain amount of prep work is required to create the standby database from RMAN backups. When performing the duplication, RMAN makes the connection to the target database (the primary database), to the catalog (if you use one), and then a third connection to the auxiliary database. The auxiliary database will become the standby database (or duplicate). What is important to note about the duplication process is that the auxiliary database instance must exist before duplication can start. Prior to Oracle 11g, the auxiliary instance had to have access to the RMAN backups. This meant your RMAN backup being used for the duplication of a given database must be locally accessible to the auxiliary instance— options here include SBT devices, physically copying the RMAN backup files, or use of a shared file system. This often resulted in a lengthy, cumbersome process. With 11g Release 1 and above, two RMAN methods are available to perform the duplication of a target database: traditional backup-based duplication and active database duplication.

Backup-Based Duplication

Backup-based duplication is the traditional method that involves creating a database and archivelog backup, copying the backup to the standby system, preparing the standby database, and using the RMAN **duplicate** function to instantiate the standby. This method is often used when a backup of the database already exists.

If backup-based duplication is being used and the backup is stored on a shared file system or copied to a local file system (must be the same path), the duplication is straightforward: invoke RMAN, connect to the target database, connect to the auxiliary database, and run the **duplicate target database** command (as shown earlier).

If the backups have been taken to a media management server (SBT) accessible by the target node and the auxiliary node, you'll have little problem with the requirements. The only trick to remember involves permissions to backups at the media management server. Typically, computer systems are registered at the media management server as *clients* and the backups are encoded with a *client name* at the time of backup. So when you attempt to access backups at the auxiliary node that were taken from your target node, you might expect the server to respond that "no such backups exist." To resolve the issue, you pass the name of the target server from the auxiliary server, like so:

```
RMAN> allocate channel sbt1 type sbt
parms='env=
(nb_ora_server=lnx01,nb_ora_class=oracle,nb_ora_client=target_node)';
```

NOTE
This example shows the syntax for passing a client name if you are using Symantec NetBackup for Oracle. Other media managers have different ways of handling client-to-client restores. Consult your media management vendor's documentation.

7555755

Active Database Duplication

RMAN active database duplication was a much sought after feature that was introduced in Oracle Database 11g Release 1. This feature greatly simplifies the database duplication and/or standby database creation process by copying the active datafiles from the primary database directly to the standby (or auxiliary) site via Oracle Net. This process totally eliminates the need to take a disk-based backup, thus eliminating the need for a shared file system, copying of backups, or the use of a media management server (SBT). This can be a huge time-saver because it has eliminated the need to take the backup at all.

The requirements for Active Database Duplication are virtually the same as backup-based duplication, except we must log into both the target and auxiliary databases via Oracle Net. Once logged in, we can duplicate a target database with the following:

```
RMAN> duplicate target database to <clone_db_name> from active database;
```

Similarly, we can duplicate a target database for use as a standby as follows:

```
RMAN> duplicate target database for standby from active database;
```

For a full description on how to use Active Database Duplication to create a standby database, see the MAA workshop "Creating an Oracle RAC Physical Standby Database" in Chapter 9.

Using the Physical Standby Database to Create Backups

If you have a physical standby database configured, you should consider putting it to work for you by offloading your database backups to the standby. RMAN can connect to the standby database and take the backups at the standby, allowing for offloading of the disk I/O and memory utilization associated with running backups on your primary database servers. These backups can then be used to restore files at the primary database. Doing so provides yet another way to maintain an extremely high level of availability by eliminating the impact of backup processing.

In this scenario, you must use a recovery catalog to back up your database files from the standby. By using the catalog, you can connect to the standby database, take the backups, and have them recorded in the catalog. Then, when you connect to the primary database and the catalog, RMAN will have access to the metadata about the backups taken at the standby.

The trick to performing backups at the standby is to know the nature of the standby databases and the nature of RMAN backups. A standby database is an exact replica of the primary database, meaning it has the DBID as the primary. RMAN uses the DBID to identify unique databases in the recovery catalog. So when RMAN connects to the standby, it considers the standby to be the primary database in most ways, with the same exact file structure and content. A file backed up at the standby is a file that can be restored to the primary, because they are identical.

Don't think that you are somehow "faking out" RMAN when you connect to the standby. RMAN is standby aware; it knows when it's connected to a standby and acts accordingly. For instance, if you use a **db_file_name_convert** parameter at your standby to rename files to new locations, RMAN knows that it backed up a file from, say, /u02/oradata on the standby, but that it must restore the file to, say, /u04/oradata on the primary.

The backups with which you need to be careful will be archivelog backups. Naturally, a copy of every archivelog must by rule exist at the standby database for recovery. So you can back up the archivelogs from the standby. That's not the issue. The issue is archivelog cleanup—typically, an archivelog backup strategy employs the delete input option, which removes archivelogs after they have been backed up. But if you back up from the standby, the archivelogs will never be removed from the primary. You will have to employ another script to delete archivelogs from the primary database site.

MAA Workshop: *Back Up Directly to Tape from the Standby*

Workshop Notes

This workshop assumes that you have a physical standby database configured, with archivelogs streamed to the standby site via an Oracle Data Guard configuration, and you have implemented a recovery catalog database (per MAA workshop "Implementing a Recovery Catalog"). This workshop steps through a process of backing up datafiles directly to tape; it also addresses archivelog backup and cleanup at both sites (primary and standby).

Step 1. Before taking any backups, we must set our RMAN persistent configuration parameters. As always, we will describe each of these parameters as we set them (unless they have already been described). Keep in mind that for this exercise we must use a recovery catalog. To refresh your memory, to invoke RMAN with a recovery catalog, we would use the following (EZCONNECT syntax is show here):

```
# rman target / catalog rman/rman@//ratgc01:1521/gcrep
```

Then we need to configure connectivity of the primary to the standby database to allow remote resynchronization of the catalog. To do so, we will configure the connect identifier for the standby db_unique_name as follows:

```
RMAN> configure db_unique_name cosp connect identifier 'cosp';
```

Next, we configure our media management layer and our tape backup channels. For media manager configuration, see "Media Management Considerations" earlier in the chapter. This needs to be performed at both the primary and standby database. We configure the SBT channels on the standby to reflect the client name of the primary so that the backups taken at both sites are organized and stored the same at the media management server.

```
RMAN> configure default device type to sbt;
RMAN> configure channel device type sbt parms =
   SBT_LIBRARY=/fileloc/libobk.so,
   ENV=(NB_ORA_SERV=ratlnx01, NB_ORA_CLIENT = ratlnx02)";
RMAN> configure device type sbt parallelism 4;
```

Configure the archivelog deletion policy on the primary database to delete only archivelogs that have been applied to the standby database.

```
RMAN> configure archivelog deletion policy to applied on all standby;
```

On the standby database, we want to delete any archivelog that has been backed up one time:

```
RMAN> configure archivelog deletion policy to backed up 1 times to
device type sbt;
```

Step 2. Back up the controlfile and SPFILE from the primary database site, and then clean out archivelogs based on our archivelog deletion policy. (If you are using the FRA for archivelog storage, you do not need to explicitly delete the archivelogs, because Oracle will automatically delete these logs when there is space pressure in the FRA. Even if you are using the FRA, it is perfectly acceptable to manually delete archivelogs.)

```
rman> backup current controlfile;
rman> delete archivelog all;
```

Step 3. Back up the database and archivelogs from the standby site. With the following command, we will be deleting all archivelogs that are backed up using the configured archivelog deletion policy. (Again, if you are using the FRA for archivelog storage, you do not explicitly need to delete the archivelogs, because Oracle will automatically delete these logs when there is space pressure in the FRA. Even if you are using the FRA, it is perfectly acceptable to manually delete archivelogs.)

```
RMAN> backup database tag 'full_to_tape' plus archivelog tag 'arch_to_
tape' delete input;
```

Backup and Recovery Using the Standby Database with an FRA

If you have employed a FRA and are staging your backups in the FRA and then going to tape, or you are not going to tape at all, the preceding workshop obviously will change a bit. You might be asking, if I am backing up from the standby and go to the FRA with my backups, how in the world am I suppose to recover the primary database? Well, prior to 11g, you would have to copy the backup to the primary database prior to restoring/recovering. This led to a lot of DBAs creating their FRAs on shared file systems. Although this is an acceptable solution, it is not necessary with 11g because of the same functionality that makes Active Database Duplication possible.

Let's say that our LunarTrax database has corruption in the datafile housing the USERS tablespace. Since this is not a critical tablespace for the application functionality, it does not warrant a failover to the standby (which may or may not be faster than restoring the datafile). With 11g, we can perform the following to restore the corrupt datafile on the primary from the datafile at the standby site. Do take note that the TARGET database is the standby and the auxiliary database is the primary.

```
RMAN> connect target sys/<password>@<standby_db>
RMAN> connect auxiliary sys/<password>@<primary_db>
RMAN> connect catalog rman/<password>@<catalog_db>
RMAN> backup as copy datafile 4 auxiliary format '+DBDATA';
Starting backup at 06-AUG-10
allocated channel: ORA_DISK_1
channel ORA_DISK_1: SID=16 instance=maadb1 device type=DISK
channel ORA_DISK_1: starting datafile copy
input datafile file number=00004
name=+DBDATA/cosp/datafile/users.278.726269839
output file name=+DBDATA/pitt/datafile/users.299.726294579
tag=TAG20100806T002902
channel ORA_DISK_1: datafile copy complete, elapsed time: 00:00:03
Finished backup at 06-AUG-10
RMAN> exit
```

At this point, we have successfully copied the datafile from the standby to the primary. We now need to connect to the primary database as the TARGET, catalog the datafile copy (note the output filename from the previous listing), and switch the datafile to the copy:

```
RMAN> connect target sys/<password>@<primary_db>
RMAN> connect catalog rman/<password>@<catalog_db>
RMAN> catalog datafilecopy +DBDATA/pitt/datafile/users.299.726294579';
RMAN> run {
set newname for datafile 4 to '+DBDATA/pitt/datafile/
users.299.726294579';
switch datafile 4;
}
RMAN> recover datafile 4;
RMAN> sql 'alter database datafile 4 online';
```

That's it; we are now back in business. If you failed to notice, we are not even using our database backup, or FRA for that matter. This procedure actually pulls the datafile from the standby to the primary using no manual copies or shared FRA.

RMAN and Oracle RAC

Thus far in this chapter, every RMAN strategy we have discussed is applicable to Oracle RAC as well as single-instance database. In fact, if we left out this section you would still have an excellent MAA backup strategy for your Oracle RAC database. That said, it is worth noting some backup and recovery features as well as challenges of an Oracle RAC database.

RMAN Configuration for the Cluster

You must make some configuration decisions prior to implementing an RMAN backup strategy for the Oracle RAC database. These decisions are predicated on how the backup will proceed, and then how the recovery will proceed.

RMAN makes an Oracle Net Services connection to a node in the database. This connection must be a dedicated connection that is not configured for failover or load balancing across the cluster. In other words, RMAN does not connect to the cluster—it connects to one node in the cluster. All RMAN server processes related to job building, controlfile access, and controlfile updates will reside at the node of connection. However, we can configure automatic channel allocation within our static configuration parameters to allocate channels on a per-node basis by specifying a connect string in for the channel allocation:

```
RMAN> configure channel 1 device type disk connect '@node1';
RMAN> configure channel 2 device type disk connect '@node2';
```

In this configuration, we did not specify a username/password; we will inherit this from the target connect string. Note that a **show all** command will display a * for the connect string.

Allocating channels on specific nodes can distribute the workload of a backup operation across the nodes of the cluster. The decision to put a single node in charge of backup operations, or to share the work across all (or some) nodes, is an architectural decision you must make based on how you use the nodes in your cluster. It might make sense in some environments to restrict backup overhead to a less-used node in the cluster; likewise, if you have a well-tuned load-balancing technique for all nodes, distributing the backup workload evenly might make the most sense.

The Snapshot Controlfile in Oracle RAC Environments

If you plan on running backups from more than one node, you might move the snapshot controlfile to a shared location. Unfortunately, ASM disk groups are not supported by the snapshot controlfile, so if you are in an ASM-only environment, you could create an ACFS mount point for this purpose or you could leave the snapshot controlfile set to its default location of $ORACLE_HOME/dbs, which will exist on all cluster nodes. If you're not using a cluster file system, the snapshot controlfile directory path must exist on all cluster nodes.

```
RMAN> show snapshot controlfile name;
```

To change the value, use the **configure** command:

```
RMAN> configure snapshot controlfile name to
      '/ora01/app/oracle/product/11.2.0/db_1/dbs/snapcf_maadb1.f';
```

Datafile Backup

Datafiles can be backed up from any node in the cluster, because they are shared between instances anyway. So you can run a datafile backup from any node, or from all nodes, and not run into any problems.

If you are backing up to tape, you must configure your SBT interface at each node that will have channels allocated for backup. If you back up from only a single node, then only that node will have to be configured with the MML, but be aware that if this node fails, the SBT interface must be configured on a surviving node prior to you being able to perform backups and/or recovery. That being said, it is highly recommended that the SBT interface be configured on all cluster nodes.

If you are backing up to disk without using an FRA, you should configure a shared disk location on which to write your backups so that if a node is lost, the backups taken at any node will be available to any other node. You could do this through NFS mounts to a network-attached storage (NAS) or Oracle Cluster File System (OCFS2) (not recommended). If you are thinking ASM Cluster File System (ACFS)—well, ACFS does not support RMAN backups so that is not an option here. We highly recommend the use of the FRA stored in ASM.

Archivelog Backups

If you have taken our advice and are archiving to a shared location (preferably the FRA), the archivelog backups are really no different in Oracle RAC than single-instance. Now if you are in the cluster stone ages and are archiving to local destinations on each cluster node, this is where things get a little sticky. Because every node generates its own thread of archivelogs, each thread is required for backup and/or recovery. Let's assume that you have not taken our advice of using a shared location for archival, and as a result you are archiving to a local file system on each node in the cluster. The problem here is that RMAN reads a shared controlfile that lists all archivelogs, and RMAN will fail when it tries to back up archivelogs that exist on unreachable disks of other nodes.

```
RMAN-6089: archived log <name> not found or out of sync with catalog
```

Although you can perform some tricks to get these archivelogs backed up, what happens if node 1 of your cluster falls off the face of the earth and you are in a recovery situation with your database? The answer here is we have lost data and management is *not* going to be happy. For this reason, we hope you have taken our suggestion of storing archivelogs in an ASM-based FRA. For more information on configuring archivelog destinations in an Oracle RAC environment, please refer back to Chapter 4.

If you are using shared storage for your archivelog backups, the RMAN backup command is simple:

```
RMAN> backup archivelog all delete input;
```

The **delete input** command means that after RMAN backs up the archivelogs, it will delete those files that it just backed up. You'll read about the **delete all input** attribute in the next section.

Archivelog Housekeeping with RMAN   The **backup archivelog** command will check v$archived_log for all archivelogs with a status of A (for available) and then back them up. If the archivelog record has a status of D (deleted) or X (expired), RMAN will not attempt to back up that archivelog. There is a widely held misperception that RMAN determines which archivelogs to back up by checking the log_archive_dest for available files. This is not the case, however, because RMAN uses views in the controlfile to determine the status and availability, and these views can be updated only by RMAN. So if you clean out archivelogs at the OS level (instead of using RMAN), the archivelog backup will fail as it tries to back up nonexistent files, and will issue the RMAN-20242 error.

If you find yourself in this situation (RMAN-20242), you must use the RMAN **crosscheck** command to tell RMAN to validate what recovery files physically exist against what RMAN has a record of.

```
RMAN> crosscheck archivelog all;
```

Upon successful completion of the **crosscheck** command, any files that failed validation (that do not physically exist) will be marked as expired. The metadata for the expired files can be deleted with the following command:

```
RMAN> delete expired archivelog all;
```

Although the context of the **crosscheck** and **delete expired** commands in this example is related to archivelogs, similar commands would be executed for a backup, backup set, backup piece, and so on. After executing **crosscheck** and **delete expired**, the RMAN metadata will be synchronized to reflect those recovery files that physically exist.

To avoid the RMAN-20242 errors, it is highly recommended that you use RMAN to clean up after your archivelogs even if you don't use RMAN to back them up. Not only does RMAN mark the status of the archivelogs in the controlfile (something you can do *only* with RMAN), but RMAN will also never delete an archivelog while it is being written by the ARC*n* process. It knows more about the archivelogs (and the database for that matter) than any other utility.

If you use RMAN to back up archivelogs that are not stored in the FRA (more on this shortly), you should use the **delete input** command at some level to automate archivelog cleanout. That said, you may want to back up archivelogs, but not delete them immediately—in the case of recovery, obviously, it's best to have them on disk, not tape. What you can do is automate a process that backs up archivelogs older than a certain number of days and then deletes them:

```
RMAN> backup archivelog until sysdate-7 delete all input;
```

This will back up archivelogs older than seven days, and then delete them from all archive destinations (due to the all keyword). If you want to back up archivelogs up to the current point, but delete those older than seven days, you can do that, but it takes two separate commands:

```
RMAN> backup archivelog all;
RMAN> delete archivelog all completed before sysdate -7;
```

The only problem with this approach, however, is that if you run it every day, you will get approximately seven backup copies of every archivelog, because you back up all the archivelogs every day, but you don't delete them for seven days. So you can specify how many times to back up archivelogs, after which they will be skipped. Then you issue your delete command:

```
RMAN> backup archivelog not backed up 2 times;
RMAN> delete archivelog completed before sysdate -7;
```

You have now achieved archivelog maintenance nirvana: you back up every archivelog to tape twice, you keep the last few days' worth on disk, and you delete persistently from all backup locations archivelogs that are older than seven days.

From the Oracle RAC perspective, archivelog housekeeping follows all guidelines outlined previously unless you are archiving locally to each node. But you are not going to do that, are you?

Flash Recovery Area and Oracle RAC

As stated in several chapters throughout this book, it is extremely advantageous to use the FRA, especially in an Oracle RAC environment. The FRA can ease the headaches associated with multithread archivelog generation, as well as provide simplicity during stressful recovery situations. With the FRA, you can set your **log_archive_dest** of each node to a shared location that is accessible by all other nodes. You can also employ a backup strategy in which backups are spread across each node, and the backups still go to a single location, or you can use a single-node backup strategy. With the FRA in place, you can have the backups accessible to all other nodes if a node failure occurs, regardless of your backup strategy. The benefits are simplicity in design and availability as the goal.

On top of the advantages provided by the shared storage nature of the FRA, there is also a distinct advantage of Oracle being able to perform automatic cleanup of files not needed for recovery of the database (defined by retention policies) when space becomes tight. Did you forget to add the delete archivelog procedure in your backup routine, or did your database generate more redo data than usual? Typically, these situations would result in the filling up of the disk used to house the archived redo logs, resulting in an unnecessary database outage. With the FRA, Oracle can prevent such an outage by properly maintaining the recovery files based on the retention polices that you define. This is seamless to Oracle RAC and a feature that is available only with the FRA.

At this point, you may be asking, "Do I need to delete these obsolete recovery files manually when using the FRA?" Well, the preference here is to perform manual cleanup (**delete obsolete**, and so on), allowing for automatic cleanup if and when it is necessary. By taking this approach, you can ensure that your FRA is always available and that no overhead is incurred by automatic cleanup during high load periods.

Thinking Forward to Recovery

The single-node connection that limits RMAN's connection to the Oracle RAC database determines how recovery proceeds. Let's consider three situations that will result in either the inability to recover the database or in complexity in performing recovery:

- We perform backups only from node 1 of our cluster and these backups are stored locally on a file system. The end result is the inability to recover the database.

- Similarly, if we archive locally (not to a shared location) and we completely lose a cluster node, our database is not recoverable (at least to the current point in time) due to the missing archivelog threads.

- Finally, we archive locally and must perform a point-in-time recovery. All cluster nodes are available, but before we can perform this recovery, we must move all archivelogs to the node in which we are going to perform recovery. If the path is not identical on all nodes, we must manually register each archivelog. Our database is indeed recoverable, but we are facing an increased recovery time due to the manual intervention required here.

If we "share everything," these recovery issues are completely avoided—*everything,* meaning all recovery files, whether they be on tape or on disk (recent archivelogs will be on disk); the media should be accessible from all cluster nodes. And as you know, the FRA is the preferred disk location for the recovery files.

Summary

We hope you've updated your perception of backup and recovery and its integral role in the MAA environment. You have learned that using RMAN, you can easily recover from corruption without enduring lengthy restoration procedures by using technologies such as block level recovery, single datafile recovery, backup datafile copies, and automatic block recovery in Oracle Data Guard environments. These features allow for recovery to take place without a full database outage—and in some cases without any noticeable impact to the end users. We also discussed how RMAN seamlessly integrates with Oracle RAC and Oracle Data Guard to support your MAA backup and recovery requirements. Specific to Oracle Data Guard, you can offload backup processing to a physical standby database with minimal to no impact on the recoverability of the primary database. These are all key features that every MAA DBA needs to maintain those desired 5 9s, and the only thing that can provide them is RMAN. RMAN is the premier backup and recovery utility for the Oracle MAA environment. To date, nothing else compares.

CHAPTER
11

Flashback Recovery

edia recovery, as outlined in Chapter 10, provides us with safeguards against all kinds of unforeseeable problems—block corruption, hardware failure, even complete database loss. But you may have noticed that Chapter 10 didn't cover the largest cause of media recovery operations: user error.

We know. We *know* that user-induced outages are the most frustrating, because we expect humans to catch their own mistakes, whereas hard drives and motherboards all fail. They just do. But user errors happen, too. For this reason, the MAA DBA must be prepared to handle user errors efficiently.

User errors can be roughly defined as errors caused by a human mistake, rather than a software or hardware malfunction: tables updated with wrong values, tables dropped, tables truncated. These are the kinds of errors that, in our honest moments, we realize that everyone makes, but in the heat of an outage, we need to know *who* did *what* and just how soon they can be verbally reprimanded by someone important.

Being Prepared for the Inevitable: Flashback Technology

An MAA DBA needs to be prepared for the inevitable user-induced problem. That said, media recovery should not be our first line of attack; typically, user error is not something that we can recover from, because the action is not interpreted as an error by the database. **delete * from scott.emp** is not an error; it's a perfectly legitimate Data Manipulation Language (DML) statement that is duly recorded in the redo stream. So if you restore the datafile and then perform recovery, all you will do is, well, delete * from scott.emp again.

Point-in-time recovery can be a solution, but not for the MAA DBA committed to avoiding full restore of the database—way too much outage. *Tablespace-point-in-time-recovery* (TSPITR) offers a toned-down version of media recovery for user error, but it still requires a full outage on the tablespace being recovered, and TSPITR carries several limitations. This is where Flashback Technology comes in.

Flashback Technology makes up for the frightening lack of options available to a DBA when faced with user-induced database trauma. Flashback Technology is a suite of features that allow a multitude of different ways to survive user errors. These features have as a unifying concept only the simple idea that user errors occur, and recovering from them should be simple and fast. The following Flashback features are available with 11*g*:

- Flashback Query
    - Flashback Transaction Query
    - Flashback Versions Query

- Flashback Table

- Flashback Drop

- Flashback Database

- Flashback Transaction (new for 11*g* Release1 and enhanced in 11*g* Release 2)

In this chapter, we will discuss the functionality of each of the Flashback Technologies as well as provide working examples of each of these Flashback types.

Laying the Groundwork

The heading of this section sounds much more important than it really is, and although we don't mean to disappoint you, Flashback Technology is all about recovery from user error. In other words, recovering from that "delete * from my_very_important_table" without incurring addition data loss and downtime from a point-in-time recovery. That said, you do need to have a basic schema in place to follow along with this chapter. The schema (let's consider it a subschema) involves two tables in a parent-child relationship from our LunarTrax database. The parent table is the space_ship table with the child table being the space_ship_maint table. Here is the schema definition and sample data:

```
SQL> create table space_ship
( ship_id          number not null,
ship_name          varchar2(25) not null,
comission_date     date not null,
status             varchar2(10) not null,
decom_date         date);

SQL> alter table space_ship add constraint space_ship_pk primary key
(ship_id);

SQL> create table space_ship_maint
( maint_id         number not null,
ship_id            number not null,
maint_desc         varchar2(100) not null,
maint_complete     varchar2(3),
maint_date         date not null,
complete_date      date);

SQL> alter table space_ship_maint add constraint space_ship_maint_pk
primary key(maint_id);

SQL> alter table space_ship_maint add constraint space_ship_maint_fk1
foreign key(ship_id) references space_ship (ship_id);
```

```
SQL> create index space_ship_maint_idx1 on space_ship_maint(ship_id);
SQL> insert into space_ship values (1, 'Joleen','01-JUN-2002-
','ACTIVE',null);
SQL> insert into space_ship values (2, 'Hayden','01-APR-2001-
','ACTIVE',null);
SQL> insert into space_ship values (3, 'Delaney','21-AUG-2010-
','ACTIVE',null);
SQL> insert into space_ship values (4, 'Scott','20-JAN-2002-
','MAINT',null);
SQL> insert into space_ship values (5, 'Bill','01-OCT-2009-
','MAINT',null);
SQL> insert into space_ship values (6, 'Hagen','18-JUL-1994-
','DECOM','21-AUG-2010');

SQL> insert into space_ship_maint values (1, 1,'Major Crash
Repair','YES','11-SEP-2002','11-SEP-2002');
SQL> insert into space_ship_maint values (2, 1,'Oil Change','YES',
'09-AUG-2010','09-AUG-2010');
SQL> insert into space_ship_maint values (3, 4,'Engine
Repair','NO','01-AUG-2010',null);
SQL> insert into space_ship_maint values (4, 5,'Broken
Windshield','NO','19-AUG-2010',null);
```

Now that we have defined our schema and associated data, we are now ready to get to work on recovering from all of these pesky user-induced errors.

Flashback Query and Flashback Table

Flashback Query (and its relatives) and Flashback Table are grouped into a single section because both have their functionality based entirely on technology that has existed in the Oracle Database for years: undo segments. Historically, undo (previously known as rollback) was used for transaction consistency and to provide the ability to "undo" uncommitted transactions. While this functionality is a key component to the functionality of the database, as of Oracle 9*i*, we can put this undo data to an additional use with Flashback Query and Flashback Table. Before defining each of these Flashback technologies and subsequently diving into details about each, let's talk briefly about undo management in the Oracle Database, because this knowledge is the basis of making undo-based Flashback Technologies work in your environment.

Two types of undo management are available: automatic and manual. Oracle highly discourages the use of manual (as do we), so the focus here is on automatic. With automatic undo management, all new transactions look for unused space in the undo tablespace before overwriting previously used segments. When no free space is found in the undo tablespace, the oldest remaining extents will be overwritten first. This means that before images of rows in the database last as long as possible.

At this point you might be wondering, "What about that undo retention parameter?" It depends on the underlying undo tablespace configuration. With 10*g* and above, we will always use automatic tuning of the undo retention as long as undo management is set to auto. If you set your undo tablespaces to autoextend, the value of undo retention will be the minimum guaranteed undo retention (unless you have consumed *all* available space, including autoextend). If you are not using autoextend for your undo tablespace, the undo retention will be honored only if you have set the retention guarantee attribute for the undo tablespace; otherwise, the undo retention will be tuned to the maximum retention based on transaction load and the undo tablespace size. To view the current autotuned undo retention for a database, you can run the following:

```
SQL> select to_char(begin_time, 'mm/dd/yyyy hh24:mi:ss') begin_time,
tuned_undoretention from v$undostat;
```

The threshold for how far back you can use a Flashback Query or Flashback Table is considered the Flashback Window and is defined by the **tuned_undoretention** value passed back by the previous query.

Configuring for Flashback Query and Flashback Table

The guidelines for using Flashback Query demand that you first have automatic undo enabled—no rollback segments are allowed. (Okay, that's a lie. It is feasible to use flashback operations with old-school rollback segments, but Oracle discourages it and so do we. There is no reason to try and set up rollback segments manually anymore.) Oracle is best left to control undo management using new algorithms that emphasize retention of transactional history—algorithms that do not exist in rollback segments. Therefore, you need to set the following parameters:

- UNDO_MANAGEMENT = AUTO

- UNDO_TABLESPACE = <UNDO TABLESPACE NAME>

- UNDO_RETENTION = <value in seconds>

Recall our brief discussion on undo and the **undo_retention**. If you are using autoextend for your undo tablespace, you can specify the **undo_retention** parameter and it will honored. However, if you have not set autoextend for your undo tablespace, you should consider setting the **retention guarantee** attribute for the undo tablespace(s) (available for 10*g* and above) to allow for the **undo_retention** setting to be honored:

```
SQL> alter tablespace <undo tablespace> retention guarantee;
```

Once you have set the retention guarantee for your undo tablespace(s), you can validate the setting as follows:

```
SQL> select tablespace_name,retention from dba_tablespaces;
```

When setting your undo tablespace for retention guarantee, you must ensure that your undo tablespace is properly sized for the transaction volume of your database to prevent those pesky ORA-1555 errors. If you want to disable the retention guarantee for your undo tablespace(s), you can execute this:

```
SQL> alter tablespace <undo tablespace> retention noguarantee;
```

With this configuration in place, we are ready to go with Flashback Query, Flashback Versions Query, and Flashback Table, but if we want to make use of Flashback Transaction Query, we must enable database minimal and primary key supplemental logging. This is required because LogMiner is used behind the scenes to mine through the undo and redo streams to facilitate this functionality; these rows must be uniquely identifiable to LogMiner. To enable minimal and primary key supplemental logging, execute the following:

```
SQL> alter database add supplemental log data;
SQL> alter database add supplemental log data (primary key) columns;
```

If you plan on using more complex flashback operations that involve parent-child dependencies, you might want to enable foreign key supplemental logging also:

```
SQL> alter database add supplemental log data (foreign key) columns;
```

If you are unsure of your current supplemental logging configuration, you can query v$database as follows:

```
SQL> select supplemental_log_data_min,
       supplemental_log_data_pk, supplemental_log_data_fk
     from v$database;
```

Flashback Query

Flashback Query allows queries to be run against the database at a previous point in time. This historical view of the data can be used to retrieve "accidentally" delete data or to troubleshoot data integrity types of issues.

Suppose we have production table in our LunarTrax database called space_ship containing the following:

```
SQL> select * from space_ship;
   SHIP_ID SHIP_NAME COMISSION STATUS     DECOM_DAT
---------- --------- --------- ---------- ---------
         1 Joleen    01-JUN-02 ACTIVE
         2 Hayden    01-APR-01 ACTIVE
```

```
   3 Delaney   21-AUG-10 ACTIVE
   4 Scott     20-JAN-02 MAINT
   5 Bill      01-OCT-09 MAINT
   6 Hagen     18-JUL-94 DECOM        21-AUG-10
```

Now let's assume that our application developer is logged into the wrong database and issues a delete against ship_id 2, 3, and 6 at around 18-AUG-2010 22:38. We can easily see the deleted records by specifying the **as of timestamp** clause in our query:

```
SQL> select * from space_ship as of timestamp
   to_timestamp('18-AUG-2010 22:37:00', 'DD-MON-RRRR HH24:MI:SS');
```

We could then take note of the values and reinsert them if necessary or automate the process by using Flashback Query in our insert statement:

```
SQL> insert into space_ship
   select * from
   space_ship as of timestamp
     to_timestamp('18-AUG-2010 22:37:00', 'DD-MON-RRRR HH24:MI:SS')
   where ship_id in (2,3,6);
```

Pretty neat, huh? There are better ways to recover lost data due to user errors (as you'll soon see), but this feature does come in handy as a first step in the troubleshooting process or for simply querying a previous view of the data for a given table.

Flashback Versions Query

Flashback Versions Query allows users to view the history of a given row in a table over a specified time interval. The row history information available is the operation performed, starting system change number (SCN), start time, ending SCN, end time, transaction ID of the modifying transaction, and the actual table column values for each of the versions.

For this example, we will focus on a specific row in our space_ship table. The ship_id is our primary key for this table, so we will focus on the space ship with the ID of 4.

```
SQL> select * from space_ship where ship_id=4;
    SHIP_ID SHIP_NAME COMISSION STATUS      DECOM_DAT
---------- --------- --------- ---------- ---------
          4 Scott     20-JAN-02 AVAILABLE
```

When running a space ship maintenance report we see that Scott (that's the name of the ship if you haven't been paying attention) is showing that maintenance has not been completed, but the space_ship table shows it as available. We clearly have a data integrity issue here, so let's use Flashback Versions Query to see what happened. First we establish a timeline. For this issue, we know that ship Scott was showing maintenance at 19-AUG-2010 00:21 based on a space ship report. Now that we have our approximate timeline of 19-AUG-2010 00:21 to present, we can use Flashback Versions Query to see what happened and when. In this example, we use the **to timestamp** clause—alternatively, you could use **to scn**.

```
SQL> select versions_xid xid, versions_operation operation,
to_char(versions_starttime,'DD-MON-RR HH24:MI:SS') starttime,
to_char(versions_endtime,'DD-MON-RR HH24:MI:SS') endtime, ship_id, status
from space_ship VERSIONS BETWEEN TIMESTAMP
to_timestamp('19-AUG-2010 00:21:00', 'DD-MON-RRRR HH24:MI:SS')
AND
systimestamp
where ship_id = 4;
XID               O STARTTIME          ENDTIME            SHIP_ID STATUS
---------------- - ------------------ ------------------ ------- ---------
07000600664C0000 U 19-AUG-10 00:22:54                          4 AVAILABLE
04000900034C0000 U 19-AUG-10 00:22:35 19-AUG-10 00:22:54       4 DECOM
                                       19-AUG-10 00:22:35       4 MAINT
```

As you can see from the second column, two update transactions (operation of **U** with distinct transaction IDs) were performed on this row of the space_ship table within the specified time window. Cleary, we have a rogue developer! It is worth noting that we could have also queried the start and end SCN numbers, but these columns were omitted to preserve the readability of the output. So we know that our table was updated. Now what? How do we fix it? This is where Flashback Transaction Query comes in!

Flashback Transaction Query

There is more than one way to organize a manhunt for bad data in the database. Flashback Transaction Query is used to view all the changes made by a specific transaction or all the changes made by all transactions over a specified time interval. Unlike the previous flashback types, Flashback Transaction Query is actually a query on the flashback_transaction_query view as opposed to the base table in which the logical error has occurred. The flashback_transaction_query view contains the transaction ID, operation that was performed, start SCN (and timestamp), commit SCN (and timestamp), logon user, as well as the SQL required to back off the change. Taking the output from the preceding example of Flashback Versions Query, we can see that the first transaction to occur after the table was in a known "good" state was transaction ID 04000900034C0000. Using this transaction ID, let's use Flashback Transaction Query to find out who made the change and to generate the SQL to correct the logical error:

```
SQL> select operation, logon_user, undo_sql
from flashback_transaction_query
where xid = HEXTORAW('04000900034C0000');
```

```
OPERATION   LOGON_USER       UNDO_SQL
----------  ---------------  -------------------------------
UPDATE      BVONGRAY         update "LUNAR"."SPACE_SHIP"
                             set "STATUS" = 'MAINT'
                             where
                             ROWID = 'AAATjfAAGAAAACjAAD';
BEGIN       BVONGRAY
```

Uh oh! It turns out that the rogue developer actually is a rogue DBA, and that DBA is me! I'm fired! In all seriousness, this is a really cool feature. To correct our logical error, we would simply execute the **undo_sql** provided by this query, and we are back in business.

Alternatively, we could have pulled all of the transactions within the given time range by combining our Flashback Versions Query from the preceding example as a sub-select for our Flashback Versions Query (shown in the previous section). Sure beats a point-in-time recovery, doesn't it?

Flashback Table

Now for our last Flashback Technology feature that is dependent on undo data, Flashback Table, which allows for an entire table to be restored to a previous point in time. Let's say Bryan (our rogue DBA), for some reason, is working in the production schema and is trying to delete one row from our space_shuttle table. He fat fingers the delete and it executes without a where clause. All of the rows in our space_shuttle table are wiped out. Having space shuttles available for scheduling is of the utmost importance for the LunarTrax business. The loss of this table is absolutely disastrous! As you are probably aware, this would typically be grounds for a point-in-time recovery. But those days are behind us, because with Flashback Table, we can restore this table to its state prior to the "disaster" in a matter of seconds (depending on the size of the table).

Prior to performing the Flashback Table operation, we must know the approximate time that the table was in a known good state (use Flashback Query to assist here). We then must enable row movement on the table that is to be rewound. We know that Bryan issued the delete statement around 19-AUG-2010 00:54, and since we have an approximate time of the logical error, we can execute the following to bring the table back to the last known good state:

```
SQL> alter table space_ship enable row movement;
SQL> flashback table space_ship
to timestamp to_timestamp('19-AUG-2010 00:54:52', 'DD-MON-RRRR
HH24:MI:SS');
```

In this example, we used the **to timestamp** clause, but we could have used the **to scn** clause if we knew the SCN of when the logical error occurred.

Keep in mind that Flashback Table will not protect you from all user errors. Certain Data Definition Language (DDL) operations that occur against a table cannot be undone; most importantly, you cannot flashback a table to before a truncate table operation. This is because a truncate does not produce any undo—that is why truncate exists, versus a delete. Also, Flashback Table cannot be used for a dropped table (you'll use Flashback Drop for that). Also note that if the table has changed in structure within the desired Flashback window, it cannot be flashed back.

We were successful in recovering from all of the logical errors induced on our space_ship table while still maintaining 100 percent database availability by using undo-based Flashback Technologies. Let's move on to explore the remaining non-undo–based Flashback Technologies.

Flashback Drop

Flashback Drop allows you to "undrop" database objects. No longer will users be desperate for the entire database to be restored to a point in the past because they thought they were on the dev database when they were really on prod.

There's nothing all that magical about how Flashback Drop has been implemented. When you drop a table, it merely gets renamed to a system-identifiable string and then placed in the Recycle Bin. The physical segment remains in the tablespace it was dropped from and will remain there until you undrop the object, purge it manually, or the tablespace runs of out space for regular objects. If space pressure exists in the tablespace, Oracle will begin to age out dropped objects from oldest to newest.

When you drop an object, Oracle doesn't just rename the object itself. All dependent objects move to the Recycle Bin as well: indices, triggers, and constraints. Therefore, when you undrop the table, the table as well as all of its dependents come back with it.

The Recycle Bin

Oracle's Recycle Bin is similar to the Windows Recycle Bin, except without the pretty waste basket icon. The Recycle Bin is a virtual directory of all dropped objects in the database—nothing more than a list of objects that have been dropped but not purged. It is a logical container and does not require a specific storage location— actual storage for all dropped objects is in the tablespace the object was in prior to drop. Here's an example: User Scott drops the table lunar.space_ship_maint. The space_ship_maint table and associated indexes are in the tablespace lunar_data. When the space_ship_maint table is dropped, it is renamed to a system-generated name, and so are the indexes that were on the table. Both the table and the indexes appear in the DBA_RECYCLEBIN view. However, the actual space_ship_maint table and index segments still exist in the lunar_data tablespace. They are logically part of the Recycle Bin, but they physically exist in the same place they always have.

The Recycle Bin is able to be turned on or off with the **recyclebin** initialization parameter. The default of this parameter is on and we recommend leaving it on to enable the Flashback Drop functionality.

The Recycle Bin is quickly viewed via data dictionary views:

- USER_RECYCLEBIN

- DBA_RECYCLEBIN

Purging the Recycle Bin

Manually purging dropped objects from the Recycle Bin is not necessary, because the objects are automatically purged as the space is required by other segments in the tablespace. In other words, dropped objects continue to take up space in a tablespace until other objects in that tablespace run out of free space elsewhere (space pressure). The dropped objects will automatically be purged in date order (oldest first). Oracle automatically looks to purge indices before tables, so that actual data is the last thing to be lost. Recycle Bin objects will also be dropped before a tablespace autoextends, if autoextend is turned on.

If you want to empty the recycle bin manually, Oracle lets you do so with the **PURGE** command. You can purge by user, by object, by tablespace, or purge the entire Recycle Bin.

```
SQL> purge index lunar.space_ship_maint_idx1;
SQL> purge table lunar.space_ship_maint;
SQL> purge tablespace lunar_data;
SQL> purge recyclebin;
```

Undropping Objects in the Recycle Bin

Getting objects back from the Recycle Bin is pretty simple—a simple SQL command renames the object, along with any dependent objects, to their original names.

```
SQL> flashback table lunar.space_ship_maint to before drop;
```

Of course, sometimes it's not that simple. For instance, if multiple dropped objects have the same name, you would have to refer to the object by its new and improved Recycle Bin name.

```
SQL> select object_name, original_name, droptime, dropscn from user_recyclebin;
OBJECT_NAME                     ORIGINAL_NAME      DROPTIME              DROPSCN

------------------------------  -----------------  --------------------  ----------
BIN$jogU/VwlQBjgQI8KJFpPmg==$0  SPACE_SHIP_MAINT       2010-08-23:20:46:14   18118461
BIN$jogU/VwkQBjgQI8KJFpPmg==$0  SPACE_SHIP_MAINT_PK    2010-08-23:20:46:14   18118449
BIN$jogU/VwjQBjgQI8KJFpPmg==$0  SPACE_SHIP_MAINT_IDX1  2010-08-23:20:46:14   18118438
BIN$jogU/VwdQBjgQI8KJFpPmg==$0  SPACE_SHIP_MAINT       2010-08-23:20:45:33   18117920
BIN$jogU/VwcQBjgQI8KJFpPmg==$0  SPACE_SHIP_MAINT_PK    2010-08-23:20:45:33   18117908
BIN$jogU/VwbQBjgQI8KJFpPmg==$0  SPACE_SHIP_MAINT_IDX1  2010-08-23:20:45:32   18117895
SQL> flashback table "BIN$jogU/VwlQBjgQI8KJFpPmg==$0" to before drop;
```

Note the quotation marks around the Recycle Bin object name ("**BIN$jogU/ VwlQBjgQI8KJFpPmg==$0**"); these are required due to special symbols in the name.

If you have dropped an object and then created a new object with the same name, you can still flashback the first object with a different name. Syntax in the Flashback SQL lets you rename the object when you pull it from the Recycle Bin:

```
SQL> flashback table lunar.space_ship_maint to before drop rename to
space_ship_maint_hist;
```

Flashback Transaction

Although Flashback Transaction Query lets us view transactional changes made to the database and use SQL to back out a specific transaction, it left the actual execution of the back-out SQL to the DBA. This is an excellent feature, but it does have shortcomings in the fact that it did not allow us to deal with sets of transactions or dependent transactions—not to mention the fact that we manually had to run the back-out SQL provided by Flashback Transaction Query. Flashback Transaction was introduced in Oracle Database 11*g* Release 1 to fill this void: it let us back out a transaction as well as dependent transactions, but it did have a restriction on foreign key dependencies. With 11*g* Release 2, Flashback Transaction has been enhanced to track foreign key dependencies allowing for complete transaction back-outs.

Behind the scenes, this Flashback Transaction puts LogMiner to use to mine the redo data necessary to back out a given transaction. A couple of requirements must be met to make use of Flashback Transaction, however. First, the database must be in archivelog mode (see Chapter 10 to enable archivelog mode). Also, supplemental logging must be enabled. To enable minimal and primary key supplemental logging, execute the following:

```
SQL> alter database add supplemental log data;
SQL> alter database add supplemental log data (primary key) columns;
```

If you plan on using more complex Flashback Transactions operations that involve foreign key dependencies, you must also enable foreign key supplemental logging:

```
SQL> alter database add supplemental log data (foreign key) columns;
```

To view the current supplemental logging settings for your database, issue the following in SQL*Plus:

```
SQL> select supplemental_log_data_min,
       supplemental_log_data_pk, supplemental_log_data_fk
       from v$database;
```

You should understand that Flashback Transaction does have data type restrictions on BFILE, BLOB, CLOB, NCOLB, and XML data types. In addition to these restrictions, Flashback Transaction will also adhere to the LogMiner data type and storage attribute restrictions: basically, if it is not supported by LogMiner, it is not supported by Flashback Transaction. The LogMiner data type and storage attribute restrictions are dependent on the setting of the compatible parameter of the database; assuming a compatible setting of 11.2.0, we are presented with restrictions on BFILEs, VARRAYs, abstract data types (ADTs), and Object Refs.

Now let's dive into how to use Flashback Transaction. It is executed through the TRANSACTION_BACKOUT procedure of the DBMS_FLASHBACK package. The procedure takes the following four arguments:

- **Number of transactions (NUMTXNS)**   Used to specify the number of transactions to be backed out. This parameter is required.

- **Transaction list (XIDS or NAMES)**   List of transaction IDs or transaction names to be backed out. This parameter is always defined as an input array (regardless of whether you are using transaction IDs or transaction names). This parameter is required.

- **Back-out options (OPTIONS)**   Used to specify how dependent transactions are handled. The options here include the following:

  - **NOCASCADE**   Used when no transaction dependencies are expected. Should a transaction dependency be found, an error will be thrown. This is the default option if the parameter is not specified.

  - **CASCADE**   Allows for a full back-out of all transactions and dependent transactions in the reverse order of the original transaction set.

  - **NOCASCADE_FORCE**   Transactions are forcefully backed out without looking at dependent transactions. As long as no constraint violations are encountered, the back-out can be committed or rolled back.

  - **NONCONFLICT_ONLY**   Only nonconflicting rows are backed out. If a conflicting row is the result of a dependency, the conflicting row will not be backed out.

- **Time or SCN hint (TIMEHINT or SCNHINT)**   This parameter allows for the specification of an approximate SCN or timestamp before the start of transaction to be backed out. This parameter is optional but recommended, because it can improve performance of the transaction recovery by minimizing the data that LogMiner must sift through to find the transaction(s). If left at the default, **UNDO_RETENTION** will be the starting point.

When executed the TRANSACTION_BACKOUT procedure will perform the DML operations necessary to back out the specified transactions in accordance with the rules you have defined. Each transaction that is backed-out is logged in the DBA_FLASHBACK_TXN_STATE view, and details about the backed-out transactions are visible in the DBA_FLASHBACK_TXN_REPORT view. We will demonstrate the use of these views in the upcoming MAA workshop "Using Flashback Transaction." It should be noted that TRANSACTION_BACKOUT does not automatically commit the back out and will hold a row lock on the modified rows to preserve transactional consistency until an explicit commit or rollback statement is issued.

MAA Workshop: *Using Flashback Transaction*

Workshop Notes

This workshop will walk you through the execution of Flashback Transaction. This workshop assumes that the database is already in archivelog mode and minimal, primary key, and foreign key supplemental logging has been enabled. We will make use of the space_ship and space_ship_maint tables within our LunarTrax schema, so be sure that you have created these tables within your database prior to starting this workshop.

Step 1. Let's have some fun and destroy some valuable data. To make things easy for ourselves, we will take note of the SCN before and after we delete the "valuable" data. We could use a date instead of SCN, but all the examples thus far used a date, so we are going to change things up for all you number lovers out there.

```
SQL> select dbms_flashback.get_system_change_number begin_scn from dual;
BEGIN_SCN
----------
  18966981
SQL> delete from lunar.space_ship_maint where ship_id=1;
SQL> commit;
SQL> delete from lunar.space_ship where ship_id=1;
SQL> commit;
SQL> select dbms_flashback.get_system_change_number end_scn from dual;
   END_SCN
----------
  18968808
```

If you have defined the two LunarTrax tables as outlined in the beginning of this chapter, you should have deleted two rows from the space_ship_maint table and one row from the space_ship table. If you remember correctly, the space_ship table is the parent table to the space_ship_maint table, and we defined this relationship as a foreign key on the ship_id column. As you can see in the preceding code, we performed a commit after each delete for a total of two independent transactions. For the sake of your understanding the bigger picture here, let's pretend that this trauma was induced by a rogue batch job.

Step 2. Now that we have injected user induced trauma into our schema, we need to identify the transaction ID of the transaction that caused our issue. We will focus on the child table to demonstrate the 11*g* Release 2 enhanced functionality of Flashback Transaction in its ability to resolve foreign key dependencies. To find the transaction ID for the rogue transaction that created our issue with the space_ship_ maint table, we will use Flashback Transaction Query:

```
SQL> select distinct xid, start_scn, start_timestamp
from flashback_transaction_query
where table_name='SPACE_SHIP_MAINT'
  and start_scn > 18966981 and commit_scn < 18968808;
XID               START_SCN START_TIMESTAMP
---------------- ---------- ----------------
11001D00A0690000   18967595 08-26-10 23:01:40
```

Note that for this example we pulled the transactions between our begin and end SCNs from step 1. Similarly, we could have specified the begin and end dates using the START_TIMESTAMP and END_TIMESTAMP columns.

Step 3. Using Flashback Transaction, we will now reverse the erroneous transaction on the space_ship_maint table using the cascade option to allow for the dependencies to be undertaken as part of the operation. Notice that we are using the **scnhint** option with its value set to the **BEGIN_SCN** from step 1. You may be wondering why we did not use the **START_SCN** from the actual transaction—we want to ensure that we capture all transaction dependencies, so we are going back in time far enough to cover all our bases.

```
SQL> declare
  v_xid_arr sys.xid_array;
begin
  v_xid_arr := sys.xid_array('11001D00A0690000');
  dbms_flashback.transaction_backout (
    numtxns => 1,
    xids => v_xid_arr,
    options => dbms_flashback.cascade,
    scnhint => 18966981
  );
end;
/
```

Nothing is official here until we explicitly commit the back-out, but keep in mind that we are holding row locks on the rows that were backed out. If we had specified the **nocascade** option (default), the result would have been "ORA-55504: Transaction conflicts in NOCASCADE mode" error due to the foreign key dependency on the table (remember, we are backing out the transaction on the child table).

Step 4. Now we will validate the Flashback Transaction operation by querying the DBA_FLASHBACK_TXN_STATE and DBA_FLASHBACK_TXN_REPORT views:

```
SQL> select * from DBA_FLASHBACK_TXN_STATE where
xid=HEXTORAW('11001D00A0690000');
COMPENSATING_XID XID              DEPENDENT_XID    BACKOUT_MODE     USERNAME
---------------- ---------------- ---------------- ---------------- --------
03001200CA750000 11001D00A0690000 0B000A0043690000 CASCADE          SYS
```

From DBA_FLASHBACK_TXN_STATE, we can see that the Flashback Transaction completed and our backed-out transaction did have a dependency with a transaction ID of 0B000A0043690000. If we ran the same query against the dependent transaction ID, we would see the details about that transaction (it would show null for DEPENDENT_XID).

Now let's look at the Flashback Transaction report; we'll focus on the XID_REPORT column, which is in XML format stored as a character large object (CLOB):

```
SQL> set long 30000
SQL> set heading off
SQL> select xid_report from DBA_FLASHBACK_TXN_REPORT
where compensating_xid=HEXTORAW('03001200CA750000');
. . .
<EXEC_USQL>insert into "LUNAR"."SPACE_SHIP"("SHIP_ID","SHIP_NAME","COMISSION_DAT
E","STATUS","DECOM_DATE") values ('1','Joleen',TO_DATE('01-06-2002:00:00:00', 'D
D-MM-YYYY:HH24:MI:SS'),'ACTIVE',NULL)
</EXEC_USQL>
<EXEC_USQL>insert into "LUNAR"."SPACE_SHIP_MAINT"("MAINT_ID","SHIP_ID","MAINT_DE
SC","MAINT_COMPLETE","MAINT_DATE","COMPLETE_DATE") values ('2','1','Oil Change',
'YES',TO_DATE('09-08-2010:00:00:00', 'DD-MM-YYYY:HH24:MI:SS'),TO_DATE('09-08-201
0:00:00:00', 'DD-MM-YYYY:HH24:MI:SS'))
</EXEC_USQL>
<EXEC_USQL>insert into "LUNAR"."SPACE_SHIP_MAINT"("MAINT_ID","SHIP_ID","MAINT_DE
SC","MAINT_COMPLETE","MAINT_DATE","COMPLETE_DATE") values ('1','1','Major Crash
Repair','YES',TO_DATE('11-09-2002:00:00:00', 'DD-MM-YYYY:HH24:MI:SS'),TO_DATE('1
1-09-2002:00:00:00', 'DD-MM-YYYY:HH24:MI:SS'))
</EXEC_USQL>
</EXECUTED_UNDO_SQL>
. . .
```

We have shortened the output to show only the executed SQL; the full output would list all transaction IDs that were backed out (including all dependent transactions). As you can see from this output, we reinserted first into the parent space_ship table, then we reinserted into the child space_ship_maint table. Thus, the foreign key dependency was automatically taken care of, even though we only specified the transaction ID for the child table. Pretty slick!

Step 5.   The last step in this process is one not to be forgotten, because we are still holding row locks on the backed out row changes. In other words, don't walk away from your terminal without typing commit or your cell phone will start ringing off the hook!

```
SQL> commit;
```

As you can see from our simple MAA workshop, Flashback Transaction can be an invaluable tool to back out lengthy complex transactions with the database online. Backing out of these transactions without Flashback Transaction would require a point-in-time recovery or the use of Flashback Database (covered shortly), which both require an outage. I suppose another option would be to pin the task of reversal on some poor developer, but that may be days' worth of work, depending on the complexity of the rogue transactions.

Flashback Database

The most revolutionary Flashback Technology may also be the one that gets used the least often: Flashback Database. Flashback Database lets you quickly rewind the entire database to a previous point in time. This operation's end result is the same as what you'd get from doing point-in-time recovery using RMAN or user-managed recovery, except you don't have to take the time to restore all of the database's datafiles from the most recent backup, followed by a roll-forward using all the archivelogs that have accumulated since that backup. By avoiding these costly operations, Flashback Database can perform a point-in-time recovery in a fraction of the time typically required for such an operation.

Flashback Database works by incrementally recording all blocks that have changed at a timed interval. These Flashback "checkpoints" then provide the points to which the database can be "rewound." After rolling back to the flashback checkpoint, archivelogs can be used to roll forward to the exact time or SCN specified by the **FLASHBACK DATABASE** command. So the operation uses new technology as well as our old trusty archivelogs to provide a fast way to perform point-in-time-recovery.

Typically, there is less archival to be applied after a Flashback checkpoint than must be applied to the last backup (typically taken every night, versus every few minutes for Flashback logs), so the recovery stage of Flashback is quick.

With 11g, Flashback Database can be enabled with the database online (it had to be at mount state in 10g) as follows:

```
SQL> alter database flashback on;
```

Flashback Logs

Flashback Database is made possible by logging database block changes in binary log files (kind of like archivelogs) called the Flashback logs. Flashback logs are generated by the database at regular intervals and accumulate in the Flash Recovery Area (aka Fast Recovery Area, or FRA). You must have an FRA for Flashback Database; the logs cannot be created anywhere else. The Flashback log contains a copied image of every block that has been changed since the last Flashback log was generated. These blocks are then able to be reinstated into the database when a **FLASHBACK DATABASE** command is issued to rewind the database to its state at the time specified in the **FLASHBACK DATABASE** command.

Because entire blocks are being dumped to the Flashback logs, they can accumulate very quickly in extremely active databases. Therefore, setting an appropriately sized FRA is crucial to the success of meeting your Flashback Database needs. In addition, you can manually turn off Flashback logging for certain tablespaces that could be manually re-created after a Flashback Database operation, and thereby decrease the amount of logging that occurs:

```
SQL> alter tablespace users flashback off;
```

You can turn it back on at any time, but note that you cannot rewind backward through a Flashback logging gap for the tablespace you turned off.

```
SQL> alter tablespace users flashback on;
```

Any tablespace that has Flashback logging turned off for any period of time within the **FLASHBACK DATABASE** command would need to be off-lined prior to performing the Flashback Database operation; otherwise, you will receive a "ORA-38753: Cannot flashback datafile x; no flashback log data" error.

Note that Flashback logs are Oracle Managed Recovery Files. Recall our discussion of the usage of the FRA in Chapter 10: Oracle will automatically delete the files based on a user-defined retention period (see the next section) and space utilization rules for the FRA. There is no command to purge Flashback logs manually (other than shortening the retention window or disabling Flashback Database).

Flashback Retention Target

The lifespan of Flashback logs correlates directly to how far back in time you would like to have the Flashback Database option. By default, the Flashback logs will be kept long enough so that you can always flashback 24 hours from the current time (1440 minutes). If this is too long or too short a time, you can change it by setting the **db_flashback_retention_target** parameter to the desired value:

```
SQL> alter system set db_flashback_retention_target=720 scope=both;
```

The value is specified in minutes (720 would be 12 hours). If you're working in an Oracle RAC environment, this parameter value must be the same for all database instances (**sid='*'**).

MAA Workshop: *Enabling Flashback Database*

Workshop Notes

This workshop will walk you through the steps necessary to configure the database for using Flashback logging for Flashback Database operations. This workshop assumes that the database is already in archivelog mode, as this is a requirement for Flashback Database.

Step 1.   Set the values for **db_recovery_file_dest** and **db_recovery_file_dest_size** (FRA parameters). Note that if you have already set these for your RMAN backup strategy as outlined in Chapter 10, you should review the parameters now. Flashback logs increase FRA usage significantly. It would behoove you to at least double the given size of the FRA.

```
SQL> alter system set db_recovery_file_dest_size=12g scope=both sid='*';
SQL> alter system set db_recovery_file_dest='+DBFLASH' scope=both sid='*';
```

Step 2.   Set the Flashback retention target to your desired value. We will use 12 hours as the window:

```
SQL> alter system set db_flashback_retention_target=720 scope=spfile sid='*';
```

Step 3.   Turn on Flashback logging. In releases prior to 11*g*, the database would have had to be in mount state. This restriction was lifted in 11*g*, thus making it possible to enable and disable this powerful feature without an outage.

```
SQL> alter database flashback on;
```

Flashback Database: Tuning and Tweaking

You've determined that Flashback Database gives you a fallback position you want for your database, and you have determined how far back you want your fallback position to be. You've set your **db_flashback_retention_target**. Now, the question comes up: How do you know if you have enough space in your FRA to handle the volume of Flashback logs being generated? And, for that matter, how much flashback logging is occurring? Let's take a look.

Using V$FLASHBACK_DATABASE_LOG

Oracle provides built-in analysis for you to use in determining whether you need to increase the size of your FRA. After you enable Flashback logging, Oracle begins to keep track of the amount of Flashback logging that is occurring, and stores this information in the view V$FLASHBACK_DATABASE_LOG. This view actually provides an estimate for the total Flashback size:

```
SQL> select estimated_flashback_size from v$flashback_database_log;
```

Notice that this view gives the size for Flashback logs, not for all users of the FRA, so you will need to add this value to whatever size you need for archivelogs and RMAN backups. This estimated value only gets better with age, meaning that as the database runs through its day-to-day (and then month-to-month) operations, Oracle can provide a better estimate of the size. So it is a good idea to check back in with this estimator to find out if you still have the right specifications in place.

V$FLASHBACK_DATABASE_LOG also provides you with the actual oldest time to which you can flashback the database, given the current size of the FRA and the currently available Flashback logs. You can use this as another indicator of space issues in the FRA.

```
SQL> select oldest_flashback_scn, oldest_flashback_time
from v$flashback_database_log;
```

Using V$FLASHBACK_DATABASE_STAT

Oracle has built in a monitoring view so that you can keep your trained MAA DBA eye on Flashback logging activity. V$FLASHBACK_DATABASE_STAT provides information on Flashback data generated during a period of time (typically, a one-hour window extending back from sysdate). In addition to showing how much Flashback logging occurred, this view posts the redo generated and the actual database data generated over the same period.

```
SQL> select * from v$flashback_database_stat;
```

MAA Workshop: *Perform Flashback Database*

Workshop Notes

It's time to give Flashback Database a test drive. We are going to introduce a fault that cannot be handled by any of the other less-intrusive forms of Flashback: the table truncate. Because the truncate does not produce any redo, we cannot do a Flashback Table. So we are forced to do a Flashback of the entire database. This MAA workshop will make use of the space_ship_maint table within our LunarTrax schema, so if you have not created the table, you can use any table in your database that contains data.

This workshop assumes that you have successfully completed the MAA workshop "Enabling Flashback Database." Also following the concept of this book, the workshop assumes you're using an Oracle RAC database. The big difference between Oracle RAC and single instance is that we must shut down all database instances prior to the Flashback Database operation (instead of the obvious one in a single-instance environment).

Step 1. To start off, we must introduce our fault by issuing the **truncate** command against the space_ship_maint table. Prior to performing the truncate, we will take note of the SCN; similarly, we could take note of the sysdate for use in this procedure. Either will work just fine.

```
SQL> select dbms_flashback.get_system_change_number begin_scn from dual;
BEGIN_SCN
----------
  19122640
```

Now that we have our SCN to which we want to flashback, we can truncate the space_ship_maint table:

```
SQL> truncate table space_ship_maint;
```

Step 2. Shut down the database (all instances), and then mount a single instance of the database. The database must be mounted on a single instance (all other instances must be shut down) for Flashback Database.

```
# srvctl stop database -d pitt
SQL> startup mount;
```

Step 3. Issue the **flashback database** command:

```
SQL> flashback database to scn 19122640;
```

Step 4. Open the database read-only to confirm that the table has been flashed back to the appropriate SCN:

```
SQL> alter database open read only;

SQL> select count(*) from space_ship_maint;
  COUNT(*)
----------
        12
```

Step 5. Shut down the database and open with the **resetlogs** option to complete the Flashback Database operation:

```
SQL> shutdown immediate;
SQL> startup mount;
SQL> alter database open resetlogs;
```

Step 6. Open the remaining database instances:

```
# srvctl start database -d pitt
```

Different Uses of Flashback Database

One of the most interesting things about Flashback Database that makes it so compelling is a rewind button for the database. You can flashback to a certain point and open the database read-only to have a look. If you haven't gone back far enough, you can do another flashback. Then, you can also use the database's existing "fast-forward" button—database recovery using archivelogs—to move forward, if you have flashed back too far into the past. So when trying to come to terms with a user-induced trauma, you can move back and forth in the database until you isolate the perfect moment to open the database.

For Consistent Load Testing

Using Flashback Database to provide a consistent data set for application load testing is perhaps the most popular use of the technology. To do this, you would use a Flashback feature called a *guaranteed restore point*. This tells Flashback Database to retain all Flashback logs from the define guaranteed restore point forward. Here's the syntax to create a guaranteed restore point:

```
SQL> create restore point before_test guarantee flashback database;
```

Once the guaranteed restore point has been created, you can perform the load test. Once finished, simply flashback the database to the guaranteed restore point (you must shut down the database and start a single instance in mount state):

```
SQL> flashback database to restore point before_test;
```

You can do this over and over, and each test will be run against the identical set of data resulting in a true apples-to-apples load test.

As a Historical Data Extraction Tool

In the preceding MAA workshop "Perform Flashback Database" at step 5, after we opened the database read-only and confirmed that the space_ship_mait table was back, we opened the database with resetlogs. This would be required if we needed to get the database back up and operational in as little time as possible. All data generated after the Flashback time would be sacrificed on the database altar.

But there is another option. If you can live without the lost table until you can schedule emergency downtime (at end of business day, for instance), then you might be able to get the space_ship_maint table back and not be forced to lose data from any other tables in the database. To do this, you would flashback until the appropriate time and then open the database read-only. Then, instead of opening resetlogs, you would use export to do a table-level dump of the space_ship_maint table. After the export completed, you would only have to issue a **RECOVER DATABASE** command, and Oracle would fast forward to the time of the clean shutdown. Once recovery is complete, you could open the database, import the space_ship_maint table, and be back in business. An outage of the entire system would last for the duration of the export, but it can be a decent trade-off to get data from a lost table and still retain the rest of the database data up to the current time.

For Standby Database Reinstatement

Another intriguing possibility for Flashback Database comes in relation to the standby database function of your Oracle Data Guard implementation. The standby database can also be flashed to a previous time. Therefore, if you failover to the standby to overcome a logical failure, you can flashback the standby if the failure has already been propagated from the primary database.

Remember back in Chapter 9 we used Flashback Database to reinstate a failed primary database. When a failover occurs from the primary to the standby, in the past you were forced to use backups to restore a copy of the new primary back to the old primary and make it a standby, and then fail back over. Now, you can instead use Flashback Database on the old primary to move it back to the exact SCN where the standby database was prior to activation. Then you set up the flow of archivelogs from the new primary to the old primary, tell the old primary it is now a standby, and you are back in business in minutes. If you are planning on using or are already using the Oracle Data Guard Broker to manage your standby, Flashback Database and the Broker are like bread and butter, they just go together. After a failover, a simple one-line command will reinstate the failed primary as a physical standby. This will be covered in Chapter 12.

Summary

This chapter has introduced each of the Flashback Technologies available to the MAA DBA. We showed variations of Flashback Query that can be used to gain a historical insight into tables and transactions on those tables. We have successfully backed out complex transactions (OK, our example was not all that complex) using Flashback Transaction. And we have restored a table to a past point in time. And all of these operations were performed with 100 percent database uptime. Although Flashback Database does require an outage, take the time to compare the overall elapsed time of a full database restore/recovery to the overall elapsed time of the same using Flashback Database. The overall outage window between the two will definitely prove that Flashback Database will truly help you achieve those ever so desired 5 9s of up time.

PART
IV

Enhancing Availability
with Additional Features

CHAPTER
12

Oracle Data Guard Broker

hink back to what you learned in Chapter 9: You learned how to create both a physical and logical standby, how to configure log transport services, how to create standby redo logs, how to manage both a physical and logical standby, and how to perform role transitions. When we created a physical or logical standby, we had to configure numerous parameters and various attributes. Switchover to a physical standby requires about nine steps. What if a switchover or failover could be reduced to a single command? How about completely automated failovers? You can have it all by using the Oracle Data Guard Broker.

Oracle Data Guard Broker is a centralized framework that automates the configuration, management, and monitoring of an Oracle Data Guard configuration. Oracle Data Guard Broker further enhances Oracle RAC by providing apply instance failover for Oracle RAC standby databases. If your apply instance fails, the broker automatically starts recovery on a surviving instance. With Oracle Database 11g Release 2, seamless database role transitions are now possible with its integration of Oracle Clusterware.

The Oracle Data Guard Broker can be accessed locally or remotely by using either of the two clients: the command line interface (DGMGRL) or the Oracle Data Guard page of Oracle Enterprise Manager (OEM). Once it's configured, you can modify any attribute of the configuration, monitor the configuration, perform health checks, and perform role changes with a single command. Truly a wonderful thing.

In this chapter, you'll learn how to configure the Oracle Data Guard Broker in an Oracle RAC environment and how to perform various management tasks using the Oracle Data Guard Broker DGMGRL interface. Growing numbers of DBAs are big fans of GUIs, so if you fall into this category, don't worry; we'll discuss the Oracle Data Guard OEM interface in the Chapter 13.

Oracle Data Guard Broker Architecture Overview

The Oracle Data Guard Broker is a feature of the Oracle database that consists of two client interfaces (OEM and DGMGRL) and the Oracle Data Guard Monitor (DMON) process. The Oracle Data Guard OEM and DGMGRL interfaces allow you to monitor and manipulate the configuration. The DMON is a background process that runs on every database instance in the configuration. When you make a change via one of the two interfaces, the DMON process interacts with the database to effect the actual change. The DMON process also reports back on the health of the configuration. All of the information that the DMON process needs to maintain the configuration is stored in metadata files.

Oracle Data Guard Broker Configuration

An Oracle Data Guard Broker configuration is a logical definition of an Oracle Data Guard configuration allowing for centralized management and configuration of the physical resources involved in the configuration. With 11*g* Release 2, an Oracle Data Guard Broker configuration will contain a single primary database and up to 30 standby databases. The standby databases can be any combination of physical, logical, or snapshot. The configuration may also contain combination of Oracle RAC or single-instance databases.

Once a broker configuration has been implemented, modification of the Oracle Data Guard attributes such as log apply services and protection levels should be managed using one of the Oracle Data Guard Broker clients (DGMGRL or OEM). If Oracle Data Guard attributes are modified outside the broker, this will cause an inconsistency between the broker configuration and the database configuration. In most cases, these inconsistencies are resolved on the next startup of the DMON process by overriding the database attributes with those stored in the broker configuration.

MAA Workshop: *Creating a Physical Standby Oracle Data Guard Broker Configuration*

Workshop Notes

Although the DGMGRL interface can be used to modify the Oracle Data Guard configuration, it cannot actually create the standby database. This being the case, the prerequisite for this section is to have completed the physical standby build process following the procedures in the MAA workshop "Creating an Oracle RAC Physical Standby Database" in Chapter 9.

Step 1. First, we'll set the required initialization parameters on the primary and standby databases. The majority of the required initialization parameters were properly set as part of the build of our physical standby, but we need to specify the storage location for the broker configuration files and start the DMON process. Since we are working in an Oracle RAC environment, the broker configuration files *must* be stored in a location that is accessible by all database instances of our Oracle RAC database. In our case, this will be within Automatic Storage Management (ASM). Set the following initialization parameters on the primary and standby databases:

```
SQL> alter system set dg_broker_config_file1='+DBDATA/dr1maadb.dat'
scope=both sid='*';
SQL> alter system set dg_broker_config_file2='+DBFLASH/dr2maadb.dat'
scope=both sid='*';
SQL> alter system set dg_broker_start=TRUE scope=both sid='*';
```

Step 2. So that the Oracle Data Guard Broker can communicate with instances during startup/shutdown operations (such as during a switchover or a failover), the **SID_LIST_<listener_name>** clause in the listener.ora on each node must be updated with a static service having the **GLOBAL_DBNAME** set to **db_unique_name_DGMGRL .db_domain**. Add the following to the $GI_HOME/network/admin/listener.ora file on all the nodes on which the primary database is running, replacing <sid> and <oracle_home> with the appropriate SID and Oracle Home for that particular node:

```
SID_LIST_LISTENER =
  (SID_LIST =
    (SID_DESC =
      (GLOBAL_DBNAME = pitt_DGMGRL)
      (ORACLE_HOME = <oracle_home>)
      (SID_NAME = <sid>)
    )
  )
```

Add the following to the $GI_HOME/network/admin/listener.ora file on all the nodes on which the standby database is running, replacing <sid> and <oracle_home> with the appropriate SID and Oracle Home for that particular node:

```
SID_LIST_LISTENER =
  (SID_LIST =
    (SID_DESC =
      (GLOBAL_DBNAME = cosp_DGMGRL)
      (ORACLE_HOME = <oracle_home>)
      (SID_NAME = <sid>)
    )
  )
```

After making these configuration changes to the listeners, reload each of the listeners to pick up the changes. The following command must be run on all nodes as the Grid Infrastructure (GI) software owner:

```
# lsnrctl reload
```

Step 3. To create the Oracle Data Guard Broker configuration, we must invoke the DGMGRL CLI and connect to a database instance that will participate in the configuration as the sys user. Invoke DGMGRL and log into first instance of the primary database, as follows:

```
# dgmgrl sys/oracle123@pitt
```

Create the Oracle Data Guard Broker configuration named mydg by running the following DGMGRL commands:

```
DGMGRL> create configuration mydg as primary database is 'pitt' connect
identifier is 'pitt';
DGMGRL> add database 'cosp' as connect identifier is 'cosp' maintained
as physical;
```

The broker is fully Oracle RAC aware, so when the configuration is created, it will automatically detect the individual database instances at each site and add these instances into the configuration.

Once the configuration has been created, enable the configuration as follows:

```
DGMGRL> enable configuration;
```

We are now able to monitor, manage, and administer our Oracle Data Guard configuration with Oracle Data Guard Broker.

Monitoring an Oracle Data Guard Broker Configuration

Monitoring Oracle Data Guard when using the Oracle Data Guard Broker is almost as easy as configuring it. When you use DGMGRL, the current status and configuration details can be viewed using the **show** command specifying the desired target. Targets of the **show** command are configuration, database, instance, and fast_ start failover. The **verbose** command can be used with the configuration, database, and instance targets to show details on the properties of each. To display the details of configuration we just created and determine the current status, we would use the following command:

```
DGMGRL> show configuration;
Configuration - mydg
  Protection Mode: MaxPerformance
  Databases:
    pitt - Primary database
    cosp - Physical standby database
Fast-Start Failover: DISABLED
Configuration Status:
SUCCESS
```

This shows a high-level overview of our Oracle Data Guard configuration. Notice the Configuration Status; this is the current status of the Oracle Data Guard configuration. The status for **show configuration** will return one of the following values:

- **SUCCESS**   All databases in the configuration are functioning as specified with no errors or warnings.

- **WARNING**   A database(s) in the configuration is not functioning as defined in the configuration. The **show database <database_name>** command can be used to identify the database that is the source of the issue. Once the database is identified, **the show database <database_name> statusreport** command can be used to display the errors.

- **ERROR**   A database(s) in the configuration has failed. Again use the **show database <database_name>** command to identify the database that is the source of the issue. Once the database is identified, the **show database <database_name> statusreport** can be used to display the errors.

- **UNKNOWN or DISABLED**   The broker configuration is not monitoring the databases in the configuration.

From the **show configuration** output, we can see that our cosp database is our physical standby in the configuration. To see details such as the current transport lag, apply lag and apply instance, and to determine if Real-Time Query is enabled, we can issue the following:

```
DGMGRL> show database 'cosp'
Database - cosp
  Role:             PHYSICAL STANDBY
  Intended State:   APPLY-ON
  Transport Lag:    0 seconds
  Apply Lag:        0 seconds
  Real Time Query:  OFF
  Instance(s):
    maadb1 (apply instance)
    maadb2
Database Status:
SUCCESS
```

This output shows that maadb1 is our current apply instance, and, as mentioned, the broker will automatically failover SQL or redo apply to a surviving instance should the current instance fail. If you want, you could test this now by killing the PMON process for the maadb1 instance of our standby database.

So how do we monitor the monitor? The DMON process produces a trace file for its operations, and this trace file will exist for every database instance in the configuration under the trace directory of the diagnostic destination (typically $ORACLE_BASE/diag/rdbms/<db_unique_name>/<sid>/trace). This trace file will have a filename in the format of drc<sid>.trc.

Modifying a Broker-Managed Oracle Data Guard Configuration

Recall the discussion about Oracle Data Guard log transport in Chapter 9, and that several attributes are available to customize your Oracle Data Guard configuration to meet the needs of your particular business application. Each of these Oracle Data Guard attributes/parameters and more are represented within in the broker configuration as properties. Oracle Data Guard configuration properties are specific to a particular database or database instance. As with the status, the properties for a particular database can be viewed using the **show** command with the **verbose** keyword:

```
DGMGRL> show database verbose cosp;
```

The available attributes are dependent on the type of standby database (logical, physical, snapshot) being managed. As covering all attributes is not practical for this chapter, we will only briefly describe some of the more frequently used properties:

- **DGConnectIdentifier**   The attribute corresponds to the **SERVICE_NAME** attribute of the **LOG_ARCHIVE_DEST_*n*** parameter. This parameter is automatically populated to the appropriate value with the **add database** and **create configuration** broker commands. Note that when executing the **create configuration** and **add database** commands for an Oracle RAC Oracle Data Guard configuration, you need to specify a service name with which all database instances will register.

- **ArchiveLagTarget**   Increases the availability of the standby database by forcing a log switch after the amount of time specified (in seconds).

- **LogXptMode**   The method used for log file shipment to the standby. The valid values for this parameter in 11*g* are **SYNC** or **ASYNC**. When set to **SYNC**, log transport to the standby will use the **SYNC** attributes. **ASYNC** will cause the **ASYNC** and **NOAFFIRM** attributes for log transport to be used.

- **NetTimeout**   Tells the log network server (LNS) process how long to hang (in seconds) in the event of a network timeout.

- **ReopenSecs**   Specifies the minimum number of seconds before a previously failed destination is retried.

■ **PreferredApplyInstance**   Allows for specification as to which database instance is used for redo or SQL Apply on Oracle RAC standby databases.

■ **ApplyInstanceTimeout**   Specifies the period of time that the broker will wait to failover redo or SQL Apply to a surviving instance. This parameter is applicable only when the standby database is an Oracle RAC database and defaults to a value of 0.

Remember that when a broker configuration is in place, it will dynamically and persistently set the necessary database parameters in accordance with the properties defined in the broker configuration.

In addition to the ability to set database properties to control the functionality of our Oracle Data Guard configuration, the broker also lets you modify the protection level of a configuration to any one of the three available protection modes.

MAA Workshop: *Modifying the Oracle Data Guard Protection Level with DGMGRL*

In this MAA workshop, we will first set required database properties to support the Maximum Availability protection mode. Once the properties have been set, we will set the protection level of our standby database to Maximum Availability.

Step 1.   If you recall our discussion on protection modes, you will remember that the Maximum Availability protection mode requires the use of the **SYNC** attribute to be set for the **log_archive_dest_n** parameter on the primary database. In the broker, we define these attributes by setting the **LogXptMode** property to **SYNC**:

```
DGMGRL> edit database pitt set property 'LogXptMode'='SYNC';
```

Step 2.   As stated in Chapter 9, with Oracle Database 11g, you can modify the protection mode from Maximum Performance to Maximum Availability without restarting the primary database. To modify the protection mode to Maximum Protection will require a database restart if the protection level is not at Maximum Availability and if the standby database is not synchronized. To set the protection level to Maximum Availability in a broker-managed configuration, execute the following within the DGMGRL interface:

```
DGMGRL> edit configuration set protection mode as MAXAVAILABILITY;
```

We can now view our new protection level and validate that our configuration is functioning properly using the **show configuration** command.

Role Transitions with Oracle Data Guard Broker

At this point, you should be familiar with the concepts around switchover and failover operations with Oracle Data Guard and understand the steps required to perform each of these tasks. In this section, we are going to make your life easier by introducing role transitions using the Oracle Data Guard Broker. We'll start with three MAA workshops to cover switchover, failover, and reinstatement of a failed primary database using DGMGRL. We will then discuss increasing availability with the enablement of automatic failovers using the Fast-Start Failover feature of the broker.

MAA Workshop: *Performing a Switchover Using the Broker*

In this MAA workshop, we will cover the tasks necessary to perform a switchover in a broker-managed Oracle Data Guard configuration using the DGMGRL CLI. If you have multiple standby databases in your Oracle Data Guard configuration, you need to decide which standby database to switch over to. Here are a few tidbits of information to assist you with this decision:

- If you have a logical standby in your configuration, you will have to rebuild all physical standby databases upon switching over to a logical standby.

- A snapshot standby must be converted back to a physical standby prior to performing the switchover.

- If you are in a Maximum Protection configuration, switchover to a logical standby is not allowed until the protection mode is downgraded to Maximum Availability or Maximum Performance.

- The higher the apply lag of the standby database, the longer a switchover to that standby will take. To determine the apply lag for a given standby, we can execute the **show database <standby>** command within DGMGRL.

Given this information, your decision should be easy. We will switchover the physical standby database in our Oracle Data Guard configuration that has the lowest apply lag. Now that you've chosen the appropriate target standby database for our switchover, we can get started with our MAA workshop.

Workshop Notes

When performing any role transitions using DGMGRL, you must log into the database as the sys user (not /). Failure to do so will mean that the broker will not be able to authenticate with the databases remotely, resulting in its inability to start and stop the databases as required by the switchover operation. In this workshop, the pitt database is the primary database and cosp is the target physical standby database for the switchover.

> **NOTE**
> *If you are in a user/role separated environment, you must be running 11.2.0.1 PSU #1 (or higher) to avoid BUG #8751289. Otherwise, you will receive the following error on switchover: "ORA-16535: Oracle Restart or Oracle Clusterware prevented completion of broker operation. CRSD log shows: CRS-2576: User 'oracle' is not a member of group 'asmadmin'."*

Step 1.   Assuming you have already chosen a target standby database to which you will switch over, you could jump right into the switchover, but if the Oracle Data Guard configuration is in an error state, the broker will immediately throw an error stating switchover is not possible. For this reason, we will use a methodical and controlled approach: we'll validate that our configuration is in good standing prior to performing the switchover. To validate the configuration is error free and ready for switchover, execute the following **show** commands after logging into DGMGRL:

```
DGMGRL> show configuration
DGMGRL> show database verbose 'cosp'
DGMGRL> show database verbose 'pitt'
```

As discussed in the "Monitoring an Oracle Data Guard Broker Configuration" section, we expect that these three commands will return a status of SUCCESS. If a status other than SUCCESS is returned, some type of issue with the configuration will likely cause the switchover operation to fail.

Step 2.   The following switchover command will perform all the tasks necessary to reverse the roles of our primary and target standby databases. When executed, you may see ORA-01109 errors, which are informational and normal as part of the process.

```
DGMGRL> switchover to 'cosp'
```

Upon success of the switchover, take note of the following:

■   All Oracle RAC instances (primary and standby) will be started in their intended state assuming that all instances were running prior to the switchover.

- The database role defined for the clusterware resources will reflect its current role.

- Managed recovery will automatically be started on the new standby database.

- If you are not in an Oracle Active Data Guard environment, you will need to modify the start mode for the databases to ensure that the standby is mounted and the primary is open on restart.

Recall the MAA workshop for the manual switchover: we executed a total of nine steps on two different systems using numerous lines of syntax. We have now achieved the same exact goal in a total of two steps using the broker.

MAA Workshop: *Performing a Failover Using the Broker*

Two types of failovers are available with the Oracle Data Guard Broker: complete and immediate. Complete failover is the preferred and default type because it applies all available redo data prior to failover, reducing the amount of data loss. Immediate failover is faster but at the cost of potential data loss, because it immediately terminates recovery.

At this point, a couple decisions have to be made: the type of failover to be performed (complete or immediate) and which database will be the designated target for the failover (applicable in an Oracle Data Guard configuration involving multiple standby databases). Here are a few key points to assist you in making this decision:

- A complete failover will not be allowed if errors are present on the target standby database. Immediate failovers are possible even when errors are present on the target standby.

- Failover to a snapshot standby database can significantly lengthen the time to failover because of the automatic conversion and recovery of the snapshot standby failover process.

- Complete failovers will only disable standby databases (requiring them to be reinstated) if redo beyond the time of failover has been applied, while immediate failovers will disable all standby databases.

- If the failover target is a logical standby, all other standby databases must be rebuilt after the failover. The failed primary can be reinstated via Flashback Database if available.

- It is recommended that you *always* attempt a complete failover to minimize or even eliminate data loss.

When performing a failover, keep in mind all these considerations as well as those laid forth in the "Oracle Data Guard Failover" section in Chapter 9. They all apply even though this workshop comprises a single simplistic step.

Workshop Notes

Prior to beginning this workshop, you should enable Flashback Database on the primary. Flashback Database will be used for reinstatement of our failed primary database in the next MAA workshop.

```
SQL> alter database flashback on;
```

As with the broker switchover workshop, we must connect to the database as sys through the Transparent Network Substrate (TNS) to allow the broker to start and stop the databases as required.

The Only Step   Our uninterruptible power supply (UPS) in the data center housing primary database is oozing battery acid onto the floor. We have only one decision to make—complete or immediate failover. We have been diligently monitoring our standby database and know that we have only seconds of latency, so we can't waste time by trying to figure out how long a complete failover will take. We know that it will be a maximum of only a few minutes extra to perform a complete recovery, so that's what we are going to do. In the words of a famous athletic shoe manufacture, "Just Do It."

```
DGMGRL> failover to 'pitt'
```

Upon success of this command, our target standby database has assumed the primary role. All Oracle RAC instances are available to handle client connections. Should we have wanted to perform an immediate failover, we would simply specify the **immediate** keyword at the end of the statement.

In a multiple standby database configuration, those standby databases that have applied redo beyond the point of recovery of our new primary database will have to be reinstated. It should also be noted that Maximum Protection configurations will reset to Maximum Performance after a failover; therefore, the protection level of the configuration must be upgraded. Maximum Availability and Maximum Performance configurations are not impacted.

MAA Workshop: *Reinstatement of a Broker-Managed Database*

Well, the technical folks at our data center have cleaned up the battery acid and replaced the UPS. Our servers at this data center are up and available for us to work our DBA magic. Recall that in a reinstatement of databases in an Oracle Data Guard configuration, we have two options: rebuild from a backup of the new primary database or use Flashback Database. In this MAA workshop, we will use DGMGRL to perform reinstatement of our failed primary database as a standby database in our Oracle Data Guard configuration.

Workshop Notes

Assuming you followed the workshop notes in the MAA workshop "Performing a Failover Using the Broker," you enabled Flashback Database on what was your primary database and are ready to perform the tasks in this workshop.

> **NOTE**
> *If Flashback Database has not been enabled prior to the failover, the DGMGRL reinstate command will fail. In this case, you must rebuild the failed primary database as a standby (following the procedures in the MAA workshop "Creating an Oracle RAC Physical Standby Database" in Chapter 9) and enable the database in DGMGRL once the rebuild is complete.*

Step 1. We can use **srvctl** to perform this task, but we need to make sure that we specify the **–o mount** option of the command to ensure the database is mounted and not opened. Assuming the proper configuration of the clusterware database resources in a broker configuration, this should not be the case, but better safe than sorry.

```
# srvctl start database -d cosp -o mount
```

Step 2. Assuming Flashback Database was enabled prior to the failover, issue the following command to reinstate the failed primary database as a standby:

```
DGMGRL> reinstate database 'cosp'
```

After reinstatement, we will once again have a valid Oracle Data Guard configuration. Keep in mind that if the protection level prior to failover was Maximum Protection, it was reset to Maximum Performance during failover and must be reset.

Increasing Database Availability with Fast-Start Failover

Fast-Start Failover is a feature that allows the broker to failover a failed primary database automatically to a predetermined standby database. This feature increases the availability of the database by eliminating the need for DBA involvement as part of the failover process.

Let's consider what happens in a typical failover scenario: First, the DBA will receive a notification that the primary database has failed. At that point, the DBA must log into the system and execute the required commands to failover the database and if possible reinstate that failed primary as a standby. At best, we are looking at a 15 minute outage—that is, if a DBA is on site, monitoring every move of the standby. Fast-Start Failover enables the broker to perform these tasks automatically in the same time that it would typically take a DBA to log into the system.

The key to this feature is a monitoring process appropriately named the Observer. The Observer is a component of the DGMGRL interface that is configured on a system outside the systems actually running the Oracle Data Guard configuration, which monitors the availability of the primary database. Should it detect that the primary database (all instances in an Oracle RAC environment) has become unavailable or a connection with the primary database is not able to be made, it will issue a failover after waiting the number of seconds specified by the **FastStartFailoverThreshold** property. Under this circumstance for failover, the Oracle Data Guard Broker will attempt to reinstate the failed primary database as a standby when connectivity is re-established. Note that Fast-Start Failover will not be initiated when a database is shut down using normal, transactional, or immediate options.

Oracle 11g introduced user-configurable failover conditions. When one of the following user configurable conditions are met, the broker will bypass the **FastStartFailoverThreshold**, immediately initiating failover:

- **Datafile Offline**   Failover is initiated if a datafile on the primary database experiences an I/O error resulting in a datafile being taken offline. This option is enabled by default.

- **Corrupted Dictionary**   Failover is initiated if corruption of a critical database object is found. This option is enabled by default.

- **Corrupted Controlfile**   Enabled by default, the detection of controlfile corruption will result in immediate failover.

- **Inaccessible Log File**   This parameter, disabled by default, allows for failover to be initiated in the event that LGWR is unable to write to a member of a log group.

- **Stuck Archiver**   Failover is initiated should the archiver on the primary database become hung. The default setting of this parameter is disabled.

- **Application Induced Failover**   This type of failover is induced by calling the **dbms_dg.initiate_fs_failover** function, allowing for applications to invoke the failover operation.

When failover is induced from one of these user-configurable conditions, the failed primary database will be left in the down state. Reinstatement of the failed primary database will not be attempted by the broker.

To enable Fast-Start Failover, your Oracle Data Guard configuration must meet the following requirements:

- Flashback Database must be enabled for both the primary and standby database target.

- An observer server (server outside of the Oracle Data Guard configuration) should be established to monitor the environment. This requires installation of the Oracle Database 11*g* Release 2 RDBMS binaries or the 11*g* Release 2 Administrator Client binaries on the monitoring server.

One notable change from 10*g* is that the requirement to run in Maximum Availability or Maximum Protection has been lifted. To control the amount of data loss when in a Maximum Performance configuration, you should set the **FastStartFailoverLagLimit** property to the number of seconds of data you are willing to lose. (I know, you are not willing to lose any data. If that were truly the case, you wouldn't be running in Maximum Protection mode.)

The following are the high-level steps necessary to implement Fast-Start Failover for your Oracle Data Guard configuration:

1. Establish connectivity to primary and standby database sites from the system that will be running the Observer.

2. If you have multiple standby databases in your Oracle Data Guard configuration, you must set the **FastStartFailoverTarget** property on the primary and standby databases. We are promoting good habits here, so even though we have a single standby database in our configuration, we will set this parameter. The setting for the primary database will be the target standby database. The setting for the target standby database will be the primary database. This property can be set as follows:

```
DGMGRL> edit database 'pitt' set property 'FastStartFailoverTarg
et'='cosp';
DGMGRL> edit database 'cosp' set property 'FastStartFailoverTarg
et'='pitt';
```

3. Configure the Fast-Start Failover database properties to meet the needs of your application. Available properties for Fast-Start Failover are as follows:

■ **FastStartFailoverThreshold**   Used to specify the number of seconds to delay failover after the detection of a primary database failure. This parameter defaults to 30 seconds.

■ **FastStartFailoverPmyShutdown**   In its default setting of true, this parameter causes the primary database to shut down when **FastStartFailoverThreshold** has been reached for a particular database. This parameter setting is ignored in the case of a user-configurable condition failover.

■ **FastStartFailoverLagLimit**   Allows for definition of the number of seconds the standby database is able to fall behind. When this threshold is exceeded, automatic failover will not be allowed.

■ **FastStartFailoverAutoReinstate**   When set to its default of true, this parameter enables the automatic reinstatement of a failed primary database as a standby. Automatic reinstatement is not possible for user-configurable failover conditions regardless of this parameter setting.

These parameters can be set on the primary and standby databases using the **edit database set property** command; here's an example:

```
DGMGRL> edit database 'cosp' set property
' FastStartFailoverLagLimit '='60';
```

4. Configure the desired Fast-Start Failover user configurable conditions. As previously stated, these conditions include Datafile Offline, Corrupted Dictionary, Corrupted Controlfile, Inaccessible Logfile, and Stuck Archiver. These user-configurable conditions can be set as follows:

```
DGMGRL> ENABLE FAST_START FAILOVER CONDITION 'Inaccessible
Logfile';
```

To unset a user configurable condition, do this:

```
DGMGRL> DISABLE FAST_START FAILOVER CONDITION 'Inaccessible
Logfile';
```

To view the current settings for the user configurable conditions, use the **show** command as follows:

```
DGMGRL> show fast_start failover
```

5. Start the Observer on the designated server. The Observer should be run on a system within the same network segment that the application or application middle tiers run on to ensure that the Observer and the application have the

same view of the database (in terms of connectivity). The requirement to run the Observer on a server other than the primary or standby systems is to have the 11*g* Release 2 RDBMS binaries or 11*g* Release 2 Administrator Client binaries on the system and to define tnsnames.ora entries for connectivity to the databases participating in the configuration. Multiple Observers can run from a single 11*g* Release 2 (Admin Client or RDBMS) installation as long as the configuration file is uniquely identified on startup.

```
DGMGRL> start observer file='/tmp/fsfo_mydg.dat'
```

The Observer is a foreground process; therefore, control will not be returned to the user until the Observer has been stopped. For this reason, it is recommended that the Observer be run in the background and that its actions are logged to a file. On a Linux/Unix system, you can do the following:

```
# nohup dgmgrl -logfile /tmp/fsfo_mydg.log  sys/oracle123@pitt
"start observer file='/tmp/fsfomydg.dat'" &
```

How do we make the Observer resilient towards failure to enhance our MAA goals? The answer is Grid Control (or custom scripts if you are so inclined), which gives us out-of-the-box functionality to restart a failed Observer as well as the ability to failover an Observer to an alternate host. Should you not be running Grid Control to provide high availability for the Observer, don't worry, because a failed Observer is not a show-stopper for your overall Oracle Data Guard configuration. In such a situation, the broker will report a ORA-16658 or ORA-16820, letting you (the MAA DBA) know that Fast-Start Failover is not operational and manual intervention is required.

6. Finally, we enable Fast-Start Failover for the configuration:

```
DGMGRL> enable fast_start failover
```

You are probably wondering why we took the time and effort to dive so deeply into Oracle Data Guard without the broker when the broker clearly makes things much more simple while enhancing availability. Understanding the details of how Oracle Data Guard works is a valuable asset when you're troubleshooting issues in high-pressure situations. If we explained a switchover process as "switchover to standby," you would never see what steps are actually performed. Should the broker not be available for one reason or another, you will know what to do. Should the broker throw an error, you will know how to resolve it. Those who are successful are those who have prepared.

Enhancing Application Availability with Fast Application Notification and Role-Based Services

With all this automation, we should be able to avoid all those dreaded late-night phone calls. However, although our job as DBA is covered by automating failovers, how does an application know that a database failover has occurred? With Oracle 11g Release 2, the Oracle Data Guard Broker had been enhanced to publish Fast Application Notification (FAN) events (via Oracle Notification Service, or ONS), allowing for clients to be notified in the event of a failover. In addition, another new feature called Role-Based Services allows for applications to failover from a failed primary database to a designated standby with no user intervention and with little or no service interruption. ONS and FAN were covered in Chapter 8, so we are not going to dive into the details of these features here; we will describe how they can be used within an Oracle Data Guard Broker configuration to provide seamless failover of the application when a database failover has occurred.

When in an Oracle Data Guard Broker configuration, the broker will publish FAN events when a failover occurs. Oracle Java Database Connectivity (JDBC), Oracle Call Interface (OCI), or Oracle Data Provider for .NET (ODP.NET) clients can subscribe to these FAN events, allowing the application to handle the failover of the database gracefully (Fast Connection Failover). The overall end result is the ability for a failover to take place at the database level without user intervention (no need for application server reconfigurations and/or restarts). It is true that you will have to "code" this into your application for full functionality, but the extra effort will truly prove to be worth it for those who require those 5 9s.

To take this one step further, Role-Based Services lets database services run on a designated database when that database is in a specific role. For example, if we wanted a service called myoltp (serving JDBC connections) to run on our primary database, we would define a role-based service on our primary system and standby system, specifying the database role with the **–l PRIMARY** option.

NOTE
Since JDBC-based connections are serviced by the myoltp service, Transparent Application Failover (TAF) has not been configured (as it should not be). For more details on FCF and FAN, refer to Chapter 8.

Here's the configuration on a primary cluster:

```
# srvctl add service -d pitt -r "maadb1,maadb2" -s myoltp -l PRIMARY -q
FALSE -e NONE -m NONE -w 0 -z 0
```

Here's the configuration on a standby cluster:

```
# srvctl add service -d cosp -r "maadb1,maadb2" -s myoltp -l PRIMARY -q
FALSE -e NONE -m NONE -w 0 -z 0
```

NOTE
If the myoltp service is servicing ODP.NET or OCI client connections, we would want to enable subscription to AQ Notifications by specifying **—q TRUE**.

Assuming that cosp is our current standby database, this service will be enabled on that database only when it is in the primary role. The current database role is stored in the OCR and automatically managed by the broker in such a configuration.

For those making use of the Oracle Active Data Guard option, Role-Based Services can be used to provide service functionality of read-only applications directed toward Real-Time Query–enabled standby databases. For demonstration purposes, assume that we want to create a service called *reporting* with TAF enabled for a ODP.NET application. This service will run only on our Real-Time Query standby database. To achieve our goal, we would perform the following:

On the primary cluster:

```
# srvctl add service -d pitt -r "maadb1,maadb2" -s reporting -l
PHYSICAL_STANDBY -q TRUE -e SELECT -m SESSION -w 10 -z 150
```

On the standby cluster:

```
# srvctl add service -d cosp -r "maadb1,maadb2" -s myoltp -l
PHYSICAL_STANDBY -q TRUE -e SESSION -m BASIC -w 10 -z 150
```

In addition to creating the service on both the primary and standby clusters, we must create the service definition on the primary database (it will not be running on the primary) to allow for the service definition to be propagated to the standby through Redo Apply. To do so, we would execute the following SQL statement on our primary database:

```
SQL> EXECUTE DBMS_SERVICE.CREATE_SERVICE('reporting', 'reporting',
NULL, NULL,TRUE,'BASIC', 'SESSION', 150, 10, NULL);
```

Keep in mind that if this reporting service were servicing JDBC connections, we would have set AQ Notifications (**—q**) to **FALSE** and set the TAF-related entries to **none**. For an example of JDBC-based services, see the earlier example for the myoltp service.

Given the fact that these are application design considerations, this is about as far as we are going to take this subject. After all, we are DBAs! However, this topic is definitely one that should be discussed with your application developers or application vendor, because it opens a new world of possibilities, such as zero downtime patching, zero downtime upgrades, and uninterrupted application availability in the event of a failover. With this feature fully integrated with Fast-Start Failover, we might be able to turn off our on-call phones at night, and we can finally give LunarTrax the 99.999 percent availability management has been begging for.

Summary

You've learned both the easy way (Oracle Data Guard Broker) and the hard way (SQL*Plus) to use Oracle Data Guard within an Oracle MAA environment. Although the levels of data protection are identical with both methods, using the broker is not only easier but adds additional MAA functionality to your Oracle Data Guard configuration with Fast-Start Failover, Broker FAN notifications, and Redo Apply Failover. As for the hard way, we all need to learn to walk before we run. A sound understanding of the fundamentals of Oracle Data Guard lays the foundation for the automation that the Oracle Data Guard Broker provides.

Not only does the Oracle Data Guard Broker provide a easy-to-use centralize framework for managing and monitoring your Oracle Data Guard configuration, but it further enhances your MAA configuration by providing apply instance failover for Oracle RAC standby databases. With Oracle Database 11g Release 2, it provides seamless database failover with the integration into Oracle Clusterware. On top of these key MAA features, Fast-Start Failover allows for automated failover of a failed primary database to a designated standby without any involvement of a DBA. These key features of the Oracle Data Guard Broker will enhance capabilities of any Oracle MAA environment.

CHAPTER
13

Oracle Grid Control

t has been six months since we implemented 11g Release 2 Oracle RAC and Oracle Data Guard for LunarTrax's database. So far, we have exceeded our goal of 99.999 percent availability, thanks to our Oracle MAA configuration and the implementation of features such as Role-Based Services. We even applied the latest patchset update (PSU) to our database last month without any downtime whatsoever. With the performance and scalability of Oracle RAC, we were easily able to support the rapidly growing business of LunarTrax, and thanks to that logical standby, Max is happily running reports.

Now let's think about this scenario and the resources that we are in charge of maintaining. Holding true to the MAA concepts laid out in the preceding 12 chapters, we would have an Oracle RAC production database of, say, three nodes to support those three new distribution centers; a two-node Oracle RAC logical standby for reporting; and for disaster recovery (DR) purposes, we have a three-node cluster for our physical standby database. This is just our production environment!

Chances are you are not going to run Oracle Data Guard in development or QA, so let's assume that each of these is a two-node Oracle RAC system. That's a total of 12 servers just for the database. Each of these servers possess multiple resources including Grid Infrastructure (GI) resources such as Automatic Storage Management (ASM), Single Client Access Name virtual IPs (SCAN VIPs), VIPs, Listeners, and so on, and database resources such as database instances and services. Multiply all of these resources by 12, and that is approximately how many resources we as modern-day MAA DBAs are in charge of monitoring. Although they are not usually part of a DBA's responsibility, application servers and web servers are included in the overall architecture. If you are truly administering and monitoring all of these systems, you probably spend significant time on a daily basis jumping from server to server, reviewing logs, and running various queries. Some of you are probably ambitious and adept at script-writing, and you have automated some of this monitoring and now find yourself maintaining these clever scripts. Every day when you log into that first system, you think that there has to be an easier way—and there is: Oracle Enterprise Manager (OEM) Grid Control.

The overall goal of this chapter is to provide you with a general overview of Grid Control 11g Release 1. To do this, we will start off with a brief introduction of the product and architecture. We will then walk you through the installation and configuration of Grid Control 11g Release 1. The chapter concludes with a high-level description of the management of MAA environments using Grid Control 11g Release 1. This discussion will complement the preceding 12 chapters of the book.

What Is Oracle Grid Control?

OEM Grid Control 11g enables centralized administration and monitoring of "the grid." Out of the box, Grid Control provides end-to-end monitoring and administration of the Oracle Database (including 11g Release 2 new features), Oracle Clusterware, Linux OS, Oracle Middleware components including Oracle WebLogic Server, and much more. When combined with the numerous available management packs and system monitoring plug-ins, the Grid Control platform can be extended to cover integration management from application to disk.

The Oracle Grid Control platform is fully extensible through Oracle-supplied, Oracle partner–supplied, or custom-built management plug-ins. Grid Control can also integrate with third-party management systems, allowing you to take advantage of the strengths of monitoring and administering the Oracle Grid with Oracle while allowing the third-party management system to monitor and administer the components of the grid that fit within its strengths. An example of this integration is HP Operations Center via the OpenView Operations (OVO) management connector.

In addition to simple database administration, other key features of Grid Control 11*g* include the following:

- **Centralized system monitoring**   Finally, you can stop maintaining all of those legacy database and system monitoring scripts. Grid Control allows for notification of hundreds of predefined metrics for configured targets (targets in Grid Control are database instances, ASM instances, servers, application servers, and so on). Should you not find a metric you need to monitor for a target, you can create a user-defined metric. Properly configured notifications will allow for notification and/or corrective action to be taken prior to any application impact.

- **Group management**   Thinking along the lines of the grid, Production would be a group that encompasses all the production web server, app server, and database server targets. This group can then be viewed as a single logical entity within Grid Control and could include the members of the administration staff in charge of the production systems; a similar scenario would follow for development and QA.

- **Job System**   You can replace those 50-plus cron jobs defined on all those systems with the Grid Control Job System. Jobs such as database backups, OS backups, and log file rotations are available at your disposal. The Job System also is extremely flexible in the fact that user-defined OS and/or SQL commands can be run. The execution history of each job is stored in the Management Repository for later reporting or viewing.

- **Information Publisher**   Numerous canned reports are available with Grid Control. Should these reports not meet your needs, you can write custom reports on the data available within the Management Repository.

- **Integration with My Oracle Support**   Direct access to My Oracle Support is offered through the Grid Control UI.

This unified solution keeps the grid at your fingertips, making your life as the modern-day DBA much easier.

Grid Control Architecture

Grid Control 11g Release 1 comprises three components: the Oracle Management Service (OMS), the Oracle Management Repository, and the Oracle Management Agent. We will briefly explain the purpose of each of these components to provide insight into how they function as a single unit known as Grid Control.

- **Oracle Management Agent**   The Management Agent software is deployed to each monitored host. This agent collects data about the configured targets (such as the database, ASM, and so on) on that host and uploads that data via HTTP or HTTPS to the OMS for processing. The Management Agent is also responsible for executing host- or target-level tasks as instructed by the OMS.

- **Oracle Management Service**   You're probably thinking that this is the component that generates the web interface for Grid Control. Although you are entirely correct, the OMS is a Java 2 Platform, Enterprise Edition (J2EE) application that does much more than that. It is the brain behind Grid Control. It instructs the Management Agents on what aspects of a given target to monitor, at what interval to monitor the targets, what credentials are to be used for monitoring, and so on. In addition to sending directives to the Management Agents, it is also in charge of storing data uploaded from Management Agents for storage in the Management Repository (later to be used for historical trending, reporting, and so on), rendering of charts/graphs from this data, and sending of user notifications via e-mail. All communication between the OMS and agents is via HTTP or HTTPS.

- **Oracle Management Repository**   This component is a schema comprising various tables, views, packages, procedures, and jobs within an Oracle database. The Management Repository processes and stores the information received by Oracle Management Server. All target configuration information and collected data from the Management Agents is stored within this Management Repository, allowing for multiple Oracle Management Servers to access the same information simultaneously.

With Oracle Grid Control's centralized management of the grid, you will depend on it for monitoring and administration. For this reason, Grid Control is easily configurable in a MAA implementation involving an Oracle RAC/Oracle Data Guard Management Repository and multiple Oracle Management Servers accessed centrally using a load balancer. Although this type of implementation is well beyond the scope of this chapter, it is definitely a topic for consideration as your dependency on Oracle Grid Control grows.

Preparing to Install Oracle Grid Control 11*g* Release 1

Numerous installation and configuration options are available for Oracle Grid Control 11*g* Release 1, such as multitier installations, repository database versions, Oracle RAC or single instance, ASM or file systems, as well as various OMS High Availability configurations. In this chapter, we will install Grid Control in a single-tier configuration using a single-instance database. From an OS standpoint, our focus thus far has been centered around the Linux operating system; we will stay within this focus for our Grid Control installation by installing on OEL 5.2 x86_64.

Two high-level prerequisites are necessary before installing Oracle Grid Control 11*g* Release 1 regardless of the installation platform:

■ Oracle WebLogic Server 10.3.2 (other versions are not currently supported) must be installed on the machine that will run the Oracle Management Server.

■ A Oracle Database version certified for use as the 11*g* Grid Control repository must be installed, and a database must be pre-created for use as the Management Repository. The preferred database release for the OMS is 11*g* Release 2; at present, the preferred version is 11.2.0.1. Therefore, this is the version we will be using for our installation. To determine what database versions are certified, review MOS Note 412431.1.

These requirements are quite a change from previous versions of Grid Control, because the Application Server and Management Repository Database were included with the Grid Control software distribution. At this point, you might be wondering, "I am a DBA, what the heck do I know about installing WebLogic?" This chapter takes you through the steps necessary to meet these prerequisites, but first we need to ensure that our OS is configured properly to install and run all of these components.

OS Prerequisites

The platform for installing Grid Control is OEL 5.2 x86_64; therefore, the system requirements described later pertain specifically to this platform. For a listing of supported platforms, consult MOS Note: 412431.1. The OS prerequisite information for each of the supported platforms can be found on Oracle Technology Network (OTN) within "Oracle Enterprise Manager Grid Control Advanced Installation and Configuration Guide 11*g* Release 1."

Chapter 4 of this book discussed how to configure the Linux OS to meet the prerequisites for installation of the GI and Oracle RAC software, so we won't go into detail on configuring the OS to meet the Grid Control prerequisites here. Instead, these prerequisites are listed briefly.

Hardware Requirements

The hardware requirements for Grid Control on Linux x86_64 depend on the number of targets that Grid Control will be monitoring. Our configuration will be rather small, less than 100 monitored targets, allowing us to implement the database and management server on a single system.

Oracle Management Server

Size	Hosts	CPUs	Memory
Small (< 100 targets)	1	1@3GHz	4GB
Medium(< 1000 targets)	1	2@3GHz	>= 4GB
Large(< 10,000 targets)	2	2@3GHz	>= 6GB

Oracle Management Repository Server

Size	Hosts	CPUs	Memory
Small	Shared with OMS	Shared with OMS	Shared with OMS
Medium	1	2	4GB
Large	2	4	6GB

Oracle Management Repository Tablespace Sizing

Size	system	mgmt_tablespace	mgmt_ecm_depot_ts	mgmt_ad4j_ts	temp
Small	600MB	50GB	1GB	100MB	10GB
Medium	600MB	200GB	4GB	200MB	20GB
Large	600MB	300GB	> 4GB	400MB	40GB

OS Packages

The following are the required minimum version Red Hat Package Managers (RPMs) for installing 11g Grid Control on an OEL 5 or Red Hat Enterprise Linux (RHEL) 5 x86_64 platform. Prior to installing, ensure that all RPMs listed next are installed on the target system. A complete listing of these RPMs is also available in Appendix B of "Oracle Enterprise Manager Grid Control Basic Installation Guide 11g Release 1 (11.1.0.1.0)." As with all other documentation, this can be found on OTN.

- binutils-2.17.50.0.6 (x86_64)
- compat-libstdc++-33-3.2.3 (x86_64)
- compat-libstdc++-33-3.2.3 (i386)
- elfutils-libelf-0.125 (x86_64)

- elfutils-libelf-devel-0.125 (x86_64)

- gcc-4.1.2 (x86_64)

- gcc-c++-4.1.2 (x86_64)

- glibc-2.5-24 (x86_64)

- glibc-2.5-24 (i386)

- glibc-common-2.5 (x86_64)

- glibc-devel-2.5 (x86_64)

- glibc-devel-2.5 (i386)

- glibc-headers-2.5 (x86_64)

- ksh-20060214 (x86_64)

- libaio-0.3.106 (x86_64)

- libaio-0.3.106 (i386)

- libaio-devel-0.3.106 (x86_64)

- libaio-devel-0.3.106 (i386)

- libgcc-4.1.2 (x86_64)

- libgcc-4.1.2 (i386)

- libstdc++-4.1.2 (x86_64)

- libstdc++-4.1.2 (i386)

- libstdc++-devel 4.1.2 (x86_64)

- make-3.81 (x86_64)

- numactl-devel-0.9.8.x86_64 (x86_64)

- sysstat-7.0.2 (x86_64)

- unixODBC-2.2.11 (x86_64)

- unixODBC-2.2.11 (i386)

- unixODBC-devel-2.2.11 (x86_64)

- unixODBC-devel-2.2.11 (i386)

OS Users and Groups

Falling in line with the required users and groups for a typical RDBMS installation, we will perform our Grid Control installation as the oracle user who has a primary group of oinstall and a secondary group of dba. The default umask setting for the oracle user must be 022.

File User Shell Limits

Ensure that the hard and soft file descriptor limits for the oracle user are set to a minimum of 4096. To refresh your memory, these settings are in /etc/security/limits.conf in the following format:

```
oracle soft nproc 2047
oracle hard nproc 16384
oracle soft nofile 4096
oracle hard nofile 65536
```

Now edit the /etc/pam.d/login file, adding the following entry:

```
session    required    pam_limits.so
```

Kernel Parameters

The following kernel parameters must be set to a minimum of the values listed. Make the appropriate modifications in /etc/sysctl.conf and run **sysctl** –p to implement the changes.

```
kernel.sem = 250 32000 100 128
semmsl 250
semmns 32000
semopm 100
semmni 128
shmmni 4096
net.ipv4.ip_local_port_range = 9000 65500
fs.aio-max-nr = 1048576
fs.file-max = 6815744
kernel.shmall = 2097152
kernel.shmmax = 536870912
kernel.shmmni = 4096
net.core.rmem_default = 262144
net.core.rmem_max = 4194304
net.core.wmem_default = 262144
net.core.wmem_max = 1048586
```

Temp Space

Ensure that a minimum of 400MB of temp space is free on the system.

Because we are installing the RDBMS and OMS on the same server (single tier), the OS prerequisites for the 11g Release 2 database that were defined in previous chapters also need to be met on our Grid Control Server. Should you have already configured the OS for the 11g Release 2 RDBMS, most of the requirements listed are already met or exceeded.

Creating and Configuring the Repository Database

In Grid Control versions prior to 11g, you could use the database provided with the Grid Control installation or use an existing database. With Oracle Grid Control 11g, this is no longer an option: you are now required to create the repository database in an existing database. Although database versions 10g Release 2 (10.2.0.4) and 11g Release 1 (11.1.0.7) are supported for use as the repository database, 11g Release 2 (11.2.0.1 at the time of this writing) is the preferred database version for the repository database for ease of deployment. For a full up-to-date listing of supported repository database versions, consult MOS Note 412431.1.

To use an 11g Release 2 database for the repository database, the Oracle Database Software installation must meet the following criteria:

- Oracle Enterprise Edition 11.2.0.1 must be installed, Standard Edition is not supported.

- One-off patches 9002336 and 9067282 must be installed on top of 11.2.0.1.

- For those feeling ambitious who want to create the repository database on a different system than the Grid Control Server, ensure that the network latency between the systems is less than 1ms.

The installation and patching of the 11g Release 2 database should be nothing new to you, so this will not be covered in this section.

Repository Database Creation

Once the Oracle database software installation is completed and the required one-off patches have been installed, use the Database Configuration Assistant (DBCA) to create a database with the name of GCREP. The database should have the following characteristics:

- Minimum of 8k block size

- Redo logs should be a minimum of 512MB with two members for each group

- A minimum of two control files created.

■ Specify a Flash Recovery Area (FRA); this specification will automatically mirror the control files and redo logs a database create time

■ Enable Archiving, required for hot backups of the database

Post–Database Creation Configuration

After the database creation is complete, ensure that 400MB is free in both the SYSTEM and the UNDO tablespaces and that the TEMP tablespace has at least 200MB of free space available.

Following are instructions for each step of the configuration process.

Configure Initialization Parameters Configure the Grid Control repository database with the following initialization parameters (SPFILE) by logging into the database as sysdba:

```
SQL> alter system set open_cursors=300 scope=spfile;
SQL> alter system set job_queue_processes=10 scope=spfile;
SQL> alter system set log_buffer=10485760 scope=spfile;
SQL> alter system set statistics_level=typical scope=spfile;
SQL> alter system set processes=500 scope=spfile;
SQL> alter system set session_cached_cursors=200 scope=spfile;
SQL> alter system set timed_statistics=true scope=spfile;
SQL> alter system set undo_management=auto scope=spfile;
SQL> alter system set workarea_size_policy=auto scope=spfile;
```

Once these initialization parameters have been set, restart the database to allow the parameters to take effect.

Remove Existing Enterprise Manager Schema Depending on how the database was created, the sysman schema may or may not already exist in the database regardless of whether DBControl was ever configured. To check whether the sysman schema already exists, run the following query as the sys user:

```
SQL> select count(*) from dba_users where username='SYSMAN';
```

If the sysman user exists, drop the schema and related objects by running the following at a command prompt as the Oracle user:

```
# $<ORACLE_HOME>/bin/emca -deconfig dbcontrol db -repos drop -SYS_PWD
<sys password> -SYSMAN_PWD <sysman password>
```

If you were feeling ambitious and created an Oracle RAC database for the repository, specify the **–cluster** option in this command.

Prepare the DBSNMP User   If one of the presupplied database templates was used to create your repository database and DBControl was not configured, the DBSNMP account will be locked. To prevent issues monitoring the repository database reset the DBSNMP password and unlock the account.

```
SQL> alter user dbsnmp account unlock;
SQL> alter user dbsnmp identified by oracle123;
```

We have now met all of the prerequisites to install 11g Grid Control.

MAA Workshop: *Installing WebLogic for Use by Grid Control 11g*

It might be obvious, but prior to beginning the installation, we must download the Oracle WebLogic Server 10.3.2 (this is the only supported version at this time) software, which can be obtained on Oracle Technology Network at www.oracle.com/technetwork/middleware/weblogic/downloads/wls-main-097127.html. Because our target OS for installation is Linux x86_64, we must download the Generic platform installation package. Although the platform-specific WebLogic installation packages come with the necessary Java Development Kit (JDK) to perform the install, the Generic version does not. Therefore, we must also download the JDK to our Linux x86_64 Grid Control Server. JDK 1.6.0_18 is recommended due to potential issues with newer versions. This version of the JDK can be found at http://java.sun.com/products/archive. After all of the necessary packages are downloaded, we are ready to begin.

Workshop Notes

As mentioned, Oracle WebLogic Server 10.3.2 is a required prerequisite to installing Oracle Grid Control 11g Release 1. We must also install WebLogic Server Patch WDJ7. In this workshop, we will perform the installation of WebLogic Server 10.3.2 and apply the required WDJ7 patch using the Oracle Smart Update utility.

Step 1.   We'll first install JDK 1.6.0_18. For this installation, we have downloaded the .bin JDK 1.6.0_18 installation package, a self-extracting executable package. The installation directory of the JDK is where the package was extracted. To keep things simple, the JDK was installed under /ora01/java as the oracle user.

Step 2.   The WebLogic 10.3.2 installation requires a graphical interface such as XWindows or Virtual Network Computing (VNC), with the latter being our preference.

To launch the installer, execute the following within a VNC connection to the server:

```
# /ora01/java/jdk1.6.0_18/bin/java -d64 -jar wls1032_generic.jar
```

On the Welcome screen, click Next to continue.

Step 3. On the Choose Middleware Home Directory screen, only one option should be available for the Middleware Home Type: Create A New Middleware Home, as shown next. If the Use Existing Middleware Home option is not grayed out, an existing WebLogic installation is on the system that should be removed prior to continuing. Assuming the former and not the latter, enter the desired location for the WebLogic Server Home Directory —such as /ora01/app/oracle/middleware. Click Next to confirm the selection.

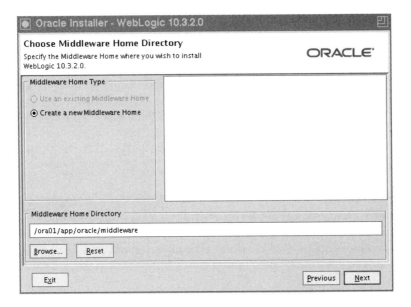

Step 4. The screen shown next will prompt for an e-mail address where you can be notified of security issues and to enable Oracle Configuration Manager. If you do not want to be notified or use Oracle Configuration Manager, leave the e-mail box

blank and uncheck the checkbox. After entering the desired information, click Next to continue.

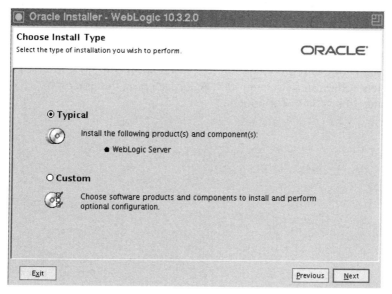

Step 5. On the Choose Install Type screen, shown next, you have the options of a Typical or Custom installation type. The Typical installation type includes all of the necessary components to run Grid Control. Choose the Typical option and click Next to continue.

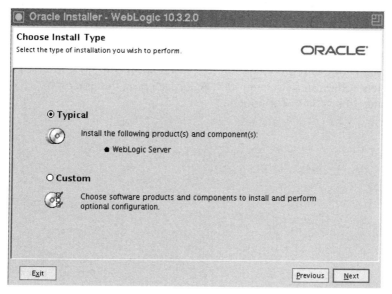

Step 6. As mentioned, the generic WebLogic installer used for Linux x86_64 does not come with a bundled JDK, so on the JDK Selection screen, shown next, this field will be blank. The Local JDK field will contain the JDK that was used to launch the installer. Ensure JDK 1.6.0_18 is checked and click Next to continue.

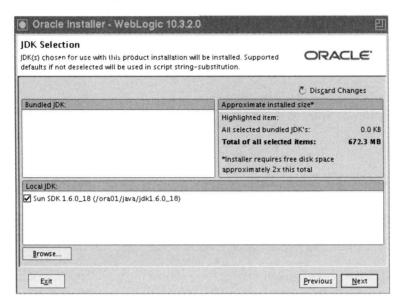

Step 7. On the Choose Product Installation Directories screen, shown next, you can define the directory location to install WebLogic Server 10.3.2. The preferred directory for installation will default to the wlserver_10.3 directory that resides in the Middleware Home Directory. Assuming /ora01/app/oracle/middleware is the Middleware Home Directory, the Product Installation Directory will be at /ora01/app/oracle/middleware/wlserver_10.3. Again, keeping things simple, accept the default and click Next to continue.

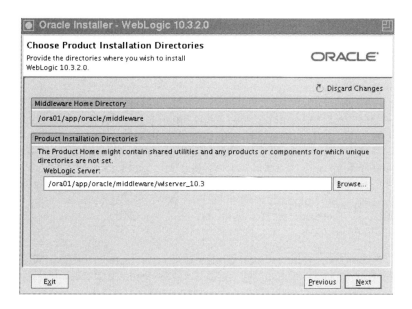

Step 8. Review the Installation Summary screen to ensure that no typos or errors were made in the previous steps. Once satisfied all information is correct, click Next to perform the installation.

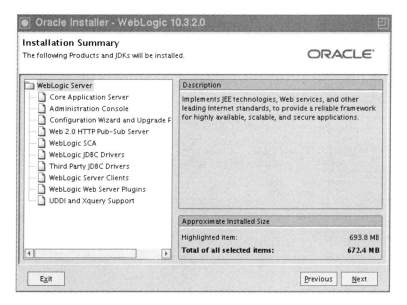

Step 9. Once the installation is complete, uncheck the Run Quickstart checkbox and you're finished. On to the patch process, which is even simpler than the installation process.

Workshop Notes

Now that we have successfully installed WebLogic Server 10.3.2, we must apply the required WDJ7 patch. We will use the Oracle Smart Update utility. Note that the steps outlined here assume that WebLogic has been installed on a system that does have access to MOS via the Internet. If you are on a system that does *not* have access to MOS (offline system), you must follow the procedures outlined in MOS Note 876004.1 to install the patch. It is also worth mentioning that if you are installing Grid Control on an offline system, you will be missing out on the powerful MOS-integrated features of Grid Control 11*g*; therefore, we highly recommend that Grid Control is installed on a system with Internet access.

Step 1. To launch the Oracle Smart Update utility, navigate to the $MIDDLEWARE_ HOME/utils/bsu directory using a VNC or XWindows display and execute the following:

```
# ./bsu.sh
```

Upon invoking the Smart Update utility, a window will be displayed stating that you must update the utility. Click OK to continue.

Step 2. At the Login screen, enter your My Oracle Support username and password. Once your username and password have been entered, click Login to continue.

Step 3. You are once again prompted to be notified of security issues and to enable Oracle Configuration Manager. Again, if you do not want to be notified or use Oracle Configuration Manager, leave the e-mail box blank and uncheck the checkbox. After entering the desired information, click Continue.

Step 4.   Once logged into the Smart Update utility, click the Get Patches tab, shown next. The available WebLogic patches for 10.3.2 are displayed here. Click the Select checkbox next to the WDJ7 patch, and then click Download Selected.

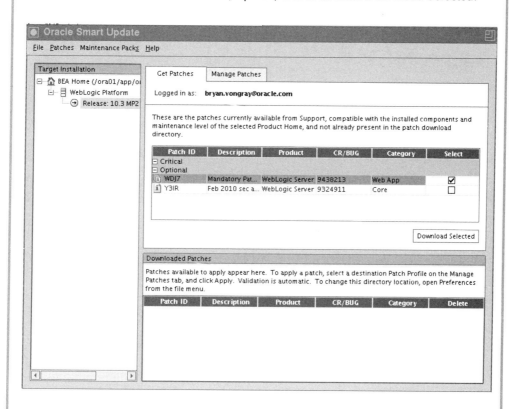

Next, you'll be prompted to perform a conflict check on the patch. If you choose Yes, be aware that the patch will automatically be checked for conflicts prior to installation. We'll choose No to avoid performing the conflict check twice.

Step 5. Once the patch has been downloaded, the WDJ7 patch will be visible in the Downloaded Patches pane of the Smart Update window, shown next. To apply the patch, open the Manage Patches tab and click the Apply button next to the WDJ7 patch. Click OK on the Oracle Support Notice pop-up window.

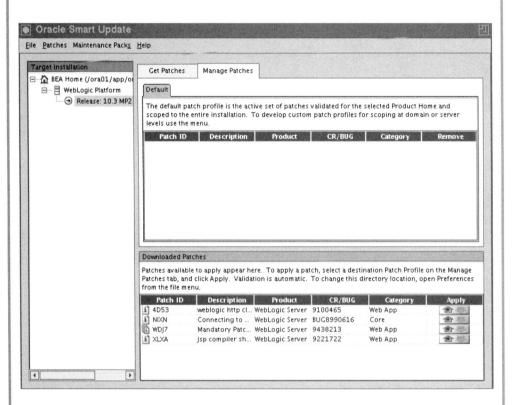

At this point, a conflict check will be performed on the patch. When the conflict check is complete, click OK to complete the patch installation. When installation of the patch is complete, the patches that were previously listed in the Downloaded Patches pane will be moved to the default active patches listing on the screen.

WebLogic 10.3.2 is now properly configured to support the installation of Oracle Grid Control 11g.

MAA Workshop: *Installing Oracle Grid Control 11g Release 1*

To install EM Grid Control 11*g*, we must first download and stage the software on our Grid Control Server. The Grid Control 11*g* Release 1 binaries can be found under the following OTN link: www.oracle.com/technetwork/oem/grid-control/downloads/index.html.

Workshop Notes

Many techies like to cut to the chase and jump right into the installation, so you may have just skipped to this MAA workshop. If you fit into this category of readers, take a step back. The 11*g* Release 1 Grid Control requirements are quite different from those of previous versions. That said, before beginning this MAA workshop, ensure that you have met all of the requirements laid out in the "Preparing to Install Grid Control 11*g* Release 1" and have successfully installed Web Logic 10.3.2.

Step 1.   As you should know from downloading the software, Grid Control 11*g* Release 1 comprises three separate zip files. To perform the installation, these zip files must all be extracted in the same directory. Use unzip to perform the extraction.

Step 2.   Within a VNC or XWindows terminal session, navigate to the staging location of the extracted Grid Control 11*g* Release 1 software and launch the OUI:

```
#./runInstaller
```

Step 3.   On the next screen, you are prompted for your MOS login credentials to be informed of security issues and to configure Oracle Configuration Manager. By now you are probably familiar with this process, but just to be thorough, if you don't want to be notified or use Oracle Configuration Manager, leave the e-mail box blank and uncheck the checkbox. After entering the desired information, click Next to continue.

Step 4.   Grid Control 11*g* Release 1 lets us check for updates and subsequently download and install updates for the product during the installation. To use this feature, we choose either the Download and Install Updates From My Oracle Support or the Install Updates From A Staging Location radio button. If you are downloading through the OUI, you can configure a proxy server for the connection should you be in an environment that requires this. The software updates that are applicable to this procedure are prerequisite updates, CPUs, and PSUs, as well as other interim patches that are deemed required by Oracle. The latest required patches that are to be downloaded (either manually or automatically by the OUI) are maintained in MOS Note 1101208.1. This functionality not only saves time by eliminating the need for post-install patching, but it also allows for you to take proactive action on known issues/bugs.

We choose Download And Install Updates From My Oracle Support, as shown next, allowing the OUI to download the required patches for us. Click Next to continue.

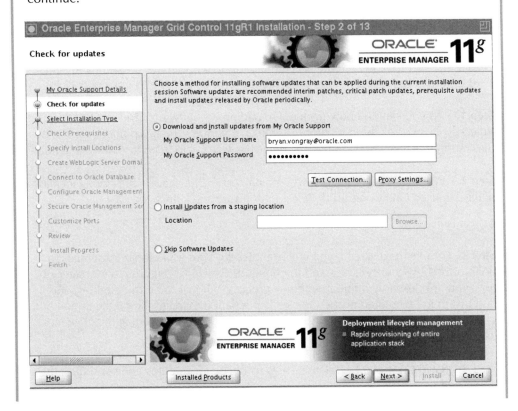

Step 5. On the Select Installation Type screen, shown next, choose Install A New Enterprise Manager System; the Add an Additional Management Service would be used for subsequent OMS installations. If you require a language other than English, click the Product Languages button and choose the appropriate language. Click Next to perform the system prerequisites check.

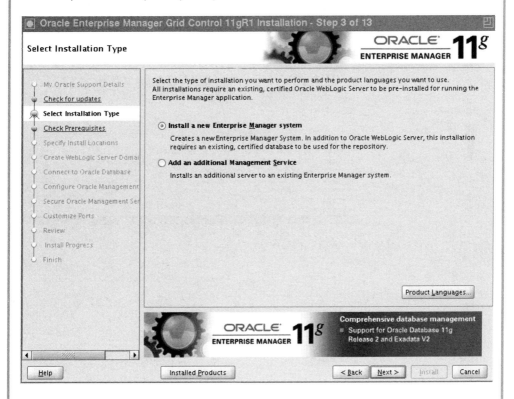

Step 6. The Inventory Location screen will be displayed only if this is the first Oracle product to be installed on the system. In our case, this screen is not displayed due to us having installed Oracle Database 11g Release 2 for our management repository database on our Grid Control Server.

Step 7. The OUI will validate that all system prerequisites have been met. Correct any failed or warning prerequisites prior to continuing. Once the corrections are made, you can click the Check Again button to rerun the prereq checks. After all prerequisites have passed, click Next to continue.

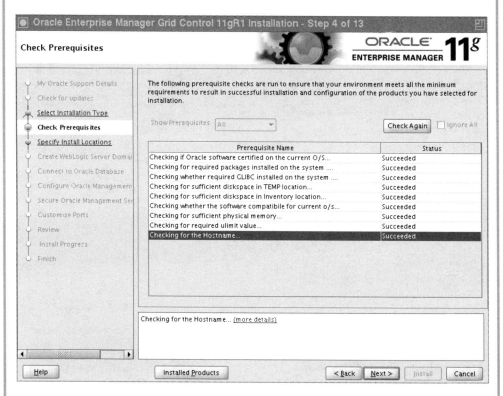

Step 8. On the Specify Install Locations screen, shown next, the Middleware Home will be automatically populated with the Middleware Home specified in the WebLogic Installation—in our case, /ora01/app/oracle/middleware. The OMS Home (oms11g) and Agent Home (agent11g) directories will be created as subdirectories of the specified Middleware Home. Although you may modify this Middleware

Home, the default location is our preferred location so we will not be making any changes here.

The OMS Instance Base Location (domain) will default to a directory called gc_inst, which resides one level under the Middleware Home directory. This directory will house the WebLogic Domain for our Grid Control installation (see step 9). These are the desired locations for our installation, so we will simply click Next to continue.

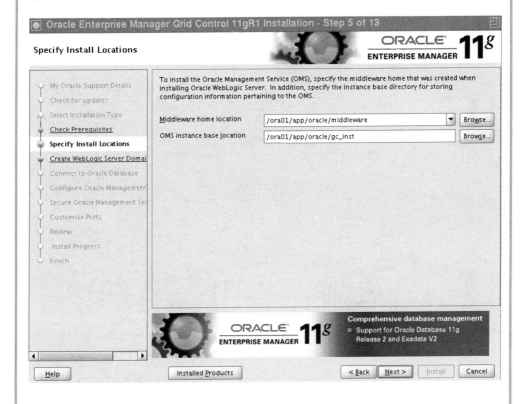

Step 9. In the Create a WebLogic Server Domain screen, shown next, the WebLogic Domain Name is GCDomain. On this screen, you can modify the WebLogic username

if want; for our purposes, we'll keep the default username of weblogic. This screen also mentions the Node Manager, because as part of the Grid Control installation, a new node manager will be created. This node manager will be used to remotely administer the WebLogic Server. Enter the desired passwords and click Next to continue.

Step 10. On the Connect to Oracle Database screen, enter the appropriate connectivity information to connect to the pre-created repository database, and click Next to continue.

NOTE
If you are connecting to an Oracle RAC database, enter the VIP name for a single node. Upon the connection, tests performed by the OUI Oracle RAC will automatically be detected and you will be prompted for the full connect string for the database.

Step 11. We must now provide the configuration details for the OMS repository. Enter a password for the sysman user (Grid Control super user) of at least eight characters, including at least one uppercase letter, one lowercase letter, and one number.

In the tablespaces section, you will see three required tablespaces: Management, Configuration Data, and JVM Diagnostics data. Enter the appropriate datafile names for each of these tablespaces. If ASM is being used, be sure to specify the appropriate disk group name (such as +DBDATA); the actual file location and name will be handled by OMF. Click Next after entering the appropriate information.

Step 12. Communication between the Oracle Management Agents and the OMS will use Secure Sockets Layer (SSL) by default; therefore, to allow registration of new Management Agents, we must use a password to authenticate. This password will be required for deployment of all new Management Agents, so be sure to enter a password you will remember.

It is recommended that you allow only SSL communication for Grid Control to ensure that modern security protocols are met. To do so, check the Allow Only Secure Agents To Communicate With The OMS and Allow Only Secure Access To The Console checkboxes, as shown. Click Next to continue.

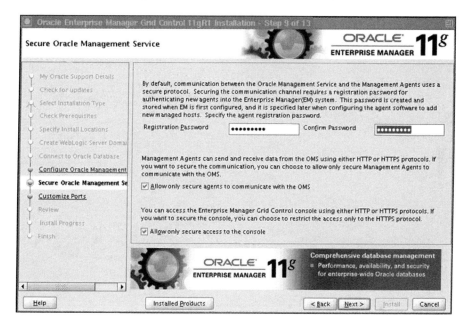

Step 13. The Customize Ports screen, shown next, will be displayed. Unless you have unique environmental requirements, no changes should be necessary on this screen. If modification to the default ports is necessary, you should choose a port in the port range listed in the Recommended Port Range column of the table of components. By default, the first port in the port range for each component is chosen. Click Next to continue.

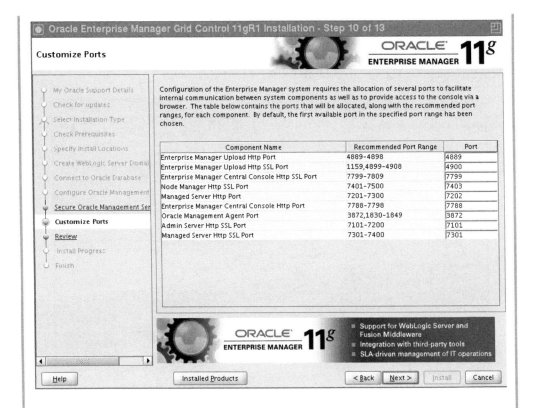

Step 14. Review the Installation Summary to ensure accuracy of the information you thought you entered and what was actually entered. Changes can be made by clicking the Back button. Once you're satisfied, click Install to perform the installation. Both the OMS and the Agent will be installed on the server running the OMS.

Step 15. After installation completes, you will be prompted in a pop-up window to run the allroot.sh configuration script as the root user:

```
# /ora01/app/oracle/middleware/oms11g/allroot.sh
```

After the script completes, click OK in the pop-up window to allow the configuration assistants to run. As each assistant completes, it will be updated in the OUI with a status of Succeeded. This is the step in which the rubber meets the road.

Step 16. We have successfully installed Oracle Enterprise Manager Grid Control 11g Release 1 and deployed the 11g Management Agent on the OMS server. Before we click that close button, we need to take note of the information on the screen. It contains the URLs for the management console.

Oracle Management Agents

Now that we have successfully installed and configured Enterprise Manager Grid Control 11*g* Release 1, we now must deploy the management agents to the servers we want to administer and monitor. But first let's learn a little about these management agents.

Grid Control Management Agents are the means of monitoring and administration of targets managed by Oracle Grid Control. These agents are platform-specific; therefore, prior to deployment, you must download the appropriate binaries for the target system before performing any of the previous installation methods. The Management Agent binaries are available for download within the Grid Control UI after you click the Download Management Agent link on the Deployments tab; alternatively, the Management Agents can be manually downloaded from OTN. At a high level, four methods are available to deploy a Grid Control Management Agent:

- Direct install from installation media (DVD/CD)

- Push install from Grid Control

- Pull install whereby a script is run locally to download the binaries from the Grid Control, install, and configure the agent

- Installation from a shared Management Agent home

To prevent this chapter from becoming its own book, we are going to keep a narrow focus, limiting Agent Deployment to the preferred method of push installation on Linux x86_64 targets. Since our OMS platform is also Linux x86_64, we can deploy agents without any additional media downloads.

MAA Workshop: *Installing Management Agents Using the Push Method*

Workshop Notes

This workshop assumes the following:

- The Management Agent will be deployed on an 11*g* Release 2 Oracle RAC system; therefore, a cluster installation will be performed.

- Domain Name System (DNS) or proper configuration of the /etc/hosts file is in place to allow for connectivity between the OMS and target systems using hostnames.

If the installation is performed on a system running a 10g or 11g Database, the OS prerequisites will already have been met. Should you be installing on a system that does not have the Oracle Database installed, ensure that the system prerequisites are met from Appendix B of "Oracle Enterprise Manager Grid Control Basic Installation Guide 11g Release 1 (11.1.0.1.0)." As with all other documentation, this can be found on OTN.

Step 1.   Log into the Grid Control Web interface as the sysman user.

Step 2.   Once in the Grid Control UI, navigate to the Deployments tab. Under the Deployments tab, locate the Agent Installation section and click the Install Management Agent link.

Step 3.   Within the Agent Deploy Application screen, choose Fresh Install.

Step 4.   On the Provide Installation Details screen, you will define the installation parameters for the Agent Deployment, as follows:

- **Source Software**   Keep the default location.

- **Version**   Select 11.1.0.1.0 from the drop-down menu.

- **Hosts**   Select Linux x86-64 from the Platform drop-down menu and provide the comma-delimited list of hosts, cluster node list, and cluster name. If the Cluster Name field is left blank, the cluster name defined when GI was installed will be used.

- **OS Credential**   Provide Oracle user credentials. Uncheck Run root.sh; since we have not configured sudo, we will manually run this after installation.

- **Destination**   Enter the location for the installation base directory. The Agent Home will be in a subdirectory (agent11g) of this installation base. For this installation, we enter **/ora01/app/oracle/product/11.1.0**.

- **Port**   Modification will be necessary only if unique environmental requirements must be met.

- **Load Balancer Host and Port**   Leave these fields blank. This would be used if we were running Grid Control in a HA configuration.

- **Additional Parameters**   This field is left blank.

- **Management Server Security**   At install time, we specified that the OMS/Agent communication will be secure, so we must provide the agent registration password that we defined during the OMS installation.

- **Additional Scripts**   This field is left blank.

Once all the appropriate information has been entered, click Continue.

Step 5.   In the My Oracle Support Details screen, you are asked for your MOS login credentials to be informed of security issues and to configure Oracle Configuration Manager. By now, this is an all too familiar screen and you know what to do. After entering the desired information, click Submit to perform the Agent Deployment.

Step 6.   Review the summary screen to ensure successful installation of the agents. Once you're satisfied that the install was successful, click Done to exit the wizard. The servers on which the agents were deployed will now appear under the Targets tab under the hosts section.

Step 7.   If sudo was not configured at agent install time, we must manually run the root.sh script located in the Agent Home directory on *all* cluster nodes. First, we shut down the agent as the oracle user:

```
# $AGENT_HOME/bin/emctl stop agent
```

Next we execute root.sh as the root user:

```
# $AGENT_HOME/root.sh
```

Finally, we restart the agent as the oracle user:

```
# $AGENT_HOME/bin/emctl start agent
```

We've deployed our Oracle Grid Control agent using the Push installation method.

Administration of Grid Control

The next logical step is to cover basic administration tasks, such as starting and stopping the OMS and Agents. Prior to performing any administration tasks, we must first understand a little about the environment for the installation that we have just performed:

- **Middleware Home**   This is the location of the Oracle WebLogic Home (MW_HOME). The location for our WebLogic Home is at /ora01/app/oracle/middleware.

- **OMS Home**   The OMS Home (OMS_HOME) is the location of the Oracle Grid Control software. For our installation, the OMS Home is at /ora01/app/oracle/middleware/oms11g.

- **Agent Home**   This directory structure houses the Oracle Grid Control Agent software (AGENT_HOME). On our OMS server, the Agent Home is located at /ora01/app/oracle/middleware/agent11g. For our target Agent installations, we used /ora01/app/oracle/product/11.1.0/agent11g for the Agent Home.

- **Grid Control Configuration Home**   This is the location of the configured Oracle Management Web Server (EM_CONFIG_HOME). The location for this home within our installation is /ora01/app/oracle/gc_inst.

Common OMS Administration Tasks

In this section, we will briefly discuss common OMS administration tasks. These tasks are very high level and will get you started with your Grid Control configuration. Therefore, we'll focus on starting, stopping, obtaining the current status, and creating Grid Control users. Advanced topics such as emcli are well beyond the scope of this chapter, so they will not be covered.

Starting the OMS

Before jumping into the steps to start the OMS manually, let's talk about server reboots. While Grid Control 11g does use init scripts (/etc/init.d/gcstartup) to start the OMS and Agent on server startup, the repository database will be automatically restarted only if the database is running in an Oracle RAC or Oracle Restart configuration. If your configuration is similar to ours and you would like the database and listener to be automatically started on boot, you can write a simple shell script to perform this task.

As a prerequisite for starting the OMS, the repository database and listener *must* be running. Once the repository database and listener are running, perform the following tasks to start the OMS:

1. Start the OMS using emctl from the OMS_HOME as follows:

   ```
   # $OMS_HOME/bin/emctl start oms
   ```

2. Start the Agent on the OMS server using emctl from the Agent Home:

   ```
   # $AGENT_HOME/bin/emctl start agent
   ```

Stopping the OMS

1. Stop the OMS using emctl from the OMS_HOME as follows:

   ```
   # $OMS_HOME/bin/emctl stop oms -all
   ```

   Omitting the **–all** option will stop only the OMS and the WebTier; to bring down the WebLogic Administration Server for the GCDomain, the **–all** option must be specified.

2. Stop the Agent on the OMS server using emctl from the Agent Home:

```
# $AGENT_HOME/bin/emctl stop agent
```

3. If necessary, stop the repository database and listener; depending on your configuration, you may use SQL*Plus and lsnrctl or srvctl.

Obtaining the Status of the OMS

On occasion, you might need to obtain a status OMS and WebTier, perhaps to ensure proper startup or when diagnosing a page not found error. To obtain the status of the OMS and WebTier, use the emctl utility, specifying the **status** keyword as follows:

```
# $OMS_HOME/bin/emctl status oms
```

Creating OMS Users

Since the sysman user is the repository schema owner, it is considered best practice *not* to use the sysman user for general usage of Oracle Grid Control. Since Grid Control security is a complex, in-depth topic that is often specific to a corporate environment, we are simply going to create a new Super Administrator to avoid the usage of the sysman user.

To create a new Super Administrator for Grid Control, perform the following steps:

1. Log into the Grid Control console as the sysman user and navigate to the setup screen by clicking the setup link at the upper-right of the screen.

2. In the setup screen, click the Administrators link to display the listing of current administrators defined within Grid Control as well as various options for administration of the users.

3. Click the Create button to create a new Administrator.

4. Populate the Username, Password, and Email Address fields and be sure to check the Super Administrator checkbox. You can also choose to configure a non-default password profile or select the other password options, but this is not necessary because we are not adhering to any security requirements in our configuration. Click Next to confirm the creation of the new Super Administrator user.

Common Agent Administration Tasks

Holding true to our brief introduction to Grid Control, let's have a quick introduction to administration of the Management Agents.

Starting and Stopping Management Agents

As with the OMS installation, the installation of the 11*g* Grid Control Agent includes init scripts (/etc/init.d/gcstartup) to start the agent automatically as part of the server startup. On occasion, it may be necessary to stop or start an agent manually. The command syntax to do so is identical to that for the agent on the OMS server (it is the same agent). To refresh your memory, here is the syntax:

```
# $AGENT_HOME/bin/emctl <start|stop> agent
```

Obtaining the Status of a Management Agent

While the OMS will automatically monitor the status of the configured agents, it may be necessary to obtain a detailed status of a Management Agent to diagnose latent alerts, an improper status of a target, or some other issue. To obtain the status of an agent, use the emctl utility, specifying the **status** keyword as follows:

```
# $AGENT_HOME/bin/emctl status agent
```

Managing Targets

The *target* is a managed component within Grid Control. These targets include (but are not limited to) the following: database, host, cluster, listener, and application server. Some of these targets were discovered as part of the Grid Control and Agent installation process. This section provides an overview of configuring database and ASM targets, adding new database targets, and deleting database targets.

Configuring Database and ASM Targets

As part of the Agent installation process, target discovery was automatically performed on the hosts on which the Agent was installed. If you have been poking around in the Grid Control UI, you have probably seen these automatically discovered targets and noticed that the ASM and Database targets are reporting metric collection errors, because the targets have not yet been configured. Configuration for the ASM and Database targets involves setting the proper monitoring credentials for the ASM and Database instances. The easiest way to configure the ASM and Database targets monitored by a particular agent is as follows:

1. Log into the Grid Control UI as the sysman user.

2. Click the Setup link on the upper-right side of the screen just above the tabs to navigate to the Grid Control setup screen.

3. Click the Agents subtab to display the Management Agents registered with Grid Control.

4. Choose the newly discovered agent to display the targets of that agent.

5. Review the Monitored Targets section of the Agent Properties screen. Targets that require configuration will have a red *X* next to them with a note stating "unconfigured." To configure the target, select the radio button next to the unconfigured target and click the Configure button. Oracle 11*g* Release 2 ASM targets should be monitored using the sysdba role and the asmsnmp username. Database instances should be monitored by the dbsnmp user using the normal role unless the database is part of an Oracle Data Guard configuration, in which case we use sys and the sysdba role to allow monitoring the database while in managed recovery mode. Enter the appropriate information for the target to be configured and click the Next (or OK in the case of ASM) button to save your changes.

6. Repeat the preceding steps until all ASM and Database targets are configured.

Adding Database Instance Targets

Suppose you have just created a new database on one of your target servers and for some reason you did not choose to manage the database with Grid Control when asked in DBCA. In this case, you must add the new database target to Grid Control. The following steps outline the process of adding a new database instance target to Grid Control. In this example, you will be adding a cluster database.

1. Log into the Grid Control UI as a Super Administrator.

2. Click the Targets Tab and select the Databases subtab.

3. On the Databases Screen, click the Add button.

4. Specify the host on which the database you want to add is running and click Continue.

 NOTE
If the target is an Oracle RAC database, enter
a single host in the cluster.

5. If the target host is a member of a cluster, you can perform the discovery on all hosts in the cluster or just the host specified on the previous screen. Assuming the target is an Oracle RAC database, perform the discovery on all hosts in the cluster. Click Continue to perform the target discovery.

6. Once target discovery has completed, all new targets for the specified host (or cluster) will be displayed. Database targets will require additional configuration. To perform this configuration, click the Configure link and follow the instructions in step 5 of the "Configuring Database and ASM Targets" instructions.

Deleting Database Instance Targets

The development team has decided they no longer need their database, so to allow reuse of the server resources, you have deleted the database from the server. You must now delete the target from Grid Control to prevent all of those pesky notifications that your deleted database is down. The process for deleting a database target is as follows:

1. Log into the Grid Control UI as the sysman user.

2. Click the Targets Tab and select the Databases subtab.

3. On the Databases Screen, choose the radio button next to the database you want to remove and click the Remove button.

4. On the confirmation screen, ensure you have chosen the appropriate database and click Yes to remove the database from Grid Control.

Monitoring

Nobody monitors Oracle better than Oracle! Think back on all of the MAA concepts and components we have discussed in this book that allow you to maintain those ever so desired 5 9s and meet those tight performance SLAs that have become common place in today's IT world. Monitoring is arguably the most critical component in meeting these strict business requirements. Proper proactive monitoring of an environment can mean the difference between an outage versus no outage, or a two-minute outage versus a two-hour outage.

Let's take the case of a former DBA at LunarTrax named Minimus, aka Min, whose idea of monitoring is reviewing disk space reports every morning. He knows it is the end of the quarter and quarterly reports will be run tonight, but generally the data growth is not in excess of 500MB, and more than 2GB is free in the DATA disk group. At midnight, Min gets the call that the production database has been down for 10 minutes. After logging into the system and investigating the issue, he discovers that a custom report was run and caused the TEMP and UNDO tablespaces to grow to the point that the DATA disk group became full, causing the entire database to freeze. At this point, the database has been down for 20 minutes and he'll need about 40 minutes to correct the issue. Max's 5 9s for the year have become 4 9s, and as a result Min has begun the job hunt.

Oracle Grid Control has built-in functionality to monitor and notify on these conditions, thus preserving those 5 9s and keeping us as DBAs happily employed. While this is a rather simplistic example, in reality, it does happen. Let's discuss monitoring of MAA environments using Oracle Grid Control.

How Does Grid Control Do It?

Essentially, the process is quite simple: The Management Agent gathers metrics for all targets on its respective host. These metrics are then uploaded to the OMS server and stored in the management repository database for use in displaying various UI screens, historical trend reporting, and so on. This is out-of-box functionality of Grid Control, which automatically occurs for a given target as soon as target discovery is performed. Grid Control, by default, supplies predefined warning and/or critical thresholds for key metrics for a given target. Should one of these key metrics meet or exceed the defined threshold, an alert is raised. These alerts are displayed in various screens (such as home page or target home page) within the Grid Control UI and can be sent to administrators who subscribe to the alerts once notification methods have been configured (we will discuss this in the next section).

The predefined collected metrics and metric thresholds for a target can be viewed by navigating within the Grid Control UI to the home page of a specific target and clicking the All Metrics link in the Related Links section of the bottom of the page.

Modifying Default Metric Settings

Although the default metric settings are generally sufficient for most configurations, they will not meet the needs for all configurations. Luckily, collected metrics and metric thresholds are able to be customized to meet the needs of your environment. Should the predefined metrics not include exactly what you are looking to monitor, Grid Control lets you create custom metrics.

Customization of metrics can be performed on a per-target basis or can be mass deployed to multiple targets through the use of monitoring templates, which are created using a specific target that has the desired metric settings already defined. Oracle Data Guard Apply Lag is an example of a metric without a predefined threshold, so let's take a look at how we would configure a threshold for this metric.

1. Log into the Grid Control console as a super administrator or a user with the privileges necessary to administer the target being configured.

2. Navigate to the home page for the standby database. To get to the home page for a database, click the Targets Tab and then click the Databases subtab.

3. Click the Metric and Policy Settings link within the Related Links section at the bottom of the database home page.

4. In the View drop-down box at the top of the screen, choose All Metrics.

5. Locate the Apply Lag (seconds) metric and enter a threshold value for Warning and Critical, and then click OK to save the changes.

NOTE
When performing this task, notice that you can also modify the collection schedule and configure metrics for specific objects. Should you want to deploy this change to all physical standby databases, you would do so through the use of a monitoring template. Monitoring templates can be created and deployed within the Grid Control Setup screen. In the screen's EM Configuration subtab, click the Monitoring Templates link.

Notifications

Grid Control can send out notifications to administrators when an alert is raised on a metric threshold. Notification methods can be sent via e-mail, SNMP traps, or custom scripts. For notifications to be sent, the desired notification method(s) must be configured by the sysman (or a Super Admin) user. Once the notification method(s) are defined, individual administrators can then subscribe to existing notification rules or create custom notification rules and a define notification schedule. These notification rules allow administrators to be notified for warning/critical states of targets pertaining to their particular business area (DBAs receive database alerts, and so on), while the notification schedule can be used to accommodate on-call rotations.

Configuring Notification Methods

As mentioned, the first step in configuring notifications is a one-time configuration of the notification methods for Grid Control. We'll use e-mail notifications for our configuration. The following steps are necessary to configure the e-mail notification method:

1. Log into the Grid Control console as a super administrator.

2. Navigate to the Setup screen by clicking the Setup link in the upper-right corner of the page. On the Setup screen, click the Notifications Method link on the left side of the screen.

3. Populate the Mail Server properties required for your specific environment and click the Test Mail Servers button to test connectivity and send a test e-mail to the Sender's Email Address. It is recommended that the Sender's Email Address field be populated with a valid e-mail address to ensure the validation e-mail is received.

4. Assuming the test has succeeded and the validation e-mail has been received, click Apply to save the changes.

Customizing Notification Rules

Notification rules are independent of configured metric thresholds because they do not (by default) include notification for all collected metrics with thresholds. Therefore, it is often necessary to create custom or modify existing notification rules when tailoring Grid Control monitoring to meet the needs of your environment. Oracle Data Guard–related metrics are among those in which notification rules are not defined by default, so you must create a custom rule or modify an existing notification rule so that notifications are sent when these thresholds are met. Although the creation of custom notification rules is not difficult, it is a topic we will allow you to explore on your own. We'll use the preconfigured notification rule for Database Availability and Critical States and add the Oracle Data Guard Status into this notification rule.

1. Log into the Grid Control console as a super administrator.

2. Navigate to the Preferences screen by clicking the Preferences link in the upper-right corner of the page. In the General screen, click Rules under Notification on the left side of the screen.

3. In the Notification Rules Screen, click the radio box next to Database Availability and Critical States and then click the Edit button.

4. In the Edit Notification Rule screen, click the Metrics tab. Here you can see that out-of-the-box, 29 notification rules are defined for Database Availability and Critical States. Review the list and you'll notice that Oracle Data Guard is not in the listing; therefore, you must add the Oracle Data Guard Metrics.

5. Click the Add button. Locate the Oracle Data Guard Status metric in the listing of available metrics. Select all the Oracle Data Guard Status checkboxes and choose a severity of warning, critical, and/or clear (clear will send notification when the metric drops below the threshold) for the metric. Click Continue to return to the Metrics tab and click OK to save the change.

Subscribing to Notifications

After the notification methods and rules have been defined, other administrators will be able to receive notifications by defining their desired Notification Schedule and subscribing to Notification Rules. Log into the Grid Control UI as the administrator you want to receive notifications. This user must have the proper privileges for the targets on which you want to receive notifications.

1. Log into the Grid Control console as the user to which you want notifications to be sent—typically, this would be yourself.

2. Navigate to the General Preferences screen by clicking the Preferences link in the upper-right corner of the page. Ensure that your e-mail address is configured in the E-mail Addresses section of the page. Multiple e-mail addresses can be configured to allow for notifications to be sent to a PDA/mobile phone and corporate e-mail accounts. If you are configuring notifications to a PDA or mobile phone, you can choose a Message Format of Short to allow for ease of reading. Click Apply to save any changes.

3. Navigate to the Notification Rules screen by clicking Rules under Notifications on the left side of the screen. You'll see a listing of all notification rules to which you can subscribe, based on the security settings of the rules and your user privileges. To subscribe to notification rules, click the checkbox within the Subscribe (Send E-mail) column next to the rule to which you want to subscribe. If you are the Grid Control Administrator, it is recommended that you subscribe to the Grid Control–related rules so that you can monitor the monitoring solution! Once you are satisfied with your selections, click Apply to save the changes.

4. By default, with Grid Control 11g, the Notification Schedule will be prepopulated with 24/7 notifications if an e-mail address was specified during the user creation process. If you modified the e-mail address settings discussed in step 3 or simply do not want 24/7 notifications, you will need to update your notification schedule. You can do so under the Grid Control Preferences screen by clicking Schedule under Notifications on the left side of the screen. To edit the current schedule, click the Edit Schedule Definition button and follow the on-screen instructions.

MAA Environment Administration Using Grid Control

Throughout this book, you've learned how to implement and administer Grid Infrastructure Components, Oracle RAC Databases, Oracle Data Guard, Backup and Recovery, and Flashback Features. The majority of the configuration and administration tasks we've performed were at the command line. While we, as DBAs, should never forget about the command line, Grid Control can and will make the daily life of a modern day DBA much easier.

In the remainder of this chapter, we will build upon the concepts that we have discussed throughout this book with Grid Control. As you move through each of the remaining sections, you will probably realize that many methods and options can be employed to perform outlined tasks, but our goal here is to simply say "you can do this." If we were to expand our focus to topics other than what was covered in this book or go into details on the topics we do cover, this chapter would quickly evolve into its own book. You will quickly realize that Grid Control is truly so powerful that a single chapter does not do it justice.

Managing Oracle VM

This topic is a bit beyond the life of a day-to-day DBA, but if you remember back to Chapter 2, we discussed Oracle VM and how you can leverage the technology to build yourself a test Oracle RAC cluster. If you decided to deploy Oracle VM to build your Oracle RAC cluster(s) as we have done in this book, you should be familiar with Oracle VM manager. With Oracle Grid Control, we can move the management of our Oracle VM servers into Grid Control using the Oracle VM Management Pack.

In addition to the Oracle VM management and administration functionality within Grid Control, which mimics that of VM Manager, Grid Control extends the functionality by proving end-to-end monitoring of Oracle VM deployments. To take advantage of this functionality, you must first download and install the Oracle VM Management Pack for Grid Control 11g. Then, you will need to migrate the management of your Virtual Machines from VM Manager to Grid Control by following My Oracle Support Note 807091.1. After the migration is completed, you can administer your Oracle VM configuration by clicking the Virtual Machines Target tab.

Managing Grid Infrastructure

As you know from reading Chapters 3 and 4, Grid Infrastructure (GI) consists of many different components, including Oracle Clusterware, Oracle ASM, Server Pools, and VIPs. Oracle Grid Control 11g Release 1 provides administration and monitoring of the GI resources. Here we will highlight some of the more frequently used capabilities of Grid Control for GI management.

Cluster Management

Many components other than hosts, database instances, listeners, and ASM make up a GI cluster. Server pools, cluster resources (VIPs, SCAN VIPs, eONS, ONS, and so on), and resource types are also included. Grid Control 11g Release 1 monitors all of these components and allows for administration of user-created resources and management of GI server pools from the cluster home page within the Grid Control Console.

Although there are probably ten different ways to navigate to the home page of a particular cluster, the most direct route is from the All Targets tab. Once you have navigated to a particular cluster's home page, you will notice that you can drill down on just about any target that is part of that particular cluster, and you can also monitor the health and performance of the cluster as a whole with a convenient interface.

ASM Management

Grid Control 11g provides full administration and monitoring functionality for ASM. ASM administration and monitoring is performed at the ASM instance level through the instance's home page. This home page is accessible from numerous places, including the cluster database home page, cluster home page, and the All Targets tab. Some of the more common ASM administration and/or monitoring tasks that you can perform with Grid Control 11g include but are not limited to the following:

- **Performance monitoring**   ASM performance can be monitored at the disk group level as well as the individual disk level. Metrics that are collected include response time (ms), throughput (MB/sec), operations per second, operation size, number of I/O calls, and errors.

- **Disk group management**   Disk group management within Grid Control 11g (accessible under the Disk Groups tab of the ASM home page of an ASM instance) includes the ability to mount/dismount, create new, drop existing, perform consistency checks, and rebalance. When drilling down on a specific disk group, additional options are available, including add/ remove disks, create/delete/manage ADVM volumes, review performance, create/delete/ manage templates, and view files that reside in the disk group.

- **ACFS management**   Grid Control 11g Release 1 introduces the ability to manage ASM Clustered File Systems (accessible through the ASM home page of 11g Release 2 ASM instances). With this feature, you can create/delete, mount/dismount, register/deregister, create snapshots, and check/repair ASM Cluster File Systems.

Listener Administration

With Grid Control 11g you can now monitor and administer the SCAN listener as well as the local listeners for each node. Local listener administration lets you configure logging, static database registration, address lists, and so on. Since the whole goal of SCAN is dynamic, no configuration is necessary, so drilling down on a SCAN listener target will allow you to monitor performance and availability. Listener monitoring and administration is accessible from many locations within Grid Control.

Provisioning and Patching

Grid Control can be used to patch existing and deploy new GI and Oracle RAC environments. In addition to the patching of existing and deployment of entirely new clusters, Grid Control can also extend (add nodes) and scale down (delete nodes) within existing clusters that are targets of Grid Control. This functionality is also backward-compatible with pre-11g Release 2 clusters. Although the provisioning pack does require an additional license, it is installed as part of the standard Grid Control 11g installation process. The provisioning procedures for GI and Oracle RAC are accessible under the Deployments tab.

Managing Oracle RAC Databases

As Oracle DBAs, we understand all the administration and monitoring tasks involved in managing our databases. Adding Oracle RAC into the mix just makes life a little more interesting. The centralized management capabilities of Grid Control are guaranteed to make life much easier for a DBA administering Oracle RAC databases—not to mention the GUIs into RDBMS tools such as SQL Advisors, Automatic Database Diagnostic Monitor (ADDM), Segment Advisor, Memory Advisors, and so on. In addition to GUIs into the RDBMS Advisory tools, Grid Control provides extended MAA functionality with the MAA Console and MAA Advisor.

Since the focus of this book is MAA and the scope of this part of the book is to enhance availability with additional features, the MAA Console and MAA Advisor are the topics of the next discussion.

High Availability Console

The High Availability Console (shown in Figure 13-1) is a centralized point of access for monitoring the status of the MAA components of a target database. The console displays recent High Availability events, availability history, backup status, Flash Recovery Area usage, Database Service details, and Oracle Data Guard statistics (assuming Oracle Data Guard is configured). The easiest way to access the MAA Console is by clicking the Console Details link under the High Availability section of a database target.

FIGURE 13-1. *Grid Control High Availability Console*

As with the majority of the Grid Control console screens, several hyperlinks here allow you to drill down on details of a particular focus area. This screen can be displayed from either the primary database or standby database when in an Oracle Data Guard environment. If you are not running Oracle Data Guard, the MAA Console is available for any database target.

MAA Advisor

The MAA Advisor allows for a real-time assessment of your MAA environment, allowing you to achieve the highest availability possible for your given environment. The MAA Advisor is located within Advisor Central for a particular database target, or you'll find it under the Availability Summary section of the MAA console.

Upon accessing the MAA Advisor, you'll see a table of outage types with a recommended solution (see Figure 13-2). Each outage type will have an associated recommendation level and benefits provided from implementing the recommended solution. Above the recommendations table is a MAA Summary with a high-level overview of the potential issues with your MAA configuration and a brief description of recommendations that are detailed in the table.

As you can see in Figure 13-2, our MAA configuration that does include Oracle Data Guard is not protected from human errors and data corruption. If you decide to implement Oracle's recommended solutions, you can do so by clicking the solution link. If you have configured your environment as outlined in this book, the MAA Advisor will hopefully come up with no recommendations.

Are you achieving your MAA goals? Are there gaps in your MAA architecture? With Oracle Grid Control 11g, the answers to these questions is as simple as a few clicks of the mouse.

Managing Oracle Data Guard Configurations

Chapter 9 went into great detail on configuring Oracle Data Guard to meet the requirements of specific environments, and in Chapter 12 we enhanced the availability of our Oracle Data Guard configuration with the Oracle Data Guard Broker. To this

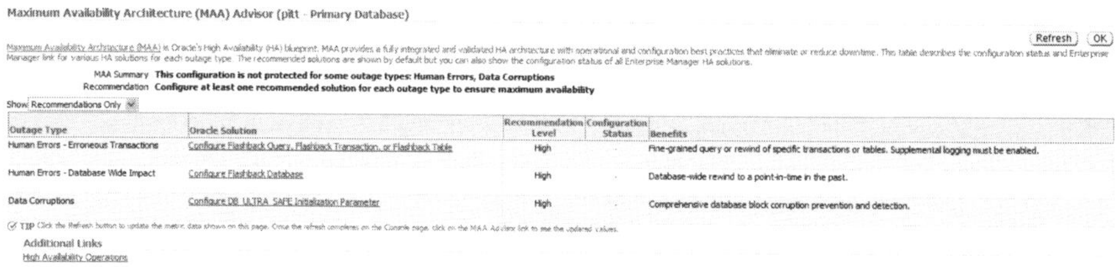

FIGURE 13-2. *MAA Advisor screen*

point, all the administration tasks have been performed at the command line. For you GUI fans out there, it is finally time to introduce the GUI into your Oracle Data Guard environment.

Although a complete end-to-end Oracle Data Guard configuration can be performed with Grid Control, we have already completed an end-to-end Oracle Data Guard configuration. Therefore, our focus in this section is purely on monitoring and administration of the Oracle Data Guard environment within Grid Control. If for some reason you skipped over Chapter 12, go back and read it now.

The Oracle Data Guard Broker is required for monitoring and administration of an Oracle Data Guard environment within Grid Control. Grid Control 11g lets you take a non-Broker–managed standby and enable broker management, but we believe that a little extra knowledge of command line interfaces is a good thing in a GUI world. Therefore, we will not be discussing the GUI Broker configuration—plus, at present, it does not support configuration of an Oracle RAC standby, so what's the point?

Oracle Data Guard administration and monitoring within Grid Control is accessed through the Availability tab of either your primary or standby database.

To determine how Oracle Data Guard is performing and whether we are meeting our RTO, we can look at the Oracle Data Guard performance screen (see Figure 13-3).

Check out the Test Application section. A test application will put a load on the primary database, allowing you to ensure that the performance of your Oracle Data Guard configuration is in check without having any type of application load. This is extremely handy for tuning new Oracle Data Guard configurations.

Chapter 9 walked you through performing role transitions (switchover and failover) the hard way via SQL*Plus. Chapter 12 introduced you to role transitions the easy way using the Oracle Data Guard Broker. With Grid Control, this task is even easier. Simply navigate to the Oracle Data Guard administration screen and click the appropriate button (Switchover or Failover).

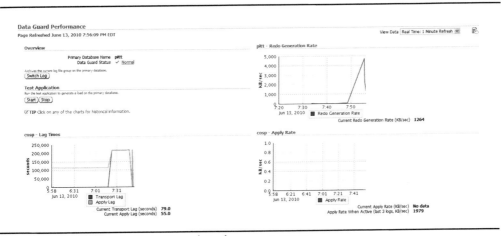

FIGURE 13-3. *Oracle Data Guard Performance screen*

A couple of confirmation screens later, and you have successfully performed a role transition. Snapshot standby—simply click the Convert button on the Oracle Data Guard administration screen. Easy!

Managing Database Backups

Grid Control lets you centralize the scheduling, reporting, scripting, and maintenance of backup and recovery tasks discussed in Chapter 10. With Grid Control, you could run OS scripts to take a non-RMAN backup of your database, but the recommended approach is to use RMAN because of its seamless integration with Grid Control (not to mention all of the advantages of RMAN mentioned in Chapter 10). Within the Grid Control console are numerous backup and recovery configuration options, such as custom backups using user-created scripts, custom backups using Oracle supplied scripts, and Oracle recommended backups. All options are available for each database target within Grid Control and can be accessed under the Database Availability tab of the target Database. The actual backups that are performed when using Grid Control are handled within the Grid Control Job subsystem, allowing for job reporting, maintenance, and monitoring to be centrally managed within the Grid Control console.

My Oracle Support and Grid Control

We'll close out this chapter, and subsequently this book, with what we consider one of the most valuable new features of Oracle Grid Control 11*g* Release 1: full integration with My Oracle Support (MOS). You have probably noticed the My Oracle Support tab within the Grid Console. Once you have specified login credentials for MOS, you will be provided with seamless access to My Oracle Support through the Grid Control console. Features of this integration include the following:

Patch Recommendations Oracle strongly recommends that customers adopt a proactive patching strategy to stay on top of known critical issues. Typically, we would consult various MOS notes to obtain information on the latest recommended patching. With this seamless integration of MOS in Grid Control (under the Patches & Updates tab) on the MOS screen, you can view and download recommended patches for the Oracle products that are targets within Grid Control. No Knowledge Base searches required.

Patch Plans Because this section of the MOS Patches & Updates screen takes up the most space on the screen, it must be important. Patch plans promote proactive patching of Oracle products. They allow you to group recommended patches (or user chosen patches) logically to apply during an outage window. A patch plan can be created for a single target or multiple targets. Once a patch plan has been created, you can validate the plan to check for conflicts between currently installed patches and patches within the plan, conflict check the patches within the patch plan, and ensure all prerequisites to apply the patches in the plan have been met. Should validation reveal any patch conflicts, you can directly request a replacement patch (commonly referred to as a MLR [Merge Label Request]) to resolve the conflict. This will virtually eliminate any surprises that can occur when you apply the patches in the patch plan. Even with validation, it is still *highly* recommended that patches be tested on nonproduction environments prior to installation on production systems. Oracle Configuration Manager is required to use the Patch Plan feature.

Knowledge Base Searches   With the integrated MOS functionality, you can troubleshoot and resolve issues without leaving the Grid Control console. This feature is available on the Grid Control MOS screen under the Knowledge tab.

Service Request Management   If you need to check the status of the service request (SR) you filed yesterday on that pesky 7445 error, you can simply click the Service Requests tab on the Grid Control MOS screen. This screen lets you create/update and close SRs for Customer Support Identifiers specified in your MOS profile.

Automatic Diagnostic Repository Integration   Automatic Diagnostic Repository (ADR) is an infrastructure introduced with 11*g* Release 1 to assist in detection, diagnosis, prevention, and resolution to problems. At the database server level, ADR is available via a command-line utility called ADRCLI. Basically, when a problem occurs (referred to as an *incident*), you can collect all diagnostic information for that incident for Oracle Support to analyze the issue. Grid Control provides a GUI into ADR that is accessible through the Enterprise Manager Support Workbench link on the Grid Control home page. This GUI allows for the packaging of an incident and directly uploading that incident data to MOS for association with an existing SR; or, if it is a new incident, a new draft SR can automatically be created. Once a draft SR is created, you can navigate to the MOS tab within Grid Control to finalize and submit the SR. This feature can greatly reduce the turnaround time of a SR by avoiding all of the manual data collection associated with database related SRs. As with Patch Plans, Oracle Configuration Manager is required to use this feature.

Summary

You now know that the power of Oracle Grid Control 11*g* Release 1 cannot be harnessed in a single chapter. Our overall goal here was not to teach you how to use Grid Control but rather to provide instruction on the installation of the utility and present an overview of how you can enhance your MAA environment with the various features available with Grid Control. If during your day-to-day life as an Oracle MAA DBA you find yourself saying, "Hey, I can do this in Grid Control," we have achieved our goal. Good luck, MAA DBA!

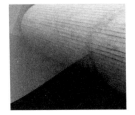

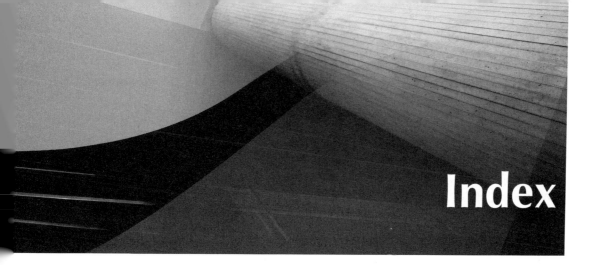

Index